TAKING SIDES

Clashing Views in

Gender

FOURTH EDITION

TAKING SIDES

Clashing Views in

Gender

FOURTH EDITION

Selected, Edited, and with Introductions by

Jacquelyn W. White
University of North Carolina at Greensboro

 **Higher Education**

Boston   Burr Ridge, IL   Dubuque, IA   New York   San Francisco   St. Louis
Bangkok   Bogotá   Caracas   Kuala Lumpur   Lisbon   London   Madrid   Mexico City
Milan   Montreal   New Delhi   Santiago   Seoul   Singapore   Sydney   Taipei   Toronto

Higher Education

TAKING SIDES: CLASHING VIEWS IN GENDER, FOURTH EDITION

Published by McGraw-Hill, a business unit of The McGraw-Hill Companies, Inc., 1221 Avenue of the Americas, New York, NY 10020. Copyright © 2009 by The McGraw-Hill Companies, Inc. All rights reserved. Previous edition(s) 2000–2007. No part of this publication may be reproduced or distributed in any form or by any means, or stored in a database or retrieval system, without the prior written consent of The McGraw-Hill Companies, Inc., including, but not limited to, in any network or other electronic storage or transmission, or broadcast for distance learning.

Some ancillaries, including electronic and print components, may not be available to customers outside the United States.

Taking Sides® is a registered trademark of the McGraw-Hill Companies, Inc.
Taking Sides is published by the **Contemporary Learning Series** group within the McGraw-Hill Higher Education division.

1 2 3 4 5 6 7 8 9 0 DOC/DOC 0 9 8
MHID: 0-07-351529-9
ISBN: 978-0-07-351529-8
ISSN: 1526-4548

Managing Editor: *Larry Loeppke*
Production Manager: *Faye Schilling*
Senior Developmental Editor: *Jill Peter*
Editorial Assistant: *Nancy Meissner*
Production Service Assistant: *Rita Hingtgen*
Permissions Coordinator: *Lori Church*
Senior Marketing Manager: *Julie Keck*
Marketing Communications Specialist: *Mary Klein*
Marketing Coordinator: *Alice Link*
Project Manager: *Jane Mohr*
Design Specialist: *Tara McDermott*
Senior Administrative Assistant: *DeAnna Dausener*
Cover Graphics: *Kristine Jubeck*

Compositor: Hurix Systems Private Limited
Cover Image: (c) Farinaz Taghavi/Getty Images

Library of Congress Cataloging-in-Publication Data
Main entry under title:
Taking sides: clashing views in gender/selected, edited, and with introductions by Jacquelyn W. White.—4th ed.

Includes bibliographical references.
1. Sex (Psychology). 2. Sex Differences. White, Jacquelyn W., *comp.*

306.7

www.mhhe.com

Preface

Issues having to do with females and males, "femaleness" and "maleness," are omnipresent in Western culture and around the world. Our lives revolve around presumed distinctions between females' and males' attitudes, characteristics, emotions, behaviors, preferences, abilities, and responsibilities. We have clear definitions of what females and males can and should do differently from one another. In some cultures, there are third and fourth gender categories, complete with their own expectations and proscriptions. What has triggered such a deep gender divide? Is it rooted in our biology? Is it a cultural creation that gets reproduced through socialization practices and interpersonal interaction? What is the future of gender? Controversy abounds.

Taking Sides: Clashing Views in Gender is a tool for stimulating critical thought about females and males, femaleness and maleness, and beyond. Consideration of the complexity of sex and gender necessitates a multidisciplinary perspective. Thus, you will learn about definitions and views of sex and gender from such fields as sociology, ethnic studies, women's studies, men's studies, gay and lesbian studies, queer studies, gender studies, transgender studies, education, language, political science, global studies, religion, history, medicine, law, psychology, and biology. The multidisciplinarity of inquiry on sex and gender has created a rich, exciting, and emotionally and politically charged body of theory, research, and practice. The study of sex and gender is so dynamic that it is one of the most fast-paced areas of inquiry, characterized by great fervor and rapid growth. It is also one of the most contentious areas of thought, distinguished by deep theoretical and philosophical differences. Such division also marks public discourse on sex and gender.

This book contains 20 issues, organized into 6 parts, that are being hotly debated in contemporary scholarly and public discourse on sex and gender. They are phrased as yes/no questions so that two distinct perspectives are delineated and contrasted. Each issue is prefaced by an *issue introduction* containing background material contextualizing the dual positions. Additional perspectives are presented in a *postscript* following each issue to enrich and enliven debate and discussion. No issue is truly binary, adequately represented by only two points of view. Considering other perspectives will broaden your understanding of the complexity of each issue, enabling you to develop an informed ideology. The *suggestions for further reading* that appear in each issue postscript should help you find resources to continue your study of the subject. At the back of the book is a listing of all the *contributors to this volume*, which will give you information on the various writers whose views are debated here. Also, on the *Internet References* page that accompanies each part opener, you will find Internet site addresses (URLs) that are relevant to the issues in that part. These Web sites should prove useful as starting points for further research.

You begin this quest with an existing personal gender ideology of which you may not even be aware. It serves as a filter through which you process information about females and males, femaleness and maleness. It draws your attention to some information and points of view and allows you to disregard other more dissonant perspectives. Your challenge is to probe your personal gender ideology (and intersecting ideologies such as ethnicity, sexual orientation, social class, gender identity) so that you can open your mind to other perspectives and information and develop a more informed ideology. To do so takes courage and active thought. As you work through this book, note your reactions to different points and perspectives. Exchange reactions and relevant experiences with your peers. "Try on" different perspectives by trying to represent a view with which you initially disagree. Explore *suggestions for further reading* and Web sites provided for each part or issue. Challenge yourself to explore all angles so that your own theories or views become more reasoned and representative.

No matter what field of study, career path, and/or other personal choices you pursue, issues of sex and gender will be pervasive. Great sociohistorical change in sex and gender marked the twentieth century, catalyzing even greater momentum for the twenty-first century. The goal of this book is to help you develop an ideological tool chest that will enable you to intelligently and responsibly navigate the changing gender landscape. Collectively, you will chart the course of the future of gender.

Changes to this edition   This edition contains 20 issues organized into six parts. The book outline has changed substantially, with the addition of 5 new issues, and 18 new, more current selections added to reflect the YES and NO perspectives. Part openers, issue introductions, and issues postscripts have been revised accordingly. Each issue opener calls attention to the consideration of cross-cutting issues that enrich and complicate in meaningful ways the clashing views presented in each part. Students and instructors are encouraged to discuss each of these questions:

1. *The role of biology*: What does emerging research on brain differences tell us about gender-related patterns of behavior? How can one separate cause, consequence, and correlates in this growing body of knowledge?
2. *Intersecting identities*: How do race, ethnicity, class, culture, and other status-defining attributes relate to gendered-patterns of behavior? Does the consideration of how multiple identities intersect contribute to new understandings of gender?
3. *Media representations*: How do media portrayals of gender-related issues affect our understanding of the phenomenon? How and when do media portrayals, including images and language, reinforce or defy gender stereotypes?

A word to the instructor   An *Instructor's Resource Guide with Test Questions* (multiple-choice and essay) is available through the publisher for the instructor using *Taking Sides* in the classroom. A general guidebook, *Using Taking Sides in the Classroom,* which discusses methods and techniques for integrating the pro-con approach into any classroom setting, is also available. An online version of *Using Taking Sides in the Classroom* and a correspondence service for *Taking Sides* adopters can be found at http://www.mhcls.com/usingts/.

Taking Sides: Clashing Views in Gender is only one title in the Taking Sides series. If you are interested in seeing the table of contents for any of the other titles, please visit the Taking Sides Web site at http://www.mhcls.com/takingsides/.

Acknowledgments   First and foremost, the contributions of Elizabeth Paul, editor of the first two editions, are acknowledged. The insights and knowledge she brought to this project have provided a solid platform from which to move forward into the third edition. Her understanding of the issues facing the study of gender and her ability to cogently frame the issues set a high standard, one to which I hope the fourth edition can measure up. I also want to express great appreciation to my many undergraduates who helped me understand which issues resonate most with them. Many colleagues in the Women's and Gender Studies program at UNCG provided an articulate sounding board as I debated which issues to include and how to frame them. Also, the comments and feedback from my doctoral students Ashlyn Gollehon and Kevin Swartout have been invaluable in developing the set of issues selected for this edition. I must also acknowledge Jill Peter at McGraw-Hill/Contemporary Learning Series who provided me with expertise, support, and encouragement at each step of the process. Lastly, my husband and children Ian and Elaine were enormously supportive and patient, filling in for all those household tasks I simply ignored. I have learned much from them about what it means to have an equal partner and to attempt to raise children free of gender constraints in a society that really does not want that to happen.

Jacquelyn W. White
University of North Carolina at Greensboro

Contents In Brief

Contents

Social psychologist Jacquelyn W. White and her colleagues conclude, based on a review of the literature, that girls and women are highly likely to be the targets of male aggression and are less likely to use physical aggression than men due to different developmental experiences. Social psychologist Richard B. Felson argues that aggression is related to physical strength and a general tendency toward violence, not male domination, and that there is not an epidemic of violence against women.

Murray A. Straus and his colleague Ignacio Luis Ramirez argue that women are just as likely to commit physical aggression against dating partners as are men, suggesting that gender symmetry exists in different cultural contexts. On the other hand, social psychologist Suzanne C. Swan and colleague David L. Snow argue that women's use of aggression does not equate to gender symmetry. Rather cultural context, motives, and history of trauma must be considered.

Professor of law Anthony D'Amato highlights statistics from the most recent National Crime Victimization Survey that demonstrate a correlation between the increased consumption of pornography over the years with the decreased incidence of rape. Some people, he argues, watch pornography in order to push any desire to rape out of their minds, and thus have no further desire to go out and actually do it. Judith Reisman, president of the Institute for Media Education, asserts that sex criminals imitate what they see depicted in the media, providing examples of serial rapists and killers who had large stores of pornography in their possession, and research in which approximately

33 percent of rapists said that they had viewed pornography immediately prior to at least one of their rapes.

Sarah S. McLanahan and Marcia J. Carlson, examine the negative effects of father-absence in children's lives and offer suggestions for how to increase father involvement. In contrast, Peggy Drexler studied what she terms "maverick" moms to show how boys can succeed in homes without fathers.

Dena S. Davis argues that fetal sex selection is an ethical issue because it is really about gender selection that promotes traditional stereotypes and can interfere with a child's right to an open future. Rosamond Rhodes describes the acceptable scope of fetal sex selection, as well as professional responsibilities of practitioners of reproductive medicine.

Brigham Young University colleagues E. Jeffrey Hill and Vjollca K. Martinson, along with Maria Ferris of IBM and Robin Zenger Baker at Boston University, suggest that women in professional careers can successfully integrate family and career by following a new-concept part-time work model. In contrast, Mary C. Noonan, an assistant professor in the department of sociology at the University of Iowa, and Mary E. Corcoran, a professor of political science at the University of Michigan, document the various costs of the mommy track for female attorneys, including lower salaries and decreased likelihood of promotion to partner.

Hilda Kahne, professor emerita at Wheaton College in Massachusetts and a member of the Scholars Program and a Resident Scholar at Brandeis University, makes the argument that incomplete education and few training programs, rather than gender discrimination, makes it more difficult for low-wage single mothers to raise their earnings. In contrast, Hadas Mandel of the department of sociology and anthropology and Moshe Semyonov of the department of sociology and labor studies anthropology at Tel Aviv University review extensive data from 22 countries and conclude that social policies have the counterintuitive impact of decreasing women's opportunities for access to more desirable and powerful positions.

Issue 16   Is the Gender Wage Gap Justified?   278

June O'Neill suggests that the gender gap is largely due to nondiscriminatory factors, most notable those associated with women's choices due to the division of labor in the home. Hilary M. Lips documents the continuing gender gap in wages and argues that a continuing undervaluing of women's work due to stereotypes and prejudice maintains the wage gap.

Issue 17   Are Barriers to Women's Success as Leaders Due to Societal Obstacles?   292

Alice H. Eagly and Linda L. Carli contend that barriers exist for women at every stage of their career trajectories, resulting in, not a glass ceiling, but a labyrinth. Kingsley R. Browne asserts that the division of labor by sex is rooted in biologically based differences between women and men. Evolutionarily based natural selection has led to inclinations that make women and men better suited for different types of jobs.

UNIT 6   GENDER AND SEXUALITY: DOUBLE STANDARDS?   311

Issue 18   Is Female Circumcision Universally Wrong?   312

Gerald Mackie takes a scientific approach to challenge the argument that female genital cutting is not always harmful, citing multiple examples of physical and psychological harm. Carla M. Obermeyer argues that a lack of research precludes us from fully understanding female circumcision and claiming that it is responsible for a variety of harmful health outcomes. She includes examples of no harm.

Issue 19   Should "Abstinence-Until-Marriage" Be the Only Message to Teens?   334

YES: **Bridget E. Maher,** from "Abstinence Until Marriage: The Best Message for Teens," Family Research Council (2004)   *336*

NO: **Debra Hauser,** from *Five Years of Abstinence-Only-Until-Marriage Education: Assessing the Impact* (2004)   *342*

Bridget E. Maher argues that far too much funding has gone into programs that teach young people about sexuality and contraception—programs that she concludes are ineffective. Debra Hauser, in an evaluation of numerous abstinence-only-until-marriage programs that received funding under the Title V Social Security Act, concludes that they show few short-term benefits and no lasting, positive effects; rather such programs may actually worsen sexual health outcomes.

Issue 20   Can Women's Sexuality Be Free from Traditional Gender Constraints?   351

YES: **Elizabeth Sheff,** from "Polyamorous Women, Sexual Subjectivity and Power," *Journal of Contemporary Ethnography* (2005)   *353*

NO: **Yuko Yamamiya, Thomas F. Cash, and J. Kevin Thompson,** from "Sexual Experiences Among College Women: The Differential Effects of General Versus Contextual Body Images on Sexuality," *Sex Roles* (2006)   *362*

Elizabeth Sheff conducted an ethnographic study that suggests that engaging in nontraditional relationships can help women reject sexual objectification and enlarge their sexual subjectivity. In contrast, Yuko Yamamiya, Thomas F. Cash, and J. Kevin Thompson suggest that the objectification of women's bodies in Western culture results in lower sexual self-efficacy and sexual difficulties.

Correlation Guide

The *Taking Sides* series presents current issues in a debate-style format designed to stimulate student interest and develop critical thinking skills. Each issue is thoughtfully framed with an issue summary, an issue introduction, and a postscript. The pro and con essays—selected for their liveliness and substance—represent the arguments of leading scholars and commentators in their fields.

Taking Sides: Clashing Views in Gender, 4/e is an easy-to-use reader that presents issues on important topics such as *gender identity, gender in the workplace and gender* and *sexuality.* For more information on *Taking Sides* and other *McGraw-Hill Contemporary Learning Series* titles, visit www.mhcls.com.

This convenient guide matches the issues in **Taking Sides: Gender, 4/e** with the corresponding chapters in two of our best-selling McGraw-Hill Psychology textbooks by Hyde/DeLamater and Lips.

Taking Sides: Gender, 4/e	Understanding Human Sexuality, 10/e by Hyde/DeLamater	Sex & Gender, 6/e by Lips
Issue 1: Is Anatomy Destiny?	**Chapter 2:** Theoretical Perspectives on Sexuality **Chapter 12:** Gender and Sexuality **Chapter 13:** Sexual Orientation: Gay, Straight, or Bi?	**Chapter 2:** Theoretical Perspectives on Sex and Gender **Chapter 5:** Biology and Environment: The Process of Becoming Female and Male **Chapter 10:** Sex and Gender and Childhood: Constructing Gender
Issue 2: Is Gender Identity Innate?	**Chapter 2:** Theoretical Perspectives on Sexuality **Chapter 12:** Gender and Sexuality **Chapter 13:** Sexual Orientation: Gay, Straight, or Bi?	**Chapter 2:** Theoretical Perspectives on Sex and Gender **Chapter 5:** Biology and Environment: The Process of Becoming Female or Male **Chapter 10:** Sex and Gender and Childhood: Constructing Gender
Issue 3: Do Sex Differences in Careers in Mathematics and Sciences Have a Biological Basis?		**Chapter 1:** Masculinity and Femininity: Myths and Stereotypes **Chapter 3:** Researching Sex and Gender: Exploring the Whys and Hows **Chapter 6:** Perceptual and Cognitive Abilities: Gender Similarities and Differences **Chapter 10:** Sex and Gender and Childhood: Constructing Gender

Taking Sides: Gender, 4/e	Understanding Human Sexuality, 10/e by Hyde/ DeLamater	Sex & Gender, 6/e by Lips
Issue 4: Are Women and Men More Similar Than Different?	**Chapter 12:** Gender and Sexuality	**Chapter 2:** Theoretical Perspectives on Sex and Gender **Chapter 3:** Researching Sex and Gender: Exploring the Whys and Hows **Chapter 4:** Worlds Apart? Gender Differences in Social Behavior and Experience **Chapter 6:** Perceptual and Cognitive Abilities: Gender Similarities and Differences **Chapter 7:** Sexual Lives and Orientations **Chapter 9:** Mental and Physical Health: Stress, Change, and Adaptations **Chapter 10:** Sex and Gender and Childhood: Constructing Gender **Chapter 11:** Family and Friends: Attachment, Intimacy, and Power
Issue 5: Are Different Patterns of Communication in Women and Men Innately Determined?	**Chapter 11:** Attraction, Love, and Communication **Chapter 12:** Gender and Sexuality	**Chapter 4:** Worlds Apart? Gender Differences in Social Behavior and Experience **Chapter 10:** Sex and Gender and Childhood: Constructing Gender **Chapter 11:** Family and Friends: Attachment, Intimacy, and Power **Chapter 12:** Economic and Political Life: Power, Status, and Achievement
Issue 6: Are the Fight-or-Flight and Tend-and-Befriend Responses to Stress Gender-Based?		
Issue 7: Are Expressions of Aggression Related to Gender?	**Chapter 12:** Gender and Sexuality	**Chapter 4:** Worlds Apart? Gender Differences in Social Behavior and Experience
Issue 8: Gender Symmetry: Do Women and Men Commit Equal Levels of Violence Against Intimate Partners?	**Chapter 12:** Gender and Sexuality	**Chapter 4:** Worlds Apart? Gender Differences in Social Behavior and Experience **Chapter 7:** Sexual Lives and Orientations **Chapter 11:** Family and Friends: Attachment, Intimacy, and Power
Issue 9: Does Pornography Reduce the Incidence of Rape?	**Chapter 15:** Sexual Coercion **Chapter 16:** Sex for Sale	**Chapter 7:** Sexual Lives and Orientations
Issue 10: Should Same-Sex Couples Be Able to Marry?	**Chapter 20:** Sex and the Law	**Chapter 7:** Sexual Lives and Orientations

Taking Sides: Gender, 4/e	Understanding Human Sexuality, 10/e by Hyde/DeLamater	Sex & Gender, 6/e by Lips
Issue 11: Can Lesbian and Gay Couples Be Appropriate Parents for Children?	**Chapter 13:** Sexual Orientation: Gay, Straight, or Bi?	**Chapter 11:** Family and Friends: Attachment, Intimacy, and Power
Issue 12: Are Fathers Essential for Children's Well-Being?	**Chapter 2:** Theoretical Perspectives on Sexuality	**Chapter 11:** Family and Friends: Attachment, Intimacy, and Power
Issue 13: Is Fetal Sex Selection Harmful to Society?	**Chapter 6:** Conception, Pregnancy, and Childbirth	
Issue 14: Does the "Mommy Track" (Part-Time Work) Improve Women's Lives?		**Chapter 11:** Family and Friends: Attachment, Intimacy, and Power **Chapter 13:** Issues in the Workplace
Issue 15: Can Social Policies Improve Gender Inequalities in the Workplace?		**Chapter 12:** Economic and Political Life: Power, Status, and Achievement **Chapter 13:** Issues in the Workplace **Chapter 14:** Justice, Equity, and Social Change
Issue 16: Is the Gender Wage Gap Justified?		**Chapter 1:** Masculinity and Femininity: Myths and Stereotypes **Chapter 2:** Theoretical Perspectives on Sex and Gender **Chapter 4:** Worlds Apart? Gender Differences in Social Behavior and Experience **Chapter 10:** Sex and Gender and Childhood: Constructing Gender **Chapter 12:** Economic and Political Life: Power, Status, and Achievement **Chapter 13:** Issues in the Workplace **Chapter 14:** Justice, Equity, and Social Change
Issue 17: Are Barriers to Women's Success as Leaders Due to Societal Obstacles?		**Chapter 1:** Masculinity and Femininity: Myths and Stereotypes **Chapter 2:** Theoretical Perspectives on Sex and Gender **Chapter 4:** Worlds Apart? Gender Differences in Social Behavior and Experience **Chapter 10:** Sex and Gender and Childhood: Constructing Gender **Chapter 12:** Economic and Political Life: Power, Status, and Achievement **Chapter 13:** Issues in the Workplace **Chapter 14:** Justice, Equity, and Social Change

Taking Sides: Gender, 4/e	Understanding Human Sexuality, 10/e by Hyde/ DeLamater	Sex & Gender, 6/e by Lips
Issue 18: Is Female Circumcision Universally Wrong?	**Chapter 1:** Sexuality in Perspective **Chapter 4:** Sexual Anatomy	
Issue 19: Should "Abstinence-Until-Marriage" Be the Only Message to Teens?	**Chapter 9:** Sexuality and the Life Cycle: Childhood and Adolescence **Epilogue:** Looking to the Future: Sexuality Education	
Issue 20: Can Women's Sexuality Be Free from Traditional Gender Constraints?	**Chapter 2:** Theoretical Perspectives on Sexuality **Chapter 12:** Gender and Sexuality	**Chapter 1:** Masculinity and Femininity: Myths and Stereotypes **Chapter 2:** Theoretical Perspectives on Sex and Gender **Chapter 3:** Researching Sex and Gender: Exploring the Whys and Hows **Chapter 4:** Worlds Apart? Gender Differences in Social Behavior and Experience **Chapter 5:** Biology and Environment: The Process of Becoming Female or Male **Chapter 6:** Perceptual and Cognitive Abilities: Gender Similarities and Differences **Chapter 7:** Sexual Lives and Orientations **Chapter 10:** Sex and Gender and Childhood: Constructing Gender **Chapter 12:** Economic and Political Life: Power, Status, and Achievement **Chapter 13:** Issues in the Workplace **Chapter 14:** Justice, Equity, and Social Change

Introduction

Sex and Gender: Knowing Is Believing, but Is Believing Knowing?

As people go through their day-to-day lives, when is their sex or gender relevant, that is, in the foreground, and when is it in the background? Think about this question regarding your own life. Are you always aware of being a female or a male? Probably not. Does your femaleness or maleness cause you to behave the way you do all the time? Probably not. Thus, we arrive at the perplexing and complicated question: When do sex and gender matter? To begin to answer this question we need to consider what we mean by the terms *sex* and *gender*. We also need to identify and make explicit the fundamental assumptions that lead us to put so much importance on questions regarding sex and gender.

Within any species of living organisms, there is variation. In Western thought, a primary individual difference is sex. What do we "know" about the ways in which individuals differ by sex? Of course, an obvious response is that individuals are either female or male. We treat it as fact. What else do you *know* about human variation by sex? Are there other *facts* about human females and males? Perhaps you will state such facts as males' greater physical strength than females, males' taller stature than females, and females' unique capacity for childbearing. Make a list of what else you *know* about human variation by sex.

Most of us have a vast network of knowledge about human variation by sex. Many of the claims stem from knowledge of the differential biology of females and males and extend to variation in human emotion, thought, and behavior. In fact, some individuals maintain that females and males are so different that they are from different planets! For most of us, this is an interconnected network of "givens" about the far-reaching effects of femaleness and maleness. Given that we consider human sex variation to be an undeniable fact, we rarely question these claims. Instead we see them as essential truths or facts—unquestionable, unchangeable, and inevitable. The goal of this book is to guide your critical evaluation of this network of knowledge. What you may discover as you critically consider the controversial issues in this book is that many of the things we believe to be factually true and objectively provable about human sex variation are instead unsupported beliefs.

Knowledge and Beliefs in the Study of Sex and Gender

Cross-cutting Issue: The Role of Biology

For decades, in public discourse and in numerous academic disciplines, there has been widespread debate and discussion of the extent of human variation by sex. In addition, there is extensive consideration of the cultural meaning and significance attached to femaleness and maleness. The terms *sex* and *gender* are used to refer to these various phenomena. Although sex and gender are commonly thought to be synonyms, many scholars attempted to assign different meanings to these terms. Sex was often used to refer to the biological distinction between females and males. Gender referred to the social and cultural meaning attached to notions of femaleness and maleness. Depending on one's theory of how sex and gender were related, there were varying degrees of overlap or interconnection between these two terms. Many scholars now question the usefulness of the distinction, suggesting that the notion of biological sex itself is socially constructed. This more contemporary view rests on two arguments. First, biological organisms cannot exist or be studied devoid of a social context, making the sex and gender dichotomy arbitrary. Second, as Myra Hird has suggested, there is a persistent, yet unchallenged belief that biological sex is the "original sign through which gender is read." That is, what we know about a person's anatomy provides the basis for prescriptions and proscriptions regarding appropriate behaviors.

Gender has been employed in theory and research in various ways and toward various goals. The study of gender has been used to assess the validity of claims of human sex differences. It has also been used to challenge assertions of biological roots of gendered behavior by testing alternate causal theories (e.g., environmental, learning, cognitive theories). Some studies of gender aim to analyze the social organization of female/male relations, elucidating gendered power dynamics and patterns of dominance and subordination. Gender studies have also been used to show how burdens and benefits are inequitably distributed among females and males in society. Other scholars have used conceptions of gender to explain the structure of the human psyche, individuals' sense of self, identity, and aspiration.

How are elements of gender produced? Biological essentialists believe that biological sex differences directly lead to behavioral, cognitive, and emotional differences (i.e., gender affects) between females and males. In other words, there are *essential* differences between females and males that stem from biology and pervade human psychology and sociality. Evolutionary theorists believe that ancestral responses to environmental challenges created physiological differences between females and males that underlie contemporary behavioral differences. In contrast, social constructionists believe gender to be a social or cultural creation. Infants and children are socialized and disciplined so as to develop sex-appropriate gender attributes and skills. As individuals mature, they develop a gender identity or a sense of self as female or male. They internalize the dominant cultural gender ideology, develop expectations for self and others, and assume sex-congruent gender roles, behaving in gender-appropriate ways. Symbolic interactionists point to the power of pervasive cultural gender symbolism in the production and reproduction of gender in cultures. They show how gender metaphors are assigned to cultural artifacts and how language structures gender meanings and dynamics creating to a dominant cultural meaning system. Standpoint theorists show us how our position in the social hierarchy impacts our perspective on and involvement in cultural gender dynamics. Throughout all the issues in this book, you will see these various perspectives being contrasted.

The concept of gender has been construed in many ways, spawning a highly complex field of inquiry. Some scholars perceive gender as an attribute of individuals or something we "have." Others see gender as something we "do" or perform; gender is seen as a product of interpersonal interaction. Gender has also been construed as a mode of social organization, structuring status and power dynamics in cultural institutions. Some see gender as universal; others believe gender to be historically—and culturally—specific. The latter perspective has yielded a proliferation of investigations into how, why, when, where, and for whom gender "works." Recently similar logic has been applied to biological sex. That is, the concept of biological sex itself is a social construction.

Biological features of sex have been assumed to include genetic factors of female and male chromosomes, hormones and the endocrine system, internal and external sexual and reproductive organs (appearance and functionality) and central nervous system sex differentiation. The assumption or the defined norm was that there is consistency among these different biological factors, differentiating individuals into females and males. However, research with transgendered people and intersexed individuals challenges the assumption that various biological features of organisms "naturally" co-occur. Research suggests that variations among these features occur naturally. Defining these variations as "normal" or "deviant" is a social construction.

Recent technological advances are permitting greater opportunities to examine genetic constitution and expression, as well as neurological and hormonal functioning in humans. Sophisticated methods provide for careful evaluation of cardiovascular and immune functions as well. All of these have been applied to the study of sex differences. The big debate is whether this work is clarifying or confusing the study of sex and gender.

Intersecting Identities

Adding to the complexity is a growing appreciation that what it means to be female or male in a given culture is affected by one's race, ethnicity, social class, and sexual orientation with some scholars arguing that these too are social constructs. Contemporary analyses suggest that the fundamental construct is *oppression*—that is, those in power have the authority to declare who is and is not "acceptable," with access to resources (such as education or political influence) based on criteria defined by the powerful. Thus, gender is seen as one system of power intersecting with other systems of power (such as race, ethnicity, heterosexuality and social class).

The concept of intersecting identities suggests that some people may experience status incongruence as they forge a sense of identity. Identity is a dynamic ongoing process involving the negotiation of social relationships across time and contexts. The view that people's identities are dynamic and negotiated indicates that one's senses of self (e.g., psychological characteristics or traits, physical features, roles, abilities) are contextually dependent. The negotiation of power relationships can be informed by the dynamic process of identity development and maintenance and vice versa. Theories of identity bring social structural variables (e.g., ethnicity, gender, class) associated with varying degrees of status, to the individual and interpersonal levels. In any given situation, a person's perception of how social structural variables are incorporated into her/his identity may inform the perception of relative power. Different levels of social power may produce different behavioral, cognitive, and affective consequences, making the presentation of self, even at the biological level, fluid across time and context. It is likely that as we more consciously consider the notion of intersecting identities into discussions of sex and gender, much of what we think we know will need to be reevaluated. Such analyses provide opportunities to challenge the essentialist notion of the universal male and female.

Media Representations

Consider what constitutes "proof" for you. What are your standards of "truth"? How do we know that a piece of information is a fact rather than a belief? Do we base our classification on evidence? What kind of evidence do we require? What constitutes enough evidence to classify a claim as a fact rather than a belief? Starting with what we *know* to be the most basic fact about human variation by sex, that humans are either female or male, how do you know that? Did someone tell you (e.g., a parent, a teacher)? Did you read it some where, in a magazine or a scientific journal? Did you observe differences between yourself and others or among others? How did this information or observation get generalized from a few individuals to all humans? How have your observations played out in movies or television programs? Is this kind of generalization warrantable, based on human variation? Are there any exceptions (i.e., individuals that do not fit neatly into the categories of female or male? Would such exceptions lead you to question the *fact* of sex as female or male? For something to be fact, must it be universally true of all individuals within a given species? Have you ever thought critically about this before? How have media portrayals challenged gender constructions? Think of *M. Butterfly* or *Broke back mountain?*

What is the difference (if any) between facts and beliefs? Do we treat knowledge differently if we classify it as fact versus belief or opinion? Are facts more important to us than beliefs? Do we question the veracity of facts as much as that of beliefs? Why not? What are the ramifications of not submitting facts to critical questioning? Rethink the facts you listed about human variation by sex. How do you know these are facts? What is your evidence? Does your evidence indisputably support the claim as fact? Do you detect defensiveness about or resistance to critically questioning facts? Why?

Most people do not read scientific journals to get their facts. They rely on various media—magazines, television, and increasingly, the Internet. A fundamental question is whether the media reflect reality or contribute to the creation of reality. Consider the marketers of Halloween costumes for children. Adie Nelson (*Psychology of Women Quarterly*, 2000) did a content analysis of 469 children's costumes and sewing patterns. She found that less that 10 percent was gender neutral. Costumes for both girls and boys were predominately hero costumes. Costumes for girls tended to depict beauty queens, princesses, and other traditionally feminine images (including animals and foodstuffs). Costumes for boys often followed a warrior theme, featuring villains (agents or symbols of death). She concluded that "children's fantasy dress reproduces and reiterates more conventional messages about gender." The same conclusion can be said about many media messages. Exposure to sexist media has been shown to lead to less achievement in girls and more sexist attitudes in boys.

It is important to also consider what media messages say to members of various racial, ethnic, and cultural groups. How do these messages frame and reinforce the marginalized status of many groups? For example, to be beautiful is to be thin, blond, and heterosexual. One study found that the more mainstream TV young white women watch the more negative their body image, but that the more black-oriented TV that young black women watch the more positive their body image.

Also, consider how current media reports of scientific findings may privilege an essentialist, causal role of biological forces in gender differences over social constructionist views. For example, an ABC News report proclaimed, "Scientists find sex differences in the brain" (Jan. 19, 2000). "The New Sex Scorecard" in *Psychology Today* (July/Aug, 2003) proclaimed that "men and women's minds really do work differently." What is the impact of such headlines from supposedly reputable sources on everyday people's understanding of the women and men?

As you can see from this brief review of many of the ways in which gender has been construed and studied, there are differences and even contradictions among the various perspectives and approaches. Some individuals champion gender as stimulating complementarity and interdependence among humans; others see gender as a powerful source of segregation and exclusion. Some scholars emphasize differences between females and males; others allow for greater individual variation that crosses sex and gender boundaries or they even emphasize similarity between females and males. Some people think of gender as invariant and fixed; others think of gender as malleable and flexible. Some scholars see gender as politically irrelevant; others see gender as the root of all social and political inequities. Some view "gender-inappropriate" behavior with disdain and fear, labeling it problematic and pathological and in need of correction; others see gender variance as natural and cause for celebration. Some individuals believe "traditional" differentiated sex roles should be preserved; others believe that these conventional notions of gender should be redefined or even transcended. Some individuals view gender processes and dynamics as personally relevant; others have little conception of the role of gender in their lived experience. How do we deal with this controversy? How can we evaluate and weigh different assertions and arguments?

Tools for Argument Analysis

Each pair of selections in this volume present opposing arguments about sex and gender. How do you decide which argument is "right" or, at least, which argument is better? Argument analysis is a field with many approaches and standards. Here a few major components and criteria are briefly presented to help you in making judgments about the quality of the arguments advanced in the book.

To assess an argument's quality it is helpful to break it down into seven components, including its *claim, definitions, statements of fact, statements of value, language and reasoning, use of authority,* and *audience.* However, first we must touch on the issue of *explicit versus implicit elements* within an argument. Real-world arguments contain many implicit (unstated) elements. For example, they may use unstated definitions of key terms or rely on value judgments that are not made clear within the body of the argument itself. Occasionally these elements are left out because the author wants to hide the weaknesses of her or his argument by omitting them. However it is probably more often the case that they are omitted because the author assumes the audience for their work knows about the missing elements and already accepts them as true. The job of the argument analyst begins with identifying implicit elements in an argument and making them explicit. Since we usually do not have direct access to the argument's author, making implicit elements explicit requires a good deal of interpretation on our part. However, few arguments would stand up to analysis for long if we did not try our best to fill in the implicit content. Specific examples of making implicit elements explicit are provided in what follows.

Claim

The first component one should look for in an argument is its claim. What, specifically, are the authors trying to convince us of? The notion of a claim in an argument is essentially the same as that of a thesis in a term paper. In almost all cases it is possible to identify a single overarching claim that the authors are trying to get their audience to accept. For example, in Issue 3 Thornhill and Palmer claim that males' propensity to rape has an evolutionary basis. Once the claim of an argument is identified, the analyst can begin to look for and evaluate supporting components. If no claim can be identified, then we do not have an argument that is well formed enough to evaluate fairly.

Definitions

At first thought, an argument's definitions might not seem a very interesting target for analysis. However, definitions are often highly controversial, implicit, and suspect in terms of their quality. This is especially the case in the study of sex and gender. How are the key terms in an argument's claim and supporting reasons defined, if at all? Does the author rely on dictionary definitions, stipulative definitions (offering an original definition of the term), definition by negation (saying what the term does not mean), or definition by example? Dictionary definitions are relatively uncontroversial but rare and of limited application. Stipulative definitions are conveniently explicit but often the subject of controversy. Other types of definitions can be both implicit and not widely accepted. Once you have identified definitions of the key terms in an argument's claim and supporting reasons, ask yourself if you find these definitions to be acceptable. Then ask if the argument's opponent is using these same definitions or is advocating a different set. Opposing arguments cannot be resolved on their merits until the two sides agree on key definitions. Indeed many long-term debates in public policy never seem to get resolved because the two sides define the underlying problem in very different ways. For example, in Issue 19 on repartive therapy consider the centrality of each author's definition of "sexual desire."

Statements of Fact

Claims have two fundamentally different types of supporting reasons. The first type is statements of fact. A fact is a description of something that we can presumably verify to be true. Thus the first question to be answered about an argument's factual statements is how do we know they are true? Authors may report original empirical research of their own. With an argument that is reporting on original research, the best means of checking the truth of their facts would be to repeat, or replicate, their research. This is almost never realistically possible, so we then must rely on an assessment of the methods they used, either our own assessment or that of an authority we trust. Authors may be relying on facts that they did not discover on their own, but instead obtained from some authoritative source.

Aside from the question of the truth of facts is the question of their sufficiency. Authors may offer a few facts to support their claim or many. They may offer individual cases or very broad factual generalizations. How many facts are enough? Since most arguments are evaluated in the context of their opponents, it is tempting to tally up the factual statements of both arguments and declare the one with the most facts the winner. This is seldom adequate, although an argument with a wealth of well-substantiated factual statements in support of its claim is certainly preferable to one with few statements of fact that are of questionable quality. In persuasive arguments it is very common to see many anecdotes and examples of individual cases. These are used to encourage the audience to identify with the subject of the cases. However, in analyzing these arguments we must always ask if an individual case really represents a systematic trend. In other words, do the facts offered generalize to the whole or are they just persuasive but isolated exceptions? On the other hand, it is also common to see the use of statistics to identify general characteristics of a population. The analyst should always ask if these statistics were collected in a scientific manner and without bias, if they really show significant distinct characteristics, and how much variation there is around the central characteristics identified. Debates about the gender pay gap are highly influenced by how the pay gap is measured (see Issues 12 and 13).

A final question about statements of fact concerns their relevancy. We sometimes discover factual statements in an argument that may be true, and even interesting reading, but that just don't have anything to do with the claim being advanced. Be sure that the forest is not missed for the trees in evaluating statements of fact—in other words, that verifying and tallying of factual statements does not preempt the question of how well an author supports the primary claim.

Statements of Value

The philosopher David Hume is famous for his observation that a series of factual statements (that something "is" the case) will never lead to the conclusion that something "ought" to be done. The missing component necessary to move from "is" to "ought," to move from statements of fact to accepting an argument's claim, are statements of value. Statements of value declare something to be right or wrong, good or bad, desirable or undesirable, beautiful or ugly. For example, "It is wrong for boys to play with dolls."

Although many people behave as if debates can be resolved by proving one side or the other's factual statements to be true, statements of value are just as critical to the quality of an argument as are statements of fact. Moreover, because value statements have their roots in moral and religious beliefs, we tend to shy away from analyzing them too deeply in public discourse. Instead, people tend to be *absolutist*, rejecting outright values that they do not share, or *relativist*, declaring that all values are equally valid. As a result, statements of value are not as widely studied in argument analysis and standards of evaluation are not as well developed for them as for factual statements.

At the very least, the argument analyst can expect the value statements of an argument to be part of what has been referred to as a "rational ideology." A rational ideology is one in which value statements are *cogent* and *coherent* parts of a *justifiable* system of beliefs. A cogent value statement is one that is relevant and clear. Coherent value statements fit together; they are consistent with one another and help support an argument's claim. A system of beliefs is justifiable if its advocate can provide supporting reasons (both facts and values) for holding beliefs. A morality that makes value judgments but refuses to offer reasons for these judgments would strike us as neither very rational nor very persuasive. Although we rarely have the opportunity to engage in a debate with authors to test their ability to justify their value statements, we can expect an argument's value statements to be explicit, cogent, coherent, and supported by additional statements of fact and value as justification. As in the case of definitions, it is also fruitful to compare the value statements of one argument with those of the opposing view to see how much the authors agree or disagree in the (usually) implicit ideology that lies behind their value statements.

Throughout the issues in this book you will see an implicit clash of values: The sexes *should* be different versus opportunity for variations should be encouraged.

Language and Reasoning

There are a vast number of specific issues in the use of language and reasoning within arguments. Any introductory book on rhetoric or argumentative logic will provide a discussion of these issues. Here just a sample of the most common ones will be touched on. The analyst gives less weight to arguments that use language that is overly emotional. Emotional language relies on connotation (word meanings aside from formal definition), bias or slanting in word choice, exaggeration, slogan, an cliché. Emotional language is sometimes appropriate when describing personal experience but it is not persuasive when used to support a general claim about what should be believed or done in society.

The analysis of reasoning has to do with the logical structure of an argument's components and usually focuses on the search for logical fallacies (errors in logic). A common fallacy has already been discussed under statements of fact: hasty generalization. In hasty generalizations claims are made without a sufficient amount of factual evidence to support them. When authors argue that one event followed another and this proves the first event caused the second, they are committing the *post hoc* fallacy (it may just be a coincidence that the events happened in that order). Two fallacies often spotted in arguments directed at opponents are *ad hominem* and straw man. The first involves attacking the person advocating the opposing view, which is generally irrelevant to the quality of their statements. The second is unfairly describing an opponent's argument in an overly simplified way that is easy to defeat. Fallacies directed at the argument's audience include false dilemma, slippery slope, and *ad populum.* Authors commit the fallacy of false dilemma when they argue that only two alternatives exist when, in fact, there are more than two. Slippery slope is an unsupportable prediction that if a small first step is taken it will inevitably lead to more change. An appeal to public opinion to support a claim is an *ad populum* argument if there is reason to believe that the public is prejudiced or plain wrong in its views, or if what the public believes is simply not relevant to the issue. In general, the argument analyst must not only look at the individual statements of an argument but must also ask how well they are put together in an argument that is logical and not overly emotional.

Use of Authority

The issue of authority is relevant in argument analysis in two places. The first has to do with the authority of the argument's author. Analysts should use whatever information they can gather to assess the expertise and possible biases of authors. Are authors reporting on an issue that they have only recently begun to study, or have they studied the issue area in considerable depth? Do they occupy a professional position that indicates recognition by others as authorities in the field? Do you have reason to believe that their work is objective and not subject to systematic biases because of who pays for or publishes their work? Be careful not to commit *ad hominem* on this one yourself. The brief biographies of contributors to this volume give you a bit of information about the authors of the arguments that follow.

The second place authority enters into analysis is the citation of authorities within the body of the argument itself. To a greater or lesser degree, all arguments rely on citation of outside authorities to support their statements. We should ask the same questions of these authorities as we ask of authors. In general, we want authorities that are widely accepted as experts and that do not have systematic biases. Even if we do not have the time or resources to check out the authorities cited in an argument, it is reasonable to expect that an argument makes very clear whom it is citing as an authority.

Audience

The final component of argument analysis is consideration of an argument's intended audience. Clues to the intended audience can be found in the type of publication or forum where the argument is presented, in the professional standing of its author, and in the type of language that the author uses in the argument itself. Knowledge of audience is critical in evaluating an argument fairly. Authors writing an argument for an audience that shares their core values and general knowledge of the subject tend to leave definitions and statements implicit and use language that is highly technical, dense, and symbolic. This applies equally well to scientists writing for a journal in their field and politicians addressing their supporters. Authors writing for an audience that is very different from them tend to make the various components of their arguments much more explicit. However if an author believes the audience disagrees with them on, for example, an important value statement, they tend to make statements that are both explicit and yet are still very general or ambiguous (this is a skill that is highly developed in politicians). It is difficult to make a fair judgment across these two basic types of author-audience relationships, since the former requires much more interpretation by the evaluator than the latter.

Analyzing arguments by evaluating their quality in terms of the seven components listed above is by no means guaranteed to give you a clear answer as to which argument is better for several reasons. The relevant criteria applicable to each component are neither completely articulated nor without controversy themselves. In the process of making implicit elements explicit, analysts introduce their own subjectivity into the process. It should also be clear by this point that argument analysis is a very open-ended process—checking the truth of statements of fact, the justifiability of statements of values, the qualifications of authorities—could go on indefinitely. Thus the logic of argument analysis is underdetermined—following each step exactly is still no guarantee of a correct conclusion. However, if you apply the analytical techniques outlined above to the essays in this volume you will quickly spot implicit definitions, hasty generalizations, unsupported value statements, and questionable authorities as well as examples of well-crafted, logical, and persuasive argumentation. You will be in a much stronger position to defend *your* views about the arguments you find in this book.

Issues in This Volume

The critical examination of sex and gender in this text is segmented into six units. In Unit 1, fundamental assumptions about sex and gender are considered, revealing that "simple" definitions of sex as female or male and gender as directly derivative from biology are shortsighted. Moreover, debate over these fundamental assumptions has yielded some of the most contentious controversy in this field. In Unit 2, the "difference model," the primary paradigm for conceptualizing and studying sex and gender is critically analyzed. Sex and gender are usually construed as binary oppositions: female versus male, feminine versus masculine. Thus, a primary way in which sex and gender are studied is the comparison of groups of females and males (i.e., sex comparison or sex difference). In this section, you will grapple with underlying theoretical rationales for excavating such differences (including biological, evolutionary, and learning theories), and you will critically evaluate the difference model in terms of methodology, social meaning and significance, and political impact. Is the search for differences between females and males a useful approach to elucidating gender or is it meaningless and even politically dangerous?

Unit 3 focuses on violence in the daily lives of women and men. One of the most pervasive stereotypes is that of sex differences in aggression. It is often assumed that males have an inborn predisposition toward aggression and females do not. As a result, girls and women should give up authority to men in exchange for their protection. This section addresses the issue of the extent to which aggression is gender-based, whether girls and boys, women and men do or do not express aggression equally and in similar or dissimilar ways. In what ways does patriarchy, that is, that masculine (male) ways lead to dominance and control? Two issues related to gender and violence are gender symmetry and pornography. Gender symmetry, as used in the domestic violence domain, reflects the assertion that women and men are both aggressive toward intimate partners; hence, domestic violence is not about gender. Various perspectives on this issue influence research agendas, intervention programs, arrest policy (i.e., dual arrest), and services (should there be shelters for battered men?). Similarly affecting research agendas, intervention programs, public policy, and services is the debate over the causal role of pornography in rape. Does viewing pornography increase men's proclivity to rape or do men with a propensity to rape prefer to view pornographic material?

Unit 4 examines gender in a critical social domain—family. Gender is influential before conception, in making decisions to carry a fetus to term, and in the life expectancy of female and male children. Sex selection is a common practice in many cultures, including Western cultures. Why is higher value placed on female versus male offspring? From some theoretical perspectives, gender begins with early socialization and is affected by family composition.

One of the most gendered social institutions is the family. Traditional Western family ideology is heterosexist (regarding the heterosexual union as the only acceptable family context) and sexist (prescribing different roles for husbands and wives). In Unit 4 these fundamental values and assumptions are examined. Gender ideology riddles the construction of parenthood. Does gender influence women's and men's capacities for and approaches to parenting? How are traditional family gender ideologies challenged by same sex parents?

In Unit 5 the world of work is explored. It is a well-established fact that women on average earn 75 cents for each man's dollar. We want to know why. Is it career choice, and if so, what factors determine individuals' career choices? It is highly likely that advanced training in mathematics and the sciences opens more doors of opportunity and increases the likelihood of a larger paycheck. How do gendered factors, be they biological or societal, affect girls' and boys' career choices and opportunities for advancement? Do these factors justify the gender wage gap? It is well understood now that most families cannot achieve a comfortable lifestyle without two paychecks. What are the implications of this for single parents, especially poor women?

In Unit 6 issues of gender and sexuality are explored. In particular, this section is interested in exploring the double-standard and double-bind that women and men often find themselves in. What does it mean to be a sexual person and how can society go about teaching young people about responsible sexual behavior? Throughout history there has been greater acceptance of female than male sexuality. Some societies have practiced female circumcision as a means of blunting female sexual desire. Some have argued that there are circumstances under which adult-child sexual relationships may be healthy. Even without such extreme measure societies traditionally have endorsed various explicit and implicit means of controlling sexual expression. For example, sex education programs in the schools are explicitly aimed to control adolescent sexuality whereas media messages about beauty and sexuality provide more subtle, yet very pervasive and often harmful, messages about sexuality.

Conclusion

Equipped with your new tools for analyzing arguments, begin your exploration of knowledge and belief in the study of sex and gender. Remain open to considering and reconsidering beliefs and knowledge in ways that you never imagined. Your "gender quest" begins now; where you will end up, no one knows!

Internet References . . .

The True Story of John/Joan

This Info-Circumcision Web site by the Circumcision Information Resource Centre includes John Colapinto's original article entitled, "The True Story of John/Joan," *Rolling Stone* (December 11, 1997). This article reveals details of the John/Joan case.

http://www.infocirc.org/rollston.htm

Gender Talk

Gendertalk.com is a resource for trans persons and folks interested in learning about trans persons. Gendertalk.com provides comprehensive access to GenderTalk Radio, the leading radio program on transgender issues.

http://www.gendertalk.com/radio/about.shtml

The Office on Violence Against Women

The Office on Violence Against Women (OVW) handles the Department of Justice's legal and policy issues regarding violence against women, coordinates Departmental efforts, provides national and international leadership, and receives international visitors interested in learning about the federal government's role in addressing violence against women.

http://www.usdoj.gov/ovw/

The New York Times

Read an article in the *New York Times* by Cornelia Dean that discusses the problems girls who are good at math encounter.

http://www/nytimes.com/2005/02/01/science/01math.html

Center for 21st Century Teaching Excellence, University of South Florida

The Center provides opportunities for scholarly dialogue on the art, science, and craft of university teaching. It sponsors publications, workshops, and research that critically examine and promote instructional excellence. The Gender, Race and Ethnicity Bibliography: Natural and Physical Science website provides a bibliography of research articles related to factors associated with relationships between sex, achievement, and science self-concept to the science career preferences of Black students.

http://www.cte.usf.edu/bibs/gre/science/
bib_science.html

Council for Media Integrity

The Council for Media Integrity is comprised of a network of distinguished international scientists, academics, and members of the media concerned with the balanced portrayal of science in the media.

http://www.csicop.org/cmi/

Definitions and Cultural Boundaries: A Moving Target

*W*hat is sex? What is gender? What is gender identity? Must *there be congruence between biological aspects of sex (chromosomes, hormones, internal organs, and genitals) and social aspects of gender (assigned sex, gender identity, sexual orientations, and career aspirations)? These are controversial questions with a diversity of answers. In fact, the vast array of contradictory "answers" loosens the boundaries of these concepts to the point of losing any sense of certain definition. Definitions often reveal important theoretical standpoints underlying much of the controversy in the study of sex and gender. Moreover, they raise the question of cultural relativity of definitions. Can these concepts be objectively defined or is the most objective and scientific definition still product of culture? This section will explore the limits and limitlessness of definitions and boundaries of sex and gender within biology, psyche, and culture. As you read these selections, consider the role of biology. Is the newest scientific evidence convincing regarding the causal role of biological factors? Does correlation mean causation? Do issues of gender identity and career choice based on biological factors play out the same way across race, ethnicity, class, culture, and other status-defining categories? How do the media shape the public's understanding of these issues?*

- Is Anatomy Destiny?

- Is Gender Identity Innate?

- Do Sex Differences in Careers in Mathematics and Science Have a Biological Basis?

ISSUE 1

Is Anatomy Destiny?

YES: Anne Campbell, from "X and Y: It's a Jungle Out There," *Psychology, Evolution, and Gender* (August 2001)

NO: Richard Wilson, from "Puncturing the Genome Myth: Why the Genetic Code Fails to Explain Gendered Behaviour," *Psychology, Evolution, and Gender* (December 2001)

ISSUE SUMMARY

YES: Psychologist Anne Campbell argues that gene-level discoveries about the X and Y chromosomes give insight into differences between females and males.

NO: Richard Wilson suggests that environmental and social factors explain gendered behavior better than the genetic code.

Do we really know what constitutes one's "sex" and "gender"? Typically people assume that being male or female is a clear and absolute distinction. Biologically based theories of sex differentiation support the argument that genetic make-up and resultant hormonal influences determine fundamental differences between women and men. Given the ethical constraints associated with doing research on humans, researchers have had to rely on animal experimentation to demonstrate that hormones contribute to sexual dimorphism (i.e., sexual differentiation) on neural systems, brains, temperament, and behavior. The assumption is that sexual is an unquestionably natural dichotomy rooted in an organism's genetics.

In contrast, a large body of research with numerous species of animals, as well as with humans, suggests that environmental factors provide the major determinants of gender-related patterns of behavior. That is, gender is a socially constructed constellation of feelings, attitudes, and behaviors, thus, strongly influenced by cultural forces.

Critics have begun to question the immunity of biological constructs from cultural analysis, urging that we must recognize that the practice of science occurs within a sociopolitical context. Therefore, biological notions of sex are cultural, social, and political creations.

The dominant Western definition of sex delineates two "normal" categories: male and female. Notions of gender follow suit, typically contrasting masculine and feminine behavior patterns. Is this dichotomy universal? Anthropologists have uncovered compelling evidence that dichotomous definitions of sex are not universal, arguing instead that many cultures have multiple genders. They argue that when looking for binaries, we observe a dichotomous reality. But what remains unseen—gender diversity—is also an important reality. Will Roscoe argues that gender diversity is a natural, worldwide phenomenon.

Some revisionists have begun to "reinvent sex" by replacing dichotomous conceptions of sex with arrays reflecting the complexities of sexual variability in natural characteristics of humans. For example, concepts such as "gender-crossing" have been coined. The problem with such concepts is that they still rely on the fixed binary of male/female, and they problematize deviations. In contrast, construing diversity as multiple genders enables the transcendence of this binary and notions of deviance associated with non-male and nonfemale genders.

In the following selections, two different perspectives on the human genome project are presented. On the one hand, Campbell marvels at how a very small number of genes, and the very small and outnumbered Y chromosome, can accomplish so much with regard to masculinizing a male fetus. Her view of the differences between women and men are clearly rooted in an evolutionary perspective. On the other hand, Wilson bemoans the fact that the human genome project has revealed so little with regard to gendered behavior. First, he questions whether the practice of science can be immune to social influences. Second, he questions the claim that genes are determinants of behavior in humans—that expressions of gender differences are "hard-wired into the fabric or our being."

YES

Anne Campbell

X and Y: It's a Jungle Out There

Almost as astonishing as the modest number of human genes uncovered by the human genome project (a mere 31,000) is confirmation of the astonishing disparity between the size of the X and Y chromosome. The Y has a humble 231 genes compared to a generous 1,184 on the X. From the point of view of evolution, size matters. It tells us much about the conflict between males and females.

The Y chromosome now carries little else but the gene complex called testes determining factor (TDF). Its job, as you might reasonably suppose, is a straightforward but very significant one—it instructs genes on other chromosomes to build the testes. From the testes comes a significant quantity of testosterone, starting in the second trimester of foetal growth and continuing for several months post-partum. From this testosterone come a variety of morphological changes to the brain as well as the body. It builds a brain with greater lateralization of function and smaller channel of communication between the two hemispheres. It builds a larger bed nucleus of the stria terminalis from which comes the ineffable sense of being male.

These masculinizing alterations to the female 'default' option are substantial yet they are accomplished by a very small number of genes. Sex differences are principally sex limited (dependent on the effect of hormones on autosomal genes) rather than sex linked (residing on the X or Y). How and why did the Y shrink to its current size? The answer seems to be that it is hiding.

It's hiding partly because it is unable to generate new versions of itself with the speed and efficiency of the X. The Y chromosome cannot recombine as the X can. To see why, we have to consider the notion of sexually antagonistic genes. These are genes that benefit one sex but are a burden for the other. Wide hips help females give birth but slow down running speed in males. Growing antlers is an efficient use of calories for a stag (who needs them for intrasexual competition) but a waste of calories for hinds. So antler genes link themselves to Y chromosomes but not to X chromosomes. During meiosis (the production of sex cells) most pairs of corresponding chromosomes line up together and exchange segments of genetic material ensuring variability in the gamete. But if X and Y were allowed to do this it would produce all sorts of inappropriate combinations—wide-hipped males and antler-bearing females. So selection operates against genetic recombination between X and Y (except on a very small section called the pseudoautosomal region). The Y chromosome now has a real problem—evolutionary biologists call it Muller's Ratchet. A gene that cannot recombine starts to degenerate and has no way to fix itself. Take a high resolution photograph, now make a photocopy of it and a photocopy of the photocopy. . . . That is the fate of the Y chromosome. It accumulates deleterious mutations much faster than beneficial ones and there is no recombination available to patch them back up. So there is selection for non-expression of these degenerate genes. The human genome project has discovered large repeated chunks of genetic material on the TDF. Perhaps they are extra insurance against the loss of accurate instruction for testes building.

The Y chromosome is not only undersized but also outnumbered. For every one Y chromosome in a population, there are three Xs. The Y is under attack from a strong army and one that has the advantage of recombination—the two X chromosomes can exchange genes during meiosis and the result is variability which is the fodder of natural selection. And there is evidence that the recombining X does indeed mount attacks on the Y. Biologists use the term 'driving' to describe a gene that behaves in such a way as to increase its chance of being transmitted to the next generation. It is a lawless gene and the law that it is breaking is Mendel's. Instances of driving X have been found in many species. An X-linked gene that killed Y-bearing sperm would be doing itself a good turn by decreasing the number of Ys and increasing the number of Xs in the next generation. Fortunately when the sex ratio veers in favour of females the results are not catastrophic—it takes just a few males to impregnate many females. Some species survive with a 97 per cent female population. When sex ratios depart from parity, it is usually in the female direction that they move. And they usually return to 50:50 because a male mutation that can fight this driving X has massive reproductive success and this version of Y sweeps across the male population.

But although Y may be small and outgunned, it does have the advantage of never finding itself in a female body. This means that it can be quite ruthless about exploiting females. If females were not good at fighting back, the Y would have killed us long ago. William Rice used fruit flies, who have a conveniently short lifespan for experimental purposes, to demonstrate the selfish strategies of males and the crucial importance of female resistance. Seminal fluid not only kills off rival males' sperm, it also carries proteins that make their way to the female's brain where they increase her rate of ovulation and diminish her interest in having sex again: This is good for a male but not so good for the female. Worse still is the fact that the fluid is toxic to her. Rice took a group of females out of the evolutionary process for forty-one generations while the males were allowed to continue competing, mating and evolving. When he returned the original females, he found that sex literally killed them. The experimental males had got better and better at producing sperm that caused the female to reject matings with other males and better at overcoming the females' reluctance to mate with them after a previous mating with a rival. Their sperm had also become more and more toxic. The males were killing the females who had been denied the opportunity to co-evolve and develop resistance. The relationship between males and females is an antagonistic one in which both sexes lose if one fails to keep up their side of the hostilities. It is like two upright wrestlers locked together—it only takes one to release their grip for both to collapse.

This same principle has been demonstrated in another genetic discovery called genomic imprinting. Here a gene is expressed or silenced ('imprinted') depending on which parent donated it. From a polygynous, mammalian male's viewpoint, reproduction involves installing his genes in a foetus which resides in a female body. From then on, the female takes responsibility for pregnancy, parturition and lactation. He may never have another child with this particular woman and so he is indifferent to her long-term reproductive success. But his genes do want to look after their own—in the form of the foetus. He wants to ensure that it is well nourished even if that costs the mother more than she can afford. (Mothers are not callous but they are cautious. They have to think ahead—they will have other children, who they can be certain will carry their genes, and they cannot squander everything on this one foetus.) The father wants more calories given to this foetus than to any other she will carry, while the mother must ration out her energy over a whole career. It is for this reason that the father's placenta-building gene is expressed over the mother's. As Matt Ridley puts it '. . . the father's genes do not trust the mother's genes to make a sufficiently invasive placenta; so they do the job themselves'. The father also tries to take control of the growth of the embryo— at least in mice. IGF2 (insulin-like growth factor two) promotes the transition of metabolites across the placenta and so is vital in acquiring resources from the mother. Predictably enough, it is the father's version of this gene that is activated. But this time, the mother fights back. Her gene for a receptor that mops up IGF2 is expressed and the father's is imprinted. And the necessity of this female counter-ploy is evident in individuals who lack the maternal receptor gene—they are 16 per cent larger than normal.

And while the father concerns himself, genetically speaking, with building a bigger body, the mother devotes a greater part of her genetic energy to controlling the growth of the brain. Keverne and his colleagues created mice where two different genomes were fused into the same body. To build a chimerical baby, they fused a normal embryo with an embryo made from two egg pronuclei. The result was a mouse with a very large head. But when they fused the normal embryo with one derived from an embryo made from two sperm pronuclei, they grew a mouse with a big body and small head. Indeed the body of the paternal chimeras grew so large that they had to be delivered by Caesarean section. So fathers contribute more to bodies and muscle while mothers specialize in brains.

But not just brains—particular parts of them. By biochemically marking the maternal and paternal cells, the researchers were able to see where they ended up. The input of the paternal cells to brain construction was to the hypothalamus, amygdala and preoptic area—the areas that control emotion and evolutionarily critical 'automatic' behaviours such as sex, reproductive behaviour, aggression and fear. The mother's cells migrated and proliferated in the cortex, striatum and hippocampus—areas implicated in reasoning, thought and behavioural inhibition. (If you are now blaming your father for inheriting his emotional tempo remember that half the hypothalamus-building genes that he bequeathed to you came from his mother. They may not have been expressed in him but they were inherited from his mother, re-tagged in him as paternal instead of maternal and then passed on to you.)

For me, these gene-level discoveries reflect the complicated and paradoxical relationship between men and women; distinctive and yet complementary, at war yet in alliance, so similar in areas where natural selection has worked and so different where sexual selection has been the driving force. The preferred sexual strategy of masculine prehistory has been sexual opportunism and with that has come selection for dominance, aggression and men's more casual regard for their own safety and longevity. For women it is offspring survival, not insemination, that has been paramount and with it has come commitment to the long haul and a cautious approach to danger. Women are no less competitive than men but their genes have 'learned' through differential reproductive success that, while cohabiting fathers are not obligate for children's survival, mothers are. I do not doubt that this tension in reproductive priorities is reflected in evolved psychological differences mediated through genes. (Nor do I doubt that they are usually embellished and occasionally opposed by culture.) But it is not all unalloyed competition. The altricial nature of human infants has also selected for a degree of paternal investment that is much higher than that seen in other primates. And the advantages of monogamy, how ever much self-denial it requires, have been elegantly shown at the gene's eye level.

The humble house fly is normally promiscuous. But Brett Holland and William Rice randomly selected some of these flies to have monogamy forced upon them. The experimenters acted as marriage brokers, teaming up and housing together individual males and females over thirty-two generations. Monogamy means not only that the reproductive success of males and females is identical but also that their reproductive interests should converge. While polygyny means that males can exploit females quite ruthlessly without suffering themselves, monogamy means that anything that hurts a female (prevents her from achieving her reproductive potential) hurts her male partner just as much. After several generations of monogamy, Holland and Rice performed the key tests. First, they introduced non-experimental, traditional females to mate with the monogamous 'new males'. They found that monogamy had led to a decrease in the toxicity of the male's seminal fluid and also to a reduction in male courtship—an activity that is harmful to females. Then they looked at the effect of monogamy on the experimental females. During monogamy, these females' male partners had behaved in a less exploitative way toward them and so the monogamous females had not needed to evolve counter-strategies of resistance. As expected, when these monogamous females mated with normal males, a larger proportion died than among traditional females that had been allowed to co-evolve with male polygyny. Freed from the antagonistic tussle, monogamous males became more benign and females produced more offspring and suffered lower mortality.

Men and women are different morphs but they are not from different planets. They both have representational thought—they see into each other's minds, recognize their differences and manage to bridge them more often than not. And they both have foresight, a uniquely human gift. The combination of these two human abilities mean that men and women, unlike genes, can choose to cooperate rather than compete.

Richard Wilson  **NO**

Puncturing the Genome Myth: Why the Genetic Code Fails to Explain Gendered Behaviour

I have been following the developing and ongoing story of the human genome project, admittedly at a distance, for a few years now. The project seemed to promise, on the one hand, the possibility of cures for all known (and probably some unknown) ills and, on the other, to provide definitive answers to thorny questions of human social behaviour, explaining, for example, the differences between the sexes in their social presentation, and many others.

In arriving at a sceptical approach to the genome project there have been two lines of critical analysis which actively fuelled my doubt and disbelief. The first of these concerns the actual practice of science itself as the process by which this knowledge is generated and passed back into the wider social world. The second is related to the genetic code and the influence that it has, or might have, on human behaviour.

It often seems, or at least is often implied, that the scientific process is the only means by which a reliable and accurate understanding of the physical world may be generated. Scientific practitioners might advance many reasons for this contention but may well include the following: an inquiring and experimental approach to knowledge determining and gathering; an openness to testing and discarding ideas or theories about the way the world works if they are shown to be false; and a commitment to search for and work with facts rather than conjecture. Looking at the facts is an important component of the scientific method, and Chalmers notes that there is a conception of scientific knowledge being '. . . based on the facts established by observation and experiment . . .' and that this sets it apart from knowledge created by other means.

There is then still the question of whether this process of observation and experiment does produce something that is true in an objective sense or indeed whether science can ever produce a final truth. It is a debatable point. For Popper these are not possibilities. He talks of science not being knowledge and says '. . . it can never claim to have attained truth, or even a substitute for it. . . .' Science is, in his eyes, a painstaking process of groping toward the truth without necessarily ever arriving at it. The ideas science generates about

From *Psychology, Evolution & Gender*, December 2001, pp. 273–277. Copyright © 2001 by Taylor & Francis Journals. Reprinted by permission.

the world can be considered nets within which to trap 'reality' and the ongoing task is to make the mesh of those nets '. . . ever finer and finer.' Work taking place on the genome project, and the theories which underpin this, is one of those nets which, while it may trap some little extra bit of reality, is also going to miss many other bits in the process. Whatever the knowledge that comes out of this whole project it will not present a complete answer, only a partial and probably poorly understood picture.

Nor can one ignore the wider social context within which scientific study is undertaken. Whatever claims may be made about open-minded approaches and impartiality it cannot be denied that scientists are social beings like all other members of society. They are steeped in the thinking, beliefs and attitudes of the wider society and their approach to science will reflect this. It is one thing to claim an open-minded attitude to the 'facts' and theories that might explain them but it is still necessary to define what things count as facts and then to specify what questions need to be asked in order to generate the theories that explain the facts. A particular orientation to the world is needed, one that is shared among the community of scientists, that gives structure to the ways of thinking and questioning that are permissible and defines those ways of thinking and questioning that are not. It is this common orientation that provides the framework or paradigm through which questions of science can be determined. Yet this paradigm is itself a social construct, prone to periodic destruction and rebuilding, shadowing the social developments and thinking of the era in which it was created.

This means that science, as a human endeavour, despite its claims to knowledge generation of a special kind, is no more immune to social influences than any other human activity. It is not particularly surprising if genomic research throws up evidence which is then used to support arguments that there are in-built differences in the presentation of gender. The genomically inspired claim that men and women are different in some fundamental, God-given and unalterable way would be well received by some (because they already believe it to be true) and accepted by others because of its cloak of scientific legitimacy. Now the science ripples back into the social fabric by serving as a useful justification for maintaining the status quo and continuing the differential treatment of men and women in the workplace or in society generally. This in turn perpetuates inequalities in earnings and life chances. If science is finding genetically ordained differences of this type it is, to a greater or lesser extent, only reflecting the structural inequalities inherent in a conflictual capitalist society.

Taking all this into account I do not believe that science can be seen as a black box that takes phenomena in one end and churns out explanations from the other in some magical way that ultimately guarantees the absolute truth of the explanations produced. If it functions as a black box at all it is as one that owes its existence to the dominant scientific paradigm of the day; a paradigm which in turn is the product of the complex social forces and currents of opinion already present in society.

So, I regard science, and the knowledge it generates, as simply one more biased, partial and idiosyncratic human endeavour like any other and of no greater validity than any other. That claims are going to be made on the back of the apparently greater understanding of human genetic composition regarding gender attributes and the extent to which these may be built in and not acquired, to me, simply reflects the social milieu from which scientists are drawn from the current of beliefs in the wider society.

However, suppose one were to accept that the information we (or at least geneticists) now possess about the genome were true, what then? Does that mean that our genetic composition really is the ultimate determinant of all that we are, in terms of our social presentations and behaviour? Again, I find some quite real problems with the knowledge, and the claims made for it, even when taken at face value.

There has been, and there continues to be, a degree of hype and spin about the genome project (although there are dissenting voices to be heard). For many it seems to come across as one of the most profound events to have happened in human history and one which will transform all our lives. Take these comments made by an MP, Dr. Ian Gibson, in the House of Commons in January 2000. In speaking of the genome project he says, 'The results of that have been described as revolutionary by scientists around the world and its implications equated with the discovery of the wheel.' Hardly a modest description but one which is accepted by a government junior minister speaking in the same debate. She follows him by saying, 'The scientific and technological achievements so far associated with the human genome project are arguably some of the finest to have been seen in the previous millennium— and the potential is greater still. . . . The potential of the human genome project cannot be overestimated.' These two members of the political elite are in no doubt as to the truth and value of genomic research. A commentator in the *Daily Telegraph* enthuses that 'it really is BIG NEWS' (his emphasis) and goes on to say that thanks to genome research we will be able 'to solve old mysteries of determinism and free will.'

All very inspiring. But despite this, and looking at the information that has now been gleaned on the genetic code, there are, I think, real problems with the thesis that genes can be considered as determinants of behaviour in humans.

It was initially thought that there may be up to 140,000 different genes in the human genome. Now, with the mapping complete, this figure seems to have been considerably over-estimated. The two bodies involved in the mapping process say that the true figure is likely to lie between around 26,000 and 40,000. Still a lot of genes, it is true, but many fewer than had been expected. And not only are there fewer genes than expected but we appear to hold most of them in common with all other living creatures. Humans apparently share 85 per cent of their genetic sequence with the dog, something that may explain the occasional urges I feel to urinate against lamp-posts and chase after sticks.

Lamp-posts aside, this reduced genetic number does have implications for explanations of human behaviour which rely on the scale and complexity of the genome to govern all aspects of our being. With the genes that are known to exist and the relationships between them, the way in which they work together must be of a complexity and subtlety that geneticists have barely begun to grasp. The influences that genes have on behaviour would be even harder to determine. It seems unlikely that it will be possible to identify one gene that can with certainty be seen to code for one protein that in turn governs one clearly identified facet of human behaviour, even if claims are being made to the contrary. Richard Lewontin chides geneticists who take this line (that genes can be said to govern behaviour) saying that they are 'supposed to know better' and arguing that if genes are determining anything at all about an organism it is patterns of variation, not of similarity.

That being the case, it seems to me that the door to environmental and social factors as primary determinants to behaviour is left wide open. I do not consider tenable the argument that our varying expressions of gender differences (that is, historically and in other human societies apart from our own) result from being hard-wired into the very fabric of our being. As discussed above, even if one ignores the validity or accuracy of the claims made about the genome, there seems insufficient 'wiring' to allow any aspect of human behaviour to be so simply or deterministically explained. That differences in the outward manifestation of genders exist is not in dispute. My final argument would be that gender attributes are the product, possibly including some inherent genetic predisposition, overwhelmingly of the complex and continuous interplay of the many social and cultural factors and influences to which we are exposed from the moment of our birth. It is here that I would seek for explanations of gender differences, not in the coiled helices of our DNA.

POSTSCRIPT

Is Anatomy Destiny?

Nature versus nurture? Biology versus social determinism? Just as some scholars argue that we need to move beyond gender binaries to better understand human complexity, we must also move beyond neat either/or propositions about the causes of sex and gender. Traditional thought dictates that biology affects or determines behavior, that anatomy is destiny. But behavior can also alter physiology. Recent advances explore the complex interaction between biology (genes, hormones, brain structure) and environment. We have learned that it is impossible to determine how much of our behavior is biologically based and how much is environmental. Moreover, definitions of gendered behavior are temporally and culturally relative. Yet why do researchers continue to try to isolate biological from environmental factors?

Advancements in the study of biological bases of sex and critiques of applications of biological theory to human behavior, such as Wilson discussed, challenge some of Campbell's assertions. Many traditional biologists recognize species diversity in hormone-brain-behavior relationships, which makes the general application of theories based on animal physiology and behavior to humans problematic. Moreover, species diversity challenges male/female binaries. The validity of the presence/absence model of sex dimorphism has been challenged. In embryonic development, do females "just happen" by default in the absence of testosterone? No, all individuals actively develop through various genetic processes. Moreover, the sexes are similar in the presence and need of both androgens and estrogens; in fact, the chemical structures and derivation of estrogen and testosterone are interconnected.

Suggested Readings

Dina Anselmi, *Questions of Gender: Perspectives and Paradox* (New York: McGraw-Hill, 2006).

Anne Fausto-Sterling, *Sexing the Body: Gender Politics and the Construction of Sexuality* (New York: Basic Books, 2000).

David C. Geary, *Male, Female: The Evolution of Human Sex Differences* (Washington, DC: American Psychological Association, 1998).

Michael S. Kimmel, *The Gendered Society* (New York: Oxford Press, 2000).

Steven Rhodes, *Taking Sex Differences Seriously* (San Francisco: Encounter Books, 2004).

ISSUE 2

Is Gender Identity Innate?

YES: **Frederick L. Coolidge, Linda L. Thede, and Susan E. Young,** from "The Heritability of Gender Identity Disorder in a Child and Adolescent Twin Sample," *Behavior Genetics*, 2002.

NO: **Carla Golden,** from "The Intersexed and the Transgendered: Rethinking Sex/Gender," in J. C. Chrisler, C. Golden, and P. D. Rozee, eds., *Lectures on the Psychology of Women*, (The McGraw-Hill Companies, 2004)

ISSUE SUMMARY

YES: In an analysis of twins, Frederick Coolidge, along with Linda L. Thede and Susan E. Young, document that gender identity disorder has a strong heritable component, suggesting that gender identity is more a matter of biology than choice.

NO: Carla Golden argues that the diagnosis of gender identity disorder is problematic. It is the socially constructed nature of sex and gender that has problematized some forms of gender expression while privileging others.

Psychosexuality, or psychological behaviors and phenomena presumably associated with biological sex, has typically been defined as having three components: gender identity, gender role, and sexual orientation. A fundamental assumption is that these are congruent.

Gender identity is one's sense of self as belonging to one sex: male or female. Cognitive developmentalists such as Lawrence Kohlberg add the criterion of gender constancy. Gender constancy starts with the ability of a child to accurately discriminate females from males and to accurately identify her or his own status correctly, and develops into the knowledge that gender is invariant. The acquisition of gender identity is often affectively loaded and sometimes marked by negative emotion, otherwise known as gender dysphoria.

The term *gender role* refers to attitudes, behaviors, and personality characteristics that are designated by society (in particular sociohistorical contexts) as appropriately masculine or feminine (i.e., typical of the male or female role, respectively). Thus, assessments of gender role behavior in children have included toy preferences, interest in physical activities, fantasy role and dress-up play, and affiliative preference for same-sex versus opposite-sex peers.

Sexual orientation refers to the match between one's own sex and the sex of the person to whom the person is erotically attracted. Typically, sexual orientation has been considered categorically as heterosexual, homosexual, or bisexual.

Gender Identity Disorder (GID) is defined as a strong psychological identification with the opposite sex and is signaled by the display of opposite sex-typed behaviors and avoidance or rejection of sex-typed behaviors characteristic of one's own sex. It is not related to sexual orientation. Distress or discomfort about one's status as a boy or a girl frequently accompanies these behaviors. The age of onset is 2 to 4 years. Some children self-label as the opposite sex, some self-label correctly but wish to become a member of the opposite sex. Other children do not express cross-sex desires but exhibit cross-sex-typed behavior. Some children cross-dress, sometimes insistently. Less characteristic are cross-sex-typed mannerisms (e.g., body movements, voice, pitch). Cross-sex peer affiliation preferences, poor peer relations, and alienation are typical.

Child referrals for GID have increased in the last two decades. Speculations about the cause of this increase include the heightened sensitivity to gender identity issues among schools, doctors, parents, and others. Boys are about six times as likely as girls to be referred for GID. Three explanations have been offered: (1) perhaps boys have greater biological vulnerability to anomalous development, (2) social factors reflect less tolerance of cross-gender behavior in boys, thereby creating greater dysphoria, or (3) different base rates of cross-gender behavior (i.e., boys are less likely to display feminine behavior than are girls to display masculine behavior) make boys' cross-gender behavior more noticeable.

There is considerable controversy concerning whether gender identity is socially constructed or innate. Researchers studying the effects of prenatal hormones on brain structure, gender identity, and gendered behavior have challenged the claim that gender identity is socially constructed.

A pivotal case was that of John/Joan, a boy (with a twin brother) who at eight months of age was injured in a botched circumcision and subsequently reared as a girl. This created the opportunity to study "naturalistically" whether or not gender identity could be socially constructed. But at the age of 14, upon learning the facts of his birth and sex reassignment, the child rejected his reassigned sex and began living as a man. In May, 2004 he committed suicide.

The study of twins has continued to be a useful method for assessing the degree of heritability of various attributes. Coolidge and his colleagues present evidence that GID has a strong heritable component. The researchers also noted that more boys than girls are diagnosed in clinical sample, but the reverse may be true for nonclinical samples, suggesting more social tolerance for cross-gender behavior in girls than boys. Countering the argument that GID is genetically based, Golden critically analyzes the classification of GID as a disorder and offers a social constructionist view as an alternative to understanding atypical gender identities.

YES ⟵   Frederick L. Coolidge, Linda L. Thede, and Susan E. Young

The Heritability of Gender Identity Disorder in a Child and Adolescent Twin Sample

Introduction

Gender identity refers to one's sense of self or conviction in being male or female. Sexual orientation refers to one's degree of sexual attraction to males or females. A gender identity disorder (GID), as defined by the *Diagnostic and Statistical Manual of Mental Disorders* (*DSM-IV;* American Psychiatric Association, 1994), consists of two components: (1) a strong and persistent cross-gender identification and (2) persistent discomfort with one's biological sex or gender role behavior associated with one's sex. Heritability studies related to gender issues, employing twin and family prevalence studies, more often have investigated genetic influences upon sexual orientation.

A review of heritability studies of sexual orientation reveals a fairly consistent finding that male homosexuality appears to be familial, is not controlled by a single major gene, is probably not X-linked, but has a genetic component. There are fewer heritability studies of female homosexuals. A review of the latter research reveals somewhat the same pattern as for male homosexuals. It appears that female homosexuality has an appreciable genetic basis, but there appears to be some evidence that the genetic etiological mechanisms for homosexuality may be different for the two genders. One of the important differences lies in the prevalence rates between the two genders for homosexuality. Female homosexuality is generally considered more rare than male homosexuality. It also appears that the prevalence of female homosexuality among the relatives of homosexual females is much greater than the prevalence of male homosexuality among the relatives of homosexual males. Both of these lines of evidence suggest different mechanisms contributing to male and female sexual orientation, but the data [are] far from convincing.

As noted earlier, there are far fewer twin and familial studies of GID compared to studies of homosexuality. One recent retrospective study reported on the heritability of childhood gender nonconformity in 1,891 adult twins (median age 29 years). They found a significantly heritable pattern for childhood gender nonconformity for both men and women, although the

From *Behavior Genetics*, July 2002, pp. 251–257. Copyright © 2002 by Springer Journals (Kluwer Academic). Reprinted by permission.

heritability estimates (univariate and multivariate) were stronger in men. . . . The authors concluded that their findings provided some support for a hypothesis by Bem that childhood gender nonconformity is the heritable component of adult sexual orientation. However, [this study] not only found different patterns of heritability for adult sexual orientation and for adult gender identity than . . . for childhood gender nonconformity, but also varying patterns between men and women. The latter findings may alternatively suggest that childhood gender nonconformity does not have a simple predictive relationship with adult sexual orientation for both genders.

The controversy continues over the issue of the relationship of a childhood GID diagnosis with an adult homosexual orientation. In study, 75% of boys who may have met criteria for GID reported homosexual or bisexual fantasies by the age of 19. About 80% of the individuals in this sample who have had sexual experiences were classified as homosexual or bisexual. [A] review of two long-term follow-up studies of 160 children with GID found that from about half to three-quarters of the children were homosexual or bisexual as adolescents or adults. However, adult retrospective studies of homosexual men and women show that most do not report a childhood history of GID. From these and other studies, [it has been] argued that the relationship "between GID and homosexuality is not a perfect one and that GID is not simply the early manifestation of homosexuality. . . ." [A] counter-argue[ment] that "A 75% homosexual outcome makes GID an unusually strong predictor . . . This means that there is a strong correspondence between GID behaviors and adult homosexuality. . . ." In summary, it appears that although GID may be a fair predictor of later adult homosexuality, most adult homosexual orientations cannot be explained by a childhood GID diagnosis. However, it is also possible that retrospective adult studies are flawed by such factors as memory, self-report, social desirability, etc., and perhaps underestimate the real childhood prevalence of GID in this population.

DSM-IV notes that the prevalence of GID is unknown, but it has been considered to be a "very rare syndrome" or "relatively rare." In children clinically referred for GID, cross-gender interests and behavior typically onsets between 2 and 4 years, and a diagnosis of GID commonly occurs about school age; 6% of nonreferred 4- to 5-year-old boys and 12% of nonreferred 4- to 5-year-old girls sometimes or frequently behaved like the opposite sex (according to mothers' ratings). Furthermore, . . . 1% of these boys and 5% of these girls sometimes or frequently wished to be of the opposite sex. In children referred for clinical evaluation, approximately 16% of 4- to 5-year-old boys behaved like the opposite sex and approximately 16% wished to be girls. [A]lthough [these] data did not define rates of GID, cross-gender behaviors are not uncommon in children, and GID symptoms may not be uncommon in clinical populations. In their gender identity clinic, they also found a male-to-female sex ratio for GID symptoms of 1.4:1 [has been found].

Studies of clinical samples of children have reported that there were five times as many boys for each girl diagnosed with GID. In adult clinical samples, GID appeared in men at about two to three times the rate of women. *DSM-IV* notes that referral bias might artificially increase the rate of GID in males, because there may be a greater stigma attached to cross-gender behavior for boys than for girls. [One] study of GID familial patterns, investigated the ratio of brothers to sisters for 444 boys with GID. They found an excess of brothers of male probands with GID and evidence that boys with GID are born relatively late among their brothers. [T]his pattern may be reversed in girls, although the latter results were based on a small sample ($N = 22$). Psychosocial explanations for these results are equivocal: some suggest that children with GID may find it difficult to identify with more masculine older brothers, predisposing them to greater femininity. However, other studies suggest that the presence of older brothers is associated with greater behavioral masculinity.

Biological explanations for sexual orientation have included an immuno-hormonal hypothesis involving maternal antibodies to testosterone. [A]n alternative immunohormonal hypothesis involv[es] the relationship between a mother's immune reaction and antibodies on the sexual differentiation of the fetal brain and a child's future gender identity and sexual orientation. . . . [M]ost immunohormonal theories suggest that there are likely to be prenatal hormonal effects on sexual-dimorphic behavior. However, most studies of sexual chromosomes or hormonal abnormalities associated with GID have typically been negative.

Another issue in GID is the comorbidity with other disorders. . . . [C]omorbid disorders may more often be related to the stress experienced by the children with GID. [It has been] counter-argue[d] that, whereas some psychological problems in children with GID are probably related to the stigma associated with the disorder, many of the problems are not simply reactive. . . . [C]hildren with GID frequently have separation anxiety disorder, depression, and other behavioral problems. . . .

[T]he first heritability study of childhood gender nonconformity in twins [was] a retrospective design. Prior speculations as to the heritability of GID appear to be based primarily upon genetic studies of adult sexual orientation. The purpose of the present study was to estimate heritability of GID in a sample of child and adolescent twins in a nonretrospective design. No twin studies to date have investigated the heritability of GID in a nonretrospective design. In addition, the present study attempted to estimate the prevalence of GID and the covariation of GID with symptoms of depression and separation anxiety. GID was measured in the present study by a six-item parent-as-respondent scale from the Coolidge Personality and Neuropsychological Inventory for children. There is substantial support from adult twin studies that heritability of many types of psychopathology may be appropriately estimated by the use of nonclinical samples.

Method

Participants and Procedures

Participants consisted of parents of twins who were recruited through advertisements on the Internet and in local newspapers and through students in psychology classes at a midwestern university who earned extra credit by identifying parents of twins. Parents completed the CPNI on each child, as well as a demographic survey. Informed consent was obtained.

There were 314 twins, 96 MZ pairs (44 male pairs and 52 female pairs) and 61 DZ pairs (20 male pairs, 20 female pairs, and 21 male/female pairs). The mean age of the MZ pairs was 9.4 (SD = 3.4), and the mean age of the DZ pairs was 10.1 (SD = 3.6). The mean age of the parents was 39.5 years (SD = 6.3), and 85% of the parents had attained a level of education beyond high school. The mean maternal age at time of birth was 29.5 years (SD = 5.3), and ethnicity was as follows: MZ twins, Caucasian (83%), Hispanic (4%), Asian (6%), African American (2%), or other (5%); DZ twins, Caucasian (93%), Asian (2%), and other (5%). Conception followed the use of fertility drugs for 12% of the twins. Some parents reported having exposed the twins to potentially harmful substances prior to birth, such as alcohol (4%), tobacco (11%), injury (1%), serious illness (1%), and prescription drugs (11%).

Materials

The parents completed the 200-item, parent-as-respondent CPNI (Coolidge, 1998). The CPNI contains a six-item GID scale, based on the criteria in *DSMI-IV* for GID. Each item is answered on a 4-point Likert-type scale ranging from (1) *strongly false,* (2) *more false than true,* (3) *more true than false,* to (4) *strongly true.* The CPNI is designed to be filled out by a primary caregiver who is intimately acquainted with the child's behavior. . . .

Zygosity was determined by a 10-item questionnaire that contained items regarding physical similarities (e.g., height, weight, hair and eye color) and confusion of the twins by parents, family, and strangers. The questionnaire has been demonstrated to be approximately 90% valid (compared to blood-typing).

In the present twin sample, the internal reliability of the GID scale was .84, the internal reliability of the separation anxiety disorder scale was .82, and the internal reliability of the depression scale was .80. . . .

Results

Genetic Analyses

Based on parsimony and a comparison of log-likelihood fit statistics, the [additive genetic component] model, which estimates heritability at .62, is considered the best fitting model for these GID data. [A nonshared environmental component accounted for the remaining 38%].

Comorbidity of GID with Separation Anxiety and Depression

Ordinal scales were generated from item scores on the separation anxiety scale [SAD] and the depression scale [DEP] resulting in three symptom levels: no symptoms, minimal symptoms, and clinically significant symptoms. . . . Parents

Table II

**Prevalence of Symptom Levels for Gender Identity Disorder (GID),
Separation Anxiety Disorder (SAD), and Depression (DEP)**

	Males			Females		
	No symptoms (%)	Minimal (%)	Clinically significant (%)	No symptoms (%)	Minimal (%)	Clinically significant (%)
GID	90.5	8.8	0.7	81.5	14.8	3.7
SAD	65.3	30.6	4.1	65.4	30.9	3.7
DEP	38.1	55.1	6.8	54.9	35.8	9.3

reported their female children as having higher levels of GID than their male children in both the minimal and clinically significant categories. In contrast, males were rated as having more depressive symptoms than females. Scores for SAD were quite comparable for males and females. . . . The correlation between the GID and the DEP was significant ($r = .20$, $CI_{(95)} = .01$ to $.37$), as was the correlation between SAD and DEP ($r = .48$, $CI_{(95)} = -.34$ to $.60$). However, the correlation between GID and SAD was nonsignificant ($r = .11$, $CI_{(95)} = -.10$ to $.31$).

Discussion

The present study appears to be the first to estimate heritability of GID in a sample of child and adolescent twins in a nonretrospective design. Although a model including only shared and nonshared environmental effects could not be rejected, the best fitting model suggested that GID is highly heritable. Although GID appears to be somewhat more heritable in the older cohort compared to the younger cohort, this difference was not significant in our sample. This finding is similar to a recent study [that] found that childhood gender nonconformity was significantly heritable for adult twins in a retrospective design. The present findings are also similar to studies that have found appreciable heritable components of other personality traits and psychopathology in children and adolescents. The present findings also complement an adult twin study [that] found a strong heritable basis for sexual orientation and homosexuality. Even if the size of the present heritability estimate may have been inflated somewhat by parental ratings as opposed to self-ratings, the estimate remains substantial and in the general range of a prior retrospective study of gender nonconformity.

A second purpose of the present study was to estimate the prevalence of GID symptomatology. Clearly, there was no external validity for high scores on the GID scale, thus any interpretation must be viewed with caution. Nevertheless, the current finding of 2.3% of the children who scored in the clinically significant range in this study would appear to counter claims that GID is a rare or very rare phenomenon. . . . There was also a modest but significant relationship between gender and GID scores and between age and GID scores in the present study. Because of the relatively small number of twins in the present study, a determination of reliable prevalence rates by age was not feasible. Thus, to be conservative, the present prevalence estimate may be considered an upper limit of GID prevalence. A final note of caution: The ratio of boys to girls with GID symptomatology in the present study was 1:5. [Other] evidence that in nonreferred children, this ratio may range from about 1:2 to 1:3. However, in clinical samples, the rates range from about 7:1 to 1.4:1. Thus, the present estimate appears to have a greater similarity to nonreferred samples rather than clinical samples. It might still be argued, however, that cross-gender behaviors in girls are more acceptable to peers and adults than cross-gender in boys. Thus, girls may have a higher threshold for clinical referral. It appears clear from the present study and previous research that GID prevalence in future studies should be estimated separately by gender and in much larger samples.

A third purpose of the present study was to investigate the hypothesis that GID would be associated with higher rates of psychopathology, specifically SAD and DEP: . . .; however, the strength of both relationships was weak. [T]he causal nature of the relationship between GID and associated psychopathology . . . is an important one as well as the issue of whether GID may be considered a precursor or prodromal stage of adult homosexuality. Certainly, both of these issues deserve further attention.

There are a few additional limitations of the present findings. The power in the present study was limited by the small sample size, although the power was sufficient to detect a heritability of the present magnitude (.62). However, because of the small sample size, we were unable to discriminate between competing models, which may be plausible and could not appropriately examine differential heritability in males and females. Nevertheless, a principal components analysis of the GID scale for gender and age did reveal a similar single factor structure and stable internal reliabilities. Future studies may wish to address the complexity of gender role development as a function of pre- and post-pubescence. Additional studies employing combinations of rater sources and clinical interviews with the parents and children are also needed. The parents in the present twin sample were also highly educated, and future studies may wish to ascertain whether less educated twin samples yield similar results. Overall, however, the central finding of this study cannot be lightly dismissed. It appears that the variation in GID has an appreciable heritable component, and the implications of the latter finding in terms of intervention, therapy, and counseling appear to loom large.

Carla Golden

The Intersexed and the Transgendered: Rethinking Sex/Gender

Let me first define what transgender means, and then I'll give you some idea of the diversity that exists under the umbrella of the transgender community. "Trans" means *across* or *beyond*, and thus transgender means that which moves across or beyond gender (as it is defined by the culture). As applied to people, it refers to someone who moves across or beyond gender boundaries. Leslie Feinberg, who first used the term and continues to elaborate on it, identifies as a transgendered person, as well as a "he-she," and a masculine female. Even as s/he travels around the country speaking and raising consciousness on transgender issues, s/he lives and passes as a man in daily life because s/he fears for her safety as an openly transgendered person. Kate Bornstein, a genetic male and a self-described "gender outlaw," sees herself as beyond gender. In both her writing and speaking, she is emphatic that she is not a man, despite having lived as one for 37 years, and "probably not a woman either," though to look at her you would think she was. Riki Wilchins adopts the label "transgender" at the same time as she rejects it. She points out that transgender is not some natural fact or true identity but a political category that people like her are forced to take on when they construct their sex and gender according to their own definitions and desires.

You may be wondering at this point what's the difference between people who call themselves transsexuals and those who call themselves transgendered. The answer is that it's very much a question of chosen identity. The word "transsexual" has been around much longer and has been used by psychologists to describe people whose gender is at odds with their biological sex. Feinberg, Bornstein, and Wilchins are politically active feminists who have self-consciously constructed their own identities as transgender. They have also used the term "transpeople" (also written as "trans people," or "trans" for short). Still, they have not completely discarded the word "transsexual." In writings from within the transgender community, one will see abundant references to ftms (female to male transsexuals, also called transsexual males) and mtfs (male to female transsexuals, also called transsexual females).

Transsexuals and transgendered people are a diverse group, and the transgender activists previously cited do not speak for all transsexuals. For example, Margaret O'Hartigan vigorously rejects a transgender identity in favor of a transsexual one because to her thinking she did not change her *gender;* she changed her *sex.* As a postoperative transsexual, she moved from one sex category (male) to the other (female), but she had always considered herself a girl or woman. In her experience of self, there are only two categories, and she is a *woman*—not a man, not in-between, not beyond gender. Many transsexuals tell the story of being "trapped in the wrong body," a powerful metaphor that rests on the essentialist belief that there exist only two sexes and two corresponding genders, each of which is fundamentally different from the other. If the gender doesn't match the body's sex, then the body is wrong (a trap) and must be altered. Although it is impossible to provide numerical estimates, it is probably the case that more transsexuals see themselves as trapped in the wrong body than think in terms of transgender identities.

This essentialist dichotomy shows up also in the diagnostic category of gender identity disorder (GID), which entered the third edition of the American Psychiatric Association's *Diagnostic and Statistical Manual of Mental Disorders* (*DSM*) in 1980. It is perhaps not surprising that the narrative told by so many transsexuals resonates with the psychiatric diagnosis they must have if they want to be considered acceptable candidates for surgical and hormonal treatments. The specific criteria that one must meet in order to be given a diagnosis of GID are completely dependent on binary models of sex and gender— specifically, the belief that a person is either male *or* female, a man *or* woman; there is no beyond or in-between. The criteria also rest on the assumption that one's sex and gender must match, and if they don't, something is profoundly wrong and warrants a psychiatric diagnosis.

It is worth considering the diagnosis of gender identity disorder in greater detail as it is presented in the *DSM-IV.* The first diagnostic criterion is "a strong and persistent cross-gender identification," which can manifest itself in a number of different ways. . . .

The second criterion is "persistent discomfort with his or her sex or sense of appropriateness in the gender role of that sex." . . .

There are two additional criteria for diagnosis; one specifies that "the disturbance" is not related to intersexuality and the other that it causes "clinically significant distress or impairment" in the life of the person so diagnosed. In the section on differential diagnosis, it is noted that gender identity disorder is not the same thing as "simple nonconformity to stereotypical sex role behavior" and that it is distinguishable from this "by the extent and pervasiveness of the cross-gender wishes, interests, and activities."

From a feminist psychological perspective, the diagnosis of gender identity disorder is both problematic and suspect. Cross-gender interests and activities? Feminist psychologists had already established that interests and activities are not, and should not, be constrained by one's sex/gender. Just because trucks are marketed to boys doesn't mean that a girl who wants to play with them (even exclusively) has "cross-gender interests." Consider another symptom: the conviction that one has the typical feelings and reactions of the other sex. Is a woman who feels angry, or sexual, or aggressive, or ambitious having the feelings of the other sex? You might agree with me that these so-called symptoms are questionable. But what about the desire to physically alter one's sexual characteristics through hormones and surgery? That's pretty extreme and a legitimate criterion of mental disturbance, isn't it? It all depends on how you think about it. What about the large numbers of non-transsexual women (i.e., biological females who consider themselves to be women) who are both dissatisfied and preoccupied with their secondary sex characteristics to the point of undergoing breast augmentation or reduction surgeries; electrolysis; frequent shaving of legs, underarms, and "bikini" lines; weight-reduction regimens; hormone replacement therapy—all of which are designed to alter the natural female body. Such practices on the part of women reflect the nonconscious ideology that females are born—if not the wrong sex—the second sex, or "the never-good-enough-as-you-are" sex, yet women who choose to change their bodies in these ways are considered quite normal in our culture!

Finally, consider the "clinically significant distress" that must be present for the person to receive a diagnosis of GID. As with any condition of difference in our culture, one can question whether the distress comes from the condition itself or from other people's reaction to the difference. If transsexuals are distressed (as required for a diagnosis of GID), is it because they have "cross-gender" identifications and interests, or because in a culture where sex and gender are dichotomized, we are intolerant of people who step outside the dichotomies? Suppose a person has a ". . . sense of inappropriateness in the gender role of that sex"? So what?! What is the appropriate gender role of each sex, anyway?! Each sex doesn't have one and only one appropriate gender role. Sex and gender aren't linked in any necessary or inevitable way. The diagnostic category of gender identity disorder, like so many other gender- and sexuality-related diagnoses, is highly problematic for feminists or anyone in the process of rethinking the meaning of sex and gender and their relation to each other.

The social constructionism of the transgender activists is more enlightening than the essentializing and pathologizing language of the *DSM*, so let me return to consideration of transgender issues as they emerge from *within* that community rather than from outside of it. One question that often arises has to do with the relative frequency of transsexualism in females and males. Early discussions of the topic pointed to a much lower frequency in biological females. The *DSM-IV* offers no data on prevalence of the disorder but does suggest that in terms of those who seek sex-reassignment surgery, the ratio is 3:1 in favor of biological males. It is difficult to know with any certainty, but recent estimates made from within the transsexual community are that there are probably as many ftms as there are mtfs. In just the past few years, numerous works have appeared that have broadened our exposure to females who cross and sometimes move beyond the gender divide. Holly Devor's (1997) book *FTM: Female-to-Male Transsexuals in Society* offers more than 600 pages of description and analysis of her interviews with 45 ftms. Loren Cameron has produced an eye-opening set of photographs of ftms under the title *Body Alchemy: Transsexual Portraits*, and a documentary film called *You Don't Know Dick*[1] features female to male transsexuals talking about their lives.

Trans people can be anywhere in the process of moving across or beyond gender, from being preoperative to postoperative to any of a number of places in-between, including nonoperative. In contrast to essentialist transsexuals, transgender activists talk about choosing their gender as well as making choices about what kinds of bodies they want. Their chosen gender may or may not correspond to their genitals. Apparently, more and more transsexuals are choosing not to have genital surgery not only because it's extremely expensive (and often results in subsequent complications) but also because it's increasingly seen as unnecessary. The belief in two sexes/genders is challenged, to say the least, by women with breasts and penises and men with beards and clitorises!

Trans people are as heterogeneous a group as any other group of people. In addition to the diversities of thought, personality, and interests that you would find in any group, there are differences among them as they relate to sex, gender, and identity. Some specifically identify as transgender, whereas others do not. They have been variously described as gender blenders (or gender benders), masculine females, feminine males, and gender variants. Among them are those who consider themselves to be women, or men, or intermediate, or neither, or in-progress, or just "different" from what their culture dictates a man or woman should be. Some say they have chosen their gender; others say it was not a choice. Some have decided to have genital surgery, and others have decided against it. Some elect to change other parts of their bodies, and some do not. Their sexualities cover a broad range of possibilities. Their performance of gender reveals its multiplicity and range of complexity. And they are only one segment of the larger whole that makes up the transgender community.

If we understand transgender to mean across or beyond gender lines, then there are many more people who might claim (or be claimed for) membership in the transgender community. The International Foundation for Gender Education (founded in 1987) estimates that 6 percent of the U.S. population are cross-dressers, also known as transvestites. In the *DSM-IV*, transvestites are identified as heterosexual males who cross-dress. I wouldn't argue that we need to expand the criteria for inclusion in the *DSM*, but clearly there are some gay men (known as drag queens) as well as women (less well known, but referred to as drag kings) who don the clothes not considered appropriate for their sex. According to the *DSM-IV*, transvestism is classified as a "fetish," which means that there is some sexual arousal that accompanies cross-dressing in men. Psychologists and others have doubted that there are parallels between men's and women's cross-dressing, believing that for women cross-dressing is more socially acceptable and has no related sexual component. Pat Califia disagrees, pointing to the discrimination, condemnation, and even violence directed toward biological females who cross-dress.[2] She also describes the sexual rush she feels when she is in male drag and notes that her conversations with other women suggest that this is not uncommon. Like transsexuals, cross-dressers constitute a diverse group of men and women with a range of identities and practices. Cross-dressers have existed across history (e.g., Joan of Arc, Mulan) and although some have attempted to claim them as trans people, it's not so easy to say how they thought of themselves. In contemporary times, cross-dressing carries many meanings, and people do it for different reasons. It may or may not be related to sexual orientation, or to transsexuality, and it may or may not include a sexual component. Whatever the case, the very notion of "cross" dressing warrants its inclusion under the umbrella of the transgender community.

In addition to transsexuals and cross-dressers, self-identified intersexuals belong within the transgender community. Intersexual activists are raising awareness about the harm done to infants and children who are subject to genital surgeries they do not need. A federal law passed in 1996 bans genital cutting in the United States, and although the law was aimed at halting the practice among recent immigrants from countries where female genital mutilation is widely practiced, intersexual activists are seeking ways to use the law to ban medically unnecessary intersex surgeries as well. Taking a stand against surgery is not a simple issue for the transgender community, which is hardly monolithic. Movement across and beyond gender lines can work in multiple and sometimes contradictory ways. While intersexual activists are organizing and calling for a halt to intersex surgery, transsexuals are fighting for the right to surgically alter their bodies. Although there is a difference in informed consent (infants can't give it), a feminist social constructionist like me resonates best to the idea of people keeping whatever bodies and genitals they have and performing gender in whatever way suits them. As I see it, the most progressive trend in the transgender community is the one that challenges the requirement that the sex of the body must match the gender of the performance.

Intimate partners of intersexuals and transgendered people deserve inclusion within the transgender community. One shouldn't assume that intersexuals and transgender people are lonely and have difficulty establishing meaningful sexual relationships with others. Nor should it be assumed that they will always or most often relate intimately with other people like them. Any person sexually involved with a man who has breasts or with a woman who has a penis is crossing gender boundaries regardless of their own particular body or identification.

There are still others to be included. Lesbians, gays, and bisexuals might consider themselves part of a broadly defined transgender community. Through their partnerships, self-presentations, and ideas, many lesbians, gays, and bisexuals cross and go beyond conventional gender lines. For that matter, so do some heterosexuals. There are a diversity of ways to cross and go beyond gender boundaries, from the mundane to the more unusual. Consider the report of a 31-year-old "normal" married heterosexual male who requested breast enlargement (which was accomplished via estrogen treatment), so that he could experience more sexual pleasure in his nipples during sexual activity with his wife.

Finally, there are contemporary boys and girls who are gender nonconformists, sometimes aided and encouraged by feminist parents and teachers, all of whom might be included within the transgender community for expanding the possibilities of what gender means. Girls especially seem to me to be stretching the boundaries, moving in-between and beyond gender. In conversations with young girls, I have found the concept of "tomboy" to be on the wane. One 7-year-old whom I asked to point out the tomboys in her class said she wasn't sure about that, but she could identify the "really girly girls" and the "sometimes girly girls" and "the kid kids," a category that included both boys and girls.

The Fluidity of Gender

I hope by now your head is spinning with the dazzling diversity of gendered expressions and with a sense of possibility. It all started out so neat and clear, with sex being defined as biological and gender as a social construction. Then I presented information on the intersexed and suggested that sex wasn't so neatly packaged into two and only two categories and that gender wasn't something we *have* or *are* but a performance. This was followed by a necessarily brief reference to members (or potential members) of the transgender community. The people I have described may or may not consider themselves to be part of a transgender community. But the fact that they might not consciously think of themselves as part of a larger coalition of gender benders or gender performers doesn't stop us from seeing them that way. Performances are seen and interpreted by others, and those of us who are in the process of learning to see differently can learn a lot from other people's performance of gender. Probably most important is that they can help us to imagine the gender possibilities for *ourselves* and to see that gender is fluid—a process, a work-in progress, something not yet finished—not just for *them*, but for *all* of us.

What we can learn from the experiences and performances of those within the transgender community is that neither bodies nor genders are fixed and unchanging. This has led some feminist psychologists to question the notion that a stable and fixed gender identity is desirable or even possible. Research over the past decade on the fluidity of women's sexuality has shown that fixed sexual orientation categories don't adequately describe many women's experience of sexual desire and identity. In the same vein, it is possible that fixed gender identities don't capture the multiplicities of our gendered selves, either. Some psychologists have begun to challenge the longstanding claim of mainstream developmental psychologists that the developing child *must* attain a fixed gender identity, and that doing so is a sign of maturity. Virginia Goldner suggested that learning to tolerate the ambiguity and instability of gender categories is a more appropriate developmental goal than achieving a gender-unified and coherent sense of self. Robert May has argued that, in men, a fixed gender identity may be the result of an inhibition of gender ambiguities and contradictions and as such reflects an impoverishment of character rather than a mature developmental outcome. Sandra Bem argued that, in a gender polarizing and androcentric culture that requires men to repress any "feminine" tendencies, the security of their gender identity will be under constant threat; thus, men will work ceaselessly to prove their masculinity. Sarah Pearlman described gender identity *destabilization* as healthy and elaborated on the opportunities for creative self-expression that can arise from such destabilization of fixed gender identity in women. For the most part, however, these views are too radical to have reached the mainstream of developmental psychology texts.

Conclusion

There are at least five "sex/gender principles" that can be extracted from this lecture, and they are based on what we have learned from the intersexed and the transgendered, broadly defined. First, there exists a lot more diversity in biological sex than we have previously acknowledged; our belief in the existence of only two sexes is a social construct. Second, because both sex *and* gender are socially constructed and because they don't always match, it is no longer so useful to distinguish between them. It made more sense to do so when we thought that gender was a social construct and sex was a biological fact, but our thinking has shifted. Third, people can choose their gender, and this includes moving away from or beyond the gender that had been imposed upon them as children. What they choose may not correspond to their genitals, and what that means is that genitals need not be the central marker of our sex/ gender. Fourth, identities are not necessarily fixed, stable, and coherent, and thus a fixed gender identity is neither necessary nor advantageous to mental health. Just as our age-related or ethnic identities can change over the life course, so, too, can our gender identities. Fifth, the possibilities for gender fluidity, as well as gender ambiguity and contradiction, are enormous, as demonstrated by the members of the broadly defined transgender community.

In my early days as a feminist, I used to think that, in order to achieve equality between the sexes, we would need to deemphasize gender by constantly refocusing attention away from the differences between women and men. But that strategy was frustrating because it wasn't effective. People still focused on the differences, despite a body of research demonstrating that there are more similarities than differences. That was before I realized that gender is a mode of performance and that *more* of it might be better than less. The more we do gender, the more we can stretch it and in the process diversify and multiply the possibilities. Rather than aiming for a gender-free utopia, my vision now is for a world that would be gender-full, where there would be so many different ways to be women, men, in-between, and beyond, that in the end the categories themselves would lose meaning and what we would be left with is a diversity of ways to be. And I don't just mean that the categories woman and man would lose meaning, but so, too, would all cultural constructs grounded in gender, and that includes femininity and masculinity as well as heterosexuality, homosexuality, and bisexuality. A world of multiple gender expressions, where bodies, selves, and desires can combine in all possible ways will be one where there is a lot to see, to be, to do, and to learn—and being female or male, woman or man will have little to do with it. If we take social construction theory seriously, we must remember that those possibilities aren't merely "out there" to be discovered; they are to be actively created by us. Gender is not just what the other presents; it is what we do and what we see. Feminism is, after all, about seeing differently.

Notes

1. This film is distributed by the University of California (at Berkeley) Extension Center for Media and Independent Learning.

2. The notion that women can wear men's clothing without negative social consequence is belied by the experience of Brandon Teena who in 1995 was killed for having a female body at the same time that s/he presented as a man.

POSTSCRIPT

Is Gender Identity Innate?

The etiology (cause) of GID is still more unknown than known. The biological perspective explores the effects of prenatal androgens and maternal prenatal distress on gender atypicality. This research is primarily conducted on lower animals or on intersexual humans (even though GID is not typical in inter-sexuals). Social scientists examine sex-related socialization practices, including parental attitudes, social reinforcement processes (consistently and without ambiguity rearing a child as a boy or a girl, including encouragement of same-gender behavior and discouragement of cross-gender behavior), and self-socialization. An interactionist perspective suggests that sexual biology makes some individuals more vulnerable to certain psychosocial rearing conditions.

Different ideologies about whether or not GID is a disorder seem to rest on this question: do we view sex, gender, and sexual orientation as distinct domains or as inextricably linked? Phyllis Burke notes in *Gender Shock: Exploding the Myths of Male and Female* (Anchor Books, 1996) that "when you look at what society pathologizes, you can get the clearest glimpse of what society demands of those who wish to be considered normal." It appears, then, that our society expects congruence among sex, gender, and sexual orientation and believes that to be the norm. But some critics caution that the biodiversity of nature is greater than our norms allow us to observe. Moreover, we have little understanding, beyond stereotype and presumption, of the association between this biodiversity and gender identity and behavior. For example, how many of us have biological evidence (beyond visible external genitalia) that we are the sex that we believe ourselves to be? There have been cases where female athletes were surprised to find that they have a Y chromosome, yet by other biological measures they are clearly female. What, then, is this individual's "appropriate" gender identity?

Throughout history all societies have had differently gendered people, with varying statuses. These range from examples of women such as Joan of Arc who presented as men, without necessarily hiding their femaleness, so they could fight in wars. The *Hijras* in India were male-to-female transgender people who were believed to be possessed with a spirit of the opposite sex and participated in a religious cult. Other societies have also presumed that transgender people had special spiritual powers, such as the Xaniths in Oman and the Berdache among Native Americans. Clearly, beyond biology, societal norms define what traits and behaviors are "normal" and what status should be accorded individuals who manifest various traits and patterns of behavior. Deviation from conventional social norms may lead either to elevation of status, such as to that of a spiritual leader in some cultures, to that of depraved in other cultures.

What is the future of gender? Are there only two genders (predetermined by the sex binary) or are genders unlimited in form and function, able to be individually and uniquely constructed? Many contemporary scholars remark that the boundaries of gender have been challenged in recent times and that the future holds promise for the "transcendence" of gender. They foretell movement beyond traditional gender roles to refashioned and more flexible gender motifs or perhaps even to the eradication of gender altogether. What would a gender-transformed or gender-irrelevant future look like and what will enable the attainment of such future visions? What do current societal trends indicate? Are our ideas about sexual deviance changing? Are we moving toward or away from gender redefinition and transcendence?

Suggested Readings

Jennifer Finney Boylan, *She's Not There: A Life in Two Genders* (Random House, 2004).

Judith Butler, *Undoing Gender* (New York: Routlege, 2004).

Paula J. Caplan, *They Say You're Crazy: How the World's Most Powerful Psychiatrists Decide Who's Normal* (Perseus Books, 1995).

J. Colapinto, *As Nature Made Him: The Boy Who Was Raised as a Girl* (HarperCollins, 2000).

Judith Rich Harris, *The Nurture Assumption: Why Children Turn Out the Way They Do* (New York: Free Press, 1999).

Sharon E. Preves, *Intersex and Identity: The Contested Self* (Piscataway, NJ: Rutgers University Press, 2003).

N. K. Sandnabba and C. Ahlberg, "Parents' Attitudes and Expectations About Children's Cross-Gender Behavior," *Sex Roles* (February 1999).

K. J. Zucker and S. J. Bradley, *Gender Identity Disorder and Psychosexual Problems in Children and Adolescents* (Guilford Press, 1995).

ISSUE 3

Do Sex Differences in Careers in Mathematics and Sciences Have a Biological Basis?

YES: **Steven Pinker,** from "The Science of Gender and Science: Pinker vs. Spelke," *The Edge* (May 16, 2005)

NO: **Elizabeth Spelke,** from "The Science of Gender and Science: Pinker vs. Spelke," *The Edge* (May 16, 2005)

ISSUE SUMMARY

YES: Steven Pinker reviews arguments supporting the claim that there is a biological basis for gender differences in math and science.

NO: Elizabeth Spelke argues that the underrepresentation of women in the sciences is due to environmental factors.

Cognition represents a complex system of skills that enable the processing of different types of information. Cognitive processes underlie our intellectual activities and many other daily tasks. For three decades, researchers have actively explored whether or not males and females differ in their cognitive abilities. The most common taxonomy of cognitive processes used in cognitive sex differences research is based on the type of information used in a cognitive task: verbal (words), quantitative (numbers), and visual-spatial (figural representations).

The study of cognitive sex differences became especially active after the publication of Eleanor Emmons Maccoby and Carol Nagy Jacklin's now famous book entitled *The Psychology of Sex Differences* (Stanford University Press, 1974). While concluding with a generally skeptical perspective on the existence of sex difference, the authors maintained that one area in which the sexes did appear to differ was intellectual ability and functioning. Specifically, the sexes appeared to differ in verbal, quantitative, and spatial abilities.

This compilation and synthesis of sex comparison findings spawned extensive research on sex differences in numerous areas of functioning but especially in the domain of cognitive abilities. Researchers began to use the quantitative technique of meta-analysis, which has been used to explore whether or not any sex differences change in magnitude over the life cycle or over time, whether or not there is cross-cultural consistency in any sex differences, and whether or not cognitive sex differences are found across various ethnic groups.

At an academic conference in January, 2005 Harvard's president Lawrence Summers gave a talk in which he suggested that innate differences in the math ability of women and men help explain why so few women are found at the highest levels in careers in mathematics and sciences. His speech has generated a huge outcry from feminists and numerous scholars who dispute such claims.

Summers's comments have refueled the ongoing debate regarding the biological basis of math and science abilities. We know that in careers in mathematics and the sciences women tend to earn 25 percent less than men. They are twice as likely to be out of a job. Consider as well that only 2.5 percent of Nobel Prize winners are female and only 3 percent of the members of the U.S. National Academy of Sciences are women.

There has been contradiction among findings. Some researchers document what they describe as important sex differences; others report negligible sex differences that have become smaller over time. When sex differences are described, males show better visual-spatial ability, especially the ability to mentally rotate three-dimensional figures. Males are also found to have greater mathematical ability. Females show better verbal fluency.

This is a politically charged area of research because the stakes are high for the more and less cognitively able. Cognitive abilities relate to valued and "marketable" occupational and societal skills, often putting males at an advantage for higher social status and advancement. This "cognitive ability hierarchy" is not determined by findings of sex differences but reflect differential societal valuation of different cognitive abilities. Critical questions are, What causes cognitive sex differences? Must cognitive ability differences between the sexes, and thus societal inequalities, continue?

A criticism of explanatory research (including both biological and socio-cultural studies) is the lack of direct testing of causal links. For example, sex differences in brain structure may exist, as might sex differences in spatial test performance. But do sex differences in brain structure *cause* sex-differentiated performance on spatial tests? Evidence is lacking for such causal claims. Observers caution that we must discriminate between causal theory and scientific evidence when evaluating causal claims.

The debate falls into the classic concern that correlation does not mean causation. Consider a study that was done examining visual-spatial skills in children. Boys on average outperformed girls. However, the sex disparity was eliminated after girls had been given training in the requisite skills. In these selections you will be reading a debate that was held at Harvard between two professors. Steven Pinker summarizes the mass of evidence supporting the claim that there is a biological basis for sex differences in math and science and believes that "social forces are over-rated as the causes of gender differences." Elizabeth Spelke could not disagree more. For her, social factors are by far the major forces causing the gap between the sexes in careers in math and science.

YES

Steven Pinker

The Science of Gender and Science: Pinker vs. Spelke, A Debate

(STEVEN PINKER:) . . . For those of you who just arrived from Mars, there has been a certain amount of discussion here at Harvard on a particular datum, namely the under-representation of women among tenure-track faculty in elite universities in physical science, math, and engineering. Here are some recent numbers:

As with many issues in psychology, there are three broad ways to explain this phenomenon. One can imagine an extreme "nature" position: that males but not females have the talents and temperaments necessary for science. Needless to say, only a madman could take that view. The extreme nature position has no serious proponents.

There is an extreme "nurture" position: that males and females are biologically indistinguishable, and all relevant sex differences are products of socialization and bias.

Then there are various intermediate positions: that the difference is explainable by some combination of biological differences in average temperaments and talents interacting with socialization and bias.

Liz [Elizabeth Spelke] has embraced the extreme nurture position. There is an irony here, because in most discussions in cognitive science she and I are put in the same camp, namely the "innatists," when it comes to explaining the mind. But in this case Liz has said that there is "not a shred of evidence" for the biological factor, that "the evidence against there being an advantage for males in intrinsic aptitude is so overwhelming that it is hard for me to see how one can make a case at this point on the other side," and that "it seems to me as conclusive as any finding I know of in science."

Well we certainly aren't seeing the stereotypical gender difference in *confidence* here! Now, I'm a controversial guy. I've taken many controversial positions over the years, and, as a member of *Homo sapiens,* I think I am right on all of them. But I don't think that in any of them I would say there is "not a shred of evidence" for the other side, even if I think that the evidence *favors* one side. I would not say that the other side "can't even make a case" for their position, even if I think that their case is not as *good as* the one I favor. And as for saying that a position is "as conclusive as any finding in science"—well, we're talking about social science here! . . .

These are extreme statements—especially in light of the fact that an enormous amount of research, summarized in these and many other literature reviews, in fact points to a very different conclusion. I'll quote from one of them, a book called *Sex Differences in Cognitive Ability* by Diane Halpern. She is a respected psychologist, recently elected as president of the American Psychological Association, and someone with no theoretical axe to grind. She does not subscribe to any particular theory, and has been a critic, for example, of evolutionary psychology. And here is what she wrote in the preface to her book:

> At the time I started writing this book it seemed clear to me that any between sex differences in thinking abilities were due to socialization practices, artifacts, and mistakes in the research. After reviewing a pile of journal articles that stood several feet high, and numerous books and book chapters that dwarfed the stack of journal articles, I changed my mind. The literature on sex differences in cognitive abilities is filled with inconsistent findings, contradictory theories, and emotional claims that are unsupported by the research. Yet despite all the noise in the data, clear and consistent messages could be heard. These are real and in some cases sizable sex differences with respect to some cognitive abilities. Socialization practices are undoubtedly important, but there is also good evidence that biological sex differences play a role in establishing and maintaining cognitive sex differences, a conclusion I wasn't prepared to make when I began reviewing the relevant literature.

This captures my assessment perfectly.

Again for the benefit of the Martians in this room: This isn't just any old issue in empirical psychology. There are obvious political colorings to it, and I want to begin with a confession of my own politics. I am a feminist. I believe that women have been oppressed, discriminated against, and harassed for thousands of years. I believe that the two waves of the feminist movement in the 20th century are among the proudest achievements of our species, and I am proud to have lived through one of them, including the effort to increase the representation of women in the sciences.

But it is crucial to distinguish the *moral* proposition that people should not be discriminated against on account of their sex—which I take to be the core of feminism—and the *empirical* claim that males and females are biologically indistinguishable. They are not the same thing. Indeed, distinguishing them is essential to protecting the core of feminism. Anyone who takes an honest interest in science has to be prepared for the facts on a given issue to come out either way. And that makes it essential that we not hold the ideals of feminism hostage to the latest findings from the lab or field. Otherwise, if the findings come out as showing a sex difference, one would either have to say, "I guess sex discrimination wasn't so bad after all," or else furiously suppress or distort the findings so as to preserve the ideal. The truth cannot be sexist. Whatever the facts turn out to be, they should not be taken to compromise the core of feminism.

Why study sex differences? Believe me, being the Bobby Riggs of cognitive science is not my idea of a good time. So should I care about them, especially since they are not the focus of my own research?

First, differences between the sexes are part of the human condition. We all have a mother and a father. Most of us are attracted to members of the opposite sex, and the rest of us notice the difference from those who do. And we can't help but notice the sex of our children, friends, and our colleagues, in every aspect of life.

Also, the topic of possible sex differences is of great scientific interest. Sex is a fundamental problem in biology, and sexual reproduction and sex differences go back a billion years. . . .

The nature and source of sex differences are also of practical importance. Most of us agree that there are aspects of the world, including gender disparities, that we want to change. But if we want to *change* the world we must first *understand* it, and that includes understanding the sources of sex differences.

Let's get back to the datum to be explained. In many ways this is an *exotic* phenomenon. It involves biologically unprepared talents and temperaments: evolution certainly did not shape any part of the mind to do the work of a professor of mechanical engineering at MIT, for example. The datum has nothing to do with basic cognitive processes, or with those we use in our everyday lives, in school, or even in most college courses, where indeed there are few sex differences.

Also, we are talking about extremes of achievement. Most women are not qualified to be math professors at Harvard because most *men* aren't qualified to be math professors at Harvard. These are extremes in the population.

And we're talking about a subset of fields. Women are not under-represented to nearly the same extent in all academic fields, and certainly not in all prestigious professions.

Finally, we are talking about a statistical effect. This is such a crucial point that I have to discuss it in some detail.

Women are nowhere near absent even from the field in which they are most under-represented. The explanations for sex differences must be statistical as well. And here is a touchstone for the entire discussion:

These are two Gaussian or normal distributions: two bell curves. The X axis stands for any ability you want to measure. The Y axis stands for the proportion of people having that ability. The overlapping curves are what you get whenever you compare the sexes on any measure in which they differ. In this example, if we say that this is the male curve and this is the female curve, the means may be different, but at any particular ability level there are always representatives of both genders.

So right away a number of public statements that have been made in the last couple of months can be seen as red herrings, and should never have been made by anyone who understands the nature of statistical distributions. This includes the accusation that President Summers implied that "50% of the brightest minds in America do not have the right aptitude for science," that "women just can't cut it," and so on. These statements are statistically illiterate, and have nothing to do with the phenomena we are discussing.

There are some important corollaries of having two overlapping normal distributions. . . . [E]ven when there is only a small difference in the means of two distributions, the more extreme a score, the greater the disparity there will be in the two kinds of individuals having such a score. That is, the ratios get more extreme as you go farther out along the tail. If we hold a magnifying glass to the tail of the distribution, we see that even though the distributions overlap in the bulk of the curves, when you get out to the extremes the difference between the two curves gets larger and larger. . . .

A second important corollary is that tail ratios are affected by differences in variance. And biologists since Darwin have noted that for many traits and many species, males are the more variable gender. So even in cases where the mean for women and the mean for men are the same, the fact that men are more variable implies that the proportion of men would be higher at one tail, and also higher at the other. As it's sometimes summarized: more prodigies, more idiots.

With these statistical points in mind, let me begin the substance of my presentation by connecting the political issue with the scientific one. Economists who study patterns of discrimination have long argued (generally to no avail) that there is a crucial conceptual difference between *difference* and *discrimination*. A departure from a 50-50 sex ratio in any profession does not, by itself, imply that we are seeing discrimination, unless the interests and aptitudes of the two groups are equated. Let me illustrate the point with an example, involving myself.

I work in a scientific field—the study of language acquisition in children—that is in fact dominated by women. Seventy-five percent of the members the main professional association are female, as are a majority of the keynote speakers at our main conference. I'm here to tell you that it's not because men like me have been discriminated against. I decided to study language development, as opposed to, say, mechanical engineering, for many reasons. . . .

Now, all we need to do to explain sex differences without invoking the discrimination or invidious sexist comparisons is to suppose that whatever traits *I* have that predispose *me* to choose (say) child language over (say) mechanical engineering are not exactly equally distributed statistically among men and women. For those of you out there—of either gender—who also are not mechanical engineers, you should understand what I'm talking about.

Okay, so what *are* the similarities and differences between the sexes? There certainly are many similarities. Men and women show no differences in general intelligence or *g*—on average, they are exactly the same, right on the money. Also, when it comes to the basic categories of cognition—how we negotiate the world and live our lives; our concept of objects, of numbers, of people, of living things, and so on—there are no differences.

Indeed, in cases where there *are* differences, there are as many instances in which women do slightly better than men as ones in which men do slightly better than women. For example, men are better at throwing, but women are more dexterous. Men are better at mentally rotating shapes; women are better at visual memory. Men are better at mathematical problem-solving; women are better at mathematical calculation. And so on.

But there are at least six differences that are relevant to the datum we have been discussing. The literature on these differences is so enormous that I can only touch on a fraction of it. . . .

1. The first difference, long noted by economists studying employment practices, is that men and women differ in what they state are their priorities in life. To sum it up: men, on average, are more likely to chase status at the expense of their families; women give a more balanced weighting. Once again: Think statistics! The finding is not that women value family and don't value status. It is not that men value status and don't value family. Nor does the finding imply that every last woman has the asymmetry that women show on average or that every last man has the asymmetry that men show on average. But in large data sets, on average, an asymmetry is what you find. . . .

2. Second, interest in people versus things and abstract rule systems. There is a *staggering* amount of data on this trait, because there is an entire field that studies people's vocational interests. . . . [T]here are consistent differences in the kinds of activities that appeal to men and women in their ideal jobs. I'll just discuss one of them: the desire to work with people versus things. There is an enormous average difference between women and men in this dimension, about one standard deviation.

   And this difference in interests will tend to cause people to gravitate in slightly different directions in their choice of career. The occupation that fits best with the "people" end of the continuum is "director of a community services organization." The occupations that fit best with the "things" end are physicist, chemist, mathematician, computer programmer, and biologist. . . .

3. Third, risk. Men are by far the more reckless sex. In a large meta-analysis involving 150 studies and 100,000 participants, in 14 out of 16 categories of risk-taking, men were over-represented. The two sexes were equally represented in the other two categories, one of which was smoking, for obvious reasons. And two of the largest sex differences were in "intellectual risk taking" and "participation in a risky experiment." . . .

4. Fourth, three-dimensional mental transformations: the ability to determine whether the drawings in each of these pairs has the same 3-dimensional shape. Again I'll appeal to a meta-analysis, this one containing 286 data sets and 100,000 subjects. The authors conclude, "we have specified a number of tests that show highly significant sex differences that are stable across age, at least after puberty, and have not decreased in recent years." Now, as I mentioned, for some kinds of spatial ability, the advantage goes to women, but in "mental rotation, spatial perception," and "spatial visualization" the advantage goes to men.

   Now, does this have any relevance to scientific achievement? We don't know for sure, but there's some reason to think that it does. In psychometric studies, three-dimensional spatial visualization is correlated with mathematical problem-solving. And mental manipulation of objects in three dimensions figures prominently in the memoirs and introspections of most creative physicists and chemists, including Faraday, Maxwell, Tesla, Kéekulé, and Lawrence, all of whom claim to have hit upon their discoveries by dynamic visual imagery and only later set them down in equations. . . .

5. Fifth, mathematical reasoning. Girls and women get better school grades in mathematics and pretty much everything else these days. And women are better at mathematical calculation. But consistently, men score better on mathematical word problems and on tests of mathematical reasoning, at least statistically. Again, here is a meta-analysis, with 254 data sets and 3 million subjects. It shows no significant difference in childhood; this is a difference that emerges around puberty, like many secondary sexual characteristics. But there are sizable differences in adolescence and adulthood, especially in high-end samples. . . .

Now why is there a discrepancy with grades? Do SATs and other tests of mathematical reasoning aptitude underpredict grades, or do grades overpredict high-end aptitude? At the Radical Forum Liz [Elizabeth Spelke] was completely explicit in which side she takes, saying that "the tests are no good," unquote. But if the tests are really so useless, why does every major graduate program in science still use them—including the very departments at Harvard and MIT in which Liz and I have selected our own graduate students?

I think the reason is that school grades are affected by homework and by the ability to solve the kinds of problems that have already been presented in lecture and textbooks. Whereas the aptitude tests are designed to test the application of mathematical knowledge to unfamiliar problems. And this, of course, is closer to the way that math is used in actually *doing* math and science.

Indeed, contrary to . . . the popular opinion of many intellectuals, the tests are *surprisingly* good. There is an enormous amount of data on the predictive power of the SAT. . . . [T]he tests predict earnings, occupational choice, doctoral degrees, the prestige of one's degree, the probability of having a tenure-track position, and the number of patents. Moreover this predictive power is the same for men and for women. . . .

6. Finally there's a sex difference in variability. It's crucial here to look at the right samples. Estimates of variance depend highly on the tails of the distribution, which by definition contain smaller numbers of people. Since people at the tails of the distribution in many surveys are likely to be weeded out for various reasons, it's important to have large representative samples from national populations. In this regard the gold standard is the *Science* paper by Novell and Hedges, which reported six large stratified probability samples. They found that in 35 out of 37 tests, including all of the tests in math, space, and science, the male variance was greater than the female variance. . . .

Now the fact that these six gender differences exist does not mean that they are innate. This of course is a much more difficult issue to resolve. A necessary preamble to this discussion is that nature and nurture are not alternatives; it is possible that the explanation for a given sex difference involves some of each.

The only issue is whether the contribution of biology is greater than zero. I think that there are ten kinds of evidence that the contribution of biology *is* greater than zero, though of course it is nowhere near 100 percent.

1. First, there are many biological mechanisms by which a sex difference *could* occur. There are large differences between males and females in levels of sex hormones, especially prenatally, in the first six months of life, and in adolescence. There are receptors for hormones all over the brain, including the cerebral cortex. There are many small differences in men's and women's brains, including the overall size of the brain (even correcting for body size), the density of cortical neurons, the degree of cortical asymmetry, the size of hypothalamic nuclei, and several others.

2. Second, many of the major sex differences—certainly some of them, maybe all of them, are universal. The idea that there are cultures out there somewhere in which everything is the reverse of here turns out to be an academic legend. In his survey of the anthropological literature called *Human Universals,* the anthropologist Donald Brown points out that in all cultures men and women are seen as having different natures; that there is a greater involvement of women in direct child care; more competitiveness in various measures for men than for women; and a greater spatial range traveled by men compared to by women.

   In personality, we have a cross-national survey (if not a true cross-cultural one) in Feingold's meta-analysis, which noted that gender differences in personality are consistent across ages, years of data collection, educational levels, and nations. When it comes to spatial manipulation and mathematical reasoning, we have fewer relevant data, and we honestly don't have true cross-cultural surveys, but we do have cross-national surveys. David Geary and Catherine Desoto found the expected sex difference in mental rotation in ten European countries and in Ghana, Turkey, and China. Similarly, Diane Halpern, analyzing results from ten countries, said that "the majority of the findings show amazing cross-cultural consistency when comparing males and females on cognitive tests."

3. Third, stability over time. Surveys of life interests and personality have shown little or no change in the two generations that have come of age since the second wave of feminism. There is also, famously, *resistance* to change in communities that, for various ideological reasons, were dedicated to stamping out sex differences, and found they were unable to do so. These include the Israeli kibbutz, various American Utopian communes a century ago, and contemporary androgynous academic couples. . . .

4. Fourth, many sex differences can be seen in other mammals. It would be an amazing coincidence if these differences just happened to be replicated in the arbitrary choices made by human cultures at the dawn of time. There are large differences between males and females in many mammals in aggression, in investment in offspring, in play aggression versus play parenting, and in the range size, which predicts a species' sex differences in spatial ability (such as in

solving mazes), at least in polygynous species, which is how the human species is classified. Many primate species even show a sex difference in their interest in physical objects versus conspecifics, a difference seen their patterns of juvenile play. . . .

5. Fifth, many of these differences emerge in early childhood. It is said that there is a technical term for people who believe that little boys and little girls are born indistinguishable and are molded into their natures by parental socialization. The term is "childless."

   Some sex differences seem to emerge even in the first week of life. Girls respond more to sounds of distress, and girls make more eye contact than boys. And in [one] study . . . , newborn boys were shown to be more interested in looking at a physical object than a face, whereas newborn girls were shown to be more interested in looking at a face than a physical object.

   A bit later in development there are vast and robust differences between boys and girls, seen all over the world. Boys far more often than girls engage in rough-and-tumble play, which involves aggression, physical activity, and competition. Girls spend a lot time often in cooperative play. Girls engage much more often in play parenting. . . . There are sex differences in intuitive psychology, that is, how well children can read one another's minds. For instance, several large studies show that girls are better than boys in solving the "false belief task," and in interpreting the mental states of characters in stories.

6. Sixth, genetic boys brought up as girls. In a famous 1970s incident called the John/Joan case, one member of a pair of identical twin boys lost his penis in a botched circumcision. . . . Following advice from the leading gender expert of the time, the parents agreed to have the boy castrated, given female-specific hormones, and brought up as a girl. All this was hidden from him throughout his childhood.

   When I was an undergraduate the case was taught to me as proof of how gender roles are socially acquired. But it turned out that the facts had been suppressed. When "Joan" and her family were interviewed years later, it turned out that from the youngest ages he exhibited boy-typical patterns of aggression and rough-and-tumble play, rejected girl-typical activities, and showed a greater interest in things than in people. At age 14, suffering from depression, his father finally told him the truth. . . .

7. Seventh, a lack of differential treatment by parents and teachers. These conclusions come as a shock to many people. One comes from Lytton and Romney's meta-analysis of sex-specific socialization involving 172 studies and 28,000 children, in which they looked both at parents' reports and at direct observations of how parents treat their sons and daughters—and found few or no differences among contemporary Americans. In particular, there was no difference in the categories "Encouraging Achievement" and "Encouraging Achievement in Mathematics."

   There is a widespread myth that teachers (who of course are disproportionately female) are dupes who perpetuate gender inequities by failing to call on girls in class, and who otherwise have low expectations of girls' performance. In fact Jussim and Eccles, in a study of 100 teachers and 1,800 students, concluded that teachers seemed to be basing their perceptions of students on those students' actual performances and motivation.

8. Eighth, studies of prenatal sex hormones: the mechanism that makes boys boys and girls girls in the first place. There is evidence, admittedly squishy in parts, that differences in prenatal hormones make a difference in later thought and behavior even within a given sex. In the condition called congenital adrenal hyperplasia, girls in utero are subjected to an increased dose of androgens, which is neutralized postnatally. But when they grow up they have male-typical toy preferences—trucks and guns—compared to other girls, male-typical play patterns, more competitiveness, less cooperativeness, and male-typical occupational preferences. However, research on their spatial abilities is inconclusive, and I cannot honestly say that there are replicable demonstrations that CAH women have male-typical patterns of spatial cognition.

   Similarly, variations in fetal testosterone, studied in various ways, show that fetal testosterone has a nonmonotic relationship to reduced eye contact and face perception at 12 months, to reduced vocabulary at 18 months, to reduced social skills and greater narrowness of interest at 48 months, and to enhanced mental rotation abilities in the school-age years.

9. Ninth, circulating sex hormones. . . . Though it's possible that all claims of the effects of hormones on cognition will turn out to be bogus, I suspect something will be salvaged from this somewhat contradictory literature. There are, in any case, many studies showing that testosterone levels in the low-normal male range are associated with better abilities in spatial manipulation. And in a variety of studies in which estrogens are compared or manipulated, there is evidence, admittedly disputed, for statistical changes in the strengths and weaknesses in women's cognition during the menstrual cycle, possibly a counterpart to the changes in men's abilities during their daily and seasonal cycles of testosterone.

10. My last kind of evidence: imprinted X chromosomes. In the past fifteen years an entirely separate genetic system capable of implementing sex differences has been discovered. In the phenomenon called genetic imprinting, studied by David Haig and others, a chromosome such as the X chromosome can be altered depending on whether it was passed on from one's mother or from one's father. This makes a difference in the condition called Turner syndrome, in which a child has just one X chromosome, but can get it either from her mother or her father. When she inherits an X that is specific to girls, on average she has a better vocabulary and better social skills, and is better at reading emotions, at reading body language, and at reading faces.

   A remark on stereotypes. . . .

Are these stereotypes? Yes, many of them are (although, I must add, not all of them—for example, women's superiority in spatial memory and mathematical calculation). There seems to be a widespread assumption that if a sex difference conforms to a stereotype, the difference must have been *caused* by the stereotype, via differential expectations for boys and for girls. But of course the causal arrow could go in either direction: stereotypes might *reflect* differences rather than cause them. In fact there's an enormous literature in cognitive psychology which says that people can be good intuitive statisticians when forming categories and that their prototypes for conceptual categories track the statistics of the natural world pretty well. . . .

To sum up: I think there is more than "a shred of evidence" for sex differences that are relevant to statistical gender disparities in elite hard science departments. There are reliable average differences in life priorities, in an interest in people versus things, in risk-seeking, in spatial transformations, in mathematical reasoning, and in variability in these traits. And there are ten kinds of evidence that these differences are not *completely* explained by socialization and bias, although they surely are in part.

A concluding remark. None of this provides grounds for ignoring the biases and barriers that do keep women out of science, as long as we keep in mind the distinction between *fairness* on the one hand and *sameness* on the other. And I will give the final word to Gloria Steinem: "there are very few jobs that actually require a penis or a vagina, and all the other jobs should be open to both sexes."

Elizabeth Spelke  **NO**

The Science of Gender and Science: Pinker vs. Spelke Debate

(ELIZABETH SPELKE:) . . . I want to start by talking about the points of agreement between Steve [Pinker] and me, and as he suggested, there are many. If we got away from the topic of sex and science, we'd be hard pressed to find issues that we disagree on. Here are a few of the points of agreement that are particularly relevant to the discussions of the last few months.

First, we agree that both our society in general and our university in particular will be healthiest if all opinions can be put on the table and debated on their merits. We also agree that claims concerning sex differences are empirical, they should be evaluated by evidence, and we'll all be happier and live longer if we can undertake that evaluation as dispassionately and rationally as possible. We agree that the mind is not a blank slate; in fact one of the deepest things that Steve and I agree on is that there is such a thing as human nature, and it is a fascinating and exhilarating experience to study it. And finally, I think we agree that the role of scientists in society is rather modest. Scientists find things out. The much more difficult questions of how to use that information, live our lives, and structure our societies are not questions that science can answer. Those are questions that everybody must consider.

So where do we disagree?

We disagree on the answer to the question, why in the world are women scarce as hens' teeth on Harvard's mathematics faculty and other similar institutions? In the current debate, two classes of factors have been said to account for this difference. In one class are social forces, including overt and covert discrimination and social influences that lead men and women to develop different skills and different priorities. In the other class are genetic differences that predispose men and women to have different capacities and to want different things.

In his book, *The Blank Slate,* and again today, Steve [Pinker] argued that social forces are over-rated as causes of gender differences. Intrinsic differences in aptitude are a larger factor, and intrinsic differences in motives are the biggest factor of all. Most of the examples that Steve gave concerned what he takes to be biologically based differences in motives.

My own view is different. I think the big forces causing this gap are social factors. There are no differences in overall intrinsic aptitude for science and mathematics between women and men. Notice that I am not saying the genders are indistinguishable, that men and women are alike in every way, or even that men and women have identical cognitive profiles. I'm saying that when you add up all the things that men are good at, and all the things that women are good at, there is no overall advantage for men that would put them at the top of the fields of math and science.

On the issue of motives, I think we're not in a position to know whether the different things that men and women often say they want stem only from social forces, or in part from intrinsic sex differences. I don't think we can know that now.

I want to start with the issue that's clearly the biggest source of debate between Steve and me: the issue of differences in intrinsic aptitude. This is the only issue that my own work and professional knowledge bear on. Then I will turn to the social forces, as a lay person as it were, because I think they are exerting the biggest effects. . . .

Over the last months, we've heard three arguments that men have greater cognitive aptitude for science. The first argument is that from birth, boys are interested in objects and mechanics, and girls are interested in people and emotions. The predisposition to figure out the mechanics of the world sets boys on a path that makes them more likely to become scientists or mathematicians. The second argument assumes, as Galileo told us, that science is conducted in the language of mathematics. On the second claim, males are intrinsically better at mathematical reasoning, including spatial reasoning. The third argument is that men show greater variability than women, and as a result there are more men at the extreme upper end of the ability distribution from which scientists and mathematicians are drawn. Let me take these claims one by one.

The first claim . . ., is gaining new currency from the work of Simon Baron-Cohen. It's an old idea, presented with some new language. Baron-Cohen says that males are innately predisposed to learn about objects and mechanical relationships, and this sets them on a path to becoming what he calls "systematizers." Females, on the other hand, are innately predisposed to learn about people and their emotions, and this puts them on a path to becoming "empathizers." Since systematizing is at the heart of math and science, boys are more apt to develop the knowledge and skills that lead to math and science.

To anyone as old as I am who has been following the literature on sex differences, this may seem like a surprising claim. The classic reference on the nature and development of sex differences is a book by Eleanor Maccoby and Carol Jacklin that came out in the 1970s. . . . At the top of their list of myths was the idea that males are primarily interested in objects and females are primarily interested in people. They reviewed an enormous literature, in which babies were presented with objects and people to see if they were more interested in one than the other. They concluded that there were no sex differences in these interests. . . .

Let me take you on a whirlwind tour of 30 years of research. . . . From birth, babies perceive objects. They know where one object ends and the next one begins. They can't see objects as well as we can, but as they grow their object perception becomes richer and more differentiated.

Babies also start with rudimentary abilities to represent that an object continues to exist when it's out of view, and they hold onto those representations longer, and over more complicated kinds of changes, as they grow. Babies make basic inferences about object motion: inferences like, the force with which an object is hit determines the speed with which it moves. These inferences undergo regular developmental changes over the infancy period.

In each of these cases, there is systematic developmental change, and there's variability. Because of this variability, we can compare the abilities of male infants to females. Do we see sex differences? The research gives a clear answer to this question: We don't.

Male and female infants are equally interested in objects. Male and female infants make the same inferences about object motion, at the same time in development. They learn the same things about object mechanics at the same time.

Across large numbers of studies, occasionally a study will favor one sex over the other. For example, girls learn that the force with which something is hit influences the distance it moves a month earlier than boys do. But these differences are small and scattered. For the most part, we see high convergence across the sexes. Common paths of learning continue through the preschool years, as kids start manipulating objects to see if they can get a rectangular block into a circular hole. If you look at the rates at which boys and girls figure these things out, you don't find any differences. We see equal developmental paths.

I think this research supports an important conclusion. In discussions of sex differences, we need to ask what's common across the two sexes. One thing that's common is infants don't divide up the labor of understanding the world, with males focusing on mechanics and females focusing on emotions. Male and female infants are both interested in objects and in people, and they learn about both. The conclusions that Maccoby and Jacklin drew in the early 1970s are well supported by research since that time.

Let me turn to the second claim. People may have equal abilities to develop intuitive understanding of the physical world, but formal math and science don't build on these intuitions. Scientists use mathematics to come up with new characterizations of the world and new principles to explain its functioning. Maybe males have an edge in scientific reasoning because of their greater talent for mathematics.

[F]ormal mathematics is not something we have evolved to do; it's a recent accomplishment. Animals don't do formal math or science, and neither did humans back in the Pleistocene. If there is a biological basis for our mathematical reasoning abilities, it must depend on systems that evolved for other purposes, but that we've been able to harness for the new purpose of representing and manipulating numbers and geometry.

Research from the intersecting fields of cognitive neuroscience, neuropsychology, cognitive psychology, and cognitive development provide evidence for five "core systems" at the foundations of mathematical reasoning. The first is a system for representing small exact numbers of objects—the difference between *one*, *two*, and *three*. This system emerges in human infants at about five months of age, and it continues to be present in adults. The second is a system for discriminating large, approximate numerical magnitudes—the difference between a set of about ten things and a set of about 20 things. That system also emerges early in infancy, at four or five months, and continues to be present and functional in adults.

The third system is probably the first uniquely human foundation for numerical abilities: the system of natural number concepts that we construct as children when we learn verbal counting. That construction takes place between about the ages of two and a half and four years. The last two systems are first seen in children when they navigate. One system represents the geometry of the surrounding layout. The other system represents landmark objects.

All five systems have been studied quite extensively in large numbers of male and female infants. We can ask, are there sex differences in the development of any of these systems at the foundations of mathematical thinking? Again, the answer is no. . . .

[Studies] support two important points. First, indeed there is a biological foundation to mathematical and scientific reasoning. We are endowed with core knowledge systems that emerge prior to any formal instruction and that serve as a basis for mathematical thinking. Second, these systems develop equally in males and females. Ten years ago, the evolutionary psychologist and sex difference researcher, David Geary, reviewed the literature that was available at that time. He concluded that there were no sex differences in "primary abilities" underlying mathematics. What we've learned in the last ten years continues to support that conclusion.

Sex differences do emerge at older ages. Because they emerge later in childhood, it's hard to tease apart their biological and social sources. But before we attempt that task, let's ask what the differences are.

I think the following is a fair statement, both of the cognitive differences that Steve described and of others. When people are presented with a complex task that can be solved through multiple different strategies, males and females sometimes differ in the strategy that they prefer.

For example, if a task can only be solved by representing the geometry of the layout, we do not see a difference between men and women. But if the task can be accomplished either by representing geometry or by representing individual landmarks, girls tend to rely on the landmarks, and boys on the geometry. . . .

Because of these differences, males and females sometimes show differing cognitive profiles on timed tests. When you have to solve problems fast, some strategies will be faster than others. Thus, females perform better at some verbal, mathematical and spatial tasks, and males perform better at other verbal, mathematical, and spatial tasks. This pattern of differing profiles is not well captured by the generalization, often bandied about in the popular press, that women are "verbal" and men are "spatial." There doesn't seem to be any more evidence for that than there was for the idea that women are people-oriented and men are object-oriented. Rather the differences are more subtle.

Does one of these two profiles foster better learning of math than the other? In particular, is the male profile better suited to high-level mathematical reasoning?

At this point, we face a question that's been much discussed in the literature on mathematics education and mathematical testing. The question is, by what yardstick can we decide whether men or women are better at math?

Some people suggest that we look at performance on the SAT-M, the quantitative portion of the Scholastic Assessment Test. But this suggestion raises a problem of circularity. The SAT test is composed of many different types of items. Some of those items are solved better by females. Some are solved better by males. The people who make the test have to decide, how many items of each type to include? Depending on how they answer that question, they can create a test that makes women look like better mathematicians, or a test that makes men look like better mathematicians. What's the right solution? . . .

A second strategy is to look at job outcomes. Maybe the people who are better at mathematics are those who pursue more mathematically intensive careers. But this strategy raises two problems. First, which mathematically intensive jobs should we choose? If we choose engineering, we will conclude that men are better at math because more men become engineers. If we choose accounting, we will think that women are better at math because more women become accountants: 57% of current accountants are women. So which job are we going to pick, to decide who has more mathematical talent?

These two examples suggest a deeper problem with job outcomes as a measure of mathematical talent. Surely you've got to be good at math to land a mathematically intensive job, but talent in mathematics is only one of the factors influencing career choice. It can't be our gold standard for mathematical ability.

So what can be? I suggest the following experiment. We should take a large number of male students and a large number of female students who have equal educational backgrounds, and present them with the kinds of tasks that real mathematicians face. We should give them new mathematical material that they have not yet mastered, and allow them to learn it over an extended period of time: the kind of time scale that real mathematicians work on. We should ask, how well do the students master this material? The good news is, this experiment is done all the time. It's called high school and college.

Here's the outcome. In high school, girls and boys now take equally many math classes, including the most advanced ones, and girls get better grades. In college, women earn almost half of the bachelor's degrees in mathematics, and men and women get equal grades. Here I respectfully disagree with one thing that Steve said: men and women get equal grades, even when you only compare people within a single institution and a single math class. Equating for classes, men and women get equal grades.

The outcome of this large-scale experiment gives us every reason to conclude that men and women have equal talent for mathematics. Here, I too would like to quote Diane Halpern. Halpern reviews much evidence for sex differences, but she concludes, "differences are not deficiencies." Men and women have equal aptitude for mathematics. Yes, there are sex differences, but they don't add up to an overall advantage for one sex over the other.

Let me turn to the third claim, that men show greater variability, either in general or in quantitative abilities in particular, and so there are more men at the upper end of the ability distribution. . . .

[However], males and females [have been found to take] equally demanding math classes and major in math in equal numbers. More girls major in biology and more boys in physics and engineering, but equal numbers of girls and boys major in math. And they get equal grades. The SAT-M not only under-predicts the performance of college women in general, it also under-predicts the college performance of women in the talented sample. These women and men have been shown to be equally talented by the most meaningful measure we have: their ability to assimilate new, challenging material in demanding mathematics classes at top-flight institutions. By that measure, the study does not find any difference between highly talented girls and boys.

So, what's causing the gender imbalance on faculties of math and science? Not differences in intrinsic aptitude. Let's turn to the social factors that I think are much more important. . . . I will talk about just one effect: how gender stereotypes influence the ways in which males and females are perceived.

Let me start with studies of parents' perceptions of their own children. Steve said that parents report that they treat their children equally. They treat their boys and girls alike, and they encourage them to equal extents, for they want both their sons and their daughters to succeed. This is no doubt true. But how are parents perceiving their kids?

Some studies have interviewed parents just after the birth of their child, at the point where the first question that 80% of parents ask—is it a boy or a girl?—has been answered. Parents of boys describe their babies as stronger, heartier, and bigger than parents of girls. The investigators also looked at the babies' medical records and asked whether there really were differences between the boys and girls in weight, strength, or coordination. The boys and girls were indistinguishable in these respects, but the parents' descriptions were different.

At 12 months of age, girls and boys show equal abilities to walk, crawl, or clamber. But before one study, Karen Adolph, an investigator of infants' loco-motor development, asked parents to predict how well their child would do on a set of crawling tasks: Would the child be able to crawl down a sloping ramp? Parents of sons were more confident that their child would make it down the ramp than parents of daughters. When Adolph tested the infants on the ramp, there was no difference whatsoever between the sons and daughters, but there was a difference in the parents' predictions.

My third example, moving up in age, comes from the studies of Jackie Eccles. She asked parents of boys and girls in sixth grade, how talented do you think your child is in mathematics? Parents of sons were more likely to judge that their sons had talent than parents of daughters. . . .

There's clearly a mismatch between what parents perceive in their kids and what objective measures reveal. But is it possible that the parents are seeing something that the objective measures are missing? Maybe the boy getting B's in his math class really is a mathematical genius, and his mom or dad has sensed that. To eliminate that possibility, we need to present observers with the very same baby, or child, or Ph.D. candidate, and manipulate their belief about the person's gender. Then we can ask whether their belief influences their perception.

It's hard to do these studies, but there are examples, and I will describe a few of them. A bunch of studies take the following form: you show a group of parents, or college undergraduates, video-clips of babies that they don't know personally. For half of them you give the baby a male name, and for the other half you give the baby a female name. (Male and female babies don't look very different.) The observers watch the baby and then are asked a series of questions: What is the baby doing? What is the baby feeling? How would you rate the baby on a dimension like strong-to-weak, or more intelligent to less intelligent? There are two important findings.

First, when babies do something unambiguous, reports are not affected by the baby's gender. If the baby clearly smiles, everybody says the baby is smiling or happy. Perception of children is not pure hallucination. Second, children often do things that are ambiguous, and parents face questions whose answers aren't easily readable off their child's overt behavior. In those cases, you see some interesting gender labeling effects. For example, in one study a child on a video-clip was playing with a jack-in-the-box. It suddenly popped up, and the child was startled and jumped backward. When people were asked, what's the child feeling, those who were given a female label said, "she's afraid." But the ones given a male label said, "he's angry." Same child, same reaction, different interpretation. . . .

I think these perceptions matter. You, as a parent, may be completely committed to treating your male and female children equally. But no sane parent would treat a fearful child the same way they treat an angry child. If knowledge of a child's gender affects adults' perception of that child, then male and female children are going to elicit different reactions from the world, different patterns of encouragement. These perceptions matter, even in parents who are committed to treating sons and daughters alike.

I will give you one last version of a gender-labeling study. This one hits particularly close to home. The subjects in the study were people like Steve and me: professors of psychology, who were sent some vitas to evaluate as applicants for a tenure track position. Two different vitas were used in the study. One was a vita of a walk-on-water candidate, best candidate you've ever seen, you would die to have this person on your faculty. The other vita was a middling, average vita among successful candidates. For half the professors, the name on the vita was male, for the other half the name was female. People were asked a series of questions: What do you think about this candidate's research productivity? What do you think about his or her teaching experience? And finally, Would you hire this candidate at your university?

For the walk-on-water candidate, there was no effect of gender labeling on these judgments. I think this finding supports Steve's view that we're dealing with little overt discrimination at universities. It's not as if professors see a female name on a vita and think, I don't want her. When the vita's great, everybody says great, let's hire.

What about the average successful vita, though: that is to say, the kind of vita that professors most often must evaluate? In that case, there were differences. The male was rated as having higher research productivity. These psychologists, Steve's and my colleagues, looked at the same number of publications and thought, "good productivity" when the name was male, and "less good productivity" when the name was female. Same thing for teaching experience. The very same list of courses was seen as good teaching experience when the name was male, and less good teaching experience when the name was female. In answer to the question would they hire the candidate, 70% said yes for the male, 45% for the female. If the decision were made by majority rule, the male would get hired and the female would not.

A couple other interesting things came out of this study. The effects were every bit as strong among the female respondents as among the male respondents. Men are not the culprits here. There were effects at the tenure level as well. At the tenure level, professors evaluated a very strong candidate, and almost everyone said this looked like a good case for tenure. But people were invited to express their reservations, and they came up with some very reasonable doubts. For example, "This person looks very strong, but before I agree to give her tenure I would need to know, was this her own work or the work of her adviser?" Now that's a perfectly reasonable question to ask. But what ought to give us pause is that those kinds of reservations were expressed *four times more often* when the name was female than when the name was male.

So there's a pervasive difference in perceptions, and I think the difference matters. Scientists' perception of the quality of a candidate will influence the likelihood that the candidate will get a fellowship, a job, resources, or a promotion. A pattern of biased evaluation therefore will occur even in people who are absolutely committed to gender equity. . . .

From the moment of birth to the moment of tenure, throughout this great developmental progression, there are unintentional but pervasive and important differences in the ways that males and females are perceived and evaluated.

I have to emphasize that perceptions are not everything. When cases are unambiguous, you don't see these effects. What's more, cognitive development is robust: boys and girls show equal capacities and achievements in educational settings, including in science and mathematics, despite the very different ways in which boys and girls are perceived and evaluated. I think it's really great news that males and females develop along common paths and gain common sets of abilities. The equal performance of males and females, despite their unequal treatment, strongly suggests that mathematical and scientific reasoning has a biological foundation, and this foundation is shared by males and females.

Finally, you do not create someone who feels like a girl or boy simply by perceiving them as male or female. That's the lesson that comes from the studies of people of one sex who are raised as the opposite sex. Biological sex differences are real and important. Sex is not a cultural construction that's imposed on people.

But the question on the table is not, Are there biological sex differences? The question is, Why are there fewer women mathematicians and scientists? The patterns of bias that I described provide four interconnected answers to that question. First, and most obviously, biased perceptions produce discrimination: When a group of equally qualified men and women are evaluated for jobs, more of the men will get those jobs if they are perceived to be more qualified. Second, if people are rational, more men than women will put themselves forward into the academic competition, because men will see that they've got a better chance for success. Academic jobs will be more attractive to men because they face better odds, will get more resources, and so forth.

Third, biased perceptions earlier in life may well deter some female students from even attempting a career in science or mathematics. If your parents feel that you don't have as much natural talent as someone else whose objective abilities are no better than yours, that may discourage you, as Eccles's work shows. Finally, there's likely to be a snowball effect. All of us have an easier time imagining ourselves in careers where there are other people like us. If the first three effects perpetuate a situation where there are few female scientists and mathematicians, young girls will be less likely to see math and science as a possible life.

. . . Let me end, though, by asking, could biological differences in motives—motivational patterns that evolved in the Pleistocene but that apply to us today—propel more men than women towards careers in mathematics and science?

My feeling is that where we stand now, we cannot evaluate this claim. It may be true, but as long as the forces of discrimination and biased perceptions affect people so pervasively, we'll never know. I think the only way we can find out is to do one more experiment. We should allow all of the evidence that men and women have equal cognitive capacity to permeate through society. We should allow people to evaluate children in relation to their actual capacities, rather than one's sense of what their capacities ought to be, given their gender. Then we can see, as those boys and girls grow up, whether different inner voices pull them in different directions. I don't know what the findings of that experiment will be. But I do hope that some future generation of children gets to find out.

POSTSCRIPT

Do Sex Differences in Careers in Mathematics and Sciences Have a Biological Basis?

From the 1940s to the 1960s boys tended to surpass girls in math and science, but those discrepancies have lessened more recently. Today girls and boys tend to be equal, especially in basic math skills. Although in advanced math, high school girls tend to outperform boys in the classroom. Even at the college level, although males receive higher scores on standardized tests such as the SAT, females tend to earn higher grades in college math courses. It has been suggested that numerous factors affect females' math performance, such as differential treatment of girls and boys in the classroom and girls' lower expectation and lower confidence because of cultural messages that math is a male domain and that girls are not supposed to do well. There was briefly a Barbie doll on the market that said "math is tough." Additionally, even highly competent girls may suffer from the stereotype threat in standardized testing situations. That is, although they may know they are good at math, the testing context arouses anxiety because of the stereotype; ironically, this can impair their performance. Research has suggested that girls who resist the pressure to conform to gender role expectations are more likely to take more math and science courses, compete in sports, and be more creative and achievement-oriented. Interestingly, it helps to not have a brother, especially an older brother. Birth order as well as the sex composition of the siblings makes a difference. Girls without brothers tend to have higher self-esteem and find it easier to resist the pressure to conform to gendered expectations. Jacquelynne Eccles has proposed an Expectancy by Values Theory that helps explain girls' and boys' differential interest in math. She explains that one's expectations for success interact with the subjective value of various options. Women, as well as men, must believe they can do it and must enjoy doing it. Her research demonstrates that parental attributions are very important. Parents very strongly influence their children's beliefs about their skills, which in turn shapes their academic and ultimately, career choices. Very frequently men are socialized to value career over family and vice versa for women. This emphasis on the development of attitudes towards math and science and their impact on career choices is important because it gives us insight into why there is a gender wage gap and why so many single mothers find themselves on welfare. Recently organizations have launched campaigns to narrow the computer technology gap, which may contribute to the math and science gap for girls and boys. For example, in 2002 the American Association of University Women began the Nebraska Girls and Technology Project in cooperation with the Girl Scouts. The project includes *Girls Click,* which is a computer-based hands-on learning experience.

What does it mean if we find that cognitive sex differences are more heavily accounted for by biology or by environmental reason? If individuals are differently predisposed for cognitive skill, should we and can we do something about it? If so, what? For example, evidence suggests that testosterone is implicated in spatial abilities. Should we give females more testosterone to boost their spatial abilities? Does this sound preposterous considering that thousands of athletes (predominantly males) inject themselves with steroids daily to boost their muscle mass?

Feminist scholars are fearful of biological causal evidence because it renders the environment irrelevant and implies that cognitive sex differences are unchangeable. Rather, they believe that sociocultural evidence provides more hope for social change. How much truth can be found in either claim? Psychosocially caused behavior has often been very difficult to reduce or eliminate (e.g., sex and racial bias). Furthermore, biological mechanisms (e.g., hormones and brain structure) change in response to environmental input. Recent evidence shows, for example, that just as brain structures and functions have been found to impact the way people select and respond to the environment, environmental input and experience alter brain structure and function throughout the life course. If so, then a radical move like injecting females with testosterone is not necessary. Simply engaging individuals in certain activities (even the performance of cognitive tasks) can boost testosterone levels naturally. Thus, many scholars have argued for an interactionist approach to studying cognition, examining the interaction of biology and environment.

Rather than think of sociocultural and biological arguments as necessarily in opposition and mutually exclusive, we must consider how they interact to explain cognitive sex differences. For example, individuals differ in their genetic potential or predisposition for good spatial skills. But genetically predisposed children might select environments that provide more spatial opportunity, augmenting brain structure and further fostering the development of spatial ability. The environment also intercedes in either developing or thwarting this potential. The biological makeup of individuals in the home may also influence the family environment (e.g., parents' and siblings' biological predisposition as impacted by past experiences and environmental inputs). Likewise, individuals might recognize and directly respond to the child's predisposition for spatial ability and provide spatial experiences. Macro-level cultural influences may also act on biological predisposition (e.g., cultural prohibition of certain experiences).

Scholars also urge that we need to go beyond descriptive and explanatory research to a consideration of what the differences *mean* for individuals and society, especially given differential societal valuation of the cognitive differences. Indeed, cognitive sex differences research has revealed the powerful effects of identification and reinforcement of sex role–appropriate behaviors, expectations, motivational variables, and explicit and implicit messages in cognitive sex differences. If individuals have poor mathematical or spatial skill, what does it mean to be excluded from opportunities because of these cognitive deficits (whether actual or presumed based on stereotypes)? Having cognitive deficits impacts identity and self-esteem: how we feel about our abilities, our role in society, and our potential for success. It also creates dependencies. (Think about how much more expensive life is for individuals who are not mechanically inclined.) Spending so much time in a devaluing environment provides constant reminders of the jeopardy incurred by cognitive sex differences to future income, status, and happiness. The restrictions to societal and occupational opportunities based on cognitive functioning have repercussions for individuals and also for society at large. How is society influenced by the fact that the majority of engineers, mathematicians, chemists, mechanics, and airplane pilots are male? Of course, critics point out that the sex differences in occupational representation are grossly disproportionate to the magnitude of cognitive sex differences. Thus, even if there is biological evidence for cognitive sex differences, there seem to be other social factors at work in creating this gulf.

Suggested Readings

Deborah Blum, *Sex on the Brain: The Biological Differences Between Men and Women* (New York: Penguin Books, 1998).

Simon Baron-Cohen, *The Essential Difference: The Truth about the Male and Female Brain* (New York: Basic Books, 2003).

Girl Scouts, *The Girls Difference: Short-Circuiting the Myth of the Technophobic Girl.* (New York: Girl Scouts Research Institute, 2001).

Barbara A. Gutek, "Women and Paid Work," *Psychology of Women Quarterly, 25* (2001): 379–393.

Diane F. Halpren, *Sex Differences in Cognitive Abilities,* 4th ed. (Mahwah, NJ: Lawrence Erlbaum, 2000).

Caryl Rivers and C. Barnett, *Same Difference: How Gender Myths Are Hurting Our Relationships, Our Children, and Our Jobs* (New York: Basic Books, 2005).

Janet Shibley Hyde and Kristen C. Kling, "Women, Motivation, and Achievement," *Psychology of Women Quarterly, 25* (2001): 364–378.

E. S. Spelke, "Sex Differences in Intrinsic Aptitude for Mathematics and Science? A Critical Analysis," *American Psychologist,* 60 (2005): 950–958.

Internet References . . .

Men, Women, and Sex Differences: The Attitudes of Three Feminists—Gloria Steinem, Gloria Allred, and Bella Abzug

A paper by Russell Eisenman entitled "Men, Women, and Sex Differences: The Attitudes of Three Feminists—Gloria Steinmen, Gloria Allred, and Bella Abzug" is presented on this website. This paper is a case study of perspectives on sex differences of three prominent feminists.

http://www.theabsolute.net/misogyny/eisenman.html

Genderlect Styles of Deborah Tannen

This Web site on the genderlect styles of Deborah Tannen provides an overview of Deborah Tannen's popular work on gender and communication.

http://www.usm.maine.edu/com/genderlect/

Feminism and Women's Studies

This link is maintained by EServer, which is an e-publishing cooperative housed at Iowa State University. Hundreds of writers, editors, and scholars gather here to publish their work free of charge. This link provides access to articles, research papers, and reports that focus on gender, communication, and Internet issues

http://feminism.eserver.org/gender/cyberspace/

The website for Life Positive describes different life stressors women and men might experience and offers suggestions for coping.

http://www.lifepositive.com/Mind/psychology/
stress/male-depression.asp

Different Strokes: The Question of Difference

*W*hat is the most fruitful approach for better understanding sex and gender? For decades, the dominant approach in social scientific research on sex and gender is studying sex differences, termed a difference model. The goal is to examine whether or not sex differences exist and to describe the differing group tendencies. In this research, sex differences are identified from a comparison of the average tendency of a group of males to the average tendency of a group of females. The result is typically expressed in the form of generalizations of ways in which males and females differ, presuming within-sex homogeneity (i.e., all females are alike). Although most of the research is descriptive, assumptions and theories of what causes these sex differences abound. The aims of this section are to explore some ways in which the difference model has shaped our understanding of gender in various domains of human functioning, including communication and responses to stress.*

As you read these selections, consider the role of biology. Are new developments in neuron-imaging that show which areas of the brain are most active during various tasks clarifying or confusing our understanding the role of biology in explanations of sex differences and similarities? How do issues of sex differences/similarities play out across race, ethnicity, class, culture, and other status-defining categories? Are women and men similarly alike or different across these various categories? Do media representations of women and men "fan the fires" of difference, especially when talking about gender and communication and responses to stress?

- Are Women and Men More Similar Than Different?

- Are Different Patterns of Communication in Women and Men Innately Determined?

- Are the Fight-or-Flight and Tend-and-Befriend Responses to Stress Gender-Based?

ISSUE 4

Are Women and Men More Similar Than Different?

YES: Janet Shibley Hyde, from "The Gender Similarities Hypothesis," *American Psychologist* (2005)

NO: Kingsley R. Browne, from *Biology at Work: Rethinking Sexual Equality* (Rutgers University Press, 2002)

ISSUE SUMMARY

YES: Psychology professor Janet Shibley Hyde of the University of Wisconsin at Madison argues that claims of gender differences are overinflated, resulting in serious consequences for women and men in the workplace and in relationships.

NO: Kingsley R. Browne, a professor at Wayne State University Law School, claims that the differences are real, rooted in biology.

Some feminist scholars warn of the overrepresentation of findings of sex differences in published scholarship. Many scholars argue that the comparison of males and females is as much a political as a scientific enterprise. Findings of similarities between groups is thought to be a "null" finding and thus not publishable in its own right. The popular press is eager to disseminate evidence of sex differences; indeed, findings of sex similarity are viewed as not newsworthy. Often, the description of a sex difference is accompanied by a presumption that the difference is innate and thus immutable.

An ongoing debate surrounds whether women and men are more similar than different and whether it is worthwhile to continue to study differences, especially if they are small. There appears to be a trade-off in the costs and benefits of each perspective. Noted feminist psychologist Rhoda Unger once said, "Consider a rainbow. Given the full spectrum of color, we perceive red and magenta as being similar. If, however, we eliminate all other hues, red and magenta are now perceived as being different. But the price of emphasizing this difference is the loss of the rest of the spectrum. Similarly, relationships relevant to both sexes have been obscured by the limitation of research to the difference between them."

Maccoby and Jacklin's work triggered other in-depth analyses of the existence or lack thereof of sex differences in numerous areas. In general, conclusions reflected skepticism about the presence of sex differences. In the 1980s this area of research took another step forward by moving from an impressionistic normative reviewing process to a more formal, quantitative technique for synthesizing research: meta-analysis. Meta-analysis provides a common metric with which studies can be directly compared and the magnitude of sex differences can be represented. Moreover, meta-analysis looks at the consistency of findings across studies and tries to identify variables (such as measurement strategies, the historical moment when the study was conducted, and sample characteristics) that explain inconsistencies and even contradictions across studies.

Researcher and psychologist Jacquelyn James in "What Are the Social Issues Involved in Focusing on *Difference* in the Study of Gender?" *Journal of Social Issues* (Summer 1997), outlines five critical issues to consider when reviewing the status of the difference model:

1. *Very Small Differences Can Be Statistically Significant.* Because of the social weight of scientific evidence, even misrepresented and statistically weak differences get exaggerated by public accounts and therefore misused.
2. *False Universalism.* Interpretations of group differences often presume within-group similarity. In fact, other individual differences (e.g., social power) may explain differences better than sex.
3. *The "Tyranny of Averages."* Sex differences are usually based on group averages, interpreted as if they represent absolutes. Within-group variability or the overlap between distributions of males and females is not examined.
4. *The Revelations of Within-Group Differences.* Careful examination of within-group variation can be very effective in challenging gender stereotypes and examining the conditions under which differences do and do not occur. Furthermore, methodological practices may skew the meaning of sex differences (e.g., measurement bias).
5. *Some Differences Are Diminishing Over Time.* Weakening differences over time suggest that sociohistorical change is relevant to the "why" of difference.

Has the difference model outlived its purpose? In the following selections Janet Hyde, using results of several meta-analyses, documents that women and men are quite similar in a number of psychological domains. Only for the domains of motor performance and physical aggression, behaviors that depend largely on muscle mass and bone size, and for sexuality (at least masturbation and attitudes accepting of casual sex) have moderate to large sex differences been found. She highlights the importance of considering social context when examining gender-related behaviors and concludes that the overinflation of sex differences is costly for girls and boys. In contrast, Kingsley Browne focuses on precisely the attributes for which Hyde claims women and men are the most similar. He claims that these domains have a biological basis and lead to inevitable differences between women and men. He argues that research on these differences can "assist us in an understanding of existing patterns as well as developing designs for change."

YES

Janet Shibley Hyde

The Gender Similarities Hypothesis

The mass media and the general public are captivated by findings of gender differences. John Gray's (1992) *Men Are From Mars, Women Are From Venus*, which argued for enormous psychological differences between women and men, has sold over 30 million copies and been translated into 40 languages. Deborah Tannen's *You Just Don't Understand: Women and Men in Conversation* argued for the *different cultures hypothesis*: that men's and women's patterns of speaking are so fundamentally different that men and women essentially belong to different linguistic communities or cultures. That book was on the *New York Times* bestseller list for nearly four years and has been translated into 24 languages. Both of these works, and dozens of others like them, have argued for the *differences hypothesis*: that males and females are, psychologically, vastly different. Here, I advance a very different view—the *gender similarities hypothesis*.

The Hypothesis

The gender similarities hypothesis holds that males and females are similar on most, but not all, psychological variables. That is, men and women, as well as boys and girls, are more alike than they are different. In terms of effect sizes, the gender similarities hypothesis states that most psychological gender differences are in the close-to-zero ($d \leq 0.10$) or small ($0.11 < d < 0.35$) range, a few are in the moderate range ($0.36 < d < 0.65$), and very few are large ($d = 0.66$–1.00) or very large ($d > 1.00$).

Although the fascination with psychological gender differences has been present from the dawn of formalized psychology around 1879, a few early researchers highlighted gender similarities. Thorndike (1914), for example, believed that psychological gender differences were too small, compared with within-gender variation, to be important. Leta Stetter Hollingworth (1918) reviewed available research on gender differences in mental traits and found little evidence of gender differences. Another important reviewer of gender research in the early 1900s, Helen Thompson Woolley, lamented the gap between the data and scientists' views on the question:

> The general discussions of the psychology of sex, whether by psychologists or by sociologists show such a wide diversity of points of view that one

From *American Psychologist*, vol. 60, no. 6, September 2005, pp. 581–582, 586–590. Copyright © 2005 by American Psychological Association. Reprinted by permission. References omitted.

feels that the truest thing to be said at present is that scientific evidence plays very little part in producing convictions.

The Role of Meta-Analysis in Assessing Psychological Gender Differences

Reviews of research on psychological gender differences began with Woolley's (1914) and Hollingworth's and extended through Maccoby and Jacklin's watershed book *The Psychology of Sex Differences*, in which they reviewed more than 2,000 studies of gender differences in a wide variety of domains, including abilities, personality, social behavior, and memory. Maccoby and Jacklin dismissed as unfounded many popular beliefs in psychological gender differences, including beliefs that girls are more "social" than boys; that girls are more suggestible; that girls have lower self-esteem; that girls are better at rote learning and simple tasks, whereas boys are better at higher level cognitive processing; and that girls lack achievement motivation. Maccoby and Jacklin concluded that gender differences were well established in only four areas: verbal ability, visual-spatial ability, mathematical ability, and aggression. Overall, then, they found much evidence for gender similarities. Secondary reports of their findings in textbooks and other sources, however, focused almost exclusively on their conclusions about gender differences.

Shortly after this important work appeared, the statistical method of meta-analysis was developed. This method revolutionized the study of psychological gender differences. Meta-analyses quickly appeared on issues such as gender differences in influenceability, and aggression.

Meta-analysis is a statistical method for aggregating research findings across many studies of the same question (Hedges & Becker, 1986). It is ideal for synthesizing research on gender differences, an area in which often dozens or even hundreds of studies of a particular question have been conducted.

Crucial to meta-analysis is the concept of effect size, which measures the magnitude of an effect—in this case, the magnitude of gender difference. In gender meta-analyses, the measure of effect size typically is d (Cohen, 1988):

$$d = \frac{M_M - M_F}{S_W},$$

where M_M is the mean score for males, M_F is the mean score for females, and S_W is the average within-sex standard deviation. That is, d measures how far apart the male and female means are in standardized units. In gender meta-analysis, the effect sizes computed from all individual studies are averaged to obtain an overall effect size reflecting the magnitude of gender differences across all studies. In the present article, I follow the convention that negative values of d mean that females scored higher on a dimension, and positive values of d indicate that males scored higher.

Gender meta-analyses generally proceed in four steps: (a) The researcher locates all studies on the topic being reviewed, typically using databases such as PsycINFO and carefully chosen search terms. (b) Statistics are extracted from each report, and an effect size is computed for each study. (c) A weighted average of the effect sizes is computed (weighting by sample size) to obtain an overall assessment of the direction and magnitude of the gender difference when all studies are combined. (d) Homogeneity analyses are conducted to determine whether the group of effect sizes is relatively homogeneous. If it is not, then the studies can be partitioned into theoretically meaningful groups to determine whether the effect size is larger for some types of studies and smaller for other types. The researcher could ask, for example, whether gender differences are larger for measures of physical aggression compared with measures of verbal aggression.

The Evidence

To evaluate the gender similarities hypothesis, I collected the major meta-analyses that have been conducted on psychological gender differences. They are . . . grouped roughly into six categories: those that assessed cognitive variables, such as abilities; those that assessed verbal or nonverbal communication; those that assessed social or personality variables, such as aggression or leadership; those that assessed measures of psychological well-being, such as self-esteem; those that assessed motor behaviors, such as throwing distance; and those that assessed miscellaneous constructs, such as moral reasoning. I began with meta-analyses reviewed previously. I updated these lists with more recent meta-analyses and, where possible, replaced older meta-analyses with more up-to-date meta-analyses that used larger samples and better statistical methods.

Inspection of the effect sizes . . . reveals strong evidence for the gender similarities hypothesis. . . . Of the 128 effect sizes, . . . 4 were unclassifiable because the meta-analysis provided such a wide range for the estimate. The remaining 124 effect sizes were classified into the categories noted earlier: close-to-zero ($d \leq 0.10$), small ($0.11 < d < 0.35$), moderate ($0.36 < d < 0.65$), large ($d = 0.66 - 1.00$), or very large (> 1.00). The striking result is that 30% of the effect sizes are in the close-to-zero range, and an additional 48% are in the small range. That is, 78% of gender differences are small or close to zero. This result is similar to [another analysis that] found that 60% of effect sizes for gender differences were in the small or close-to-zero range.

The small magnitude of these effects is even more striking given that most of the meta-analyses addressed the classic gender differences questions— that is, areas in which gender differences were reputed to be reliable, such as mathematics performance, verbal ability, and aggressive behavior. For example, . . . gender differences in most aspects of communication are small. [It] has argued that males and females speak in a different moral "voice," yet meta-analyses show that gender differences in moral reasoning and moral orientation are small.

The Exceptions

As noted earlier, the gender similarities hypothesis does not assert that males and females are similar in absolutely every domain. The exceptions—areas in which gender differences are moderate or large in magnitude—should be recognized.

The largest gender differences . . . are in the domain of motor performance, particularly for measures such as throwing velocity ($d = 2.18$) and throwing distance ($d = 1.98$). These differences are particularly large after puberty, when the gender gap in muscle mass and bone size widens.

A second area in which large gender differences are found is some—but not all—measures of sexuality. Gender differences are strikingly large for incidences of masturbation and for attitudes about sex in a casual, uncommitted relationship. In contrast, the gender difference in reported sexual satisfaction is close to zero.

Across several meta-analyses, aggression has repeatedly shown gender differences that are moderate in magnitude. The gender difference in physical aggression is particularly reliable and is larger than the gender difference in verbal aggression. Much publicity has been given to gender differences in relational aggression, with girls scoring higher. According to [an earlier] meta-analysis, indirect or relational aggression showed an effect size for gender differences of −0.45 when measured by direct observation, but it was only −0.19 for peer ratings, −0.02 for self-reports, and −0.13 for teacher reports. Therefore, the evidence is ambiguous regarding the magnitude of the gender difference in relational aggression. . . .

Developmental Trends

Not all meta-analyses have examined developmental trends and, given the preponderance of psychological research on college students, developmental analysis is not always possible. However, meta-analysis can be powerful for identifying age trends in the magnitude of gender differences. Here, I consider a few key examples of meta-analyses that have taken this developmental approach.

At [one] time, . . . it was believed that gender differences in mathematics performance were small or nonexistent in childhood and that the male advantage appeared beginning around the time of puberty. It was also believed that males were better at high-level mathematical problems that required complex processing, whereas females were better at low-level mathematics that required only simple computation. Hyde and colleagues addressed both hypotheses in [an earlier] meta-analysis. They found a small gender difference favoring girls in computation in elementary school and middle school and no gender difference in computation in the high school years. There was no gender difference in complex problem solving in elementary school or middle school, but a small gender difference favoring males emerged in the high school years ($d = 0.29$). Age differences in the magnitude of the gender effect were significant for both computation and problem solving.

[In] a developmental approach in [a] meta-analysis of studies of gender differences in self-esteem, on the basis of the assertion of prominent authors such as Mary Pipher that girls' self-esteem takes a nosedive at the beginning of adolescence [it was] found that the magnitude of the gender difference did grow larger from childhood to adolescence: In childhood (ages 7–10), $d = 0.16$; for early adolescence (ages 11–14), $d = 0.23$; and for the high school years (ages 15–18), $d = 0.33$. However, the gender difference did not suddenly become large in early adolescence, and even in high school, the difference was still not large. Moreover, the gender difference was smaller in older samples. . . .

[Another] analysis of age trends in computer self-efficacy is revealing. In grammar school samples, $d = 0.09$, whereas in high school samples, $d = 0.66$. This dramatic trend leads to questions about what forces are at work transforming girls from feeling as effective with computers as boys do to showing a large difference in self-efficacy by high school.

These examples illustrate the extent to which the magnitude of gender differences can fluctuate with age. Gender differences grow larger or smaller at different times in the life span, and meta-analysis is a powerful tool for detecting these trends. Moreover, the fluctuating magnitude of gender differences at different ages argues against the differences model and notions that gender differences are large and stable.

The Importance of Context

Gender researchers have emphasized the importance of context in creating, erasing, or even reversing psychological gender differences. Context may exert influence at numerous levels, including the written instructions given for an exam, dyadic interactions between participants or between a participant and an experimenter, or the sociocultural level.

[A]n important experiment, . . . demonstrated the importance of gender roles and social context in creating or erasing the purportedly robust gender difference in aggression. [The researchers] used the technique of deindividuation to produce a situation that removed the influence of gender roles. *Deindividuation* refers to a state in which the person has lost his or her individual identity; that is, the person has become anonymous. Under such conditions, people should feel no obligation to conform to social norms such as gender roles. Half of the participants, who were college students, were assigned to an individuated condition by having them sit close to the experimenter, identify themselves by name, wear large name tags, and answer personal questions. Participants in the deindividuation condition sat far from the experimenter, wore no name tags, and were simply told to wait. All participants were also told that the experiment required information from only half of the participants, whose behavior would be monitored, and that the other half would remain anonymous. Participants then played an interactive video game in which they first defended and then attacked by dropping bombs. The number of bombs dropped was the measure of aggressive behavior.

The results indicated that in the individuated condition, men dropped significantly more bombs than women did. In the deindividuated condition, however, there were no significant gender differences and, in fact, women dropped somewhat more bombs than men. In short, the significant gender difference in aggression disappeared when gender norms were removed.

[W]ork on stereotype threat has produced similar evidence in the cognitive domain. Although the original experiments concerned African Americans and the stereotype that they are intellectually inferior, the theory was quickly applied to gender and stereotypes that girls and women are bad at math. In one experiment, male and female college students with equivalent math backgrounds were tested. In one condition, participants were told that the math test had shown gender difference in the past, and in the other condition, they were told that the test had been shown to be gender fair—that men and women had performed equally on it. In the condition in which participants had been told that the math test was gender fair, there were no gender differences in performance on the test. In the condition in which participants expected gender differences, women underperformed compared with men. This simple manipulation of context was capable of creating or erasing gender differences in math performance.

Meta-analysts have addressed the importance of context for gender differences. [O]ne of the earliest demonstrations of context effects meta-analyzed studies of gender differences in helping behavior, basing the analysis in social-role theory. [It was] argued that certain kinds of helping are part of the male role: helping that is heroic or chivalrous. Other kinds of helping are part of the female role: helping that is nurturant and caring, such as caring for children. Heroic helping involves danger to the self, and both heroic and chivalrous helping are facilitated when onlookers are present. Women's nurturant helping more often occurs in private, with no onlookers. Averaged over all studies, men helped more ($d = 0.34$). However, when studies were separated into those in which onlookers were present and participants were aware of it, $d = 0.74$. When no onlookers were present, $d = -0.02$. Moreover, the magnitude of the gender difference was highly correlated with the degree of danger in the helping situation; gender differences were largest favoring males in situations with the most danger. In short, the gender difference in helping behavior can be large, favoring males, or close to zero, depending on the social context in which the behavior is measured. Moreover, the pattern of gender differences is consistent with social-role theory.

[S]imilar context effects [were found in a] meta-analysis of gender differences in conversational interruption. At the time of their meta-analysis, it was widely believed that men interrupted women considerably more than the reverse. Averaged over all studies, however, [only] a small effect [was found]. The effect size for intrusive interruptions (excluding back-channel interruptions) was larger: 0.33. It is important to note that the magnitude of the gender difference varied greatly depending on the social context in which interruptions were studied. When dyads were observed, $d = 0.06$, but with larger groups of three or more, $d = 0.26$. When participants were strangers, $d = 0.17$, but when they were friends, $d = -0.14$. Here, again, it is clear that gender differences can be created, erased, or reversed, depending on the context.

[A] moderate gender difference in smiling ($d = -0.41$), with girls and women smiling more [has been reported]. Again, the magnitude of the gender difference was highly dependent on the context. If participants had a clear aware-ness that they were being observed, the gender difference was larger ($d = -0.46$) than it was if they were not aware of being observed ($d = -0.19$). The magni-tude of the gender difference also depended on culture and age.

[Others have] also found marked context effects in their gender meta-analyses. The conclusion is clear: The magnitude and even the direction of gender differences depends on the context. These findings provide strong evi-dence against the differences model and its notions that psychological gender differences are large and stable.

Costs of Inflated Claims of Gender Differences

The question of the magnitude of psychological gender differences is more than just an academic concern. There are serious costs of overinflated claims of gender differences. These costs occur in many areas, including work, parenting, and relationships.

[The] argument that women speak in a different moral "voice" than men is a well-known example of the differences model. Women, according to Gilligan, speak in a moral voice of caring, whereas men speak in a voice of justice. Despite the fact that meta-analyses disconfirm her arguments for large gender differences, Gilligan's ideas have permeated American culture. One consequence of this overinflated claim of gender differences is that it reifies the stereotype of women as caring and nurturant and men as lacking in nurturance. One cost to men is that they may believe that they cannot be nurturant, even in their role as father. For women, the cost in the workplace can be enormous. Women who violate the stereotype of being nurturant and nice can be penalized in hiring and evaluations. [For example,] female job applicants who displayed agentic qualities received considerably lower hire-ability ratings than agentic male applicants ($d = 0.92$) for a managerial job that had been "feminized" to require not only technical skills and the ability to work under pressure but also the ability to be helpful and sensitive to the needs of others. The researchers concluded that women must present them-selves as competent and agentic to be hired, but they may then be viewed as interpersonally deficient and uncaring and receive biased work evaluations because of their violation of the female nurturance stereotype.

A second example of the costs of unwarranted validation of the stereo-type of women as caring nurturers comes from [a] meta-analysis of studies of gender and the evaluation of leaders. Overall, women leaders were evaluated as positively as men leaders ($d = 0.05$). However, women leaders portrayed as uncaring autocrats were at a more substantial disadvantage than were men leaders portrayed similarly ($d = 0.30$). Women who violated the caring stereo-type paid for it in their evaluations. The persistence of the stereotype of women as nurturers leads to serious costs for women who violate this stereo-type in the workplace.

The costs of overinflated claims of gender differences hit children as well. According to stereotypes, boys are better at math than girls are. This stereotype is proclaimed in mass media headlines. Meta-analyses, however, indicate a pattern of gender similarities for math performance. . . . One cost to children is that mathematically talented girls may be overlooked by parents and teachers because these adults do not expect to find mathematical talent among girls. Parents have lower expectations for their daughters' math success than for their sons' despite the fact that girls earn better grades in math than boys do. Research has shown repeatedly that parents' expectations for their children's mathematics success relate strongly to outcomes such as the child's mathematics self-confidence and performance, with support for a model in which parents' expectations influence children. In short, girls may find their confidence in their ability to succeed in challenging math courses or in a mathematically oriented career undermined by parents' and teachers' beliefs that girls are weak in math ability.

In the realm of intimate heterosexual relationships, women and men are told that they are as different as if they came from different planets and that they communicate in dramatically different ways. When relationship conflicts occur, good communication is essential to resolving the conflict. If, however, women and men believe what they have been told—that it is almost impossible for them to communicate with each other—they may simply give up on trying to resolve the conflict through better communication. Therapists will need to dispel erroneous beliefs in massive, unbridgeable gender differences.

Inflated claims about psychological gender differences can hurt boys as well. A large gender gap in self-esteem beginning in adolescence has been touted in popular sources. Girls' self-esteem is purported to take a nosedive at the beginning of adolescence, with the implication that boys' self-esteem does not. Yet meta-analytic estimates of the magnitude of the gender difference have all been small or close to zero. . . . In short, self-esteem is roughly as much a problem for adolescent boys as it is for adolescent girls. The popular media's focus on girls as the ones with self-esteem problems may carry a huge cost in leading parents, teachers, and other professionals to overlook boys' self-esteem problems, so that boys do not receive the interventions they need.

As several of these examples indicate, the gender similarities hypothesis carries strong implications for practitioners. The scientific evidence does not support the belief that men and women have inherent difficulties in communicating across gender. Neither does the evidence support the belief that adolescent girls are the only ones with self-esteem problems. Therapists who base their practice in the differences model should reconsider their approach on the basis of the best scientific evidence.

Conclusion

The gender similarities hypothesis stands in stark contrast to the differences model, which holds that men and women, and boys and girls, are vastly different psychologically. The gender similarities hypothesis states, instead, that males and females are alike on most—but not all—psychological variables. Extensive evidence from meta-analyses of research on gender differences supports the gender similarities hypothesis. A few notable exceptions are some motor behaviors (e.g., throwing distance) and some aspects of sexuality, which show large gender differences. Aggression shows a gender difference that is moderate in magnitude.

It is time to consider the costs of overinflated claims of gender differences. Arguably, they cause harm in numerous realms, including women's opportunities in the workplace, couple conflict and communication, and analyses of self-esteem problems among adolescents. Most important, these claims are not consistent with the scientific data.

Kingsley R. Browne

 **NO**

Biology at Work: Rethinking Sexual Equality

To provide biological explanations is, some say, to confuse the *is* and the *ought*, apparently ignoring the fact that the primary function of science is to explain the natural world, not to justify or defend it. If it is a fallacy to argue that the biological roots of a phenomenon demonstrate its desirability—as it surely is—then it is equally fallacious to infer that an argument for the biological roots of a phenomenon is implicitly an argument that the phenomenon is good. Put another way, it is more commonly the opponents than proponents of biological explanations who draw inferences of value from assertions of fact.

The discovery that all manner of social ills, from rape to child abuse, derive in part from biological predispositions does not justify these behaviors, especially since our desire to prevent those ills probably stems from the same kind of predispositions. Nor does the biological argument imply that attempts to reduce the prevalence of such behaviors are necessarily doomed, for a central finding of evolutionary psychology is the flexibility (albeit along predictable lines) of human behavioral responses. Nonetheless, an understanding of the deep origins of the phenomena of interest may assist us in an understanding of existing patterns as well as in developing designs for change. . . .

Aggressiveness, Dominance Assertion, Competitiveness, Achievement Motivation, and Status Seeking

The sexes are consistently found to differ in a constellation of related traits: aggressiveness, dominance assertion, competitiveness, achievement motivation, and status seeking. Each of these terms has its own somewhat different definition, but the traits are highly correlated and often overlapping. Although "aggressiveness" may be defined narrowly to mean the infliction of harm on another, a broader definition of the term encompasses most of the traits listed above. Thus, when we speak of an "aggressive soccer player" or "aggressive businessman," we are not necessarily describing a person who wishes to inflict harm on another, although we may be describing a willingness to step on competitors—literally in the former case and figuratively in the latter—in pursuit of his goals. . . .

Competitiveness

Competition seems to come more easily to males than females and to be a more unalloyed positive experience for males. Competition significantly increases the intrinsic motivation of men, while it does not do so for women. A perception that an academic program is competitive may result in poorer performance by women but better performance by men. Women also report higher levels of stress attendant to competition.

Sex differences in competition appear in early childhood. Even pre-school boys engage in more competitive activities than girls, activities that seem to elevate levels of adrenaline and noradrenaline. A study of second through twelfth graders found that girls reported more-positive attitudes toward cooperation in school and less-positive attitudes toward competition in all grades than did boys.

Sex differences in attitudes toward competition are reflected in children's play styles, as demonstrated in a well-known study of play by Janet Lever. Boys were much more likely to engage in "game" (competitive interactions with explicit goals), while girls engaged in more "play" (behaviors with no explicit goal and no winners). Even when both sexes played games, the games were of different types. Games like hopscotch and jump-rope are "turn-taking" games, in which any competition that exists is indirect. When boys competed, they were more likely to compete head-to-head in zero-sum competition. Because boys cared more about being declared the winner, their games were usually structured so that there would be a clear and definite outcome.

The boys in Lever's study seemed to display a more instrumental approach to competition. Exhibiting a difference that may have later workplace implications, boys were much better than girls at competing against friends and cooperating with teammates whom they did not like. Anecdotal accounts of childhood play suggest that when boys pick teams for games they pick the people they believe to be the best players irrespective of whether they like them, while girls are more likely to choose their friends irrespective of skill. Although Lever observed that among boys there were repeated disputes over the rules, no games were terminated as a consequence of these disputes. In fact, she concluded, boys enjoyed the rule disputes as much as the game. In contrast, quarrels among girls over application of rules were likely to terminate the game, perhaps anticipating what primatologist Sarah Hrdy has referred to as "the well-documented problem that unrelated women have working together over a long period of time."

Competition is simply a greater part of male life, even among children. If one boy tells another boy that he can spit ten feet, the response is likely to be either "I bet you can't" or "I can spit farther"; if a girl tells another girl that she can spit ten feet, the response is likely to be either "So what?" or "That's gross." Psychologist Eleanor Maccoby observes that "even when with a good friend, boys take pleasure in competing to see who can do a task best or quickest, who can lift the heaviest weight, who can run faster or farther." A study of free-play activities in fourth and sixth graders found that boys were engaged in direct competition with other boys 50 percent of the time, while among girls direct competition occurred only 1 percent of the time.

This is not to say that girls do not compete, but they often employ different means and pursue different ends. Sarah Hrdy attributes the belief that females are less competitive than males to the failure of scientists to examine "women competing with one another in the spheres that really matter to them." . . .

Dominance Assertion

Dominance assertion is, in a sense, a form of competition. Dominance behaviors are those intended to achieve or maintain a position of high relative status—to obtain power, influence, prerogatives, or resources. When children get together, even in the preschool years, dominance hierarchies emerge spontaneously: some children are more influential and less subject to aggression by others. Boys engage in a significantly greater amount of dominance-related play than girls, such as playing with weapons and engaging in rough-and-tumble play. In mixed-sex groups in nursery schools, boys end up disproportionately at the top of the hierarchy within the classroom. Even among preschoolers, the expression by girls of their ideas seems to be significantly curtailed in the presence of boys.

Although boys generally assume the dominant positions in mixed-sex hierarchies, boys and girls mostly establish separate hierarchies, a division that occurs in large part because boys and girls spend most of their time with others of the same sex. One of the most robust sex effects of early childhood is the powerful tendency that young children exhibit toward sex segregation. Up until about age two, children show little preference regarding the sex of playmates, but during the third year, same-sex preference begin to emerge in girls, followed perhaps a year later by similar preference among boys. Although girls show an earlier same-sex preference, when the preference emerges in boys it is stronger. After about age five, boys take a much more active role in policing the boundaries of sex-appropriate behavior. These findings have been replicated in a wide range of cultures.

After the preference for same-sex playmates develops, children continue to play with members of the opposite sex, especially if required to by adults or by the dearth of same-sex playmates. When children find themselves surrounded by large numbers of children of their own age, however, the impulse to self-segregation is strong. As children move into later stages of childhood, an increasingly large portion of their time is spent with same-sex others, despite pressures by teachers to require greater sexual integration. Eleanor Maccoby has suggested that part of the aversion that girls have to boys is that girls find it difficult to influence the boys. Jacklin and Maccoby found, for example, that among unfamiliar pairs for thirty-three-month-old children, boys were less likely to pay attention to instructions from girls than girls were to those from boys.

In their same-sex groups, both boys and girls establish hierarchies, but the hierarchies differ in strength and in the traits that lead to dominance. Boys' dominance hierarchies tend to be more stable and well defined than those of girls. That is, the boys largely agree about who is on top, and these rankings tend to persist over time. Among girls, on the other hand, hierarchies are more fluid and there is considerably less agreement concerning the relative rankings of individual girls. Hierarchies among boys tend to be established quickly, often during their first interaction. Among boys, the critical determinant is "toughness," both physical strength and unwillingness to back down. Among girls, however, status tends to be achieved through physical attractiveness and friendship with popular girls.

Important sex differences in dominance behaviors and aggressiveness are obscured by looking only at frequencies, since the sexes also differ in the types and causes of these behaviors. Psychologists Martin Daly and Margo Wilson, for example, have found a consistent worldwide pattern: homicides tend to be committed by and against unmarried young males. Many are what Daly and Wilson label "trivial altercations," either "escalated showing-off disputes" or "disputes arising from retaliation for previous verbal or physical abuse." Although to an outside observer the precipitating event may seem trivial, many of these disputes are "affairs of honor," in which the precipitating event "often takes the form of disparagement of the challenged party's 'manhood': his nerve, strength or savvy, or the virtue of his wife, girlfriend, or female relatives." Failure to respond to challenges to reputation or signs of disrespect leads to loss of face and of relative status.

The foregoing does not mean that women are not interested in achieving status. However, the route to female status, across history, has been quite different for men and women. Men have generally achieved status through dominance over other men; women have achieved status not primarily by achieving dominance over other women (or over men) but rather through their association with high-status men.

Achievement Motivation and Response to Failure

Although in many respects the sexes are similar in their motivation to achieve, some sex differences are consistently reported, many of which are associated with attitudes toward failure. For example, when given a choice of tasks to perform, males are more likely to select the more difficult task and females the easier one. Females tend also to be more adversely affected by failure and more likely to give up than males, and they are somewhat more likely to attribute failure to lack of ability rather than lack of effort. Males, on the other hand, are more likely than females to improve in performance after failure.

Confidence is an important contributor to achievement motivation, and competition seems to exaggerate sex differences in confidence. Anticipation of competition results in lower confidence levels in females than males. Moreover, females' performance predictions tend to be relatively unstable and subject to change with single encounters, while males are less likely to allow one failure to diminish their performance expectations.

Females seem to have a greater need than males for feedback about performance in order to achieve or maintain high levels of self-confidence in their performance capabilities. Such feedback seems to be more central to women's self-esteem than is the case for men. Who exhibit a weaker relationship between positive feedback and global self-esteem. [T]his need may contribute to the dissatisfaction that women who study science often feel in moving from high school to college, when they leave an environment in which they are lavished with attention and praise and enter an environment in which they join the relatively anonymous masses.

Competition and Dominance in Mixed-Sex Groups

Studies measuring only attributes of individuals often miss important dynamics of social interactions. Males and females sometimes exhibit different competitive and dominance behaviors in same-sex and mixed-sex groups. Within same-sex groups, for example, males engage in more dominance behaviors than females do. This tendency is moderated to some extent in mixed-sex groups, with male dominance behaviors tending to abate somewhat and female dominance behaviors to increase; still, males in mixed-sex groups continue to act more dominantly. Not surprisingly, in same-sex pairings, a high-dominance individual will assume a leadership role over a low-dominance individual. However, when a high-dominance woman is paired with a low-dominance man, the low-dominance man tends to assume the leadership role. It is not that he asserted dominance over the woman to become the leader, but rather that the dominant woman selected him to be the leader. Perhaps this represents the same phenomenon as the many examples of very able women pushing their somewhat less able husbands to be more successful than the husbands would have been on their own.

Mixed-sex competition seems to be a quite different experience for its participants from same-sex competition. A study comparing responses of competitors to male, female, and machine opponents in a video game found some interesting patterns. First, it appears that men do not like to compete against women. Men who were measured as being low in competitiveness demonstrated low physiological arousal when their competitor was a woman, apparently because they were less engaged in the competition than when their opponent was either a machine or a man. This result is consistent with suggestions that some men may reduce effort in situations in which they are concerned about being outperformed by women. High-competitive men, on the other hand, demonstrated the highest level of engagement and the highest level of negative affect at the conclusion of the competition when their opponent was a woman. Why should men feel discomfort when competing against a woman? One potential reason is that men may feel they will be criticized for playing to win against a woman. Another reason is that men may perceive these encounters as "no-win' situations for them, because they do not get the same credit for winning if their opponent is "just a woman," but losing to a woman is worse than losing to a man.

The literature dealing with female performance in mixed-sex competition is not entirely consistent, but psychologist Carol Weisfeld summarizes the literature as revealing that "it is almost always the case that some females will depress their performance levels, resulting in victory for males." This female suppression of effort does not appear to be consciously motivated. Females who perform at their highest level against males tend to be those characterized by masculine or androgynous temperaments. For them, competition against males appears to be a positive experience, perhaps for precisely the opposite reason that competitive males do not like the same competition: if she wins, the credit for beating a male is high, but if she loses, there is no shame in losing to a male.

Head-to-head competition between the sexes for status in hierarchies is a relatively recent phenomenon. Humans, like other primates, may not be "wired" in such a way as to evoke competitive responses from members of the opposite sex. Thus, perhaps it should not be surprising that neither males nor females view competition with the opposite sex as equivalent to same-sex competition.

Risk Taking

As with the other traits, . . . the sexes differ in risk taking from childhood. One of the best measures of physical risk taking in children is the incidence of accidental death and injury. In most industrialized countries, including the United States, accidents are the leading cause of death for children older than one year. A World Health organization study of accidental-death rates in fifty countries found a substantially higher rate for boys in all countries, with a ratio of male to female deaths of 1.9:1 in Europe and 1.7:1 in non-European countries. Notwithstanding greater equality and socially sanctioned androgyny, the male/female accidental-death ratio actually increased in the United States from 1960 to 1979.

Greater risk taking among boys is a robust finding. Boys are exposed to greater risks not only because they are more likely to engage in risky behaviors, but also because when engaging in the same activity as girls, they are more likely to perform it in a risky manner. Boys are substantially more likely to approach a hazardous item than girls, and they differ in how they approach them, with girls tending to look and point and boys tending to touch and retrieve them.

Several factors appear to account for the greater inclination of boys to engage in risky activity. Boys tend to have both a higher activity level and poorer impulse control, both traits that are associated with injury rates. Three factors are correlated with self-reported risk taking in both boys and girls: attribution of injuries to bad luck, a belief that one is less vulnerable to injury than one's peers, and downplaying the degree of risk. Boys score higher than girls on all three of these traits.

Boys are less likely than girls to abstain from a risky activity simply because they have seen a peer injured while engaging in the same activity. The best predictor of girls' willingness to take a particular risk is their belief about the likelihood of getting hurt, while for boys it is the perceived severity of the injury. That is, girls tend to avoid risks if they think they might get hurt, while boys seem to be willing to take risks if they do not think they will get *too* hurt. It is possible, however, that positive attitudes about risk may result in part from risk taking, rather than causing it.

In adolescence and adulthood, sex differences in risk taking increase. Men are disproportionately involved in risky recreational activities such as car racing, sky diving, and hang gliding. Indeed, sex is the variable most predictive of the extent of participation in high-risk recreation. The driving style of men also shows a greater propensity toward risk. Men are disproportionately represented in risky employment, as well. Over 90 percent of all workplace deaths in the United States are males. A list of dangerous occupations is a list of disproportionately male occupations: fisherman, logger, airplane pilot, structural metal worker, coal miner, oil and gas extraction occupations, water transportation occupations, construction laborer, taxicab driver, roofer, and truck driver.

Men's greater propensity to risk their lives is demonstrated by a study of the recipients of awards granted by the Carnegie Hero Fund Commission. Of the 676 acts of heroism recognized from 1989 through 1995, 92 percent were performed by males. Moreover, over one-half of those rescued by women were known to the rescuer, while over two-thirds of those rescued by men were strangers. Although this is not a random sample of heroes, since one must be nominated for the award, it is likely that, if anything, the sex difference is understated because acts of heroism by women would tend to attract more attention than those by men.

Risk taking is statistically correlated with a number of other stereotypically male traits. People who rate high on achievement and dominance, for example, tend to be high risk takers. Risk taking and competitiveness may be related, since competition-prone individuals tend to be willing to take greater risks in pursuit of their competitive objective. High risk takers also fight more frequently, are more socially aggressive, take more dares, and participate in more rough sports and physical activities such as hunting, mountain climbing, and auto racing. In contrast, risk taking is negatively associated with a number of stereotypically feminine traits: affiliation, nurturance, succorance, deference, and abasement.

Psychologist Elizabeth Arch has suggested that the sex differences in achievement-orientation previously discussed may be explained in part by sex differences in risk taking. From an early age, females are more averse not just to physical risk but also to social risk, and they "tend to behave in a manner that ensures continued social inclusion." This aversion to risk may be partially responsible for women's disproportionately low representation in positions involving "career risk," which may adversely affect their prospects for advancement. This pattern suggests that what is sometimes labeled women's "fear of success" is in fact the more prosaic and easier-to-understand "fear of failure."

One's willingness to take risks depends in large part upon the relative values that one places on success and failure. A person whose appetite for success exceeds his aversion to failure will be inclined toward action; a person whose aversion to failure exceeds his appetite for success will be inclined not to act. A strong motive to achieve or to avoid failure may also bias the actor's subjective probability of outcome. That is, an achievement-oriented person may have a higher expectation of success than is objectively warranted, while a person with a high motivation to avoid failure may consistently underestimate the chance of success.

Nurturance, Empathy, and Interest in Children

Females in all known societies exhibit more nurturing behavior than males both inside and outside the family. Everywhere it is women who are the primary caretakers of the young, the sick, and the old. Even among young children, girls tend to exhibit more nurturing behavior, and throughout the adolescent years, girls have a greater preference than boys for more caring, personal values. Girls' interest in infants increases substantially at menarche.

Just as the description of greater male aggressiveness, dominance assertion, and risk taking does not mean that women lack these traits altogether, to say that women seem to be higher in nurturance and empathy does not mean that men lack these traits or that they are not capable of caretaking behavior. Men are certainly as capable as women of learning many of the routine behaviors of parenthood, such as changing diapers and making dinner. The important question, however, is whether the connection to the infant and attunement to its state is the same for men as for women. There is some evidence to suggest that women's nurturant responses have a stronger physiological underpinning than men's.

Sex differences in parental care are universal across cultures. While the level of paternal involvement varies considerably among societies, there is no society in which the level of direct paternal care approaches that of mothers. Among the Aka pygmies of Central Africa, fathers provide more direct care to their children than in any other society known to anthropologists. Nonetheless, Barry Hewlett found that males, on average, hold their infants for a total of 57 minutes per day, compared to 490 minutes for mothers. The greater female contribution to child care in contemporary Western society is, of course, well known. The disparity between male and female care is exaggerated after divorce, with noncustodial mothers being far more likely to maintain close contact with their children than noncustodial fathers.

Psychological studies generally confirm that women are more empathic than men, in the sense that they experience a "vicarious affective response to another's feelings." As psychologist Martin Hoffman observed in 1977, the most striking feature of the empathy findings in a whole host of studies "is the fact that in every case, regardless of the age of the subjects or the measures used, the females obtained higher scores than did the males." While some subsequent studies have found no sex difference, they tend to be studies measuring the ability to identify other people's feelings rather than measuring the subject's emotional reaction to those feelings. Personality studies also show a substantial correlation between nurturance and empathy.

The more social orientation of females is reflected in a consistently found sex difference in "object versus person" orientation. Females of all ages tend to be "person oriented," while males tend to be more "object oriented." As early as the first year of life, girls pay more attention to people and boys pay more attention to inanimate objects. In a study of college students, male and female subjects were shown a series of pictures of human figures and mechanical objects in a stereoscope so that a picture of a human figure and a picture of a mechanical object were falling on the same part of the subject's visual field. The theory behind the experimental design is that when two stimuli are competing, subjects will pay attention to the stimulus that is more interesting to them. Males had a greater tendency to report seeing the objects, while females tended to report seeing the human figure.

Differences in orientation affect the way people perceive themselves. Women's self-identity and self-esteem tend to be centered around sensitivity to and relations with others, while men's self-concepts tend to be centered around task performance, skills, independence, and being "better" than others. In one study, 50 percent of the women but only 15 percent of the men agreed with the statement, "I'm happiest when I can succeed at something that will also make other people happy." As psychologist Carol Gilligan has argued, "Women not only define themselves in a context of human relationship but also judge themselves in terms of their ability to care." . . .

⊱✦⊰

This chapter has revealed that males and females differ, on average, in a number of temperamental traits. Men tend toward competition, women toward cooperation. Men seek to achieve dominance over others, while women seek to cement social relations. Men tend to be object oriented, while women tend to be person oriented. . . . These are just statistical generalizations, but they hold true not just in our society but also cross-culturally.

POSTSCRIPT

Are Women and Men More Similar Than Different?

The issue of similarity and difference is one of degree and perspective. Although many meta-analyses inform us that most differences between women and men are statistically quite small, there are differences. What do we make of small differences, especially when the differences within women and within men typically exceed the average difference between the groups?

Should we move beyond the difference model for studying sex and gender? Debate has focused on social costs and benefits incurred as a consequence of sex difference findings, the statistical and social meaning of sex difference findings, the overemphasis on difference and underrepresentation of findings of similarity, and the questionable efficacy of sex difference findings in elucidating the phenomena of sex and gender.

Whether or not scholars believe that the continuation of sex difference research would be beneficial or at least benign, there is widespread agreement that this research alone is insufficient to explore the complexities of sex and gender as social categories and processes. Difference research has been primarily descriptive in nature, even though assumptions abound about the "natural" causes of sex differences. But knowing what differences exist between males and females does not help us to understand why, how, when, and for whom they exist. Furthermore, descriptive research alone does not help us understand the social meaning or significance of such differences. Some assert that sex comparisons obscure an understanding of gender as social relations and do little to help us understand the processes that expand or delimit the significance of the difference. Others argue that focusing on categorical differences helps us to avoid the hard work we have to do to improve our society. At the very least, scholars urge that we move beyond the individual as the focus of difference research to examine the way gender is produced in interpersonal and institutional contexts.

In moving beyond the difference model, what other approaches can be used to better understand sex and gender? One suggestion calls for an approach to studying gender that transcends the difference model. The focus is on the *process* of gender. Research should explore and document "gender coding," or how society is gendered (e.g., unequal expectations, opportunities, power), and how individuals (particularly those who are disenfranchised) cope with or negotiate such inequality (ranging from acceptance to resistance). It is important to view individuals as having some agency to affect their environment but also as being constrained or shaped by social situations and structures.

Another suggested innovation reflects an effort to move beyond essentialist overgeneralizations about "generic" men and women as distinct groups. What does a categorical variable like sex actually mean? Many argue that such variables are too simplistic and therefore meaningless for representing the complexity among individuals, identities, and experiences that make up the group. Some state that assertions about sex differences are usually based on comparisons of white middle-class men and women and therefore have limited generalizability. Thus, some scholars advocate exploring within-sex diversity and attending to a host of contextual and structural variables that are inseparable from sex.

This kind of approach has led some to ask, Can we move to a point where difference no longer makes so much of a difference? How do we get there? One view differentiates between approaches that "turn the volume up" versus "turn the volume down" on categories of difference. Should we eliminate sex and gender dichotomies from the definition of normal and natural (turn the volume down) or proliferate categories of sex and gender into as many categories as needed to capture human complexity? Or is the focus on categories obscuring more specific and critical concepts such as privilege, conflict of interest, oppression, subordination, and even cooperation?

Suggested Readings

R. Barnett and C. Rivers, *Same Difference: How Gender Myths Are Hurting Our Relationships, Our Children, and Our Jobs* (Basic Books, 2004).

J. B. James, ed., "The Significance of Gender: Theory and Research About Difference" (Special Issue), *Journal of Social Issues* (Summer 1997).

M. M. Kimball, "Gender Similarities and Differences as Feminist Constructions," in R. K. Unger, ed., *Handbook of the Psychology of Women and Gender* (John Wiley & Sons, 2000).

C. Kitzinger, ed., "Should Psychologists Study Sex Differences?" *Feminism & Psychology* (1994).

B. Lott, "The Personal and Social Correlates of a Gender Difference Ideology," *Journal of Social Issues* (1997).

ISSUE 5

Are Different Patterns of Communication in Women and Men Innately Determined?

YES: **Louann Brizendine,** from *The Female Brain* (Morgan Road Books, 2006).

NO: **Brenda J. Allen,** from *Difference Matters: Communicating Social Identity* (Waveland Press, 2004). Long Grove: IL.

ISSUE SUMMARY

YES: Louann Brizendine argues that women's brains are hard-wired to communicate differently from men, suggesting on the jacket of her book "men will develop a serious case of brain envy."

NO: In contrast, Brenda J. Allen argues that socialization leads to forms of communication that are based on power and privilege.

Feminists view the study of communication and gender as very important because language is a powerful agent in the creation and maintenance of the gender system. In 1978, a major review of the scientific literature on gender and language by Cheris Kramer, Barrie Thorne, and Nancy Henley entitled, "Perspectives on Language and Communication," *Signs: Journal of Women in Culture and Society* (vol. 3, 1978) was published. This review summarized the three central research questions: (1) Do men and women use language in different ways? (2) In what ways does language—in structure, content, and daily usage—reflect and help constitute sexual inequality? (3) How can sexist language be changed?

Twenty-five years later, these three questions continue to dominate the field, but they have been reframed in more contemporary work because of an interest in *specificity* and *complexity*. Rather than studying "generic" groups of males and females, we must study particular men and women in particular settings and examine the interactions of gender and other identity categories and power relations.

In a recent issue of *Ladies Home Journal* (June 2005) an article on "Why Communication Counts" declared "Over and over again, communication problems are targeted as the number-one cause of marital strife. In many cases, couples think they're communicating, but the messages aren't getting through. Communication problems stem from differences in conversational styles between men and women." The article then proceeded to give readers (presumably mostly women) tips on how to communicate more effectively with their partner. The popular press is quick to agree with assertions such as these. In fact, most of these claims are based on the widely cited work on gender and language by author Deborah Tannen. Following up on her classic *You Just Don't Understand: Women and Men in Conversation* (1991), she has recently examined women and men's "conversational rituals" in the workplace in *Talking from 9 to 5: Women and Men at Work* (2001). In her writings she argues that "men and women live in different worlds . . . made of different words," and that how women and men converse determines who gets heard and who gets ahead in the workplace, via a verbal power game.

Tannen parallels male-female difference to cultural difference and regards males and females as different but equal. She explores how this cultural difference manifests itself in male-female (mis)communication. Her aim in her popular publications is to reassure women and men that they are not alone in experiencing miscommunication and communication problems because of sex-differentiated communication styles. Moreover, she says that she does not value one style over the other. If anything, she praises women's communication styles. Tannen urges that males and females need to respect each other's differences so that they understand why they misunderstand each other.

Similarly, Louann Brizendine in the selection that follows suggests that gendered communication is a result of biological differences in the brain. She agrees with Tannen that women and men live in different worlds, and these worlds differ beginning at conception.

Critics claim that analyses such as Tannen's and Brizendine's universalize and generalize, thereby creating generic individuals. Questions of difference are misguided and counterproductive not only because they are invariably marked by a political agenda but also because sex comparisons locate gender in the individual rather than in social relations and processes. Responses to claims of sex difference in communication styles frequently involve blaming women for deficiencies or minimizing conflicts between men and women by reframing them as miscommunication for which we must develop tolerance. Sociocultural inequalities are not addressed.

What do we *know* about differences between males' and females' communication styles? In the following selections, Brizendine's analysis of brain differences leads to a conclusion supporting Tannen's claims. Regarding the question of sex differentiation in communication styles she suggests, for example, that men use only 7,000 words a day compared to women's use of about 20,000. In contrast, Brenda Allen argues that gendered communication patterns are related to power and status differences.

YES

Louann Brizendine

The Female Brain

What Makes Us Women

More than 99 percent of male and female genetic coding is exactly the same. Out of the thirty thousand genes in the human genome, the less than one percent variation between the sexes is small. But that percentage difference influences every single cell in our bodies—from the nerves that register pleasure and pain to the neurons that transmit perception, thoughts, feelings, and emotions.

To the observing eye, the brains of females and males are not the same. Male brains are larger by about 9 percent, even after correcting for body size. In the nineteenth century, scientists took this to mean that women had less mental capacity than men. Women and men, however, have the same number of brain cells. The cells are just packed more densely in women—cinched corsetlike into a smaller skull.

For much of the twentieth century, most scientists assumed that women were essentially small men, neurologically and in every other sense except for their reproductive functions. That assumption has been at the heart of enduring misunderstandings about female psychology and physiology. When you look a little deeper into the brain differences, they reveal what makes women women and men men.

Until the 1990s, researchers paid little attention to female physiology, neuroanatomy, or psychology separate from that of men. . . .

The little research that was available, however, suggested that the brain differences, though subtle, were profound. . . .

What we've found is that the female brain is so deeply affected by hormones that their influence can be said to create a woman's reality. They can shape a woman's values and desires, and tell her, day to day, what's important. Their presence is felt at every stage of life, right from birth. Each hormone state—girlhood, the adolescent years, the dating years, motherhood, and menopause—acts as fertilizer for different neurological connections that are responsible for new thoughts, emotions, and interests. Because of the fluctuations that begin as early as three months old and last until after menopause, a woman's neurological reality is not as constant as a man's. His is like a mountain that is worn away imperceptibly over the millennia by glaciers, weather, and the deep tectonic movements of the earth. Here is more like the weather itself—constantly changing and hard to predict.

❧

New brain science has rapidly transformed our view of basic neurological differences between men and women. . . .

As a result, scientists have documented an astonishing array of structural, chemical, genetic, hormonal, and functional brain differences between women and men. We've learned that men and women have different brain sensitivities to stress and conflict. They use different brain areas and circuits to solve problems, process language, experience and store the same strong emotion. Women may remember the smallest details of their first dates, and their biggest fights, while their husbands barely remember that these things happened. Brain structure and chemistry have everything to do with why this is so.

The female and male brains process stimuli, hear, see, "sense," and gauge what others are feeling in different ways. Our distinct female and male brain operating systems are mostly compatible and adept, but they perform and accomplish the same goals and tasks using different circuits. . . .

Until eight weeks old, every fetal brain looks female—female is nature's default gender setting. . . . A huge testosterone surge beginning in the eighth week will turn this unisex brain male by killing off some cells in the communication centers and growing more cells in the sex and aggression centers. If the testosterone surge doesn't happen, the female brain continues to grow unperturbed. The fetal girl's brain cells sprout more connections in the communication centers and areas that process emotion. How does this fetal fork in the road affect us? For one thing, because of her larger communication center, this girl will grow up to be more talkative than her brother. Men use about seven thousand words per day. Women use about twenty thousand. For another, it defines our innate biological destiny, coloring the lens through which each of us views and engages the world. . . .

Baby girls are born interested in emotional expression. They take meaning about themselves from a look, a touch, every reaction from the people they come into contact with. From these cues they discover whether they are worthy, lovable, or annoying. But take away the sign-posts that an expressive face provides and you've taken away the female brain's main touchstone for reality. . . .

Don't Fight

So why is a girl born with such a highly tuned machine for reading faces, hearing emotional tones in voices, and responding to unspoken cues in others? Think about it. A machine like that is built for connection. That's the main job of the girl brain, and that's what it drives a female to do from birth. This is the result of millennia of genetic and evolutionary hardwiring that once had—and probably still has—real consequences for survival. If you can read faces and voices, you can tell what an infant needs. You can predict what a bigger, more aggressive male is going to do. And since you're smaller, you probably need to band with other females to fend off attacks from a ticked off caveman—or cavemen.

If you're a girl, you've been programmed to make sure you keep social harmony. This is a matter of life and death to the brain, even if it's not so important in the twenty-first century. . . .

Typical non-testosteronized, estrogen-ruled girls are very invested in pre-serving harmonious relationships. From their earliest days, they live most comfortably and happily in the realm of peaceful interpersonal connections. They prefer to avoid conflict because discord puts them at odds with their urge to stay connected, to gain approval and nurture. The twenty-four-month estrogen bath of girls' infantile puberty reinforces the impulse to make social bonds based on communication and compromise. . . .

It is the brain that sets up the speech differences—the genderlects—of small children, which Deborah Tannen has pointed out. She noted that in studies of the speech of two-to-five-year-olds, girls usually make collaborative proposals by starting their sentences with "let's"—as in "Let's play house." Girls, in fact, typically use language to get consensus, influencing others without telling them directly what to do. . . .

Boys know how to employ this affiliative speech style, too, but research shows they typically don't use it. Instead, they'll generally use language to command others, get things done, brag, threaten, ignore a partner's sugges-tion, and override each other's attempts to speak. . . .

The testosterone-formed boy brain simply doesn't look for social con-nection in the same way a girl brain does. In fact, disorders that inhibit people from picking up on social nuance—called autism spectrum disorders and Asperger's syndrome—are eight times more common in boys. Scientists now believe that the typical male brain, with only one dose of X chromosome (there are two X's in a girl), gets flooded with testosterone during develop-ment and somehow becomes more easily socially handicapped. Extra tes-tosterone in people with these disorders may be killing off some of the brain's circuits for emotional and social sensitivity.

⋰⊙⋰

By age two and a half, infantile puberty ends and a girl enters the calmer pas-tures of the juvenile pause. The estrogen stream coming from the ovaries has been temporarily stopped; how, we don't yet know. But we do know that the levels of estrogen and testosterone become very low during the childhood years in both boys and girls—although girls still have six to eight times more estrogen than boys. When women talk about "the girl they left behind," this is the stage they are usually referring to. This is the quiet period before the full-volume rock 'n' roll of puberty. It's the time when a girl is devoted to her best friend, when she doesn't usually enjoy playing with boys. Research shows that this is true for girls between the ages of two and six in every culture that's been studied. . . .

Many women find biological comfort in one another's company, and language is the glue that connects one female to another. No surprise, then, that some verbal areas of the brain are larger in women than in men and that women, on average, talk and listen a lot more than men. The numbers vary, but on average girls speak two to three times more words per day than boys. We know that young girls speak earlier and by the age of twenty months have double or triple the number of words in their vocabularies than do boys. Boys eventually catch up in their vocabulary but not in speed. Girls speak faster on average—250 words per minute versus 125 for typical males. Men haven't always appreciated that verbal edge. In Colonial America, women were put in the town stocks with wooden clips on their tongues or tortured by the "dunking stool," held underwater and almost drowned—punishments that were never imposed on men—for the crime of "talking too much." . . .

And why do girls go to the bathroom to talk? Why do they spend so much time on the phone with the door closed? They're trading secrets and gossiping to create connection and intimacy with their female peers. They're developing close-knit cliques with secret rules. In these new groups, talking, telling secrets, and gossiping, in fact, often become girls' favorite activities— their tools to navigate and ease the ups and downs and stresses of life. . . .

There is a biological reason for this behavior. Connecting through talking activates the pleasure centers in a girl's brain. Sharing secrets that have romantic and sexual implications activates those centers even more. We're not talking about a small amount of pleasure. This is huge. It's a major dopamine and oxytocin rush, which is the biggest, fattest neurological reward you can get outside of an orgasm. Dopamine is a neurochemical that stimulates the motivation and pleasure circuits in the brain. Estrogen at puberty increases dopamine and oxytocin production in girls. Oxytocin is a neurohormone that triggers and is triggered by intimacy. When estrogen is on the rise, a teen girl's brain is pushed to make even more oxytocin—and to get even more reinforcement for social bonding. At midcycle, during peak estrogen production, the girl's dopamine and oxytocin level is likely at its highest, too. Not only her verbal output is at its maximum but her urge for intimacy is also peaking. Intimacy releases more oxytocin, which reinforces the desire to connect, and connecting then brings a sense of pleasure and well-being. . . .

Why the Teen Girl Brain Freaks

Think about it. Your brain has been pretty stable. You've had a steady flow—or lack—of hormones for your entire life. One day you're having tea parties with Mommy, the next day you're calling her an asshole. And, as a teen girl, the last thing you want to do is create conflict. You used to feel like a nice girl, and now, out of nowhere, it's as though you can't rely on that personality anymore. Everything you thought you knew about yourself has suddenly come undone. It's a huge gash in a girl's self-esteem, but it's a pretty simple chemical reaction, even for an adult woman. It makes a difference if you know what's going on. . . .

Studies show that when a conflict or argument breaks out in a game, girls typically decide to stop playing to avoid any angry exchange, while boys generally continue to play intensely—jockeying for position, competing, and arguing hour after hour about who'll be the boss or who will get access to the coveted toy. If a woman is pushed over the edge by finding out that her husband is having an affair, or if her child is in danger, her anger will blast right through and she will go to the mat. Otherwise, she will avoid anger or confrontation the same way a man will avoid an emotion.

Girls and women may not always feel the initial intense blast of anger directly from the amygdale that men feel. . . . Women talk to others first when they are angry at a third person. But scientists speculate that though a woman is slower to act out of anger, once her faster verbal circuits get going, they can cause her to unleash a barrage of angry words that a man can't match. Typical men speak fewer words and have less verbal fluency than women, so they may be handicapped in angry exchanges with women. Men's brain circuits and bodies may readily revert to a physical expression of anger fueled by the frustration of not being able to match women's words.

Often when I see a couple who are not communicating well, the problem is that the man's brain circuits push him frequently and quickly to an angry, aggressive reaction, and the woman feels frightened and shuts down. Ancient wiring is telling her it's dangerous, but she anticipates that if she flees she'll be losing her provider and may have to fend for herself. If a couple remains locked in this Stone Age conflict, there is no chance for resolution. Helping my patients understand that the emotion circuits for anger and safety are differences in the male and female brains is often quite helpful.

Brenda J. Allen

 **NO**

Difference Matters: Communicating Social Identity

Communicating Social Identity

Our study of difference (and similarity!) centers on communication. I use the verb form, communicating, to represent the dynamic nature of processes that humans use to produce, interpret, and share meaning. Our study of communicating views these processes as constitutive of social reality. To see how communicating helps to create reality, we will explore various relationships between social identity and discourse. *Discourse* refers to "systems of texts and talk that range from public to private and from naturally occurring to mediated forms. . . .

Scholars from disciplines such as sociology, psychology, communication, anthropology, and philosophy study identity as an individual and/or a collective aspect of being. As sociologists Judith Howard and Ramira Alamilla observe, identity is based not only on responses to the question "Who am I?" but also on responses to the question "Who am I in relation to others?" Our exploration of difference matters focuses on *social identity*, aspects of a person's self-image derived from the social categories to which an individual perceives herself/himself as belonging. Most human beings divide their social worlds into groups, and categorize themselves into some of those groups. In addition, we become aware of other social groups to which we do not belong, and we compare ourselves to them. We often define ourselves in opposition to others: "I know who I am because I am not you." Thus, social identity refers to "the ways in which individuals and collectivities are distinguished in their social relations with other individuals and collectivities."

Because social identity stems from perceptions of social group membership, social identity is somewhat distinct from personal identity, which encompasses the conception of the self in terms of variables such as personality traits. For instance, a person may be characterized as "shy" or "outgoing." However, "a person's self actually consists of a personal identity and multiple social identities, each of which is linked to different social groups."

An individual can "belong" to numerous social identity groups. I self-identify as: professor, black, woman, homeowner, U.S. citizen, baby boomer, middle-class, and volunteer. Although infinite possibilities exist for categories of social identity groups, I focus on six that are especially significant in

From *Difference Matters: Communicating Social Identity*, September 30, 2003, pp. 10–15, 53–56, 189–190. Copyright © 2004 by Waveland Press. Reprinted by permission.

contemporary society: gender, race, social class, ability, sexuality, and age. Nationality and religion also are important aspects of identity. . . .

Central are the interconnected ideas that all identity is relational, and that human beings develop their social identities primarily through communicating. This perspective represents the *social constructionist* school of thought, which contends that "self is socially constructed through various relational and linguistic processes." In other words, "our identity arises out of interactions with other people and is based on language." Let's look at how communication helps to construct social identity.

From the time we are born (and even prior to birth, due to tests that determine a baby's sex or congenital defects), socially constructed categories of identity influence how others interact with us (and vice versa), and how we perceive ourselves. When a child is born, what do people usually want to know? Generally, they ask if "it" is a boy or a girl. Why is the sex of the child so important? Sex matters because it cues people on how to treat the baby. If the newborn is a girl, relatives and friends may buy her pink, frilly clothes and toys designated for girls. Her parent(s) or guardian(s) may decorate her room (if she's fortunate enough to have her own room) or sleep area in "feminine" colors and artifacts, or she may share a room with other family members. These actions and others will help to "create a gendered world which the infant gradually encounters and takes for granted as her social consciousness dawns, and which structures the responses to her of others."

And that's just the beginning. As she develops, she will receive messages from multiple sources, including family members, teachers, peers, and the media about what girls are allowed and supposed to do (as contrasted with boys). This process is known as *socialization*. . . .

The same scenario applies for a male child. He too will receive numerous messages, blatant and subtle, that will mold his self-perception. Simultaneously, both female and male children will learn about additional identity categories like race, class, and ability. What they learn may vary depending on their identity composites. For instance, a white Jewish boy in a middle-class family probably will be socialized differently than a Latino Catholic in a working-class family, even as they each may receive similar messages about being male. Meanwhile, as both males receive comparable lessons about masculinity, a nondisabled Asian-American boy will probably receive different messages than a white boy labeled as "developmentally challenged." These individuals also will learn communication styles particular to their groups, such as vocabulary, gestures, eye contact, and use of personal space.

As these children become indoctrinated into social identity groups, they will receive information about other groups, including contrasts between groups, and "rules" for interacting (or not) with members of other groups. They will be exposed to stereotypes about groups, and they may accept these stereotypes as facts. They also will learn about hierarchies of identity. They may learn that being young is more desirable than being elderly, or that being heterosexual is preferable to being gay. These and other "lessons" about distinctions between and within groups will recur throughout their lives.

Due to socialization, children will accept social identity categories as real and natural designations. Yet, they are not. Historically, persons in power have constructed categories and developed hierarchies based on characteristics of groups. For example, in 1795 a German scientist named Johann Blumenbach constructed a system of racial classification that arranged people according to geographical location and physical features. He also ranked the groups in hierarchical order, placing Caucasians in the most superior position.

Although scientists have since concluded that race is not related to capability, many societies in the world still adhere to various racial classification systems because the idea of race has become essentialized. *Essentialism* refers to assumptions that social differences stem from intrinsic, innate, human variations unrelated to social forces. For example, so-called racial groups are viewed as if they have an "ultimate essence that transcends historical and cultural boundaries.

Thus, while we accept social identity groups as real and natural, we also perceive them as fixed (essentialized) and unchanging. However, not only are such categories artificial, but they also are subject to change. In different times and different places, categories we take for granted either did/do not exist or they were/are quite unlike the ones that we reference in the United States in the twenty-first century. Currently, the same person identified as black in the United States may be considered white in the Dominican Republic; in the nineteenth century choices for racial designations in the United States included gradations of enslaved blacks (mulattos were one-half black, quadroons were one-quarter black, and octoroons were one-eighth black). . . .

The tendency to compartmentalize humans according to physical characteristics is logical because "labels can be helpful devices used to identify people." If we did not have labels to distinguish groups of items that are similar, we would have to create and remember a separate "name" for everything and everyone. What a pain that would be! Therefore, it makes sense that we use cues like skin color, facial features, body parts, and so forth to distinguish and group people.

However, problems can arise when people assign meaning to previously neutral descriptors. They may use categories not only to distinguish, but also to discriminate and dominate. Categorizing can lead to in-group/out-group distinctions that may negatively affect intergroup interactions. For instance, *social identity theory* (SIT) describes humans' tendency to label self and others based on individual and group identity. This theory contends that members of social identity groups constantly compare their group with others, and they tend "to seek positive distinctiveness for one's own group." When an individual perceives someone else to be a member of an out-group, that person will tend to react more to perceived *group* characteristics than to the other person *as an individual*. Stereotypes and prejudice occur more frequently in this scenario. In contrast, stereotypes and prejudice are less likely when a communicator views another person as an individual, especially when both persons belong to the same social identity group(s).

.   [I]ndividuals often use identity markers like skin color to develop hierarchies. Moreover, many people accept and reinforce such hierarchies as natural and normal. Organizational communication scholars explain: "As people *internalize* the values and assumptions of their societies they also internalize its class, race, gender, and ethnicity-based hierarchical relationships." One consequence of these perceptions is the social construction of inequality, which results in favoritism and privilege for some groups and disadvantage for others. . . .

Privilege is a key concept in understanding how difference matters. *Privilege* refers to advantaged status based upon social identity. Sociologist Peggy McIntosh coined this term to refer to men's advantages in society, based upon her experiences teaching women's studies. McIntosh noticed that while men in her classes were willing to concede women's disadvantages, they were unaware of advantages they enjoyed simply because they were men. She later extended her analysis to encompass race, and she developed the concept of white privilege. . . .

Privilege tends to "make life easier; it is easier to get around, to get what one wants, and to be treated in an acceptable manner." On the Public Broadcasting System's video *People Like Us*, which explores social class in the United States, a white male plumber describes how sales clerks tend to treat men in suits better than they respond to him when he wears his work clothes. Similarly, a working-class college student reported that he would change out of his work clothes before going to campus because he felt that faculty and staff treated him less favorably when he wore them. . . .

Opposing standpoints of privileged and nonprivileged persons can negatively impact interactions. A person who is not privileged (or who does not feel privileged) may seem hypersensitive to an individual who is privileged. In contrast, the person who is privileged (or whom the other person perceives to be privileged) may seem totally insensitive. Privileged individuals sometimes diminish, dismiss, or discount experiences of others who are not advantaged. If a privileged person witnesses an incident in which a less privileged person is demeaned or humiliated, she or he may characterize it as exceptional rather than routine and may assess the less-privileged person's complaints about this type of treatment as an overreaction or misinterpretation of the situation. . . .

Most individuals simultaneously occupy privileged and nonprivileged social identity groups. Although I may experience discrimination based upon my race and/or gender, I also reap benefits associated with being heterosexual, nondisabled, and middle-class. We will consider the concept of privilege and its complexities as we study gender, race, class, ability, sexuality, and age.

In addition to constructing inequality, another consequence of internalizing dominant values and assumptions about social identity groups is that members of nondominant groups often help to perpetuate hierarchies because they believe that their group is inferior and that the dominant group is superior. Accepting these ideas and believing negative stereotypes about one's group is known as *internalized oppression*. . . .

To summarize, social identities are created in context; they emerge mainly from social interactions. We learn communication styles and rules based upon our membership in certain groups, and we communicate with other people based upon how we have been socialized about ourselves and about them. We learn who we are and who we might become through interaction with others, within a variety of social contexts, from a variety of sources. These sources also give us information about other groups. To every interaction, we bring preconceptions and expectations about social identities that can affect what, how, when, why, and whether or not we communicate. Most of these interactions occur "within prevailing normative and structural circumstances." . . .

Power Dynamics and Gender

Although scholars have studied gender and communication for over fifty years, academic and popular writing on the topic has surged in the past two decades. Two recurring topics that reveal power dynamics are sexist language and gender differences in styles of communicating.

Language

As communication scholars Diana Ivy and Phil Backlund observe, "English is a patriarchal language." However, as they also note, we did not invent this male-dominated language; we inherited it. Therefore, referring to English as patriarchal and sexist is not an indictment against those of us (men and women) who use it: "It's nobody's fault (nobody alive anyway) that we have a language that favors one sex over the other, but it's also not something that we 'just have to live with.'" As I share examples of the sexist nature of English, I hope you will reflect on how you might avoid them.

Language reflects patriarchy and sexism in numerous ways. Some of these are subtle; others are blatant. A prevalent example is the use of generic masculine pronouns. Although proponents of "he," "him," or "his" contend that these terms are neutral and inclusive of women and men, research indicates that exclusive masculine pronoun usage helps to maintain sex-biased perceptions and shape attitudes about appropriateness of careers for women or men. Such usage also helps to perpetuate a gender hierarchy. One compelling example is the volume of derogatory words in English for women with a smaller number of such terms for men. Among negative synonyms for women/girls and for men/boys, many have sexual denotations or connotations. Moreover, pejorative terms for men/boys often are feminine.

A gender hierarchy also is implied in gendered pairs of words such as "old maid" and "bachelor." Additional examples include gendered titles such as Mrs., Ms., Miss, and Mr., which differentiate women according to marital status, but not men. Man-linked terminology such as "mankind," "foreman," "man-hours" and feminine suffixes (-ette, -ess, -enne) are other examples. These uses of language help to inculcate the idea that men are more valuable than women.

Linguistic practices also reveal patriarchy. For instance, in everyday talk and writing, communicators usually place masculine words prior to feminine words. Consider the following phrases: "boys and girls," "he or she," "his and hers," "husband and wife," and "masculine and feminine." While writing this book, I found myself routinely enacting that norm. To resist this tendency, I conscientiously placed the feminine in the first position. Exceptions to this rule include "ladies and gentlemen," "bride and groom," and "mom and dad." Why do you think these are exceptions? They may reflect patriarchal expectations about gender roles. For example, in writing or speaking contexts, placing "mom" before "dad" may emphasize the female's parental role. Although these and similar uses of language may seem trivial, they reflect deep structures of power that most people do not even realize exist.

Communication Styles

Another stream of research investigates differences in women's and men's communication styles. Rarely do such studies assess similarities between women's and men's communication. This body of research studies sex/gender differences in: (1) communication styles, and (2) perceptions about the function of communication.

A recurring depiction of women's speech as tentative encompasses several patterns. Women sometimes use tag questions such as "isn't that right?" or "don't you think?" Or, they employ question intonation in declarative contexts; that is, they say a statement as if it were a question and as if seeking approval. Other examples of speech styles frequently used by women include hesitation forms such as "um" or "like"; overuse of polite forms; and the frequent use of qualifiers and intensifiers like "sort of," "rather," "very," and "really." Some communicators overuse these ways of speaking to the extent that listeners may not take them seriously.

Rather than view these deferential differences in speech styles as gender-based, some scholars refer to them as "powerless" speech styles that anyone can employ. Although women tend to use powerless language more frequently than men, other users include poorly educated or lower status individuals. Thus, some linguists argue that this speech style is related more to women's relatively powerless position in society rather than to essentialist characteristics of females. Experimental courtroom research found that jurors and judges were less likely to view powerless speakers, regardless of gender, as credible.

Results of research on functions of communication tend to correspond with the femininity/masculinity clusters (nurturing-expressive/instrumental-active). For example, Ivy and Backlund offer a "relational/content" differentiation: "We believe that men approach conversation more with the intent of imparting information (the content aspect) than to convey cues about the relationship (the relational aspect)."

Sociolinguist Deborah Tannen offers similar perspectives on gender differences in her influential book entitled *You Just Don't Understand*. Tannen labels female communication style "rapport," meaning that women establish connections and negotiate relationships. In contrast, she terms the male style of communication "report," to indicate men's need to preserve independence and to impart information.

Communication differences between women and men may be due to socialization processes, including the proliferation of literature that asserts such differences. Men tend to be socialized to use language that is valued, while the opposite usually occurs for women. Several research conclusions support this claim: men tend to talk about their accomplishments using comparative and competitive terms, while women may understate their contributions and acknowledge others' assistance. Women often are more relational and dialogic; men tend to be more competitive and monologic. Women tend to provide support work in interaction. They offer verbal and nonverbal encouragement, such as nodding or smiling, ask questions returning to points made by earlier speakers, and attempt to bring others into the conversation.

Communication scholars Daniel Canary and Kimberley Hause criticize research on sex differences in communication for relying on and perpetuating sex stereotypes, using invalid measures of gender, a dearth of theory, and a tendency to polarize the sexes. In a meta-analysis of communication studies, they conclude, "given this research, we should *not* expect to find substantial sex differences in communication" (emphasis added). Indeed, they did not. Communication scholars Daena Goldsmith and Patricia Fulfs draw a similar conclusion in a refutation of Tannen's claims about gender differences. From their analysis of Tannen's evidence, they report that communication differences between women and men are typically minimal and are contingent upon situational factors. They conclude that differences tend to be nonverbal rather than verbal. Basically, they assert that women's and men's communication behaviors are more similar than different.

Some scholars critique researchers' propensity to denote females and males as a dualism with each embodying clear-cut, uniform characteristics. Rather than assuming a "two worlds" approach to gender interaction, they advocate research that explores different forms of femininity and masculinity. For instance, Deborah Cameron problematizes the tendency to homogenize women's and men's communication behaviors. She asserts a need in gender studies of language to consider contextual factors such as setting, purpose of communication, and relationship between communicators, as well as complex facets of communicators themselves.

Researchers have attended to both context and complexity of gendered communication. Some studies found that women and men behave differently according to context. These projects indicate differences among women or among men, instead of concentrating on differences between women and men. Men in all-male groups such as sports teams or in combat situations may exhibit caring characteristics that usually are attributed to women. Women in positions of authority often are more assertive than those who are in powerless jobs. Finally, the significance of context and complexity is evident in a volume of research projects about black women across a variety of contexts, including contemporary university students, nineteenth-century "club women" who worked for the social uplift of black people, and female hip-hop artists. The diverse perspectives shown in this collection underscore the need to consider intersections of social identity, rather than focusing only on one. . . .

Social Identities are Social Constructions

Humans create schemes to classify groups of people based on characteristics such as skin color and perceived ability. These classifications designate social identity categories that we may assume to be natural and permanent. However, social identity categories are artificial and subject to change. Meanings and classifications of gender, race, class, ability, sexuality, and age have varied throughout history. Classifications of these groups always are products of their times, as humans engage in social processes to manufacture differences, conclude that some differences are more important than others, and assign particular meanings to those differences.

We do not have to accept traditional notions that social identity groups are natural and unchangeable. We can change our beliefs and behaviors regarding social identity groups. For example, we can imagine and enact alternative meanings of our own social identities. We can affirm our "humanity as free agents with a capacity to create, to construct, to wonder, and to venture. . . ."

It seems ironic that although the United States is defined as an individualist culture, people rarely seem to behave as individuals. Even though we are relatively free to choose how we enact identity, we usually are predictable. We tend to choose occupations, clothing, food, music, recreational activities, and so forth, based on the social identity groups to which we "belong." We often seem to make decisions based on group identity rather than considering our options.

I encourage you to make conscientious choices rather than be a puppet or a parrot. Snip the invisible strings that control your behaviors. Rewrite the scripts that tell you what to say in certain situations. Resist the pressure to conform to societal expectations about the social identity groups you belong to. Remember that your attitudes and actions help to create who you are.

Power Matters

Across history, humans have enacted power relations to construct social identity classifications. Authoritative sources such as those from science, politics, medicine, religion, the media, and so forth use dominant belief systems to create and disseminate hierarchies of human differences. Most people take for granted these hierarchies and the ideologies that undergird them. Persons in positions of privilege tend to reap the benefits of these hierarchies and their consequences, while people categorized in lower levels of classification systems are more likely to be disadvantaged.

However, throughout the history of the United States, some members of nondominant and dominant groups have challenged ideological systems that discriminate against certain groups and favor others. Advocates for change have initiated social movements, campaigned for laws, developed social and economic programs, and engaged in other actions to challenge the status quo. Countless individuals have endeavored to achieve freedom and equality for everyone in the United States.

Once you realize that dominant ideologies underlie beliefs and behaviors related to difference, that you and others have been socialized to believe many ideas about matters of difference, and recognize the power of socialization and the persistence of dominant ideologies, you can make a conscious decision to contest forces that compel humans to comply with unjust dominant belief systems.

Communication Rules!

Humans use communication to construct social identities. Communication comprises discourse and discursive practices that produce, interpret, and share meaning about social identity groups. Through communication, we develop and disseminate classifications and hierarchies of gender, race, class, sexuality, ability, and age. We create labels, ascribe meaning to them, and use them to refer to one another. And, we use communication to co-create and re-create our identities as we interact with one another. A significant proportion of these interactions occurs in the various organizations that pervade our lives.

Socialization practices, which are primarily communicative, teach us about in-groups and out-groups. We inherit meanings about social identity groups from our families, peers, the media, teachers, and other sources, and we accept those meanings as our own. We use communication to create and consume media reports about social identity groups and media portrayals (factual and fictitious) of social identity groups. Many, if not most, of these reports and portrayals reinforce dominant ideologies and stereotypes.

Even as communication can reinforce dominant meanings of difference, communication can facilitate social change. For instance, the media sometimes offer alternative narratives, depictions, and information that challenge mainstream conceptions of social identity groups. In addition, advocacy groups use communication to develop and distribute information, engage in marches and rallies, and construct symbols to represent and advance their causes. Groups that oppose social change also employ these communication processes. Thus, communication can impede or facilitate progress toward equal opportunity for life, liberty, and the pursuit of happiness for everyone in the United States. Therefore, communication is central to applying what you have learned.

To summarize how to apply what you learned: appreciate and value difference, contest and re-imagine conceptions of social identities, assume agency, and acknowledge the power of communication.

POSTSCRIPT

Are Different Patterns of Communication in Women and Men Innately Determined?

It is important to situate discourse about sex differences in communication (indeed in any domain) in a sociopolitical context. Beliefs that the sexes differ, whether supported by empirical evidence or not, are deeply entrenched in our society. Indeed, while academic critics signal the lack of a scientific basis to Tannen's sweeping claims, her popular works have shot to the top of the bestseller list. We, the consumers, have to be very careful about scrutinizing how knowledge has been constructed and used. There is no such thing as a "simple" yes or no answer to a question of sex difference.

Scholarly and popular writing on sex differences is impacted greatly by what can be called the "hall of mirrors" effect. As described by Deborah Cameron in "Gender and Language: Gender, Language, and Discourse: A Review Essay," *Signs: Journal of Women in Culture and Society* (1998), "in the course of being cited, discussed, and popularized over time, originally modest claims have been progressively represented as more and more absolute, while hypotheses have been given the status of facts." Thus, for example, the originally modest claim made by researchers Don Zimmerman and Candace West in "Sex Roles, Interruptions and Silences in Conversation," in Barrie Thorne and Nancy Henley, eds., *In Language and Sex: Differences and Dominance* (Newbury House, 1975), that men interrupt women more than the reverse may have been exaggerated by constant repetition and then critiqued for being overstated (much like the "telephone" game played by children).

As another example, it turns out that no study has actually counted the number of words used by women and men in natural conversations, that is, not until July 2007. In contradiction of Brizdendine's claim that women utter 200,000 words to men's 7,000 per day, Matthias Mehl and his colleagues found over of period of 17 working hours women average 16,214 words and men averaged 15,669, a highly statistically nonsignificant finding (*Science*, vol. 31).

Currently there is less interest in examining sex differences in language and more emphasis on how people use language in everyday life to create and maintain social realities. Mary Crawford points out that feminists have worked to create a more gender-balanced language through the coining of new words and putting old words to new uses. She notes that language is power.

Suggested Readings

Daniel J. Canary and Kathryn Dindia, Eds., *Sex Differences and Similarities in Communication: Critical Essays and Empirical Investigations of Sex and Gender in Interaction* (2nd ed. New York: Lawrence Erlbaum, 2006).

Mary Crawford, "Gender and Language," in R. K. Unger, ed., *Psychology of Women and Gender* (pp. 228–244), (New York: John Wiley & Son, 2001).

K. M. Galvin and P. J. Cooper, *Making Connections: Readings in Relational Communication*, 4th ed. (Los Angeles: Roxbury Publishing Co., 2006).

Diana Ivy and Phil Backlund, *Gender Speak: Personal Effectiveness in Gender Communication* (New York: McGraw-Hill, 2003).

Charlotte Krolokke and Anne Scott Sorenson, *Gender Communication Theories and Analyses: From Silence to Performance* (Thousand Oaks, CA: Sage, 2005).

Deborah Tannen, *Talking from 9 to 5: Women and Men at Work* (San Francisco: HarperCollins, 2001).

J. Wood, (2001). *Gendered Lives: Communication, Gender, and Culture*, 4th ed. (Belmont, CA: Wadsworth Publishing, 2001).

ISSUE 6

Are the Fight-or-Flight and Tend-and-Befriend Responses to Stress Gender-Based?

YES: Shelley E. Taylor, Brian P. Lewis, Tara L. Gruenewald, Regan A. R. Gurung, John A. Updegraff, and Laura C. Klein, from "Sex Differences in Biobehavioral Responses to Threat: Reply to Geary and Flinn," *Psychological Review* (2002)

NO: David C. Geary and Mark V. Flinn, from "Sex Differences in Behavioral and Hormonal Response to Social Threat: Commentary on Taylor, et al.," *Psychological Review* (2002)

ISSUE SUMMARY

YES: Shelley E. Taylor and her colleagues, in a review of the literature, conclude that there is an evolutionarily based biobehavioral mechanism that underlies women's tend-and-befriend response to stress.

NO: David C. Geary and his colleagues extend Taylor's arguments to include men's tending and befriending behaviors and female-female competition.

Women's caring and nurturing nature is often contrasted with the stereotype of men as aggressive and competitive. In numerous theories it has been assumed that women's reproductive role as childbearers and caregivers is foundational and at the root of their affiliative nature. There is substantial empirical evidence that supports the idea that women can more reliably be depended on for meeting the long-term needs of family and friends. Women have been shown to, on average, have deeper and more intimate friendships, more extensive social networks, be more likely to discuss personal problems with friends, be more likely to seek treatment for psychological problems, and be more person-oriented rather than task-oriented in work situations. What is in dispute is the reason for these observed differences. Such generalizations oversimplify very complex patterns of gender-related patterns across cultures, at different ages, and in different contexts.

The selections here alert us to the dangers of confusing correlation with causation, an especially easy error to make when one of the correlates is biological. Shelley Taylor's writings have made a valuable contribution by noting that classic research on stress and coping relied exclusively on studies of males (animal and human research). These classic theories proposed that there are two responses to stress: flight or fight. She pondered the relevance of these two possibilities for females (animal and human). She subsequently concluded that there may be a different possible response to stress for females: tend-and-befriend, and built a new theoretical model based on this possibility. Geary and Flinn provide the counterpoint argument, showing that men can also tend and befriend. They also point out that women can be competitive. Their observations suggest that the role of sound context should not be ignored. Consider a few key findings from a recent study by Katie Kivlighan, Douglas Granger, and Alan Booth (2005). They examined gender-related patterns of hormone-behavior relationships in novice and experienced varsity rowers in a particular stressful situation, a competition. They found a complex set of interactions based on level of experience and time (pre-event, during the event, and post-event), as well as gender and type of measure. For example, higher cortisol levels pre-event in men were associated with more bonding and social affiliation with teammates. In contrast, HPA axis (i.e., "stress system") elevation pre-event was associated with social bonding in women but social withdrawal in men. During the competition, higher testosterone levels were associated with slower race times and poorer finishes in both novice female and male rowers. After the competition, novice rowers "recovered" more quickly than experienced rowers, who tended to focus their thoughts and feelings on the events, even after their hormonal levels declined. Novice male rowers showed the most rapid decline in cortisol and female rowers the slowest. They concluded that there is a "need for more sophisticated measurement of social behavior and cognitions involved in affiliation and bonding with teammates such as the timing of the behavior in relation to competitive event, the role an individual plays as a giver or receiver of social support, and the means through which bonding occurs," and in attempting to integrate their findings with Taylor's model they conclude "the model provides little guidance regarding the possibility of gender differences."

YES

Shelley E. Taylor et al.

Sex Differences in Biobehavioral Responses to Threat: Reply to Geary and Flinn (2002)

D. C. Geary and M. V. Flinn (2002) have offered a commentary on our tend-and-befriend theory that provides intriguing extensions to the stress responses of men. We concur with some of their ideas and disagree with others. Nonetheless, we believe this debate will spark constructive attention to the limitations of previous models of stress for understanding the many ways in which both men and women respond socially and biologically to stress.

Is There Male Tending?

Geary and Flinn have suggested that male paternal behavior is evidence of "tending," as we have used the term. We do not agree. Men are certainly good fathers, especially when compared with other mammalian fathers. The tend-and-befriend model is not about parenting, however; it is a model of biobehavioral responses to stress. We present evidence that hormones are released under stress that increase maternal tending, and we provide evidence that tending behavior under stress does indeed occur in human and nonhuman females. Neither Geary and Flinn nor the sources they refer to provide evidence that the hormones or behaviors associated with fight or flight in males are suppressed under stressful conditions to favor male tending instead. Given the different hormones and behaviors identified to date in males' responses to stress, whatever social behaviors males may engage in under threat may well assume quite different form than is true of females.

Male hormonal responses to stress do not appear to support tending responses, but they may lead to alternative patterns of social responding. Testosterone increases in response to some stressors, and vasopressin is also implicated in males' stress responses. Vasopressin's actions are enhanced in the presence of testosterone, and vasopressin has been tied to defense and patrolling of territory in male animal models. Consequently, one could argue for an influence on male protective behavior under stress via vasopressin, a hormone that is structurally very similar to oxytocin. As these hormonal patterns would also imply, aggression in response to stress is also more behaviorally descriptive of males than females (e.g., Mazur & Booth, 1998), suggesting that the "fight" response may better characterize men's than women's responses to threat. We believe that any model of male responses to stress will need to take evidence like this into account.

Reciprocal Altruism

Geary and Flinn have suggested that befriending in women is based more on reciprocal altruism than on tending. Reciprocal altruism is a powerful behavioral aspect of social interaction, but it is unclear what its biological underpinnings are. In our tend-and-befriend model, we present neuroendocrine evidence that implicates some of the same neurocircuitries in female friendship as are implicated in maternal tending. On this basis, we argue that befriending among women may have piggybacked onto the maternal neurocircuitry. . . . This is a conjecture on our part, not a central argument of our theoretical position, but we present empirical neuroendocrine and behavioral evidence to support this conjecture. Geary and Flinn have made a reasonable descriptive case for reciprocal altruism as a mechanism underlying tending, but it is unsupported by empirical evidence.

We believe that our argument, namely that befriending may have coevolved or been a consequence of the tending response, and Geary and Flinn's position, with respect to reciprocal altruism, are not fundamentally incompatible because they address different levels of theory. Reciprocal altruism is a broad principle that attempts to explain how, among other things, altruism gets into selfish genes. Our explanation is at the level of the neurocircuitries and specific behaviors through which befriending may occur. To set two such different levels of analysis against each other is to miss the point that these two theoretical vantage points address fundamentally different questions.

Befriending in Men and Women

Contrary to Geary and Flinn, we suggest that the patterns of affiliation under stress among men and women are quite different. Females seek and give social support at levels that are markedly, robustly, and qualitatively different from those of men. Contrary to Geary and Flinn's characterization of our position, we drew not only on evidence from Western cultures to make this assertion, but also on evidence from 18 additional cultures that found substantially the same thing. If the accumulation of cultural evidence on affiliation ultimately demonstrates that men are more affiliative under stress than women, then we are prepared to be proven wrong on this point. However, the cultural evidence to date clearly demonstrates that women are the more affiliative sex under stress by a large margin.

Philopatry

Which sex leaves the natal group to migrate to another group is certainly an important factor that influences social behavior. Among chimpanzees, bonobos, and humans—all of whom are very closely related genetically—female rather than male dispersal appears to be the typical pattern (although the evidence for early humans is largely conjectural). However, this issue may have little relevance for processes of tending and befriending under stress, except in one respect: When females are the migrators, befriending is likely to occur among nonkin rather than among kin.

Bonobos, who leave their natal troop to join a new one, represent an example. Several investigators have documented the strong nonkin bonds formed among female bonobos in their new troops. These strong ties are thought to be one reason why bonobos largely escape the abuse by males that female chimps (whose bonds in the wild are weaker) typically incur from males. Consistent with this argument, in captive populations or populations under stress, female bonds among chimpanzees are stronger, perhaps because they need more protection in geographically tight or stressful situations. In the cross-cultural literature in humans, the evidence suggests that when women emigrate and are unable to form alliances with other women, they are at heightened risk for abuse. Geary and Flinn pointed out that "men's coalitions provide a protective social ecology" for women's tending and befriending. But only to a point. Women's ties with others also serve to shelter themselves and their infants from abuse by males; both animal and human data clearly show the relation between strong female ties and lower rates of abuse by males.

In summary, we view philopatry as a moderating condition that does not fundamentally alter the existence of tending and befriending among females under stress but that may somewhat alter their form, as noted above.

Men's Befriending

Geary and Flinn suggested that male coalition formation is a counterpart to female befriending. Men do indeed form coalitions, but the extensive literature on this issue suggests that it is largely for purposes of building or maintaining a position in a dominance hierarchy, warding off or defending against aggression by other males, and protecting or creating resources that facilitate access to females. There are examples in the primate literature of females forming coalitions for some of the same purposes. However, befriending also involves activities related to child care, to food distribution, and to protection in times of threat. Coalition formation is not synonymous with befriending, nor are male coalition formation and female befriending—especially under conditions of stress and threat—likely to be guided by the same neurocircuitry and psychological mechanisms.

Women's Befriending

We have few concerns regarding Geary and Flinn's characterization of female same-sex egalitarian relationships as opposed to the dominance hierarchies related to affiliation that is characteristic of males. However, some qualifications may be in order. Geary and Flinn argued that female friendships require more investment and are more readily disrupted than are men's friendships. The empirical evidence does not support these assertions. There is no evidence that female friendships require more investment than male coalitions. Female activities are more likely to end when there is conflict than is true of males, but conflict is also less common among groups of females than among groups of males.

Female–Female Competition

Geary and Flinn credited us with the assertion that "there is not a strong evolutionary foundation for female-on-female aggression in humans," and they disagree with that statement. So do we. We never made such an assertion, nor did we make any statement that should be construed as support for such an implication. That female ties exist in the context of forces that also breed competition goes without saying. Competition characterizes both male ties and female relationships, and it exists in all primate species that have been studied.

Biological Model

Geary and Flinn's extensions to the tend-and-befriend model ignore our proposed neuroendocrine mechanisms. The neuroendocrine model does not, indeed cannot, apply to men: It draws on estrogen, which exists in very small quantities in men; oxytocin, which appears to be enhanced by estrogen and antagonized by testosterone (a hormone that increases in men in response to many stressors); and endogenous opioid peptides, which appear to have different effects on the social behaviors of men and women. These points question whether it is scientifically defensible to look at men's social behavior under stress through the biobehavioral perspective we have developed for women.

More generally, we have been concerned by the degree to which some social scientists commenting on our model have ignored the biological evidence and the data from animal models that underlie it, favoring, instead, constructions of what early humans might have been like. Such constructions are risky in the absence of direct evidence, and not surprisingly, they have varied dramatically from decade to decade. We are not opposed, in theory, to such reconstructions—many valuable insights have come from them. However, to ignore biological evidence and continuity among animal models for understanding the origins of human development is to eschew very important sources of scientific knowledge. We believe that scientific progress will come only with willingness to integrate biological and behavioral evidence. In this context, we note that both Geary and Flinn have been in the vanguard of efforts to integrate biology and behavior in masterful ways in their prior and current work. Our disagreements with them on some specific issues we discuss here do not challenge our genuine admiration of their research legacy and its biobehavioral focus. In fact, it is this form of scientific analysis that we had hoped our model would encourage.

Conclusion

We developed the tend-and-befriend position because we believed that the existing models of stress obscured important biological and behavioral differences between the sexes and overgeneralized evidence from men to women, who have faced quite different selection pressures throughout human evolutionary history. In our [work], we illustrated how a general model, fight-or-flight, is insufficiently precise to account for specific neuroendocrine and behavioral stress responses characteristic of women. We used biological and behavioral evidence to jointly constrain our model. To take the tend-and-befriend theory and try to broaden it to include men without any of the qualifying biological and behavioral precision of the original model would do a disservice to the field. Nonetheless, we agree with Geary and Flinn that the study of stress will be well served by attention to men's and women's social and biological responses to stress—both the commonalities in their responses and the differences.

David C. Geary and
Mark V. Flinn

Sex Differences in Behavioral and Hormonal Response to Social Threat: Commentary on Taylor et al. (2000)

Taylor and colleagues provided an important and, in many respects, groundbreaking evolutionary analysis of women's neuroendocrine and social responses to threats and other stressors. They proposed that women do not fit the traditional fight-or-flight stress response paradigm developed from research with men but instead tend and befriend. *Tending*, the protection and care of offspring, and *befriending*, the formation and maintenance of a small network of interpersonal relationships with other women, are proposed as an integrated and evolved strategy of women defending themselves and their offspring with protective coalitions. Tending and befriending are posited to have evolved from the attachment and nurturance systems involved in maternal care, including oxytocin and endogenous opioids, whose effects are moderated by estrogens. The behavioral and neuroendocrine mechanisms involved in tending and befriending were contrasted with the mechanisms for fight and flight, which were characterized as being more commonly expressed in men than in women and "organized and activated by androgens." Androgens may work as antagonists with respect to the neuroendocrine systems (e.g., expression of oxytocin) that dispose women toward tending and befriending.

In all, Taylor et al. have made a potentially seminal contribution to the understanding of women's social relationships and in understanding sex differences in patterns of social affiliation and neuroendocrine response to stressors. There are several areas, however, in which we disagree with Taylor et al. and other areas in which we suggest friendly elaboration of their model. We focus on the following issues: (a) the importance of male parenting; (b) evolutionary interpretations of tending and befriending, with specific questions concerning whether befriending evolved from tending; (c) patterns of philopatry and male coalitions in hominid evolution; and (d) the nature and source of female–female competition. The first two issues are addressed in the section below and the third and fourth in separate sections. Where relevant, the types of stressors that elicit tending or befriending in women and men are discussed, as these were not fully elaborated by Taylor et al.

From *Psychological Review*, vol. 109, issue 4, 2002, pp. 751–753. Copyright © 2002 by American Psychological Association via Rightslink. Reprinted by permission.

Tending and Befriending

Tending is a form of parental investment. The nature and extent of this investment by one or both sexes strongly influences the dynamics of intersexual and intrasexual relationships, termed *sexual selection.* Species in which females provide the majority of parental effort, such as chimpanzees (*Pan troglodytes*) and lions (*Panthera leo*), are characterized by intense male–male competition for access to females or for control of the resources (e.g., breeding territory) females need to raise their offspring. In these species, female tending and male fighting are salient features of reproductive dynamics. The reverse situation occurs in species in which males provide the majority of parental effort, such as red-necked phalaropes (*Phalaropus lobatus*), where sexual selection involves female–female competition over resources provided by males.

Humans are one of few mammalian species in which both females and males parent. The first section below provides consideration of how human paternal investment is related to predictions regarding tending in men, and the second focuses on the relation between tending and befriending in women. The implications of men's tending for understanding competitive relationships among women are discussed in a later section.

Men's Tending

Among primates, the expression of both paternal and maternal investment appear to be influenced by similar hormonal and contextual factors, although there are differences as well. For humans, it is likely that combinations of hormonal, experiential, and contextual factors contribute to maternal and paternal investment, some of which differ between the sexes and some of which do not. [H]igh cortisol levels are correlated with attentive and sensitive parenting of newborns in both mothers and fathers, although there are also hormonal correlates that differ for mothers and fathers. In response to infant distress cues, men who responded with concern and a desire to comfort the infant had higher prolactin levels and lower testosterone levels than did other men. "Men with more pregnancy symptoms (couvade) and men who were most affected by the infant reactivity test had higher prolactin levels and greater post-test reduction in testosterone." Added analyses suggested these hormonal patterns may have been moderated by the nature of the man's relationship with his wife.

For men, a combination of other hormonal and interpersonal factors appear to suppress testosterone levels, which, in turn, may result in the inhibition of the motivational and behavioral dispositions associated with fight or flight. The inhibition of these dispositions may enable the expression of paternal tending in some contexts. Of course, it is likely that some of the hormonal and neuroendocrine systems that support tending differ in women and men, and thus these patterns may not be completely relevant to tending in women. The point is that men do not always react to stressors with a fight or flight response, and, in fact, in some contexts show many of the same tending behaviors that Taylor et al. described for women.

Women's Tending and Befriending

We propose that the evolution of befriending may have been more strongly related to the mechanisms that support reciprocal altruism than the tending mechanisms proposed by Taylor et al. Befriending is defined by a shared ethos of equality and high levels of reciprocal intimacy, as well as the mutual sharing of time, resources, and social support. The dynamics of these relationships mirror those that define friendships and are the predicted pattern for an evolved system supporting reciprocal altruism—that is, the formation and maintenance of relationships among nonkin. Unlike women's befriending, mother–offspring relationships are not defined by reciprocity and, in fact, are characteristically nonsymmetrical in all species. Moreover, it is not clear whether the evolved tending system involves emotional nurturance, as such behaviors are not a universal feature of mother–child relationships, although the providing of emotional support is one of the defining features of women's befriending.

There are also developmental patterns that suggest different mechanisms in the evolution of tending and befriending. . . . If tending and befriending have a common evolutionary history, then there should be developmental similarities in the focus and form of these social behaviors. During childhood and adolescence, girls engage in both play parenting and actively form and maintain relationships with other same-age girls, but these social behaviors differ in both function and form. Play parenting is typically directed toward younger children, or child substitutes (e.g., dolls), and involves the rehearsal of parenting activities, such as the feeding and bathing of children. Social relationships, in contrast, are almost always with same-age peers and involve nonparental activities, such as discussion of boys or relational aggression (i.e., gossiping about and backbiting other girls).

The argument is not that there is no overlap in the behavioral and neuroendocrine systems that support tending and befriending. Clearly, there are overlaps, as aptly described by Taylor and colleagues. It is, of course, possible that the befriending system evolved from a combination of mechanisms involved in tending and in reciprocal altruism. Nonetheless, at a social and behavioral level, befriending is more similar to reciprocal altruism than to tending.

Befriending in Men and Women

Men's social affiliations were mentioned by Taylor et al. but were not the focus of their theoretical argument. Taylor et al. did, however, contrast the social behavior or women and men under stressful conditions and argued that women are more likely to affiliate under these conditions than are men. Under laboratory and in some other well-studied contexts, such as following divorce, women do indeed show .more social affiliation than do men. However, laboratory studies and studies of stressors in Western societies are not always representative of the stress-inducing contexts that were likely to have been of importance during human evolution. The goal here is to provide a theoretical elaboration of the Taylor et al. model by considering the social ecology within which humans most likely evolved, as related to men's and women's befriending.

Philopatry

An important frame for understanding the social ecology of human evolution is *philopatry*, that is, the tendency of members of one sex to stay in the birth group and members of the other sex to migrate to another group. Taylor et al. used female coalitional behavior in other primates to make inferences about the evolution of befriending in women. The reviewed studies were largely of female kin-based coalitions in several species of old-world monkey, species in which females are the philopatric sex. Female-biased philopatry results in a social ecology that favors the evolution of kin-based coalitions among females, at least when coalitional behavior covaries with survival or reproductive outcomes. These coalitions typically compete over access to high quality food sources, such as fruit trees. Offspring borne in coalitions that gain control of these resources are healthier and survive in greater numbers than do offspring borne in other coalitions. These coalitions also provide support during periods of social conflict and otherwise function to control the dynamics of social living, as described by Taylor et al. In contrast, for "most monkeys with multimale groups, tolerant or cooperative relationships among males are rare or unknown." In these species, antagonistic relationships among males are well described by fight or flight and the social coalitions of females by tend and befriend.

However, female-bonded species may not provide the most appropriate analogy for making inferences about the evolution of befriending in humans. Male-biased philopatry in chimpanzees, bonobos (*Pan paniscus*), and humans (*Homo sapiens*) suggest that the modal social ecology during hominid evolution was male philopatry, not female philopatry. . . . A male kin-based social ecology creates the potential for the evolution of motivational and behavioral dispositions for males to form kin-based coalitions, and such dispositions are expressed in humans and chimpanzees.

Men's Befriending

Male befriending and the resulting formation of kin-based coalitions is a common feature of social life in chimpanzees and humans in preindustrial societies, although it is only intermittently observed in bonobos. For humans and chimpanzees, male befriending is sometimes seen among unrelated or distantly related males, suggesting strong benefits to coalitional behavior for the males of these species. Indeed, Taylor and her colleagues described social affiliation in men, noting that "men have been observed to form groups for purposes of defense, aggression, and war . . . [they] tend toward larger social groups than is true of women . . . and these groups are often organized around well-defined purposes or tasks." The functional significance of this behavior was not the theoretical focus of their model but is nonetheless relevant to the broader issue of befriending.

For chimpanzees, humans, dolphins (*Tursiops truncatus*), and other species in which male coalitions form, coalitional behavior is related to male–male competition over access to females or for control of the resources females need to raise their offspring. In preindustrial societies, coalitional warfare is common and social politicking and alliance formation is a crucial element of the social life of men. Within this social network, men's relationships reflect a balance of cooperative and competitive behaviors. Cooperation is needed to maintain the coalition, and competition emerges from attempts to increase individual status within the dominance hierarchy of the coalition. Once established, the dominance hierarchy facilitates the social cooperation needed for coalitional competition.

For chimpanzees, humans, and other species, larger coalitions typically have a competitive advantage over smaller coalitions. The advantage of group size in male coalitional competition, and in political negotiations, places constraints on the types of mechanisms that can support men's befriending. . . . Stated differently, evolved motivational and emotional mechanisms that enable men to form large competition-related social groups based on low-intensity activities is a necessary correlate of coalitional competition. Proximity, shared activities, "horse play," and so forth often appear to be sufficient for forming the affective and affiliative ties that define befriending in boys and men, as related to coalition formation.

Again, developmental patterns appear to reflect evolutionary function. The development and maintenance of boys' friendships is often achieved through shared activities and often in social contexts in which coalitional behavior is needed to achieve mutual goals. Many of these developmental activities, such as team sports, mirror and thus provide practice for primitive warfare. Moreover, boys and men, unlike girls and women, show increased cortisol and testosterone responses with the formation of same-sex coalitions during group-level competition—the expected endocrine reactions associated with an evolved fight response, when the fight occurs in the context of group-level competition.

Low-intensity investment in boys' and men's befriending might be a consequence of male philopatry. In natural settings, most of the boys and men in the local group will be kin and thus the maintenance of these relationships will not require the same level of reciprocity as will relationships with nonkin. In any case, men's befriending and coalitional fighting are coevolving features of social life in preindustrial societies and almost certainly throughout much of recent human evolution. Finally, it must be noted that men's coalitions provide a protective social ecology within which women's tending and befriending, as described by Taylor et al., are expressed.

Women's Befriending

On the basis of male philopatry, girls and women are predicted to have an evolved motivational disposition to maintain same-sex relationships around an ethos of equality and reciprocity, as contrasted with the dominance hierarchies that form with groups of boys and men. In social contexts in which women migrate to the group of their husband, the most likely source of social support is other often unrelated or distantly related women. In this circumstance, selection will favor women who have the social competencies needed to develop relationships with unrelated women and through this maintain a supportive social network. As noted, these social competencies define friendship and reciprocal altruism—relationships with nonkin—which, in turn, well describe the dynamics of women's relationships.

On the basis of male philopatry and kinship, women's relationships are not only predicted to require more intense investment to maintain, they are also predicted—and appear—to be more readily disrupted by conflict than relationships among men. Conflicts in men's relationships are a normal aspect of the formation of within-group dominance hierarchies. Kinship and the benefits of group size in coalitional conflict result in selective advantages for men who maintain the coalition, following within-group conflict. The mechanisms for maintaining women's social networks, in contrast, evolved under a different social ecology, one that was not defined by philopatry or the benefits of large coalitions.

Female–Female Competition

Taylor and colleagues note that male-on-male physical aggression is more common than female-on-female physical aggression in many species. Indeed, extreme and life-threatening levels of female-on-female aggression are likely to be selected against, because of the associated reproductive costs, which are not born by males. At the same time, it was acknowledged that relationships among women are not always nurturing and cooperative, but it was suggested that women's "aggressive behavior may be more moderated by social norms and learning and by cultural, situational, and individual differences." The implication is that there is not a strong evolutionary foundation for female-on-female aggression in humans.

We disagree. As with other species of primate, women are predicted to compete over social and material resources, including paternal investment. Men's tending creates a more uniquely human form of female–female competition; that is, competition for high-quality men who are able and are willing to invest their resources in the woman and her children. The associated competition is typically expressed in terms of relational aggression. At the root, relational aggression functions to exclude sexual and other female competitors from the social group and to disrupt the above described social networks that women work to develop. In most preindustrial societies, female-on-female aggression, relational and otherwise, is likely to involve competition among cowives, as high-status men in these societies are typically polygynously married. Female–female competition over social and other resources may also occur between other women, such as between a wife and her husband's sister in matrilineal societies; in these societies, men are expected to invest in their sister's children.

In the United States and other Western nations, polygyny is socially suppressed. Once married, women in these cultures do not usually experience the same level of female-on-female relational, and sometimes physical, aggression as might have been common during human evolution. In other words, the befriend aspect of Taylor et al. may belie the more competitive side of adult relationships among married women, because the social context—outlawing of polygynous marriages—removes an important source of such conflict, cowives. Moreover, many women in Western society are socially isolated in comparison with women in preindustrial societies and thus removed to some extent form the above noted broader female–female competition.

Conclusion

Taylor et al. presented a groundbreaking analysis of relationships among women. Their evolutionary model proposed new adaptive explanations and underlying neuroendocrine mechanisms that support these relationships and has implications for understanding sex differences in human stress response. We suggest an elaboration of their model based on a broader evolutionary perspective that emphasizes human paternal investment and the likelihood that males were the philopatric sex throughout much of human evolution.

Parental investment appears to be an evolved feature of the reproductive strategy of men and is relevant to two issues related to tending and befriending. First, the Taylor et al. (2000) framework for understanding tending can be expanded to include men, although it is very likely that there are differences as well as similarities in the neuroendocrine mechanisms supporting tending in women and men. An important evolutionary corollary is that men's tending is predicted to—and does—occur in some stressful contexts (Storey et al., 2000). Second, across-species patterns indicate that when males parent, females compete over this investment. Taylor et al. do not deny that relationships among girls and women are sometimes competitive but do suggest that female-on-female aggression is more strongly related to learning and culture than is male-on-male aggression. Clearly, patterns of same-sex aggression differ for men and women, . . . evolved forms of female-on-female aggression follow as an evolutionary consequence of male parenting. In studies of Western girls and women, this often takes the form of relational aggression, which may belie the intensity of female-on-female aggression, relational and otherwise, in other contexts and during human evolution.

Male philopatry provides an essential frame for understanding the social ecology in which befriending mechanisms evolved in women and men. One result is the creation of a social ecology in which a motivational disposition for males to form kin-based coalitions can evolve, at least when coalitional behavior covaries with reproductive outcomes. Such a disposition exists in boys and men, although it is primarily expressed in social contexts that favor formation of male coalitions, such as group level male–male competition. One corollary is that to support coalitional competition, the fight in the fight or flight response must include an element of befriending for boys and men. Evolved mechanisms that foster befriending in boys and men under conditions of social threat, however, cannot involve all of the same befriending mechanism described by Taylor et al. for girls and women. The time-intensive befriending mechanisms found in girls and women would constrain the size of boys' and men's coalitions, hence resulting in a competitive disadvantage.

Male philopatry also leads to the prediction that the evolution of women's befriending will strongly involve the mechanisms that support reciprocal altruism. Residential groups were more likely to have included distant or unrelated females than males during human evolution. Female nonkin relationships would be based on reciprocal altruism; that is, an exchange of social and emotional support, information, resources, and so forth that are considered to be advantageous to both parties. The befriending patterns described by Taylor et al. are congruent with the view that social relationships among girls and women are strongly influenced by reciprocal altruism, whether or not tending mechanisms are also involved.

Future studies that assess sex differences in endocrine responses in different social contexts and under different social conditions—as illustrated with the elevation of boys' and men's cortisol and testosterone levels with coalitional competition—are needed to test these elaborations of the Taylor et al. model. We think it will be useful to expand the Taylor et al. model to capture additional complexities of the evolution of human social relationships and sex differences in these relationships. We suggest consideration of social dynamics in other hominoids, social patterns that are unique to humans, and social dynamics that occur in preindustrial contexts, especially those that are more similar than Western society to the social contexts in which human biobehavioral evolution occurred.

POSTSCRIPT

Are the Fight-or-Flight and Tend-and-Befriend Responses to Stress Gender-Based?

Feminist theorists have been reluctant to consider biologically based explanations of women's and men's behavior, such as Taylor's tend-and-befriend model. These explanations essentialize the nature of women's and men's behaviors. Such thinking provides the justification for the various inequalities in our society based on one's sex. It absolves society of the responsibility of seeing the inequalities as social problems. Shelley's model assumes that there is an evolutionarily based biobehavioral mechanism that underlies the tend-and-befriend response to stress. She suggests that it is an attachment-caregiving system based on women's mothering role. However, when her model is considered in light of Geary and Flinn's observation that men also may tend and befriend can begin to reconsider Taylor's claims. Typically, social scientists have viewed biological approaches to be too reductionistic to be useful; the accusation is that in search of the ultimate cause these approaches have ignored the realities of an organism's real-life context. On the other hand, proponents of the biological approach often question the scientific rigor of social scientists' methods for establishing a knowledge base.

Perhaps there is really no place for sex differences per se in such debates. It might be more useful to entertain the view that biological organisms exist in differential social contextual factors that result in different biobehavioral responses to stress in a dynamic interplay of influences across time; that is, biology and social context are both cause and effect. Thus, when males and females find themselves in different social contexts, different biobehavioral responses to stress occur. It seems more valuable to ask what are the social pressures, both current and evolutionarily based, that affect fight-flight and tend-befriend pattern's in females and males. From this purview, we might think about the number of women who are poor, who are the victims of abuse beginning in early childhood, who are dependent on men for their well-being, as well as that of their children, who are sexually harassed at work and fear losing their jobs if they complain, or who are denied access to the highest levels of power at work and in the community, including the faith community. Do such social contexts increase the likelihood of tending-and-befriending rather than flight-or-fight? What would be the social consequences for the woman who stands to fight, or where would the woman who wants to flee go? And think of the numbers of boys and men who have been expected, and even taunted, to stand and take it like a man,

113

whether on the football field or the battlefield. So, are the hormonal and neuro-endocrinological differences seen in women and men the result of evolutionally hard-wired systems or logical consequences of different positions in the status hierarchy? What is the role of power? Society gives the weaker, women, children, the elderly, permission to ask for help, but the stronger are expected to give help, to be the "hero."

Suggested Readings

Nancy Adler, M. Marmot, B. McEwen, and J. Singer (eds.), *Socioeconomic Status and Health in Industrial Nations: Social, Psychological, and Biological Pathways* (New York Academy of Sciences, 1999).

Roy Baumeister and Mark Leary, "The Need to Belong: Desire for Interpersonal Attachment as a Fundamental Human Motivation," *Psychological Bulletin* (vol. *117*, 1995) 497–529.

Michelle G. Craske, *Origins of Phobias and Anxiety Disorders: Why More Women Than Men?* (Elsevier, 2003).

Richard M. Eisler and M. Hersen (eds.), *Handbook of Gender, Culture, and Health* (Lawrence Erlbaum Associates, 2000).

Debra L. Nelson and Ronald J. Burke, eds., *Gender, Work Stress, and Health* (Washington, DC: American Psychological Association, 2002).

Jerry Suls and Kenneth A. Wallston, *Social Psychological Foundations of Health and Illness* (Malden, MA: Blackwell Publishing, 2003).

Internet References . . .

MedlinePlus: Domestic Violence

This website is presented by the U.S. National Library of Medicine and the National Institutes of Health to provide accurate data on a variety of health issues. Information ranges from basics, diagnoses, references, and resources.

> http://www.nlm.nih.gov/medlineplus/
> domesticviolence.html

National Online Resource Center on Violence Against Women

This website is the online resource for advocates working to end domestic violence, sexual assault, and other violence in the lives of women and their children. It provides resources regarding sexual violence, domestic violence, information on grants, and research. It is funded through a Cooperative Agreement with the U.S. Centers for Disease Control and Prevention and is housed within the National Resource Center on Domestic Violence (NRCDV).

> http://www.vawnet.org/

Men Against Violence

This group is a nonprofit corporation dedicated to reducing domestic violence. It is a group of committed men and women who actively provide early intervention to reduce domestic violence through the education and support of individuals who have been or may be at risk of offending.

> http://www.menagainstviolence.org/

Same-Sex Dating Violence

This website is maintained by Student Services at Brown University to provide a wide range of information and resources regarding same-sex dating violence.

> http://www.brown.edu/Student_Services/
> Health_Services/Health_Education/
> sexual_assault/ssdv.htm

Enough Is Enough

Enough.org is dedicated to protecting children and families from the Internet dangers of pornography and sexual predators. This website is the Internet safety site. It provides various resources including information on the harms of pornography and tips for parents, including information on how to report cybercrimes.

> http://www.protectkids.com/effects/

Violence in the Daily Lives of Women and Men

V iolence is an unfortunate part of many people's daily lives. It can range from exposure to violent images in the media, including television shows, movies, music videos, and electronic games, as well as pornography. Remarkably high percentages of children, adolescents, and adults report experiences with witnessing, experiencing, or engaging in name-calling, screaming, yelling, hitting, pushing, shoving, and slapping, with smaller numbers reporting violence that involves weapons. A major question regards the extent to which patterns of violence are gendered, for victims and for perpetrators. One of the most enduring stereotypes is that of aggressive men and passive women. But just how accurate is that stereotype? Research would suggest that the answer depends on how aggression is defined and whether one is looking at discrete behaviors or other forms of psychological control and abuse. Additionally, the meaning, motive, and outcome can alter how the gendered nature of violence is construed. Consistent with stereotypes it has been assumed that level of testosterone plays a causal role in aggression, supporting the stereotype of male aggressiveness. However, recent research suggests that testosterone levels may be a result, not necessarily a cause. So, does aggression have a biological basis? Can studies of neurological and hormonal functioning better help us understand gendered patterns of experiences with violence? What insights does the study of race, ethnicity, and social class lend to our understanding of violence? How do media portrayals of aggressive women and men, as well as portrayals of male and female victims, fuel or challenge stereotypes?

- Are Expressions of Aggression Related to Gender?

- Gender Symmetry: Do Women and Men Commit Equal Levels of Violence Against Intimate Partners?

- Does Pornography Reduce the Incidence of Rape?

ISSUE 7

Are Expressions of Aggression Related to Gender?

YES: Jacquelyn W. White, Patricia L. N. Donat, and Barrie Bondurant, from "A Developmental Examination of Violence Against Girls and Women," in R. Unger, ed., *Handbook of the Psychology of Women and Gender* (John Wiley & Sons, 2001)

NO: Richard B. Felson, from *Violence and Gender Reexamined* (American Psychological Association, 2002)

ISSUE SUMMARY

YES: Social psychologist Jacquelyn W. White and her colleagues conclude, based on a review of the literature, that girls and women are highly likely to be the targets of male aggression and are less likely to use physical aggression than men due to different developmental experiences.

NO: Social psychologist Richard B. Felson argues that aggression is related to physical strength and a general tendency toward violence, not male domination, and that there is not an epidemic of violence against women.

One of the most pervasive gender-related stereotypes is that of sex differences in aggression. The view that males are physically more aggressive and women are more verbally aggressive persists in spite of inconsistent findings. American society is thought by many to be a violent culture, marked by the high prevalence of family and school violence, as well as high rates of aggression and violence in the media. A host of factors likely contribute to the rise of violence in the USA, including alcohol and drug consumption, increased access to guns, and gender expectations. Are youth, especially males, learning to model the violence they see on TV and in the family? Some lament that "boys will be boys," believing that boys are aggressive by nature, while others argue that boys' aggression results from societal rules and expectations tied to masculinity. One result of these expectations is that any feminine characteristics or behaviors (e.g., emotional expression, gentleness) in males lead to rejection and ridicule. Social desirability restricts boys' public display of

118

emotions to anger, resulting in aggressive and violent behaviors. Boys face a Catch-22; expressing their fears and frustrations is unacceptable for "real men," but such expression is what they so desperately need. As noted in the Postscript to Issue 3, "culturally based socialization practices encourage men to be aggressors and women to be victims. In societies where there is no formal hierarchy that privileges one group over another and in which women and men exercise relatively equal power, general levels of aggression, male violence against women, and rape are low." In contrast, the one emotion women are not supposed to display is anger. Just as many people assume that males are by nature aggressive they likewise assume that females are by nature non-aggressive. Thus, what do girls do with their anger? Evidence suggest that there are no sex differences in level of anger experiences, but there are gendered patterns in what leads to anger and the form and function of the behavior that follows from the anger. Research on intimate partner violence and child abuse documents that women can be just as aggressive and sometimes more so than men, but the aggression is manifested differently. Recent research on relational aggression has also established a number of ways in which girls are more relationally aggressive than boys. Thus, rather than asking the question of whether men are more aggressive than women is to ask how do men and women differ in their expression of aggression and what role does gender play. Most feminist scholars, especially those in the behavioral sciences, use the principles of social learning theory to account for how sociocultural values are transmitted and learned at the individual level and to describe how individual women and men come to behave in gender typical as well as atypical ways.

White and her colleagues argue that the childhood experiences of girls and boys provide the roots for the gendered nature of aggression and violence. Gendered in this context means that the who, how, and why of violence cannot be understood without consideration of the sex of the perpetrator, the victim, their relationship, and the context of the violence. Their review of the literature leads to the conclusion that gendered aggression can be observed in childhood, adolescence, and adulthood, including the elder years. Gender role expectations, socialization, and power inequalities are central to understanding aggression and violence in both women and men. Felson in contrast argues that aggression has to do with size and strength and not gendered constructs such as status, power, and dominance.

YES ◁ Jacquelyn W. White, Patricia L. N. Donat, and Barrie Bondurant

A Developmental Examination of Violence against Girls and Women

In spite of images of loving, supportive families and caring, protective lovers, intimate relationships may be plagued by alarming levels of aggression and violence. Although men are usually the victims of nonintimate crimes, girls and women are much more likely than men to be the victims of violence in intimate relationships. Physical violence against women takes many forms, including childhood sexual abuse, dating violence, acquaintance rape, battering and wife abuse; nonphysical forms of violence include sexual harassment, stalking, and pornography. All these forms of violence share in common the fact that they frequently are committed by men known to the girls and women. Unlike other crimes, they are crimes in which others, as well as the victim herself, tend to blame the victim for what happened. By blaming the individual victims, attention and responsibility are shifted away from the perpetrators and from the social context that contributes to violence against women. The present chapter suggests that the roots of violence against women can be found in the childhood experiences of girls and boys, and that the messages learned in and the consequences of these early experiences are repeated and reinforced in adolescence and young adulthood. . . .

Gendered Violence in Childhood

The gendered nature of violence is evident early in childhood and establishes a framework for patterns of interactions between adult women and men. Children are at great risk for victimization because of their small physical stature and dependency on adults; they have little choice over whom they live with and few opportunities to leave an abusive home. From the beginning, they learn the major lesson of patriarchy: The more powerful control the less powerful. Furthermore, children learn that power is gendered and associate men and masculinity with power and dominance. Victimization is also gendered. During childhood, boys experience more physical aggression and girls experience more sexual aggression. Among adolescents, girls are at a greater risk than boys for both physical and sexual victimization. . . .

Gender and Parental Punishment

In both normal and abusive homes, children receive gendered messages about aggression and violence. Children, especially those from abusive homes, have many opportunities to learn that the more powerful person in a relationship can use aggression to successfully control the less powerful person. The majority of parents in American homes use verbal and physical aggression as disciplinary tactics. . . . [O]ver 90% of children are spanked sometime in their youth, with many parents (62%) reporting physical aggression against their children; this aggression includes pushing, shoving, and slapping. Fewer parents (11%) report using severe aggression, including hitting, kicking, beating, threatening, and using weapons against their children.

Punishment does not appear to be uniform, however; the sex of the child and the parent affect the pattern and outcome. During early childhood, boys are at greater risk than girls for severe abusive punishment, whereas during preadolescence and adolescence, girls' risk increases. This is presumably because of boys' increased ability to inflict harm on others as they physically mature. Although parents do not differ in the frequency with which they spank girls and boys, the effects of the spanking are different. Paternal spanking leads to reactive (angry) aggression in both girls and boys, but only boys show unprovoked bullying aggression against others when spanked by their fathers. . . . [F]athers' spanking of boys communicates a "gender-based approach to interpersonal disagreements, that of physical dominance, . . . explicitly transmitting gender-stereotypic notions". Moreover, parents' reactions to their children's aggressive behavior differs. Although parents generally see aggression as an undesirable attribute for children, they view it as a tolerated *masculine* behavior. Thus, boys expect less parental disapproval than girls for aggression directed toward peers although they are punished more harshly for aggression than are girls.

Childhood Sexual Abuse

The message that the more powerful can control the less powerful is also learned in a sexual context for a minority of girls and boys. . . .

The sexual victimization of children is an abuse of interpersonal power and a violation of trust. What makes the statistics even more tragic is the fact that most children are victimized by people they know and trust to protect them. Almost 90% of children who are raped are victimized by someone known to them. Boys are more likely to be sexually abused by someone outside the family, whereas girls are more likely to be sexually abused by a family member or a quasi–family member (e.g., mother's boyfriend). Betrayal of the trust vested in those who have power is central to understanding childhood sexual abuse, its consequences, and the systems that sustain it. . . .

Characteristics of Abusive Families

. . . The family system in which parent-child incest typically occurs is headed by a father who is authoritarian, punitive, and threatening. Children who are victimized often feel powerless to stop the abuse and feel they have nowhere to turn for help, comfort, and support. The child's ability to confront and refuse sexual contact is overwhelmed by the feelings of loyalty and trust that the child may have developed for the perpetrator. The adult is in a position of authority (and often one of trust as well) and communicates to the child that the behavior is part of an exclusive, secretive, and special relationship. The perpetrator may even come to believe and attempt to convince the child that the relationship is a mutually loving and caring one. For children who may otherwise be neglected and emotionally isolated, the special attention and inappropriate sexual contact with the adult may be confusing and may complicate the coping process.

Ethnicity and Childhood Sexual Abuse

The relationship between racial ethnicity and victimization is currently being studied. No statistical differences between the percentages of Black (57%) and White (67%) women reporting childhood sexual victimization have been reported. Similarly, 49% of the women in a Southwestern American Indian tribal community reported childhood sexual victimization. . . . [N]o significant differences in the prevalence of childhood sexual abuse among Hispanic and non-Hispanic women [have been found], with 27.1% of Hispanic women and 33.1% of non-Hispanic White women reporting victimization as children. Thus, girls from several ethnic groups appear to be at risk for becoming a victim of sexual abuse. . . .

Gendered Violence in Adolescence

During adolescence, young men and women experience extreme pressure to conform to traditional gender roles. Unfortunately, part of establishing a masculine identity for young men often involves distancing oneself socially and psychologically from anything feminine. "Thus, to turn away and distance oneself from a woman is what a man does because he is a man, and what boys do in relation to girls because they are boys. Such behavior is expected, is tacitly approved, often goes unnoticed, and contributes to the implicit definition or understanding of manliness in a sexist society." Young men seek out companionship from other men and distance themselves from women except in social contexts involving "power-enhancing" or sexual opportunities. . . .

Dating Violence

The gender-related patterns learned in childhood are played out in adolescent dating and committed relationships. Young people usually begin dating in high school, although children as young as kindergartners talk about having boyfriends and girlfriends. The idea of being paired with a member of the other sex is pervasive in our society. Traditionally, it has been assumed that children's "playing house" and, later, dating provide a context for socialization into later roles, including husband, wife, lover, and confidante. Dating also offers opportunities for companionship, status, sexual experimentation, and conflict resolution. However, courtship has different meanings for young women and men. Whereas for men, courtship involves themes of "staying in control," for women, themes involve "dependence on the relationship." Violence is one of the tactics used to gain control in a relationship.

Dating and Sexual Scripts

It appears that dating violence and sexual assault among adolescents and college students is so prevalent, in part, because of the overall structure and meaning of dating in our culture, which give men greater power. Adolescent dating patterns follow a fairly well-defined script that has not changed much over several decades. A dating script is a set of rules to be followed by girls and boys that affords men greater power relative to women because they are expected to initiate and pay for dates, and because relationships generally are perceived as more important to women than to men. Women are assumed to be responsible for "how far things go," and if things "get out of hand," it is their fault.

Relationship Traps for Women

Romantic relationships may become "destructive traps" for women when they feel they must put maintenance of the relationship above their own self-interests. Violence is more likely to occur in serious than in casual relationships. Women who experience ongoing victimization often report more commitment to and love for their partner; they are less likely to end the relationship because of abuse and they allow their partner to control them. These women also report more traditional attitudes toward women's roles, justify their abuse, and tend to romanticize relationships and love. Many students believe dating violence is more acceptable in serious relationships and is not sufficient grounds for ending the relationship. . . .

Incidence and Prevalence of Dating Violence

Studies indicate that dating violence during the teen years is pervasive, with as many as 35% of female and male students surveyed reporting at least one episode, with fewer experiencing recurring violence. A national survey of approximately 2,600 college women and 2,100 college men revealed that within the year prior to the survey, 81% of the men and 88% of the women had engaged in some form of verbal aggression, either as perpetrator or victim. Approximately 37% of the men and 35% of the women inflicted some form of physical aggression, and about 39% of the men and 32% of the women sustained some physical aggression. In this survey, all types of heterosexual relationships were included, from the most casual to the most serious, thus providing a comprehensive estimate of the scope of courtship violence. The measures of verbal aggression included arguing heatedly, yelling, sulking, and stomping. Physical aggression included throwing something at someone, pushing, grabbing, shoving, or hitting. The ubiquity of courtship violence among college students is apparent in that comparable rates of violence have been observed across gender, ethnic group, and type of institution of higher learning, such as private or public, religious or secular. All the evidence to date suggests that it would be unusual to find a high school or college student who had not been involved in some form of verbal aggression and a substantial number who have not been involved in physical aggression. Also, it appears that the same people who report inflicting some form of violence are the ones who report experiencing violence.

Motives for Dating Violence

Some studies suggest that women and men do not appear to differ in the frequency with which they report engaging in aggressive acts. However, this cannot be taken to mean there are no gender-related differences in aggression. On the contrary, studies have shown that the motives and consequences for such behavior are different for women and men. Most data suggest that women are more likely to engage in aggression for self-defense, whereas men report that they aggress to instill fear and to intimidate.

Predictors of Dating Violence

The underlying processes involved in courtship violence for women and for men appear different. The results of studies are quite consistent. Although the best predictor of being aggressive is having an aggressive partner, other predictors are different for women and men. Men who are quick to react to anger, believe that violence will aid in winning an argument, and have successfully used violence in other situations are likely to do so again. Similarities between men who engage in courtship violence and wife batterers have been found. Drug use, divorced parents, stressful life events, beliefs that violence between intimates is justifiable, and less traditional sex-role attitudes also have been identified as predictors.

For women, on the other hand, a history of parent-child abuse, as well as anxiety, depression, and drug use, have been related to courtship violence. It is likely that these latter factors are reactions to childhood experiences with violence, rendering women more vulnerable to being the target of a violent partner, which in turn increases the likelihood of being violent. Learning about violence in the home and associating with peers who endorse the use of violence may provide a backdrop of social norms that legitimate violence. Violence is learned as a tactic of dealing with interpersonal conflict.

However, women may be the initiator of aggression in dating relationships. [Others] have shown that prior experience with sexual victimization as well as physical victimization in a dating context during adolescence predicts being physically aggressive in dating situations during the first year of college. Prior experience with violence may disinhibit aggression, thus enabling women to overcome gender-related constraints on aggressive expression. A recently developed theory proposes that threat and perceptions of threat underlie relational violence. Past victimization experiences, including witnessing and experiencing parental aggression, may increase women's expectations of harm from male partners. Thus, offensive aggression may actually be preemptive aggression. Feelings of isolation resulting from prior victimization (reflected in passivity) may contribute to a greater awareness of threat associated with the intimidating behaviors of their male partners, resulting in the perceived need not only for self-defensive efforts, but for offensive (or initiating acts) as well.

Sexual Violence

As men and women establish intimate relationships, dominance and violence also surface in the form of sexual aggression. Although the legal definition of rape appears straightforward, both the social meaning of the term rape and the circumstances surrounding an act of forced sexual intercourse make some reluctant to use the label. The term rape has been shown to have different meanings for women and men. College students in general, and sexually aggressive men in particular, believe that sexual precedence (i.e., a past history of sexual intercourse) reduces the legitimacy of sexual refusal. Moreover, some people are hesitant to label forced sex as rape if consent was not explicitly verbalized, even if threats, intimidation, or incapacitation are present. Although a woman may not realize that forced sexual intercourse by an acquaintance during a date is rape, this does not change the legal definition of the act as rape, nor does it reduce the culpability of the perpetrator. Furthermore, whether a sexual assault is labeled rape does not alter the consequences for the victim.

Frequency of Sexual Victimization

A comprehensive survey asked over 3,000 college women from 32 institutions of higher education across the United States about sexual experiences since the age of 14. Of those surveyed, over half of the women (53.7%) had experienced some form of sexual victimization; 15.4% had experienced acts by a man that met the legal definition of rape (though only 27% labeled the experience rape), and 12.1% had experienced attempted rape. An additional 11.9% had been verbally pressured into sexual intercourse, and the remaining 14.4% had experienced some other form of unwanted sexual contact, such as forced kissing or fondling with no attempted penetration. More recent studies confirm these high numbers among college students in the United States and among Canadians, as well as among a probability sample of 8,000 women in the United States.

High school women also appear to be at greater risk for rape than previously thought. A recent survey of 834 entering college students found that 13% reported being raped between the ages of 14 and 18, and an additional 16% reported being victims of an attempted rape. Most victims knew the perpetrator, and the assaults frequently occurred in a dating context. Similar rates of reported sexual assault have been found among adolescents, indicating that sexual assault is not just a problem for college campuses. It is a frequent experience during the high school years as well.

The . . . survey described earlier also examined the sexual experiences of over 2,900 college men. Of this group, 4.4% admitted to behaviors meeting the legal definition of rape, 3.3% admitted to attempted rape, 7.2% to sexual coercion, and 10.2% to forced or coerced sexual contact; thus, 25.1% of the college men admitted to some form of sexual aggression. Similar rates have been reported in college samples and in a community college sample. . . .

Risk Factors for Perpetration

The typical acquaintance rapist appears to be a "normal" guy. He is not a crazed psychopath, although he may display psychopathy-related traits.

Among college students, alcohol use, athletic affiliation, and fraternity membership have been associated with sexual aggression toward women. Other significant correlates of sexual assault include a history of family violence; an early and varied sexual history, including many sexual partners; a history of delinquency; acceptance of rape myths; an impulsive personality; hedonistic and dominance motives for sex; lower than average sense of self-worth; and lower religiosity; as well as peers who condone and encourage sexual conquests. Finally, sexually aggressive men are more likely to perceive a wider range of behaviors as indicative of sexual interest than do nonsexually aggressive men and are attracted to sexual aggression.

It appears that sexual promiscuity and hostile attitudes combine to characterize sexually aggressive men, particularly in men who tend to be self-centered and have little regard for others (i.e., low in empathy). Sexually aggressive men tend to be more domineering with women, using "one-up" messages aimed at "gaining control of the exchange" (e.g., bragging about oneself and criticizing the other person). Domineeringness in conversation may be a test sexually aggressive men use to identify vulnerable targets. A woman who resists the domination may be seen as unavailable, but a subordinate response from a woman may indicate that she is a potential target. Furthermore, it is likely that a woman experiencing the helplessness and powerlessness associated with a previous victimization will be less likely to resist the man's domineering behavior than women without a victimization history. This may help us understand why and how perpetrators target vulnerable women.

Ethnicity and Sexual Assault

Dating violence and sexual assault pose additional problems among adolescents who are not White, middle class, and heterosexual. Although it is difficult for any young person to admit being victimized by a dating partner, it is especially so for ethnic minorities. The legacy of slavery and distrust of White authority figures have made it difficult for African American teens to report abusive dating relationships. Asian/Pacific women, too, are reluctant to disclose abuse because of cultural traditions of male dominance and reticence to discuss private relationships in public. For lesbian teens, the problem is complicated by the fact that, in reporting abuse, they may have to reveal their sexual orientation, something they may not be psychologically ready to do. . . .

Violence in Marriage and Other Committed Relationships

The patterns established during adolescence may continue in adulthood. The greatest threat of violence to adult women is from their intimate partners; for men, the greatest threat is from other men. Women are more likely to be physically or sexually assaulted by an intimate partner than by a stranger. It is estimated that 2 to 3 million women are assaulted by male partners in the United States each year and that at least half of these women are severely assaulted (i.e., punched, kicked, choked, beaten, threatened with a knife or gun, or had a knife or gun used on them). As many as 21% to 34% of women will be assaulted by an intimate partner during adulthood. Further, it is estimated that 33% to 50% of all battered wives are also the victim of partner rape. Studies have shown that 22% to 40% of the women who seek health care at clinics or emergency rooms are victims of battering.

Intimate violence may escalate, resulting in homicide. Approximately 66% of family violence deaths are women killed by their male partners; over 50% of all murders of women are committed by current or former partners. In contrast, only 6% of male murder victims are killed by wives or girlfriends. Murder-suicides are almost always cases where the man kills his partner or estranged partner and then kills himself. He also may kill his children or other family members before he kills himself. Although there are instances where a woman murders a partner who has been abusing her, this happens less frequently than men killing partners they have abused chronically.

When women kill their partners, they are often reacting to abuse rather than initiating it. A study of women who killed partners found several common factors. The women were in abusive relationships and the abuse was increasing in frequency and severity. The increased violence was associated with a rise in the number and seriousness of the women's injuries. It was common for these men to have raped their spouses, forced them into other sexual acts, and made threats against their lives. The men typically used excessive alcohol daily and used recreational drugs. The effects of this intense and repeated abuse has prompted attorneys to use "the battered-woman syndrome" in court cases to describe the psychological state of battered women who kill. . . .

Ethnicity and Intimate Partner Violence

Community-based surveys have found that 25% of African American women and 8% of Hispanic women reported at least one physical sexual assault experience in their lifetime. However, when norms regarding violence approval, age, and economic stressors are held constant, . . . [no] differences between Hispanic Americans and Americans [have been found] in the odds of wife abuse. However, . . . being born in the United States increases the risk of wife assaults by Mexican and Puerto Rican American husbands. Importantly, . . . in any group, regardless of SES, the presence of norms sanctioning wife assaults is a risk factor for wife abuse. . . .

Violence in Lesbian Relationships

Relationship abuse is not limited to heterosexual relationships. Although there have been no prevalence studies, research with convenience samples indicates that partner abuse is a significant problem for lesbian women and gay men. Gay male couples report slightly less sexual abuse than lesbian couples, but more severe physical violence. Apparently, violence in committed relationships is not simply a gender issue. Issues of power and control arise in all relationships, and provide the basis for abuse. Partner abuse has been associated with issues of power and dependency in both lesbian and heterosexual couples. For lesbians and gay men, the internalization of societal homophobic attitudes may, in part, lead to aggression against partners and reduce reporting due to threats that they may be "outed" by their partner. For gay men, the fear of AIDS or the stress of having AIDS or caring for a partner with AIDS may be associated with abuse. Fortunately, shelters and organizations are slowly beginning to assimilate information on the issue. For gay men, there are still few resources.

Elder Abuse: Violence Toward Elderly Women

Power inequalities between women and men continue into the later years and result in the continued victimization of older women by men. . . . [E]lder abuse is often spouse abuse that has continued for years. Although most data on elder abuse do not look specifically at spouse abuse or sexual assault, some patterns do emerge from the available data. In one of the only random-sample-based surveys examining elder abuse, . . . in the over-65 population of Boston, 2% were the victims of physical abuse, with 58% of those being abused by a spouse and 24% by an adult child. Victimization by adult children reflects the change in relationship dynamics as parents age. Adult children gain power and the aging lose power in a social context that values youth and devalues maturity. Although half the victims were men, women were much more severely injured than men. . . . [S]ubmissiveness, self-blame, self-doubt, and lack of social support mediate the effects of older woman abuse.

Even less is known about the sexual abuse of older women. This remains a taboo topic, although there is growing recognition that the problem needs attention. Clinical evidence suggests that older women may be raped in their homes as well as in institutions (such as residential treatment facilities and nursing homes). . . . [E]xamples of the sexual abuse of women in nursing homes [are difficult to verify] because of dementia and other memory-related problems among this group. . . . [A] study of elder sexual abuse in Great Britain [found] a ratio of 6:1 female:male victims; . . . the perpetrators were more likely to be sons than husbands. . . . [In a comparison of] the rape experiences of a group of older women (age 55 to 87) with those of a younger group . . . greater injury [was found in the older women]. Additionally, one study suggests that men who sexually assault older women may suffer from more severe psychopathological processes and that their assaults are more brutal and motivated by anger and a need for power. . . .

The American Association of Retired Persons produced a report identifying similarities between elder abuse and other forms of violence against women. The report identified power imbalances, secrecy and isolation, personal harm to victims, social expectations and sex roles, inadequate resources to protect victims, and the control perpetrators have over their actions. The report further suggested that life span factors pose unique problems for elder abuse. . . .

Understanding Violence against Girls and Women

The pattern of intimate violence, where women are the victims and men are the perpetrators, is not due to biological destiny. Women are not born victims and men are not biologically predetermined to be aggressors. Rather, stereotypes of how women and men are supposed to behave, experiences that reinforce stereotypical behaviors, and a social structure that supports power inequities between women and men all contribute to violence against women.

To understand violence against girls and women we must first recognize that culturally based socialization practices encourage men to be aggressors and women to be victims. In societies where there is no formal hierarchy that privileges one group over another and in which women and men exercise relatively equal power, general levels of aggression and male violence against women are low. As this chapter has described, gendered violence is learned early in life and continues in our different relationships as we age. Statistics allow us to examine larger social influences and overall patterns found in society. They reveal that women are the victims of intimate violence more often than men at every stage of development, with the exception of early childhood physical abuse.

Although women also may be the perpetrators of aggression, this does not destroy the argument that intimate violence is related to gender and social roles. The reason is that patriarchy as a social system carries with it the message that the more powerful are entitled to dominate the less powerful. Aggression and violence are inherently gendered; even when girls and women act aggressively, they are responding to and enacting male models of behavior and control, models our culture has endorsed. Because men more often hold higher-status positions than women, it follows that men will abuse more than women; because adults are more powerful than children, children will be victimized more than adults; and because the young are more powerful than the elderly, the aged are more at risk.

Inequality in relationships, coupled with cultural values that embrace domination of the weaker by the stronger, creates the potential for violence. The more powerful partner can control money, resources, activities, and decisions. Partner abuse has been associated with issues of power and dependency in both lesbians and heterosexual couples. Both men and women learn that violence is a method people use to get their way. When individuals use violence and get their way, they are reinforced and thus more likely to use aggression in the future; however, men have historically received greater rewards for aggression and violence than have women. Women are as likely as men to aggress in situations that are congruent with their gender identities and where they hold relatively more power.

Traditionally, secrecy and myths regarding male-female relationships trivialized and/or justified male violence against women. The women's movement has done much to bring to public awareness the extent of the harm done to women by men and has prompted redefinitions that acknowledge the violence. Thus, for example, no longer is rape defined as a sexual act, sexual harassment as standard working conditions, and wife abuse as a legitimate way to "show the little woman who is boss"; rather, each are seen as acts by men intended to dominate and control women.

Violence against women, in its various forms, is now recognized as a public health and social problem. Hence, research has moved from focusing on individual psychopathology to identifying the sociocultural factors that contribute to such violence. Also, communities, institutions, and organizations are combating violence against women by developing interventions that not only help individuals but also promote change in values and attitudes at the societal level.

Richard B. Felson

Violence and Gender Reexamined

Violence involving women is special, according to the feminist perspective and current conventional wisdom. Academic feminism includes different strands, but most feminists would agree with the following assertions about violence involving women:

1. Sexism plays an important role in male violence against women.
2. Because sexism is pervasive, male violence against women is at epidemic levels, or at least occurs with enough frequency to be considered a special social problem.
3. Violence involving women typically has special motives—sexist men use violence to control women or to demonstrate their power, whereas women use violence to defend themselves.
4. Patriarchal societies support violence against women by blaming the victim and by treating offenders leniently.

I have argued and provided evidence that each of these statements is misleading or false. There is not an epidemic of violence against women: Its frequency reflects the frequency of violence generally. Men are more likely than women to injure their partners, but the pattern reflects gender differences in strength and the tendency to engage in violence, not male domination. The frequency of partner violence reflects the inevitable conflict that exists in intimate relationships, not sexism. Finally, societies are no more likely to blame female victims than male victims or to treat those who attack women more leniently. In fact, societies make a special attempt to protect women and generally treat those who offend against them more severely. . . .

Comparative Approach

I have used a comparative approach to examine whether men's violence against women or wives is special. The approach is useful in disentangling the effects of gender of perpetrator, gender of target, and whether the perpetrator is an intimate partner of the target. It enables one to convert loosely stated arguments into clear, testable hypotheses. . . .

The comparisons should apply to both sexual and nonsexual violence. In the case of sexual coercion and partner violence, comparisons must control for the fact that there are many more heterosexual than homosexual people.

For example, in computing the frequency of homosexual partner violence, the denominator might be the number of gay men. The hypotheses implied by the feminist approach and the corresponding evidence are presented and critiqued as follows:

Hypothesis 1

The highest frequency of violence should occur [(for men aggressing against women)] because there is an epidemic of male violence against women. This hypothesis is not supported: Violence against women is much less frequent than violence against men. The most frequent type of violence involves men.

Hypothesis 2

The rate of male violence against women should vary across cultures and over time independently of other rates of violence. This hypothesis is not supported: Temporal and cross-national variation in homicide victimization rates are similar for men and women. When rates of violence against women are high, rates of violence against men are also high. Cross-national comparisons also reveal that male victimization rates dominate homicide statistics: There is much less variation in rates of homicide against women than in rates in homicide against men. Evidence from international crime victimization surveys does not support the idea that U.S. rape rates are particularly high or that they are high relative to the rate of general violence. American students do report more sexual coercion than Swedish students, but they report more violence generally.

Hypothesis 3

Men who use violence against women should be more likely to have sexist attitudes than men who commit violence against men. This hypothesis is not supported: The gender-related attitudes of men who use violence against women are similar to the attitudes of other criminals. Male criminal offenders are more likely than other men to have negative attitudes toward women, but the interpretation is unclear: Offenders express more antisocial attitudes generally.

Hypothesis 4

Men who have committed a violent act against a woman should be more likely to have a history of violence against women than men who have committed a violent act against a man. This hypothesis is not supported: Most men who commit violence against women are generalists who target both men and women. Their histories of violence against women are therefore similar to those of men who use violence against men.

Hypothesis 5

Men's violence (and other behavior) directed at female partners should be more likely to involve a control motive than similar behavior involving other gender-relationship combinations. This hypothesis has mixed support: Male assaults on female partners are more likely to be preceded by threats than assaults involving other gender-relationship combinations, suggesting a more important role for the control motive. However, studies that examine gender differences in the use of nonviolent means of control cast doubt on the idea that men have a greater desire to control their partners than women. Women are just as likely as men (and perhaps more likely) to attempt to control their partner's activities, and this behavior is just as highly related to women's violence as men's violence. In addition, women are more likely than men to complain—a verbal means of control—when they have grievances with their partners. This evidence suggests that when men use violence to control their partners, it is because of their greater coercive power—they are bigger, not bossier.

Hypothesis 6

Men involved in verbal conflicts with their female partners should be particularly likely to use violence, because many men believe that violence is a legitimate method of domination. This hypothesis is not supported: Both men and women show greater reluctance to use violence with their partners. Verbal conflicts are less, not more, likely to become physical when the antagonists are partners than when they are strangers. Only minor violence against children is legitimated according to evidence on the relative frequency of violence and verbal aggression.

Hypotheses 7a and 7b

Men should be more likely than women to engage in violence against their heterosexual partners due to sexism and men's desire for control over these partners. This difference should exceed gender differences in violence against other targets. This hypothesis is not supported: Survey research of minor violence involving heterosexual couples has found that men and women have similar rates. Men are more likely than women to engage in serious violence against their partners, probably because of their greater coercive power. However, the gender difference in partner violence is not as large as the gender difference in stranger violence. The evidence suggests that men are inhibited about using violence against female partners, not specially motivated to use it.

Hypothesis 8

Love triangles should be more likely to motivate men's violence than women's violence, particularly men's violence toward their partners, given the strong male desire to control partners. This hypothesis is not supported: When men commit homicide it is less likely to stem from love triangles than when women commit homicide. When men kill their partners, it is no more likely to stem from love triangles than when women kill their partners. The evidence suggests that women are just as angry with unfaithful partners; they just are not as violent as men. In addition, male protagonists are much more likely to kill their rivals than their partners. In love triangles involving college students, men are more likely than women to attempt to intimidate or control male rivals than to intimidate or control female partners.

Hypothesis 9

Heterosexual men should be more likely than homosexual men to engage in violence against their partners. This hypothesis is not supported. In fact, data from the [National Crime Victimization Survey] suggests that gay men are *more* likely to be violent toward their partners than are heterosexual men. In addition, there is some evidence that homosexual men are just as likely as heterosexual men to use sexual coercion. The evidence suggests that violence against women is not a function of male dominance or special attitudes toward women. Rather, men are more violent than women and they sometimes use violence with their partners or those with whom they desire sexual relations, whether the target is a man or woman.

Hypothesis 10

Men's violence against women, particularly their wives, should be less likely to be reported to the police than other violence and less likely to lead to arrest, prosecution, and punishment. Authorities and other third parties should be less likely to believe the charges of female victims and more likely to blame them for the crime. This hypothesis is not supported: No statistical interactions between gender and social relationship on reporting and legal treatment were observed. Male violence against female partners is not less likely to be reported, and the reaction of the criminal justice system is not special. There is evidence of gender discrimination in the criminal justice system, but it favors women. In general, violence against women is more likely to be reported than violence against men, and it is more likely to lead to arrest, prosecution, and punishment.

Women are less likely to report sexual assaults to the police than other crimes, particularly sexual assaults committed by acquaintances. However, evidence suggests that the underreporting of sexual assaults by acquaintances is the result of greater privacy concerns, not lack of confidence that the case will be successfully prosecuted. Research has not examined whether female victims are more or less likely than male victims to report sexual assaults to the police. However, women are probably more likely to report sexual assaults than men; research shows that they are more likely to report other crimes, and sexual assault victimization is probably more stigmatizing for male victims.

There is no evidence that the police are more skeptical when women charge their husbands with assault than when men charge their wives; the opposite may occur because of (valid) stereotypes about male violence. Anecdotal evidence suggests that the police are often skeptical of female charges of rape, but we do not know whether the police are more skeptical of female charges of rape than male charges of rape, or of male and female charges of other crimes. If the police are more skeptical about rape charges, there may be a good reason for it. Evidence suggests that rape charges are more likely to be false than charges for other crimes. We also know from DNA evidence that there are many cases of misidentification in rape.

Finally, there is evidence that female victims of rape are assigned less, not more, blame than male victims of rape. Observers assign blame to rape victims when they think victims have engaged in irresponsible behavior; however, they assign the bulk of blame to offenders. Finally, prosecution and conviction rates for rape are similar to other violent crimes, and convicted rapists are punished severely relative to most other crimes.

Hypothesis 11

Legal authorities and other observers are more tolerant of violence against women who violate gender roles than violence against men who violate gender roles, and they treat offenders more leniently. This hypothesis is not supported: There is some evidence that we judge men more harshly than women for violations of gender roles. In addition, the criminal justice system does not punish women more for violations of gender roles (e.g., sexual violations) than for other criminal behavior, and it generally punishes women less severely than men for the same crime.

Hypothesis 12

Women's violence against their male partners is more likely to be motivated by self-defense and victim-precipitated than other violence. This hypothesis is not supported: Neither victim precipitation nor self-defense is especially prevalent when women kill their male partners. Gender does have additive effects, however: Men are more likely to initiate violence in serious incidents (although not in minor incidents).

In sum, the comparative method is useful for testing theoretical claims that a particular type of violence is special. None of the hypotheses about the distinctiveness of violence against women or wives suggested by a feminist approach are supported. Many are in the opposite direction to the one predicted. The results suggest that the study of partner violence and violence against women she incorporated into the study of violence. Until future evidence suggests otherwise, the parsimony principle suggests that social scientists should prefer more general theories of violence. . . .

Race and Class

I have not said much about the role of race and social class in violence against women. Some scholars would criticize the neglect of these demographic variables, suggesting that it is critical that one study the intersection of "race, class, and gender." The comparative approach and standard statistical language are useful in considering the issue empirically and resolving the problem. We must be concerned with the intersection of race, class, and gender if we observe a three-way statistical interaction between these variables. If the effects of gender on violence depend on both race and socioeconomic status, then we must incorporate interaction terms in our equations and qualifications in our theoretical discussion. If the effects of gender depend on race alone or social class alone, then we need to incorporate two-way interaction terms. . . .

It is clear that there are class and race differences in violent behavior generally. Higher rates of violence among poor people and among African Americans are typically attributed to discrimination and lack of economic opportunity. It is therefore interesting that this same treatment does not lead women to have higher rates of violence than men—the gender difference is strong and in the opposite direction. The pattern suggests that either women are not subject to much discrimination or that discrimination does not lead to violent crime or that discrimination leads to violent crime only under as yet unspecified conditions. For example, some commentators believe that race and class effects are mediated by neighborhood effects. . . .

Both feminism and chivalry lead those who study violence involving women to attempt to protect the image of women. Scholars avoid ideas that might cast women in a negative light, because such ideas might support stereotypes and encourage sexism. For example, although we can talk about gender differences in violence, it is controversial to mention gender differences in complaining; it sounds like a negative stereotype about women. It is ironic that so many sociologists and other social scientists condemn stereotyping, when they are in the stereotype business. Any discussion of gender differences involves generalizations about men and women. Science suffers when hypotheses about group differences are evaluated according to the image they project for protected groups. The scientific analysis of group differences is often in conflict with the promotion of tolerance and diversity. In the study of human behavior, no group comes out unscathed. . . .

One could argue that, overall, feminist influence has been positive because it drew attention to a social problem. Even if their methods were inadequate and their conclusions erroneous, they influenced the public to devote attention and resources to helping female victims. I do not agree that the end justifies the means in this instance for three reasons: (1) There is no evidence that the feminist approach has had any effect on reducing rates of violence against women, (2) bad research produces bad public policy, and (3) social scientists lose credibility when they generate information on social problems that is later revealed to be false.

POSTSCRIPT

Are Expressions of Aggression Related to Gender?

Because of the notion that aggression is a predominantly male attribute, researchers have disproportionately used male as opposed to female participants in their research studies. Even when female aggression has been the research focus, the conceptualization of aggression has stemmed from the "male" perspective on aggression. For example, much of the research on aggression has focused specifically on physical aggression using the teacher-learner paradigm. In this paradigm, the participant, acting as teacher, punishes the "learner" with electric shocks for incorrect responses. Research has shown, however, that women perceive electric shock more negatively and a less-effective deterrent than do men; thus, they are more reluctant than men to administer it. Research demonstrating gender differences in aggression might be reflecting gender differences in a willingness to behave physically aggressively rather than the potential for aggression.

A continued focus on types of aggression in which men consistently emerge as more aggressive than women fails to examine those situations in which women might aggress and the modes of aggression they might adopt. Cross-cultural analyses suggest that despite tremendous cross-cultural variation, men tend to be more physically aggressive but women may use more indirect aggression. Men are more likely to use aggression that produces pain or physical harm, whereas women are more likely to use aggression that produces psychological or social harm. Because the majority of researchers have been male, they may have chosen questions and contexts regarding aggression of greatest personal relevance.

Thus, when asking questions about gender and aggression, aggression should be defined as any behavior directed toward another person or a person's property with the intent to do harm, even if the aggressor was unsuccessful. The behavior could be physical or verbal, active or passive, direct or indirect (i.e., aggressor may remain anonymous), and the consequence for the target could be physical or psychological. All forms of harm-doing behavior, including self-defense, should be considered because in some cases, such as domestic violence, it is difficult to distinguish retaliative from self-defense motives. Also, aggression, broadly defined, allows us to examine more fully the broad range of harm-doing behaviors available to human beings. Thus, whether than asking who is more aggressive, it might be more productive to ask what are the forms and functions of aggression for women and men, and to what degree is the expression of aggression shaped by cultural expectations regarding masculinity (power, dominance, strength) and femininity (nurturing, passive, weak).

Suggested Readings

Lyn Mikel Brown, *Raising Their Voices: The Politics of Girls' Anger* (Cambridge, MA: Harvard University Press, 1998).

Lyn Mikel Brown, *Girlfighting: Betrayal and Rejection Among Girls* (New York: New York University Press, 2005).

Jonathan L. Freedman, *Media Violence and Its Effect on Aggression* (Toronto: University of Toronto Press, 2002).

Sharon Lamb, *The Secret Lives of Girls: What Good Girls Really Do—Sex Play, Aggression, and their Guilt* (New York: The Free Press Simon and Schuster, 2002).

Myriam Miedzian, *Boys Will Be Boys: Breaking the Link Between Masculinity and Violence* (New York: Lantern Books, 2002).

ISSUE 8

Gender Symmetry: Do Women and Men Commit Equal Levels of Violence Against Intimate Partners?

YES: Murray A. Straus and Ignacio L. Ramirez, from "Gender Symmetry in Prevalence, Severity, and Chronicity of Physical Aggression Against Dating Partners by University Students in Mexico and USA," *Aggressive Behavior* (2007)

NO: Suzanne C. Swan and David L. Snow, from "The Development of a Theory of Women's Use Of Violence In Intimate Relationships," *Violence Against Women* (2006)

ISSUE SUMMARY

YES: Murray A. Straus and his colleague Ignacio L. Ramirez argue that women are just as likely to commit physical aggression against dating partners as are men, suggesting that gender symmetry exists in different cultural contexts.

NO: On the other hand, social psychologist Suzanne C. Swan and colleague David L. Snow argue that women's use of aggression does not equate to gender symmetry. Rather cultural context, motives, and history of trauma must be considered.

$\mathbf{O}$ne of the most contentious and emotional issues in the intimate partner violence (IPV) literature surrounds the issue of "gender symmetry" in the use of aggression in relationships. For many years the stereotype was of the male batterer and the female victim. Mental health, medical emergency room, and criminal justice data support this assumption. Many more women than men show up at shelters and emergency rooms suffering from the psychological and physical effects of abuse; many more women than men are likely to be murdered by an intimate partner. In contrast, most survey research that asks high school aged youth, college students, and community samples about their use of verbal and physical aggression in intimate relationships finds a very different pattern of results. In these studies as many, and sometimes more, women as men report aggression against their partners, at least when the Conflict Tactics Scale (CTS) is the research instrument of choice. These data have led some researchers to conclude that such "gender symmetry" indicates that gender is not a central issue in intimate partner violence and that the study of IPV should move from the study of gender to other issues such as dominance. However, the same studies that use the CTS still find that women are more likely to be injured than men, suggesting to a different group of researchers that gender is still a central construct of interest. This perspective suggests that it is important to acknowledge and study women's aggression toward male partners, but to maintain a focus on gender. In fact, feminists have suggested that maintenance of the myth of the nonaggressive female contributes to continued discrimination against women. That is, if women are not aggressive, they must turn to men for protection (giving up their independence in exchange for the protection), they are not capable of leadership positions (based on the assumption that aggression is correlated with power, authority, and assertiveness), and if they are aggressive, they must be mentally ill (i.e., deviation from expected gender roles is an indicator of mental illness). Feminist research is challenging this myth in numerous ways, as reflected in several special issues of journals (*Violence Against Women, Psychology of Women Quarterly, Sex Roles*). In the selections that follow Straus, the developer of the CTS, and his colleague demonstrate the typical pattern of gender symmetry found in survey research. In contrast, the selection by Swann and her colleagues examines the use of women's aggression toward intimate partners and presents a model for understanding female partner violence from a social contextual perspective that emphasizes one's own history of abuse along with the intersection of race, ethnicity, and class factors.

YES

Murray A. Straus and
Ignacio L. Ramirez

Gender Symmetry in Prevalence, Severity, and Chronicity of Physical Aggression Against Dating Partners by University Students in Mexico and USA

Introduction

A controversial issue in research on intimate partner violence (PV from here on) is whether this type of assault is primarily a crime perpetrated by men. A previous paper on this issue shows that when the statistics are based on data from the police or from surveys on crime victimization from 70 to 95% of PV perpetrators are men. On the other hand, the results of almost 200 studies using data from surveys of family problems and conflicts show that ". . . women are as physically aggressive, or more aggressive, than men in their relationships. . . . The aggregate sample size in the reviewed studies exceeds 58,000." The reason why police and crime survey data show PV to be a crime by males, whereas surveys of conflicts between partners in a couple relationship show that it is usually symmetrical or mutual were analyzed in a previous paper and will not be repeated here. Rather, this study is intended to move beyond tabulating the percent of men and women who had assaulted a partner during the time period covered by the study (typically the past year), by providing information on important additional aspects of PV such as the severity, chronicity of the assaults, and gender symmetry of assaults. Specifically, the purposes are:

- To determine the degree to which gender symmetry in PV is found in the diverse socio-cultural contexts in Mexico and the United States.
- To provide more detailed data on gender symmetry by
  - Providing data on the severity and chronicity of attacks by males and females.
  - Classifying couples into three groups: mutually violent, male partner only, and female partner only.
- To compare results based on data provided by male and female respondents.

From *Aggressive Behavior*, vol. 33, issue 4, 2007, pp. 281–289. Copyright © 2007 by John Wiley & Sons. Reprinted by permission.

Methods

Samples

The data [are] from the first four samples of the International Dating Violence Study for which data became available. . . . The data were obtained by administering questionnaires to students in introductory sociology and psychology classes at the Universidad Autonoma de Ciudad Juarez, Mexico, University of Texas at El Paso, Texas Technological University, and the University of New Hampshire.

The data were gathered using procedures reviewed and approved by the boards for protection of human subjects at each of these universities. The purpose of the study and the students' right to not participate were explained orally as well as in printed form at the beginning of each session. Participants were told that the questionnaire asked about their attitudes, beliefs, and experiences they may have had, and that the questionnaire included questions on sensitive issues, including sexual relationships. They were assured of anonymity and confidentiality. A debriefing form was given to each participant as they left. The form explained the study in more detail and provided names and telephone numbers of area mental health services and community resources such as services for battered women. Although 1,554 students completed the questionnaire, as in other surveys, not everyone answered every question. Indeed, to respect the privacy and the voluntary nature of participation the instructions emphasized that respondents were free to omit any question they did not wish to answer. One hundred and eight students (6.9%) did not answer all the questions on violence against a partner. The number of cases analyzed was 1,446 for most of the analyses. However, some analyses are based on as few as 159 cases because they were restricted to the relatively small proportion of respondents who severely assaulted a partner. . . .

Measures

Physical Assault

The revised Conflict Tactics Scales or CTS2 was used to measure physical assault by the respondent. . . . The CTS has been used in many studies of both married and dating partners in the past 25 years and there is extensive evidence of reliability and validity. Respondents are asked to indicate how often they did each of the acts in the CTS and how often their partner did. This allows for analysis of symmetry, as well as patterns of the respondent's behavior. The CTS2 has scales to measure Physical Assault, Injury, Sexual Coercion, Psychological Aggression, and Negotiation. The analyses in this paper used data from the Physical Assault scale.

The CTS2 includes subscales for two levels of severity. The Minor Assault scale includes acts such as slapping or throwing something at the partner. The Severe Assault scale includes acts such as punching and choking. The difference between the minor and severe subscales is analogous to the US legal categories of simple assault and aggravated assault. The following scores were computed:

Prevalence.   Prevalence refers to whether respondents carried out one or more of the 12 acts of physical assault in the CTS in the previous 12 months. The analysis used two measures of prevalence, one for any versus no assault (referred to as "?assault"), and one for severe assault versus both no assaults and minor assaults (referred to as "severe assault").

Severity level.   A problem with the Minor Assault scale is that some of the respondents who reported minor assaults probably also carried out more severe attacks on a partner. To have a variable in which the two are mutually exclusive, respondents were classified into one of three categories: 1 = none, 2 = minor only (i.e., one or more acts of minor violence but no instance of severe violence), and 3 = severe.

Chronicity.   The CTS asks respondents to indicate how many times in the previous year they have either perpetrated or been victim of each of the acts in the scale. Chronicity was calculated only for respondents who reported at least one instance of physical assault. Chronicity therefore indicates the number of times that subjects who were physically aggressive to a partner carried out acts of physical aggression. For a discussion of the rationale of the chronicity measure of the CTS2 see Straus [2001].

Symmetry types.   Three types were identified: *male-only* refers to couples in which violence in the relationship was perpetrated only by the male partner. *Female-only* violence refers to couples where the only violence in the relationship was perpetrated by the female partner. *Both* refers to couples in which both the male and female partner committed at least one of the acts of physical assault in the previous 12 months. Symmetry types were computed only if the respondent reported that they, and/or their partner had perpetrated an assault.

Social Desirability Response Bias

Criminological research that uses self-report data need to take into account defensiveness or minimization of socially undesirable behavior. The Limited Disclosure scale of the PRP [Straus and Mouradian, 1999; Straus et al., 1999] was used to control for the variation in individual respondents' tendencies to minimize socially undesirable behavior. This scale is a 13-item version of the widely used Crown–Marlow social desirability scale developed by Reynolds [1982]. The scale measures the degree to which respondents tend to avoid disclosing socially undesirable behavior.

Socioeconomic Status

Socioeconomic status was measured as a composite of the respondent's mother's and father's education, and family income. To control for differences in educational systems and for differences in incomes and purchasing power across countries and geographic regions, parent's education and family income were standardized (z-scored) separately for each sample, before being summed. For interpretability, the sum was then transformed to a z-score. Thus, in each sample, the score of a respondent indicates the number of standard deviations above or below the mean of respondents in that sample.

Results

Prevalence of Assaults on Dating Partners

Combined samples.   When all four samples are analyzed together, a third of the students (33.7%) reported they had physically assaulted a dating partner in the previous 12 months. This is consistent with many other studies of dating violence by university students.

Sample differences.   The percent of students reporting violence was high in all four samples, but also differed significantly between samples. . . . The lowest rate was in New Hampshire (29.7%), followed by Texas, Non-Mexican Whites (30.9%), Texas Mexican American (34.2%), and the highest rate of assault was in Juarez (46.1%).

Gender differences.   Although there were significant differences between samples, . . . the rates for males and females were similar. Thus, the four samples analyzed in this paper had similar rates of partner-assault by men and women. This finding is consistent with previous research on couple conflict discussed in the introduction.

Severe Assaults on Dating Partners

The similar rates of assaulting a partner by men and women could be misleading because the overall rate combines minor acts such as slapping and throwing things with more severe assaults involving punching, kicking, choking, etc. It is possible that the overall rate of assaults could be equal, but a larger proportion of the assaults by men could be in the form of attacks that are more likely to result in an injury. This possibility was investigated by examining the severity level of assaults.

Combined samples.   Overall, more than one out of ten students (11.4%) reported severely attacking a partner (acts such as punching, kicking, or choking).

Sample differences.   The samples differed significantly in the rate of severe violence. The differences were similar to the difference for the overall violence rate, i.e., the lowest rate was in New Hampshire (9.3%), followed by Mexican-Americans in Texas (12.4%), Non-Mexicans in Texas (14.2%) and highest in Juarez (15%).

Gender differences. [T]he rates of severe assault are almost identical for men and women. Thus, the similarity between men and women in the overall rate of violence against a partner also applies to severe attacks.

When severity level scores were examined, controlling for age, SES, and score on the Social Desirability Response scale no significant differences in the scores of male and female students were found. The interaction of gender and sample was also non-significant indicating that the absence of a gender difference applied to all four samples.

Chronicity of Assaults

Combined samples. The results from these four samples show that, among the couples where there was violence, it was not usually a one-time occurrence. Students who were physically aggressive to a partner carried out a mean of 14.7 acts of physical aggression in the previous 12 months. However, the mean overstates the typical pattern because of a relatively few cases in which violence occurred once a week or more, including a few where it was almost daily. Therefore, the median of four times in the previous year gives a better picture of the typical pattern of violence between dating couples.

A surprising finding was that average number of *severe* assaults (15.6) and the median number of severe assaults (4) was just about the same as mean and medians for the total assault scale. This indicates that when violence is severe, it also tends to be as chronic as minor assaults.

Sample differences. The chronicity of overall assaults was similar across samples. The chronicity of severe assaults was also similar across samples. Thus, the mean chronicity of both overall and severe assaults is similar across the four samples.

Gender differences. There was no significant difference between males and females in the chronicity of physical aggression overall. However, when severe assaults were considered separately, men hit their partner more than twice as frequently as women (mean of 21.9 times versus 9.3 times). The median for severe violence by men was four times in the previous year and for women three times. The large difference between the mean and the median indicates that for both men and women, but especially for men, the high mean score reflects a large influence of a relatively few extremely violent individuals. . . . [R]egardless of whether the mean or median is used, men who severely attacked their partner during the 12 month period covered by this study tended to do so more often than the women who engaged in severe assaults. Tests for a sample by gender interaction were non-significant for both overall and severe assaults. Thus, the analysis indicates that in all four samples, among individuals who assaulted their partners, men, and women did so with similar frequency, in contrast, among individuals who were severely violent, men severely assaulted their partners more frequently than women.

Gender Symmetry in Assaults

Combined samples.   Among the 553 couples where one or both of the partners were violent, in almost three quarters of the cases (71.2%) gender symmetry was found, that is, both partners perpetrated one or more assault. When only one partner was violent, this was more than twice as likely to be the female partner (19.0%) as the male partner (9.8%). Among the 205 couples where there was an act of severe aggression, symmetry was less prevalent (56.6%), but when only one partner was violent, it was again twice as likely to be the female partner (29.8% female only versus 13.7% male partner only).

The finding that women are more likely to be the only violent partner differs from the results of studies of married and cohabiting couples in the general population. General population studies tend to show that, when there is violence by only one partner, it is as likely to be the male partner as the female partner. . . . [F]or [a] nationally representative sample of couples almost identical rates of partner assault by males and females, except for the youngest couples [has been found.] At ages 18–19, the rate for women is 47% greater than the rate for men. At ages 20–24 women exceed men by 18%, however, among respondents 25 and over, rates of partner assault are almost identical for men and women. A meta-analysis of 37 studies of college students and 27 studies of community samples found that in the community samples the rate of PV by women exceeded the male rate only very slightly. However, among the student samples, the female rate was greater than the rate of PV by males. Thus, the younger the individual, the more the female rate of assaulting a partner exceeds the rate for males. If that generalization is correct, the tendency in this sample of students for women to more often be the only violent partner probably reflects the youthfulness of the sample.

Sample differences.   [G]ender symmetry in the overall assault rate across samples [was evident]. [T]he pattern of predominantly mutual violence described above was consistent when the four samples are examined individually. However, [there were] significant differences between samples for severe assaults. The most important difference is that students in the New Hampshire sample had by far the lowest percentage in both categories, and the highest percentage in the Female Only category.

The measure of gender symmetry was based on the questionnaire completed by one partner reporting on both their own behavior and the behavior of the partner. This procedure is open to the possibility that what seems to be symmetry could really be the result of men underreporting their violent behavior. To examine this possibility the Gender Symmetry measure was cross-tabulated by the sex of the respondent, [but] no significant difference in gender symmetry based on reports by male and female partners [emerged].

Discussion

The results of this study provide strong evidence of gender symmetry in respect to violence against a dating partner. First, the results were similar in four different samples with large differences in the socio-cultural setting. Second, the results showing gender symmetry and differences between samples remained after controlling for the age of the respondent, the severity and chronicity of violence, and controlling for socioeconomic status and for social desirability response bias. The results indicate that women and men have similar prevalence rates for both any and severe assaults, and for chronicity of minor assaults. Further, in the majority of couples where one partner is violent, both partners have committed one or more assaults. An important exception to the pattern of gender symmetry was that, among the subgroup of respondents who committed one or more acts of severe violence, men in all four samples did it more often than women. Finally, there is agreement between results based on data provided by males and females.

Methodological Implications

These results have important implications for the methodology of research on PV, and for primary prevention of PV. With respect to methodology, the results show that male or female respondents provide equivalent results. Thus, either partner can be the source of the data in research on PV in non-clinical populations. However, although it is not necessary to obtain data from both partners in a relationship, given that individuals of both sexes appear to underreport their own perpetration, and over-report assaults by partners, in any study of gender differences it is desirable to obtain data from both male and female respondents. Additionally, the parallel results in each of the four cultural settings suggests that the Conflict Tactics Scales is appropriate for use in cross-cultural research.

The robustness of the results cited, and the consistency of the results with many previous studies showing gender symmetry in PV, adds urgency to the need for steps to extend efforts at primary and secondary prevention of PV to women offenders. Also relevant are the studies showing that women initiate PV as often as men and the studies showing that women are injured more often and more seriously than men. Consequently, programs and policies aimed at primary prevention of PV *by women* are crucial for reducing the victimization of not only men but also women.

The High Proportion of Female Violence in New Hampshire

The high percentage in the Female Only and Both Violent category in New Hampshire could reflect the operation of two principles. One is the "convergence theory" of crime by women. This theory holds that as women become equal in other spheres of life, they will also tend to become more equal in respect to committing crime. The data for New Hampshire fit the convergence theory. First, New Hampshire had the highest degree of equality between women and men of the four samples. Second, although New Hampshire had the lowest overall rate of PV, among the couples where violence occurred, it had the largest proportion committed by women.

A second possibility is the cost-benefit theory formulated by Archer. He found that ". . . sex differences in partner aggression follow the perceived costs and benefits of physically aggressing in that social setting." In patriarchal social settings, violation of the male dominance principle in any form, and specifically by hitting a male partner, is likely to elicit severe physical retaliation. However, the social context in New Hampshire is almost the opposite. Women at the University of New Hampshire tend to come from high education and high-income families. Because of the small size of the state, many students live at home and even those living on campus are usually less than an hour from their home. They are thus in relatively protected positions. However, that also tends to be true of students in Ciudad Juarez and El Paso. Perhaps most important, women in New Hampshire have a relatively high degree of equality with men and physical violence against female partners is relatively low compared to other states of the USA. These characteristics may lower the costs women perceive of hitting a partner, and thus alter the cost-benefit ratio enough to produce a higher rate of violence by women than in the other samples.

These comments suggest some issues for future research. For example, why do women, who are on average weaker than men, engage in and initiate violence at least as often as men, whereas outside of family and dating relationships, women engage in a fraction of the violence perpetrated by men? Although Straus has outlined a theoretical model which might explain the discrepancy, it has yet to be tested. Another important avenue of research is twin studies which could provide information on genetic and environmental factors that predict PV. . . . Another needed type of research on gender symmetry in PV concerns the social context. One aspect of social context that has been investigated is the degree to which the society and the family system is male-dominant. However, the many other possible social context effects is illustrated by the Culture of Honor theory which states that violence in defense of honor will be more prevalent in ancestrally herding than in traditionally faming communities. The differences between samples in this study are consistent with that theory. . . .

Prevention Implications

Almost all primary and secondary prevention efforts are based on the assumption that PV is perpetrated primarily by men. There are several reasons for this false assumption. First, programs to end PV were initiated by and continue to be a major effort of the women's movement. Another reason is that women are much more likely to be physically, psychologically, and economically injured than men. Finally, about 90% of assaults and murders outside the family are perpetrated by men and it is easy to assume that this must also apply to PV.

PV by men, but not by women has been decreasing since the mid 1970s but PV by women on male partners have stayed about the same. The failure of prevention and treatment programs to address PV by women may partly explain why PV by men has decreased, but PV by women has remained constant. An ironic aspect is that although the number of male victims has remained high, there is no funding for services for male victims, and almost no research on male victims of PV.

Rather than ignoring assaults by female partners, primary prevention of PV requires strong efforts to end assaults by women. A fundamental reason is the intrinsic moral wrong of assaulting a spouse, as expressed in the fact that such assaults are criminal acts, even when no injury occurs. Second, males are the victims of about a third of injuries inflicted on partners, including about a third of homicides of partners. Third is the unintended validation by women of the traditional cultural norms tolerating a certain level of violence between spouses. A fourth reason for a strong effort to reduce PV by women is the danger of escalation when women engage in "harmless" minor violence. [I]f both partners were violent, it increases the probability that assaults are likely to persist or escalate in severity over [a] 2 year period; whereas if only one partner engages in physical attacks, the probability of a subsequent violence decreases. Finally, when a woman assaults her partner, it "models" violence for the children and therefore contributes to PV in the next generation. This modeling effect is as strong for assaults by women as is assaults by men.

Although it is essential that primary and secondary prevention of PV include a major focus on violence by women as well as men, the needed change must be made with extreme care for a number of reasons. First, it must be done in ways that simultaneously refute the idea that violence by women justifies or excuses violence by their partners. Second, although women may assault partners at approximately the same rate as men, assaults by men usually inflict greater physical, financial, and emotional injury. This means that male violence against women, on average, results in more severe victimization. Thus, a focus on protecting and assisting female victims must remain a priority; despite the fact that services for male victims (now essentially absent) need to be made available. Finally, in many societies women lack full economic, social, political, and human rights. In such cultural contexts, equality for women needs to be given priority as an even more fundamental aspect of primary prevention of PV. Otherwise focusing on PV by women can further exacerbate the oppression of women in those societies.

Suzanne C. Swan and
David L. Snow

 **NO**

The Development of a Theory of Women's Use of Violence in Intimate Relationships

Several reports appeared in the popular press in the late 1990s concluding that women are just as violent as men. These reports often cite the many studies of self-reported physical aggression based on data from the Conflict Tactics Scale (CTS), a widely used measure of physical aggression between intimate partners. Indeed, a meta-analysis of gender differences in rates of physical abuse found that women were slightly more likely than men to use physical aggression against intimate partners. These findings have generated a great deal of controversy, in part because there has been no theoretical framework to explain women's violence.

The conclusion that "women are just as violent as men" is problematic. The studies on which these media reports are based typically examined only physical aggression, not other types of abuse; and they do not place the occurrence of women's violence within a broader social, cultural, or historical context. For example, [the] meta-analysis did not examine sexual assault, stalking, or coercive control; studies that include such behaviors tend to find higher rates of these types of violence committed by males, as do crime surveys. A theoretical framework to guide research on intimate partner violence (IPV) and, therefore, the popular discourse on women's violence, is sorely needed. A comprehensive theory of women's violence with intimate partners should include all types of abuse, not just physical aggression; the woman's abuse against the partner and the partner's abuse against the woman; the woman's relationship history, including experiences of childhood abuse or previous adult relationships that were abusive; her motivations for using abuse; the outcomes of her abuse, for herself, her partner, and her children; and the larger cultural context of gender, race and ethnicity, and social class. Without an understanding of women's violence in context, policy makers and others will draw erroneous conclusions from the data and will implement misguided "gender neutral" policies that penalize women and place them in increased danger.

In fact, "gender neutral" applications of domestic violence (DV) law already harm women. Although dual arrests and mutual restraining orders are necessary in some cases, the overreliance on these practices in some courts is

From *Violence Against Women*, vol. 12, no. 11, 2006, pp. 1026–1040. Copyright © 2006 by Sage Publications. Reprinted by permission. References omitted.

misinformed at best, and at worst, it penalizes women who call on the criminal justice system because their lives are in danger. [O]ur cultural conception of a *battered woman* is that she deserves sympathy and protection by the law; however, a woman who fights back against her partner's violence violates our notion of acceptable feminine behavior. She thus shares the blame for her own victimization. However, it is likely that many battered women have used violence against their partners at some time, as a survival strategy and in retaliation for abuse and humiliation. For example, one study found that 33% of women residing in a DV shelter reported having used minor violence against their partners, and 24% reported using severe violence. [I]ntimate violence is gendered; that is, women's motivations for violence and the context in which the violence takes place are qualitatively different than those of men. A gendered, feminist theoretical approach, that is, one that "uses gender as a central organizing variable for understanding human behavior and social organization", is needed to understand women's violence.

The goal of this article is to provide an interpretive framework for women's violence by proposing a comprehensive, contextual model of women's violence in intimate relationships. A major emphasis is placed on the need for contextualism in the development of such a theory. Contextualism underscores that human behavior does not develop in a social vacuum but is situated within a sociohistorical and cultural context of meanings and relationships, like a message that makes sense only in terms of the total context in which it occurs. Without a focus on context in our development of theory, methods of inquiry, and interventions, there continues to be a strong tendency to locate problems in individuals. This increases the likelihood of "blaming the victim" and leaves us with limited understandings of complex social phenomena.

Based on these principles, the model of women's violence presented here includes: (a) women's violence in the context of their victimization by male partners; (b) factors that influence women's violence and victimization, namely, women's motivations for violent behavior and the coping strategies women utilize in response to relationship problems; (c) the historical context of women's experiences of childhood trauma; and (d) outcomes of depression, anxiety, posttraumatic stress disorder (PTSD), and substance use. This article briefly reviews the literature on each of these dimensions and presents a comprehensive model of women's violence and victimization, its antecedents, and its consequences. When developed, the model is examined within the context of *intersectionality,* that is, the intersection of important status variables, such as gender, race, and class that shape the experiences of women in violent relationships.

Women's Violence in the Context of Their Victimization

The evidence gathered to date strongly suggests that women are almost always violent in the context of violence against them by their male partners. Women's violence must be studied within this context. For example, in a study of 108 women who had recently used violence against an intimate male partner, women's self-reported rates of different types of violence were examined, including moderate and severe physical violence, sexual violence, emotional and/or verbal abuse, and coercive control behavior. Women reported the frequency of their male partners' commission of these behaviors as well. [This study] found that only six of the 108 participants experienced no physical victimization or injury from their male partners.

The types and prevalence of abusive behaviors committed by women also differ from those committed by men. [The study] found that women used equivalent levels of emotional and/or verbal abuse (e.g., yelling and screaming, name calling) as their partners used against them. Women also committed significantly more moderate physical violence (e.g., throwing something, pushing and/or shoving) than their partners used against them. However, women were more often victims of quite serious types of abuse, including sexual coercion, injury, and coercive control behaviors (e.g., restricting social contact, controlling the partner's activities and decisions).

These findings illustrate how the picture of women's violence changes with a more detailed examination of severity, frequency, and type of violence committed by both partners. [W]omen and men engaged in put-downs, insults, and yelling at equivalent rates. However, men much more frequently used coercive control tactics than women. This is not to say that women cannot be jealous or controlling; rather, it is much less common for a woman to have the ability to maintain significant control of a man's behavior because this type of control is maintained through fear. As a general rule, women simply do not inspire fear in men. Women were more frequently victims than perpetrators of the kinds of experiences that inspire terror, such as sexual violence and injury. Clearly, we cannot fully understand the nature, extent, and meaning of women's violence without considering the overall patterns of violence that occur in their intimate relationships. . . .

Women's Motivations for Violent Behavior

Self-defense.   Research suggests that the motivations for women's violent behavior in intimate relationships are often quite different from those for men. Several studies have found that women cite self-defense as a motivation for violence more frequently than men. For example, one study comparing the motivations for violence of college students found that 36% of women listed self-defense as a motivation compared to 18% of men. . . .

Fear.   Women also are more likely to report fear in DV situations. . . . This fear is well founded: In DV situations, women are much more likely than men to be injured, and injured severely. . . . Thus, some women's violence occurs in the context of fear of assault from their partners and the need to protect themselves from physical harm.

Defense of children.   It has been estimated that 30% to 60% of children whose mothers are battered are themselves victims of abuse. Children living with an abused mother have been found to be 12 to 14 times more likely to be sexually abused than children whose mothers were not abused. The effects of family violence on children, in terms of actual physical abuse of children and what children witness, affect how women behave in violent relationships. Some women behave violently toward their partners to protect their children and themselves.

Control.   Studies consistently show that men are more likely than women to use violence to regain control of the relationship or a partner who is challenging their authority. Findings from [a] study of men and women court ordered to a DV treatment program indicated that men were more likely to initiate and control the dynamics of violence, whereas women used violence but did not control those dynamics. However, this does not mean that control motives are completely absent from women's violence. [W]omen [have] stated that they had threatened to use violence at least sometimes to make their partner do the things they wanted him to do. . . .

Retribution.   Finally, several studies suggest that retribution for real or perceived wrongdoing is a common motivator of women's and men's violent behavior. . . . Women and men stated they used violence in retribution for their partners' attacks against them. However, men also reported using violence in retribution for their partners' unwanted behavior, such as infidelity or lying, while no women reported this motivation. In contrast, women stated they used violence in retribution for the partners' emotionally abusive behavior (e.g., "punishment for his insults"), while men did not. . . .

Women's Coping With Violent Relationships

The issue of how women cope with an abusive partner has received some attention in the DV literature; however, little research from a stress-and-coping framework has been conducted. In the general literature, coping is often grouped into three types: avoidant, problem solving, and support seeking. Studies relating coping to a variety of psychological and physical health outcomes typically find that avoidant strategies are related to poorer outcomes, and problem solving and support seeking are related to positive outcomes. Among victims of DV, avoidant coping strategies have been associated with the development of psychological problems such as depression. Problem-solving coping, on the other hand, has been related to well-being. Several studies document the variety of active coping strategies battered women use in response to abuse. Social support has also been found to be a protective factor for battered women; it has been found to be related to reduced symptoms of PTSD and depression.

. . . Problem-solving coping [has been found] negatively correlated with women's violence, indicating that the more problem-solving strategies women employed, the less violence they use. Avoidance coping was positively correlated with violence. . . .

Childhood Trauma

Evidence from several different studies indicates that rates of childhood trauma and abuse are very high among women who use violence. . . .

Several studies have found that experiences of childhood abuse are a risk factor for violent behavior and victimization as adults. A longitudinal study of 136 women who were treated at a hospital for sexual abuse as children examined the impact of childhood abuse on the women as adults. Childhood experiences of sexual abuse predicted women's use of violence against partners and their victimization from partners. Experiences of being hit or beaten by a parent also predicted women's violence against their partners. [D]ifferent types of childhood trauma correlated with women's violence and other related variables. Experiencing childhood sexual and physical abuse was positively correlated with women's use of violence and women's sexual victimization from their partners. Childhood emotional abuse experiences correlated with women's coercive control behavior and their use of avoidance coping strategies to deal with relationship violence. . . .

Outcomes

Four psychological outcomes have been associated with traumatic experiences in general, and DV victimization in particular: depression, anxiety, substance abuse, and PTSD. In a meta-analysis of IPV as a risk factor for mental disorders, the weighted mean prevalence of depression among battered women was approximately 50%. Battered women have a higher prevalence of anxiety disorders compared to the general female population. Battered women are also at risk for substance abuse. . . . Finally, the rate of diagnostic PTSD among women who experience IPV is around 40%. . . .

Sociocultural Context of Women's Violence

This section of the article examines women's violence within the context of the intersectionality of race, ethnicity, and culture. These contextual factors "color the meaning and nature of DV, how it is experienced by self and responded to by others, how personal and social consequences are represented, and how and whether escape and safety can be obtained". A focus on intersectionality in research on IPV enhances understanding of the phenomenon and increases the external validity of the study findings to different ethnic and cultural groups (Sokoloff & Dupont, 2005; Sue, 1999). . . .

African American Culture and Women's Violence
With Intimate Partners

The literature on family violence within the African American culture reveals several protective and risk factors that may affect women's use of violence. One area that is relatively unique to African American culture, as compared to other American ethnic groups, is the expectation that African American women are "strong" and invulnerable. . . . [The] strong Black woman [has been defined] as self-sufficient, independent, and able to survive difficulties without assistance. The strong Black woman takes care of not only her own problems but also those of her family and community. However, without a balance between self-care and care for others, vulnerability to physical and mental health problems can result.

In the context of DV, a consequence of the "strong woman" expectation is that African American women may be expected to hold the family together and protect their men from the hostile mainstream culture, regardless of the cost to themselves. A woman striving to be strong and independent may be reluctant to ask for outside help and may be accused of disloyalty to the Black community if she "airs dirty laundry to White folks" by reporting the violence. Battered African American women may also be faced with the dilemma that if they report abuse, they are reinforcing negative stereotypes that intimate relationships between Black men and women are inherently dysfunctional, and that Black men are naturally violent.

As the "strong woman" construction of African American femininity implies, gender roles in African American culture differ from other ethnic groups. Some literature suggests that African American couples may be more egalitarian in some respects (e.g., acceptance of women's employment, more equitable distribution of child care). These egalitarian gender roles may in some cases reduce the risk of violence. On the other hand, when there is violence in the relationship, some African American women may hit back because their relationships are more egalitarian; that is, if the couple believes that the woman has the same rights as her male partner, then if he hits her, she has the same right to hit him. . . .

In addition, African American women may be reluctant to use legal interventions because of the history of mistreatment of African Americans by the criminal justice system. African American women who fight back may end up getting arrested themselves. Even if African American women have not fought back, they may still be perceived as "inauthentic victims" (Bell & Mattis, 2000). The "strong woman" socialization includes hiding one's vulnerability, especially in the presence of Whites. . . .

Other social services may also be less than helpful for African American women involved in violent relationships. One common problem is that service providers may not understand or be sensitive to the experiences of Black women. Thus, Black women may be less likely to use these services or, if they do, may not find them to be helpful. However, culturally appropriate social services (such as DV support groups), particularly those run by and for African American women, have been found to be very helpful.

Another problem African American women in abusive relationships may face is the lack of possibilities of alternative relationships. Many Black women, particularly middle-class women, have noted a shortage in eligible African American men of their status. Some women may remain in an abusive relationship because they do not believe they will be able to find another partner. Another risk factor may be the financial burdens faced by many African American women. Although poverty exists in all ethnic groups, it is disproportionately high among African Americans. Women with very limited finances, particularly those with children, may remain in abusive relationships for economic reasons.

A potential resilience factor for African American women is a positive racial identity. Racial socialization is the "responsibility of raising physically and emotionally healthy children who are Black in a society in which being Black has negative connotations". [R]acial socialization to take pride in Black heritage and culture, use spirituality and religion as coping mechanisms, draw on extended family for social support, and be aware of and cope with racism will all serve as protective factors for African Americans. This protection may extend to a decreased likelihood of involvement in DV as well.

A buffer against violence among some African American families may be a greater involvement with extended kin and community. . . . The extended family network may also exert social pressure to curb a male partner's violence against a woman. On the other hand, some African American women with strong family support may forgo that support because they want to protect their families from the risks of getting involved. Other buffers that may be particularly important in African American culture include religious supports, spirituality, and a strong sense of being embedded in one's community and neighborhood.

In sum, African American women may be trapped in violent relationships for a variety of reasons, including the "strong woman's" responsibility to keep the family together, lack of access to and help from legal or social services, and economic needs. From the perspective of women's violence, then, we propose that the more a woman is trapped as a result of these various factors in a violent relationship, the more likely she will be to use violence to protect herself. This may hold especially true for African American women because of cultural expectations regarding the strength of Black women and relatively egalitarian gender roles. Potential buffers include positive racial socialization and involvement with extended family and religious communities.

Latino Culture and Women's Violence With Intimate Partners

In an examination of family violence in Latino culture, it is important to consider not only the minority status of Latinos in the United States but also immigration, country of origin, and acculturation. According to the 2000 U.S. Census, 40% of Latinos living in the United States were born in other countries. Studies have found substantial differences in the prevalence of family violence based on country of origin. One large-scale survey found the highest rates of male-to-female violence in Puerto Rican families (20.4%), followed by Mexican Americans (14.2%), Anglos (9.9%), and Cubans (2.5%). These differences in prevalence are probably confounded in part by the socioeconomic status of people emigrating from those countries.

The role of acculturation in family violence appears to be critical for many Latinos who have immigrated to the United States. *Acculturation* has been defined as the process by which an immigrant's attitudes and behaviors change toward those of the predominant cultural group as a result of exposure to the new culture. Recent studies indicate that couples who are in the midst of undergoing the acculturation process—who are in between the gender roles of the country of origin and those of the mainstream United States—may be at the highest risk of partner violence. . . .

Why does acculturation appear to affect women's aggression toward partners more than men's behavior? Migration may change the rules of behavior more for women than for men. Aggression is much less acceptable for women in Latin America than in the United States. Some studies have explored the gender role conflict that can occur when Latino couples sort out the new roles they are exposed to through acculturation. . . . Mexican American women who were born in the United States had higher levels of education, and worked outside the home experienced more violence than women who were born in Mexico, had less education, and did not work. In addition, the more acculturated, educated, working women had different expectations about their role in the family than did their husbands, leading to conflict about men's and women's roles and abuse by their husbands. In contrast, when the women and their husbands agreed on gender roles, whether egalitarian or traditional, the incidence of violence was lower.

Traditional gender roles affect Latinas' perceptions of what constitutes abuse and how to respond to it. In one study, although Latina, African American, and Anglo women living in shelters reported similar severity of abuse, Latinas reported the longest duration of abuse and the fewest attempts to seek help. . . .

Barriers to seeking outside help may also increase Latina women's risk of abuse. Immigration status frequently prevents women from reporting DV to authorities. For example, Detroit police reported a large volume of calls from Latina women who had been victims of violence; however, many women did not want to prosecute the abusers because of fear of deportation. Language barriers also prevent many Latinas from seeking or receiving help. Among battered Mexican, Mexican American, and Puerto Rican women, Latinas who sought help had greater proficiency in English. Finally, the barriers to getting out of abusive relationships created by poverty cannot be overestimated. The issues related to poverty are manifold: unemployment, lack of affordable housing, inability to afford child care, lack of transportation—all of which can trap a woman in a violent relationship.

Protective factors for Latinas include strong family supports. Latinas will often seek help and advice from their families first before seeking help from outsiders. Latinas are more likely to live in larger households with extended family, and to marry and start families earlier than other ethnic groups. The family, then, provides a strong base of support; family members watch out for one another. In the case of battering, however, if the family is not able or willing to help the woman, she may be very reluctant to "betray" the family by going outside of it for help. In some cases, the extended family may contribute to the woman's oppression. For recent immigrants who left their extended families in their home countries, family supports may be absent. . . .

Spirituality can also be an important source of support for Latina women in DV situations. . . . However, the church can be nonsupportive of battered women as well, advising them to endure the abuse. Finally, as is the case for African Americans, positive ethnic identity has been proposed as an important protective factor for the well-being of Latinas.

Class and Socioeconomic Issues

Virtually every study of DV that examines socioeconomic status (SES) finds that poverty is consistently and robustly related to higher prevalence rates of IPV. In fact, in most studies that control for the effects of SES, differences in the prevalence rates of IPV between racial and/or ethnic groups disappear. However, very few studies have explored what it is about poverty that elevates the risk of IPV.

[A] study of the impact of race, SES, and neighborhood on the prevalence of DV . . . examined a number of objective indicators of social class, including neighborhood disadvantage (e.g., number of people below the poverty line, number of unemployed people), employment instability of the male partner, insufficiency of income to meet basic needs, and a subjective measure of financial strain. [It was] found that the relationship between male-to-female partner violence and SES was not linear; rather, those women living in the bottom 25% of the most disadvantaged neighborhoods experienced twice the prevalence of partner violence compared to those in the upper 75%. . . . After entering economic distress indicators into the model, the impact of race on rates of DV disappeared; [that is,] severe economic disadvantage in a neighborhood fosters anonymity and reduced social controls on IPV—neighbors are not looking out for one another, leaving DV unchecked. These neighborhood economic factors were found to increase the likelihood of women's and men's use of violence with their intimate partners.

Discussion

This article develops a theoretical framework for furthering our understanding of the phenomenon of women's violence. Particular emphasis is placed on the need to study women's violence within social, historical, and cultural contexts. The model proposes a number of risk and protective factors that appear to be related to women's use of violence with male partners, including the male partners' violence against women, experiences of childhood trauma, women's strategies for coping with problems in their relationships, women's motivations for using violence, and the outcomes of depression, anxiety, substance abuse, and PTSD. We argue for the importance of sociocultural contexts in developing theory regarding women's use of violence with intimate partners. Although only two ethnic groups were examined in detail in this article, future research should examine the effects of culture on women's violence with other ethnic groups.

Models of IPV, such as that proposed here, should also be examined longitudinally. Interrelationships among variables in the model are clearly dynamic; variables that are shown as mediators or outcomes in the various models may also operate as antecedents. For example, one possible alternative model is as follows: Women who have experienced childhood trauma are at risk of developing PTSD. PTSD increases the likelihood of developing maladaptive coping strategies, such as avoidance coping and poor problem solving, thereby increasing the likelihood that women with PTSD will get involved in, and remain in, violent relationships.

The model proposed here includes a number of critical dimensions that are relevant to women's violence; however, there are certainly other important factors that should be examined in future research. For example, the model does not include age, which has consistently been found to be related to DV, with younger individuals more likely to use violence against partners. It also does not focus on Axis II disorders, such as borderline personality disorder, and the extent to which such disorders may be involved in women's violence. The model only examines outcomes for women, not for their male partners or their children, and is presented in the context of heterosexual relationships. The relationships among variables proposed here may or may not apply to lesbians. The model proposed in this article, although serving as a framework for advancing a theory of women's violence, needs to be tested and refined. Through this process, the field will advance in developing a more comprehensive understanding of women's violence.

POSTSCRIPT

Gender Symmetry: Do Women and Men Commit Equal Levels of Violence Against Intimate Partners?

The debate about gender symmetry is fueled in part by a continued focus on the question of sex differences rather than on the factors and processes that contribute to intimate partner violence. A shift in focus would lead to questions of why some women and some men abuse their partners. Gender can be reintroduced into the discussion by focusing on how traditional constructions of masculinity and the power associated with it contribute to both women's and men's involvement in partner aggression as victim and/ or perpetrator. For example, when women are aggressive, are they trying to gain power in a situation in which they feel powerless? Do men engage in aggression because they are attempting to counter threats to their masculinity? A shift in focus may also encourage researchers to more broadly define intimate partner violence so that it includes not only physical aggression, but also verbal and psychological aggression, as well as sexual assault. In doing so gender again enters the discussion in a way that asks whether there are different patterns of IPV. For example, men are much more likely to sexually coerce female partners than vice versa. Women may be more likely to persist in use of violence when they have partners who do not engage in aggression; this is known as the "rational choice" strategy. Maureen McHugh has suggested that a postmodern approach to conceptualizing women's use of aggression should include rejecting polarized stances in the debate on gender symmetry; that is, a sex difference approach is not useful. It ignores too much of the context and dynamic nature of intimate partner violence. Rather there should be a focus on human interactions, examining the meaning and consequences of the experience for all involved. There should be a recognition that patterns of intimate partner violence are multiple and varied, and that perpetrators can be victims and victims can be perpetrators. This latter point raises the possibility that intimate partner violence may be mutual, although it is not necessarily symmetric. Women and men may both commit acts of aggression but in the context of gendered constructions of power and status motives, meanings and consequences are highly unlikely to be symmetric.

Suggested Readings

Nicola Gavey, *Just Sex?: The Cultural Scaffolding of Rape* (Routledge, 2005).

Lisa Goodman and D. Epstein, *Listening to Battered Women: A Survivor-Centered Approach to Advocacy, Mental Health, and Justice* (Washington, DC: American Psychological Association, 2008).

Christopher Kilmartin and Julie Allison, *Men's Violence Against Women: Theory, Research and Activism* (Routledge, 2007).

Special issue: Female Violence Against Intimate Partners. *Psychology of Women Quarterly, 29*(3) (September 2005).

Special issue: Understanding Gender and Intimate Partner Abuse. *Sex Roles 52*(11/12) (June 2005).

Three-part special issue, Women's Use of Violence in Intimate Relationships. *Violence Against Women, 8*(11 & 12), *9*(1) (2006).

ISSUE 9

Does Pornography Reduce the Incidence of Rape?

YES: Anthony D'Amato, from "Porn Up, Rape Down," Northwestern University School of Law, Public Law and Legal Theory Research Paper Series (June 23, 2006)

NO: Judith Reisman, from "Pornography's Link to Rape," WorldnetDaily.com (July 29, 2006)

ISSUE SUMMARY

YES: Professor of law Anthony D'Amato highlights statistics from the most recent National Crime Victimization Survey that demonstrate a correlation between the increased consumption of pornography over the years with the decreased incidence of rape. Some people, he argues, watch pornography in order to push any desire to rape out of their minds, and thus have no further desire to go out and actually do it.

NO: Judith Reisman, president of the Institute for Media Education, asserts that sex criminals imitate what they see depicted in the media, providing examples of serial rapists and killers who had large stores of pornography in their possession, and research in which approximately 33 percent of rapists said that they had viewed pornography immediately prior to at least one of their rapes.

Since the creation of the Internet, the world has seen a huge increase in the amount and manner in which information is exchanged with others. This includes the adult entertainment industry, which has become an enormous, multi-billion dollar industry thanks in part to the anonymity and privacy that online pornography provides adults. One challenge, many argue, is that adults are far from the only ones who are able to access porn sites online. Children as young as middle school-age are accessing images online, some of which they search for and some of which is targeted to them through SPAM e-mails or pornographic Web sites that purchase the domain of a similarly sounding Web site, counting on minors to arrive at their sites by accident.

The debates about the effects of porn on its users are nearly endless: Does viewing porn encourage young people to become sexually active at earlier ages? Does viewing porn psychologically damage kids? Do adults who view porn develop unrealistic expectations of beauty and sexual expression in their own relationships? And so on.

This issue looks at the effects of visual pornography on the incidence of rape in the United States. Since pornography became available, there are many proponents who maintain that by depicting certain sexual acts, sexually explicit media encourages people to try these acts out. In particular, they say, porn that shows rape makes this type of behavior real and, in the rapists' mind, acceptable, thereby encouraging rape. Others maintain that there is no causality between viewing Internet porn and the incidence of rape, that people are exposed to a wide range of information, images, and behaviors every day and do not engage in all of the behaviors they see. These include, they say, sexual behaviors.

Still others, like one of the authors who appears in this issue, maintain that having pornography available actually *decreases* the incidence of rape. Depicting rape, which is a socially unacceptable (and criminal) behavior, this author argues, actually provides a potential rapist with an outlet for his unacceptable fantasies, thereby keeping him from acting upon them. In the following selections, Anthony D'Amato analyzes data that correlates a decrease in rapes in the United States with the increase of pornography availability. Judith Reisman counters with stories from actual rapists who discuss viewing porn immediately before raping a victim.

YES

Anthony D'Amato

Porn Up, Rape Down

Today's headlines are shouting RAPE IN DECLINE![1] Official figures just released show a plunge in the number of rapes per capita in the United States since the 1970s. Even when measured in different ways, including police reports and survey interviews, the results are in agreement; there has been an 85% reduction in sexual violence in the past 25 years. The decline, steeper than the stock market crash that led to the Great Depression, is depicted in this chart prepared by the United States Department of Justice:

Rape rates
Adjusted victimization rate
per 1,000 persons age 12 and over

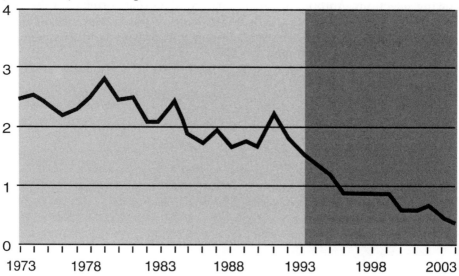

Source: *The National Crime Victimization Survey.* Includes both attempted and completed rapes.

As the chart shows, there were 2.7 rapes for every 1,000 people in 1980; by 2004, the same survey found the rate had decreased to 0.4 per 1,000 people, a decline of 85%.

Official explanations for the unexpected decline include (1) less lawlessness associated with crack cocaine; (b) women have been taught to avoid unsafe situations; (c) more would-be rapists already in prison for other crimes; (d) sex education classes telling boys that "no means no." But these minor factors cannot begin to explain such a sharp decline in the incidence of rape.

There is, however, one social factor that correlates almost exactly with the rape statistics. The American public is probably not ready to believe it. My theory is that the sharp rise in access to pornography accounts for the decline in rape. The correlation is inverse: the more pornography, the less rape. It is like the inverse correlation: the more police officers on the street, the less crime.

The pornographic movie "Deep Throat" which started the flood of X-rated VHS and later DVD films, was released in 1972. Movie rental shops at first catered primarily to the adult film trade. Pornographic magazines also sharply increased in numbers in the 1970s and 1980s. Then came a seismic change: pornography became available on the new internet. Today, purveyors of internet porn earn a combined annual income exceeding the total of the major networks ABC, CBS, and NBC.

"Deep Throat" has moved from the adult theatre to a laptop near you.

National trends are one thing; what do the figures for the states show? From data compiled by the National Telecommunications and Information Administration in 2001, the four states with the *lowest* per capita access to the internet were Arkansas, Kentucky, Minnesota, and West Virginia. The four states with the *highest* internet access were Alaska, Colorado, New Jersey, and Washington. (I would not have guessed this.)

Next I took the figures for forcible rape compiled by police reports by the Disaster Center for the years 1980 and 2000. The following two charts display the results:

Table 1

States with Lowest Internet Access[2]

State	Internet 2001	Rape 1980	Rape 2000
Arkansas	36.9	26.7	31.7
Kentucky	40.2	19.2	27.4
Minnesota	36.1	23.2	45.5
W. Virginia	40.7	15.8	18.3

All figures are per capita.

While the nationwide incidence of rape was showing a drastic decline, the incidence of rape in the four states having the *least* access to the internet showed an actual *increase* in rape over the same time period. This result was almost too clear and convincing, so to check it I compiled figures for the four states having the *most* access to the internet. Three out of four of these states showed declines (in New Jersey, an almost 50% decline). Alaska was an anomaly: it increased both in internet access and incidence of rape. However, the

Table 2

States with Highest Internet Access[3]

Alaska	64.1	56.8	70.3
Colorado	58.5	52.5	41.2
New Jersey	61.6	30.7	16.1
Washington	60.4	52.7	46.4

All figures are per capita.

population of Alaska is less than one-tenth that of the other three states in its category. To adjust for the disparity in population, I took the combined population of the four states in each table and calculated the percentage change in the rape statistics:

Table 3

Combined Per Capita Percentage Change in Incidence of Rape

	Aggregate per capita increase or decline in rape
Four states with lowest internet access	Increase in rape of 53%
Four states with highest internet access	Decrease in rape of 27%

I find these results to be statistically significant beyond the 95 confidence interval.

Yet proof of correlation is not the same thing as causation. If autumn regularly precedes winter, that doesn't mean that autumn causes winter. When six years ago my former Northwestern colleague John Donohue, together with Steven Levitt[4], found that legalized abortion correlated with a reduction in crime, theirs would have only been an academically curious thesis if they had not identified a causal factor. But they did identify one: that prior to legalization there were many unwanted babies born due to the lack of a legal abortion alternative. Those unwanted children became the most likely group to turn to crime.

My own interest in the rape-pornography question began in 1970 when I served as a consultant to President Nixon's Commission on Obscenity and Pornography. The Commission concluded that there was no causal relationship between exposure to sexually explicit materials and delinquent or criminal behavior. The President was furious when he learned of the conclusion.

Later President Reagan tried the same thing, except unlike his predecessor he packed the Commission with persons who passed his ideological litmus test (small wonder that I was not asked to participate). This time, Reagan's Commission on Pornography reached the approved result: that there does exist a causal relationship between pornography and violent sex crimes.

The drafter of the Commission's report was Frederich Schauer, a prominent law professor. In a separate statement, he assured readers that neither he nor the other Commissioners were at all influenced by their personal moral values.[5] . . .

Although the Reagan Commission had at its disposal all the evidence gathered by psychology and social-science departments throughout the world on the question whether a student's exposure to pornography increased his tendency to commit antisocial acts, I found that the Commission was unable to adduce a shred of evidence to support its affirmative conclusion. No scientist had ever found that pornography raised the probability of rape. However, the Commission was not seeking truth; rather, as I said in the title to my article, it sought political truth.

If pornography does not *produce* rape, I thought, then maybe it *reduces* rape. But no one apparently had any incentive to investigate the latter proposition. But the just-released rape statistics provide the necessary evidence.

Although neither Professor Schauer nor the other Commissioners ever responded to my William & Mary article, now they can forget it. For if they had been right that exposure to pornography leads to an increase in social violence, then the vast exposure to pornography furnished by the internet would by now have resulted in scores of rapes per day on university campuses, hundreds of rapes daily in every town, and thousands of rapes per day in every city. Instead, the Commissioners were so incredibly wrong that the incidence of rape has actually declined by the astounding rate of 85%.

Correlations aside, could access to pornography actually reduce the incidence of rape as a matter of causation? In my article I mentioned one possibility: that some people watching pornography may "get it out of their system" and thus have no further desire to go out and actually try it. Another possibility might be labeled "Victorian effect" the more that people covered up their bodies with clothes in those days, the greater the mystery of what they looked like in the nude. The sight of a woman's ankle was considered shocking and erotic. But today, internet porn has thoroughly de-mystified sex. . . .

I am sure there will be other explanations forthcoming as to why access to pornography is the most important causal factor in the decline of rape. Once one accepts the observation that there is a precise negative correlation between the two, the rest can safely be left to the imagination.

Notes

1. E.g., *Washington Post,* June 19, 2006; *Chicago Tribune,* June 21, 2006.
2. Statistics on Internet Access compiled from National Telecommunications and Information Administration. . . .
3. Statistics on forcible rape compiled from. . . .
4. Author of *Freakonimics* (2005).
5. U.S. Dept. of Justice, Final Report: Attorney General's Commission on Pornography 176–79 (1986) (personal statement of Commissioner Schauer).

 **NO**

Pornography's Link to Rape

Would you try to put out a fire with gasoline?

No? Then you might disagree with an MSNBC online article, "Porn: Good for America!" by Glenn Reynolds, a University of Tennessee law professor. Reynolds suggests that pornography *reduces* rape!

As proof, Reynolds quotes a U.S. Department of Justice claim that in 2004 rape of "people" *over age 12* radically decreased with an "85 percent decline in the per-capita rape rate since 1979" (DOJ's National Crime Victimization Survey of "thousands of respondents 12 and older").

But the FBI also estimates that "34 percent of female sex assault victims" are "under age 12" (National Incident-Based Reporting System, July 2000).

Since the DOJ data *excludes rape of children under age 12*, child rape may be *up 85 percent*, for all we know.

Although the FBI and local police departments are now swamped with teachers, police, professors, doctors, legislators, clergy, federal and state bureaucrats, dentists, judges, etc., arrested for child pornography and for abusing children *under age 12*, the Department of Justice excludes those small victims from its "rape" rates. Why?

Do DOJ, FBI Harbor Pedophiles?

You have to wonder: Are there pedophiles and other sexual predators in the governmental woodpiles?

When I worked for DOJ's Juvenile Justice and Delinquency Prevention in the 1980s, someone high up killed the order to collect crime-scene pornography as evidence in prosecutions. No Democrat or Republican administration has yet mandated such on-site pornography collections. Whom is DOJ protecting?

Reynolds, writes less like an objective scholar than a pornography defender:

> Since 1970 porn has exploded. But rape has gone down 85 percent. So much for the notion that pornography causes rape. [I]t would be hard to explain how rape rates could have declined so dramatically while porn expanded so explosively.

He opines that pornography possibly prevents rape (the old discredited "safe-outlet" theory).

The DOJ's preposterous "85 percent" decrease in rape ignores the obvious. The U.S. FBI Index of Crime reported a *418 percent increase* in "forcible rape" from 1960 to 1999. That fear means we now keep our doors, windows and cars locked. Women seldom walk alone at night. Parents rarely let children go anywhere unaccompanied. Many states let people carry guns for self-defense. Rape Crisis Centers do not report rapes to police. More women perform as sexually required. A conflicting DOJ 2002 report says "almost 25 percent of college women have been victims of rape or attempted rape since the age of 14."

Why Don't the Feds Call Child-Rape 'Rape'?

In 1950, 18 states authorized the death penalty for rape; most others could impose a life sentence. Following Alfred Kinsey's "scientific" advice in 1948, many states redefined "rape" so the crime could be plea-bargained down to a misdemeanor like "sexual misconduct."

Missouri redefined rape to mean 11 different crimes for 11 different sentences, magically lowering "rape" rates. Like all states that have trivialized rape, Missouri relied on the Kinsey-based 1955 American Law Institute Model Penal Code.

"Rape" was eliminated from New Jersey's laws and replaced with a variety of terms during a 1978 penal law revision.

For example, Dr. Linda Jeffrey notes that the charge to which child-molesting teacher Pamela Diehl-Moore pleaded guilty was reduced to a second-tier crime, "sexual assault"—i.e., sexual contact with a victim under 13, or penetration where the "actor" uses physical force or coercion, but the victim doesn't suffer severe personal injury, or the victim is 16 or 17, with aggravating circumstances, or the victim is 13 to 15 and the "actor" is at least four years older. (Whew!)

Sex Criminals Copy What Porn Depicts

DOJ experts should read reports such as "Sex-Related Homicide and Death Investigation" (2003). Former Lt. Comdr. Vernon Geberth says today's "sex-related cases are more frequent, vicious and despicable" than anything he experienced in decades as a homicide cop.

In "Journey Into Darkness" (1997), the FBI's premier serial-rape profiler, John Douglas wrote, "[Serial-rape murders are commonly found] with a large pornography collection, either store-bought or homemade. Our [FBI] research does show that certain types of sadomasochistic and bondage-oriented material can fuel the fantasies of those already leaning in that direction."

In "The Evil That Men Do" (1998), FBI serial-rape-murderer-mutilator profiler Roy Hazelwood quotes one sex killer who tied his victims in "a variety of positions" based on pictures he saw in sex magazines.

"Thrill Killers, a Study of America's Most Vicious Murders," by Charles Linedecker, reports that 81 percent of these killers rated pornography as their primary sexual interest. Dr. W.L. Marshall, in "Criminal Neglect, Why Sex

Offenders Go Free" (1990), says based on the evidence, pornography "feeds and legitimizes their deviant sexual tendencies."

In one study of rapists, Gene Abel of the New York Psychiatric Institute cited, "One-third reported that they had used pornography immediately prior to at least one of their crimes." In 1984, the U.S. Attorney General's Task Force on Family Violence reported, "Testimony indicates that an alarming number of rape and sexual assault offenders report that they were acting out behavior they had viewed in pornographic materials."

More pornography equals more rape of children and women. We need to ask whether Big Government is now selling out to Big Pornography as it did to Big Tobacco for half a century.

POSTSCRIPT

Does Pornography Reduce
the Incidence of Rape?

Throughout history, people have looked for answers to why people perpetrate violent crimes on others. Mental health professionals, law enforcement officials, politicians, parents, and others have pointed fingers at many different potential causes without coming up with a clear answer. Is a person biologically determined to be a rapist? Is a rapist "created," and if so, by what or by whom?

One of the first sources people go to for these reasons is the media. One type of indictment against the media has been made since it has existed that it causes viewers to take actions that they would not otherwise take. Some argue, for example, that depictions of violence in the media leads to greater violence in real life. These arguments have even been brought to the legal system, and used during trials. In a well-known court case at the time (*Huceg v. Hustler Magazine,* 1983), a family brought suit against *Hustler*, an adult pornographic magazine, in which a description appeared of autoerotic asphyxiation, a sexual practice in which a person restricts her or his breathing through partial hanging or other method, masturbates, and releases the air restriction at the moment of orgasm. The family's underage son tried this, did it incorrectly, and ended up hanging himself. The family sued *Hustler* magazine, arguing that if this had not been printed, their son would not have done it and died. The Court ruled for the magazine, saying that just reading a description of something does not necessarily encourage someone to do it—especially a young person for whom the material was not created.

To say, however, that the media has *no* effect on people's attitudes or behaviors would be inaccurate. Advertisers spend billions of dollars every year on television, print, Internet, and other ads to sell a wide variety of products. The ads are designed to influence people's behaviors—that if we see a particular commercial or hear a particular song, we will be more likely to purchase one product over another. If advertisers are successful at this—at actually influencing people enough to purchase something they may not have necessarily known they wanted—is it possible that the creators and producers of adult sexually explicit media could be doing the same?

For right now, the data are inconclusive—and there seem to be as many reports supporting each side of the debate. Be sure to consider a range of reasoning as you establish your own opinion on this topic. Is pornography always okay, as long as it's consumed only by adults? Is it never okay? Does it depend on what it depicts? And if there is some kind of causality shown, that pornography *does* indeed increase behavior, what role do you think the government should or should not play in regulating the industry?

Suggested Readings

M. Diamond, Pornography, Rape and Sex Crimes in Japan. *International Journal of Law and Psychiatry,* 1999, 22(1): 1–22.

S. Ehrlich, *Representing Rape: Language and Sexual Consent* (New York: Routledge Press, 2001).

D. Linz, N. M., Malamuth, and K. Beckett, *Civil Liberties and Research on the Effects of Pornography.* American Psychological Association. . . .

D. J. Loftus, *Watching Sex: How Men Really Respond to Pornography* (New York: Thunder's Mouth Press, 2002).

P. Paul, *Pornified: How the Culture of Pornography Is Changing Our Lives, Our Relationships and Our Families* (New York: Times Books, 2005).

D. E. H. Russell, *Dangerous Relationships: Pornography, Misogyny and Rape* (Thousand Oaks, CA: Sage Publications, Inc., 1998).

A. Soble, *Pornography, Sex, and Feminism* (Amherst, NY: Prometheus Books, 2002).

G. A. Walp, *The Missing Link Between Pornography and Rape: Convicted Rapists Respond With Validated Truth* (Ann Arbor, MI: ProQuest/UMI, 2006).

Internet References . . .

Tufts University's Child and Family Web Guide

This Web site provides links to the best sites on same-sex parents.

http://www.cfw.tufts.edu/topic/2/189.htm

FatherWork

FatherWork is a Web page on "generative fathering" and was developed by family science professors David Dollahite and Alan Hawkins and their students at Brigham Young University. Start with the conceptual framework for generative fathering. Included in the site are insightful personal stories about fatherhood across the life span, and ideas and activities to encourage generative fathering.

http://fatherwork.byu.edu

Work and Family: National Partnership for Women and Families

This public education and advocacy site aims "to promote fairness in the workplace, quality health care, and policies that help women and men meet the dual demands of work and family." This site includes a wealth of information about relevant public policy issues, including the Family Medical Leave Act.

http://www.nationalpartnership.org

The Family Economic Strategies

This website from The Family Economic Self-Sufficiency Project describes six strategies that families, especially women, can follow as they move from welfare to self-sufficiency. See the "Setting the Standard for American Working Families" report.

http://www.sixstrategies.org/

The Future of Children

This website is sponsored by the Woodrow Wilson School of Public and International Affairs at Princeton University and the Brookings Institution. Its goal is to promote effective policies and programs for children by providing policymakers, service providers, and the media with timely, objective information based on the best available research. Through the website one can access journal articles and other publications.

http://www.futureofchildren.org/

The Children's Defense Fund

The Children's Defense Fund's motto is "the voice of all the children of America." The nonprofit organization, begun in 1973, advocates for preventive programs to help children stay healthy and out of trouble. It pays particular attention to the needs of poor and minority children and those with disabilities.

http://www.childrensdefense.org

From *Ozzie and Harriet* to *My Two Dads*: Gender in Childhood

*I*n contemporary America, the "ideal" family continues to be defined as one in which mother and father are married, father is the breadwinner, and mother maintains the home and cares for the children. This ideal is no longer matched by actual family structure, with more and more alternative family structures, including families with same-sex parents and single-parent families being developed to meet personal desires and needs and to cope with societal pressures and changes. Nonetheless, traditional family ideology remains dominant in America. Traditional family ideology institutionalizes conventional gender roles, so much so that many gender scholars view the family as a "gender factory." The institutionalization of gender roles also extends to parental desires regarding the sex of one's children.

In this section, we examine issues surrounding what constitutes a "normal" family, from the perspective of couples themselves. In evaluating the readings in this section, consider what role biology plays in the construction of parenthood. One argument supporting traditional families rests on the assumption that women and men have biologically based attributes that renders each uniquely suited for particular parenting roles, and that having sons and daughters creates a more balanced family. Do data support such an assumption? Is there a maternal instinct? How do race, ethnicity, class, culture, and other status-defining attributes contribute to definitions of family? How might variations in family arrangements across these dimensions challenge essentialist notions of mother and father? Traditional media representations of the family supported a 1950's Ozzie and Harriet *view of a stay-at-home-mother and a working father. What views are presented in contemporary media? Consider movies such as* Three Men and a Baby *and* Transamerica. *How do media portrayals of parenting affect our understanding of healthy relationships? How and when do media portrayals, including images and language, reinforce or defy gender stereotypes?*

- Should Same-Sex Couples Be Able to Marry?
- Can Lesbian and Gay Couples Be Appropriate Parents for Children?
- Are Fathers Essential for Children's Well-Being?
- Is Fetal Sex Selection Harmful to Society?

ISSUE 10

Should Same-Sex Couples Be Able to Marry?

YES: Lawrence A. Kurdek, from "Are Gay and Lesbian Cohabiting Couples *Really* Different from Heterosexual Married Couples?" *Journal of Marriage and Family* (November 2004)

NO: Peter Sprigg, from *Questions and Answers: What's Wrong with Letting Same-Sex Couples 'Marry'?* (Family Research Council, 2004)

ISSUE SUMMARY

YES: Psychology professor Lawrence A. Kurdek reports on a longitudinal study comparing gay and lesbian partners with partners from heterosexual married couples with children. For half of the comparisons there were no differences and for 78 percent of the comparisons for which differences were found, gay or lesbian partners functioned better than heterosexual partners.

NO: Peter Sprigg, director of the Center for Marriage and Family Studies at the Family Research Council, outlines why non-heterosexual relationships do not carry with them the same validity as heterosexual relationships, and therefore non-heterosexuals should not be allowed to marry legally. He states that the rights same-sex couples would get by being able to marry are rights that are already available to them.

Many people believe that a person should have the same rights as anyone else, regardless of their race, age, gender—or sexual orientation. When this discussion moves into the arena of same-sex marriage, however, those beliefs start to waiver a bit. The past few years have seen the topic of same-sex marriage rush into the forefront of the news and other media.

Vermont became the first state to make civil unions legal between two people of the same sex. Although a same-sex couple cannot have a marriage license or refer to their union as a marriage, the benefits are the same as they would be for a heterosexual marriage. These unions are not, however, recognized in any other state. This is due in great part to the Defense of Marriage Act, which was signed into law in 1996 by President Bill Clinton. This Act says that no state is required to recognize a same-sex union, and defines marriage as being between a man and a woman only. Therefore, same-sex unions that are legal in one state do not have to be recognized as legal in another. In anticipation of efforts to have state recognition of civil unions, over 30 states have passed legislation saying they would not recognize a same-sex union that took place in another state.

In the 2004 national election few issues were more hotly debated than same-sex marriage. In that election 11 states passed constitutional amendments that effectively banned same-sex marriage. President Bush was quoted as saying "The union of a man and a woman is the most enduring human institution, honored and encouraged in all cultures and by every religious faith." Political conservatives claimed that the election results indicated that the country generally rejects same-sex marriage. However, beneath the political rhetoric are questions about what is really wrong with gays and lesbians being granted the same legal rights of heterosexual couples.

Those who oppose same-sex marriage believe that marriage is, and always has been, between a man and a woman. They believe that a key part of marriage for many heterosexual couples is reproduction or another type of parenting arrangement, such as adoption. In those cases, they believe that any child should have two parents, one male and one female (see Issue 8). Many do not oppose granting domestic partner benefits to same-sex partners, or even, in some cases, civil unions. They do, however, believe that if lesbian and gay couples were allowed to marry and to receive the legal and social benefits thereof, it would serve only to further erode the institution of marriage as it is currently defined, which, in the United States, boasts one divorce for every two marriages.

Supporters of same-sex marriage believe that if lesbian and gay couples wish to make a lifetime commitment, they should be afforded the same rights, privileges, and vocabulary as heterosexual couples. While some would be as happy with the term "civil union," accompanied by equal rights, others believe that making marriage available to all is the only way to go.

An argument that is raised in this debate is that granting same-sex couples the right to marry would open the door for adult pedophiles to petition to marry the children with whom they engage in their sexual relationships. Most lesbian and gay individuals and their supporters find this offensive, as well as an invalid comparison. What do you think?

As you read, consider what is at the base of each argument. Consider the assertions pertaining to the effects of same-sex couples or their unions on different-sex couples. Do you agree? What effect do you think the relationship status, choices, and behaviors of heterosexual couples have on lesbian and gay individuals and couples?

In the following selections, both Larry Kurdek and Peter Sprigg raise the most common questions pertaining to same-sex marriage. Kurdek's research challenges assumptions that there is something inherently "wrong" with same-sex couples. The concerns Peter Sprigg raises pertains to the expectation of heterosexual marriage to raise children, and that a same-sex couple is a harmful setting in which to do that.

YES

Lawrence A. Kurdek

Are Gay and Lesbian Cohabiting Couples *Really* Different from Heterosexual Married Couples?

Despite the current controversy surrounding same-sex marriage in the United States, there are no reliable estimates of the number of American gay and lesbian couples. Survey data indicate that between 40% and 60% of gay men and between 45% and 80% of lesbians are currently involved in a romantic relationship. Data from the 2000 United States Census indicate that of the 5.5 million couples who were living together but not married, about 1 in 9 (594,391) involved same-sex couples. Other survey data indicate that between 18% and 28% of gay couples and between 8% and 21% of lesbian couples have lived together 10 or more years. Because presenting oneself publicly as part of a gay or lesbian couple opens the door for discrimination, abuse, and even violence, these numbers are likely to be underestimates. Nonetheless, it is clear that despite a general social climate of prejudice against gay men and lesbians, being part of a couple is integral to the lives of many gay men and lesbians.

As one indication of the importance of identifying oneself as part of a couple, some gay and lesbian citizens of the United States are currently arguing that they, just like heterosexual citizens, are entitled to the privileges associated with having their relationships legalized as marriages. These privileges include access to spousal benefits from Social Security; veterans', health, and life insurance programs; hospital visitation rights; the ability to make medical decisions for partners; and exemption from state inheritance taxes. They also argue that being deprived of these privileges is unjust because it involves discriminating against a defined class of individuals. In response, some legislators have counterargued that same-sex marriages violate the sanctity of marriage as a union between a man and a woman, and that legal steps are needed to protect that sanctity. In that vein, 38 states to date have approved Defense of Marriage Acts ensuring that those states need not recognize the legality of same-sex unions effected by other states, and support is growing for an amendment to the Constitution that will define marriage as the legal union of a man and a woman.

Despite extensive media coverage of the same-sex marriage issue, the voice of relevant research is rarely heard. Consequently, my premise is that the

From *Journal of Marriage and Family*, vol. 66, November 2004, pp. 880–883, 895–897. Copyright © 2004 by National Council on Family Relations. Reprinted by permission.

complex controversy surrounding same-sex marriage can be examined, in part, as an *empirical* question of the extent to which gay and lesbian partners differ from heterosexual spouses on variables that matter to long-term relationships. I make no claims that answers to this question will provide a definitive resolution to the controversy, but I do submit that answers to this question will help to inform reasoned discussion of the controversy. If marriage is to be reserved for only unions of a man and a woman, it seems reasonable to assume that opposite-sex relationships work in ways that are radically different from the way that same-sex relationships work. Comparing partners from gay and lesbian couples to spouses from heterosexual couples on variables already known to be relevant for relationship health affords one way of testing this assumption.

Addressing the same-sex marriage issue on empirical grounds is complicated, however. Despite an increased scientific interest in gay and lesbian couples, systematic comparisons of partners from gay or lesbian couples to spouses from heterosexual couples have been characterized by several methodological and statistical problems. These include studying only one partner from the couple; averaging individual scores from both partners; using measures with unknown psychometric properties; not taking into account whether the couples had children living with them; not quantifying the size of any differences found among couples; comparing couples without first ensuring that the members of these couples were equivalent on demographic characteristics such as age, education, income, and length of relationship; and treating members of the couples as independent units of analysis.

These problems are redressed in this article by my reporting of findings from a longitudinal project involving psychometrically sound measures completed by both members of gay cohabiting, lesbian cohabiting, and heterosexual married couples. Further, I conducted comparisons between partners from both gay and lesbian couples and heterosexual couples with controls for potentially key demographic variables (i.e., age, education, income, and years living together). I assessed the size of the effects associated with type-of-couple differences, and I employed statistical analyses that took partner interdependence into account.

In the samples I recruited, partners from gay and lesbian cohabiting couples did not live with children. Because children are known to affect marital functioning, partners from heterosexual married couples were divided into those with children and those without children. In view of the complexities associated with living with stepchildren, the group of heterosexual couples identified as having children was restricted to those who lived only with their biological children.

I defend the selection of childless gay and lesbian couples on the basis of reports that the majority of gay and lesbian couples do *not* live with children. Using data from the 2000 Census, . . . [it has been] estimated that 33% of female same-sex householders and 22% of male same-sex householders lived with their own children who were under the age of 18. By extension, one can assume that the majority of gay and lesbian couples wanting to get married also would be childless. Indeed, . . . of 212 lesbians and 123 gay men who obtained same-sex civil unions in Vermont, only 30% and 18%, respectively, had children. . . . [S]uch percentages are likely to be lower than the percentages of lesbians and gay men who have children.

I conducted type-of-couple comparisons using married couples with children as the reference group for four reasons. First, an important topic in the study of cohabitation among heterosexual couples is whether such cohabitation provides a lasting arrangement in which to raise children. Second, some scholars have argued that married couples—including, potentially, gay and lesbian couples—should receive state-funded services only if they are raising children. Third, based on the 2000 Census, 46% of married householders had at least one biological child, adopted child, or stepchild living with them. It is safe to assume that the number of married householders who have *ever* had children is well over 50%. Finally, legislators who have lobbied for constitutional amendments to ban same-sex marriage have done so to promote the best interests of children. For example, in calling for a constitutional amendment protecting marriage, President Bush stated that "Ages of experience have taught humanity that the commitment of a husband and wife to love and to serve one another promotes the welfare of children and the stability of society." In sum, I compared typical partners from gay and lesbian couples not living with children to typical partners from married heterosexual couples living with their own children.

Participants in the Project

Participants were drawn from two separate longitudinal studies, one in which heterosexual married couples were participants, and the other in which gay and lesbian cohabiting couples were participants. In both studies, annual assessments were obtained by mailed surveys. Up to 11 assessments were available for heterosexual couples, whereas up to 14 assessments were available for gay and lesbian couples. Heterosexual couples were initially recruited as newlyweds from marriage licenses published in the *Dayton Daily News*. Partners from gay and lesbian couples were recruited through requests for participants published in periodicals for gay men and lesbians, and from couples who had already participated in the survey. At the sixth and eighth assessments, additional couples (recommended by couples already participating) were added to the sample. Unlike the heterosexual couples who were first studied shortly after their wedding, gay and lesbian couples were first studied at different points in their relationship careers. There were no requirements for how long gay and lesbian partners had to be cohabiting, and none of the couples lived with children. . . .

Conclusion

My major premise in this article is that the complex controversy surrounding same-sex marriage can be examined, in part, as an empirical issue. I asked whether and the extent to which partners from the most likely type of gay and lesbian cohabiting couples—those without children—differ from partners from the most likely type of heterosexual married couples—those with children. My findings are of note because both partners from gay cohabiting, lesbian cohabiting, and heterosexual married couples were assessed repeatedly with psychometrically sound measures. Further, I employed statistical techniques appropriate for analyzing data obtained from both partners of the same couple. Finally, I examined the critical issue of the extent to which gay and lesbian partners differ from heterosexual parents over a range of issues. I studied average levels of variables known to be linked to relationship health, concurrent predictors of relationship quality, and predictors of relationship stability. These issues rarely have been addressed together, even in prospective longitudinal studies of married heterosexual couples.

Despite these positive features, the data I collected were limited. I make no claim that the samples of couples are representative, all measures were open to the biases associated with self-report, partners from the different types of couples were not matched on demographic variables, and gay and lesbian partners who were also parents were not studied. Further, had I selected different variables either from the domains of interest or from different domains (e.g., sexual behavior) and used different methodologies (e.g., interviews and direct observations), I might have obtained different findings. In the context of the current controversy over same-sex marriage, however, the nonrepresentative nature of the samples in particular may not be problematic. Opponents of same-sex marriage have not indicated that marriage should be denied to only *some* types of gay and lesbian couples (such as those in short-term relationships or those living with children). Rather, opponents have objected to marriage for *any and all* same-sex couples. Because opponents of same-sex marriage have targeted gay and lesbian partners as a class of individuals, the data reported here are relevant because the gay and lesbian partners studied are members of that class.

The overall pattern of findings across the range of issues studied here is clear: Relative to heterosexual parents, partners from gay couples and partners from lesbian couples do not function in ways that place their relationships at risk for distress. In particular, there is no evidence that gay partners and lesbian partners were psychologically maladjusted, that they had high levels of personality traits that predisposed them to relationship problems, that they had dysfunctional working models of their relationships, and that they used ineffective strategies to resolve conflict. The only area in which gay and lesbian partners fared worse than heterosexual parents was in the area of social support: Gay partners and lesbian partners received less support for their relationships from family members than heterosexual parents did.

Although the rates of relationship dissolution for the heterosexual couples and gay and lesbian couples were not directly comparable, it is safe to conclude that gay and lesbian couples dissolve their relationships more frequently than heterosexual couples, especially heterosexual couples with children. Perhaps a positive side of *not* having same-sex marriage is that gay and lesbian partners confront no *formal* institutionalized barriers and obstacles to leaving unhappy relationships. Lawyers need not be consulted, court action is not required, religious vows are not broken, and no recognized kin-by-marriage ties are severed. As a result, the relatively high rate of dissolution for gay and lesbian couples might indicate that gay and lesbian cohabiting partners are less likely than heterosexual married partners to find themselves trapped in empty relationships. Nonetheless, the absence of formal institutionalized barriers for members of gay and lesbian couples does not mean that partners from gay and lesbian couples do not perceive barriers to leaving their relationships, and that gay and lesbian partners easily exit from their relationships. To the contrary, I have reported elsewhere that partners from gay and lesbian cohabiting couples are similar to partners from heterosexual married couples in both appraisals of barriers to leaving their relationships and in the personal emotional turmoil experienced subsequent to dissolution.

Given the current lack of formal institutionalized barriers to leaving a same-sex relationship, perhaps the most remarkable finding from this project is that gay men and lesbians nonetheless build and sustain durable relationships. At the time of the last available assessment, 52% of the 125 gay stable couples and 37% of the 100 lesbian stable couples had been together for more than 10 years. Further, 14% of the 125 gay stable couples and 10% of the 100 lesbian stable couples had been together for more than 20 years. To the extent that marriage is regarded as a social and legal institution, conferring the right of marriage to gay men and lesbians might actually defend their relationships against the stresses that plague any couple in the early critical stages of the relationship, stresses that may lead to premature dissolution. Because involvement in a close relationship is linked to overall well-being, protecting same-sex relationships is tantamount to protecting the well-being of the partners involved in those relationships.

That concurrent relationship quality was predicted with variables from the psychological adjustment, personality traits, relationship styles, conflict resolution, and social support domains equally well for heterosexual parents as compared to gay partners and lesbian partners is strong evidence that the processes regulating close personal relationships are robust. . . . Further, that change in relationship quality discriminated unstable couples from stable couples for both heterosexual and gay and lesbian couples is additional evidence that models of marriage and marriagelike unions should recognize change as a core relationship process.

The findings reported here should not be taken to mean that gay and lesbian cohabiting couples and heterosexual married couples do not differ from each other *in any regard*. Indeed, the findings regarding social support from family members signify that gay and lesbian couples function in a social context that is very different from that of heterosexual couples. Further, because gay men and lesbians cannot use the gender of the partner to fashion the content of their relationships, they must negotiate common couple-level issues such as household labor and family rituals in creative ways that do not involve gender. The findings reported here *can* be taken as one basis for claiming that gay men and lesbians are entitled to legal recognition of their relationships not only because, as gay and lesbian citizens, they deserve the same rights and privileges as heterosexual citizens, but also because the processes that regulate their relationships are the same as those that regulate the relationships of heterosexual partners.

Peter Sprigg

 **NO**

Questions and Answers: What's Wrong with Letting Same-Sex Couples "Marry?"

What's Wrong with Letting Same-Sex Couples Legally "Marry?"
There are two key reasons why the legal rights, benefits, and responsibilities of civil marriage should not be extended to same-sex couples.

The first is that homosexual relationships are not marriage. That is, they simply do not fit the minimum necessary condition for a marriage to exist—namely, the union of a man and a woman.

The second is that homosexual relationships are harmful. Not only do they not provide the same benefits to society as heterosexual marriages, but their consequences are far more negative than positive.

Either argument, standing alone, is sufficient to reject the claim that same-sex unions should be granted the legal status of marriage.

Let's Look at the First Argument. Isn't Marriage Whatever the Law Says It Is?
No. Marriage is not a creation of the law. Marriage is a fundamental human institution that predates the law and the Constitution. At its heart, it is an anthropological and sociological reality, not a legal one. Laws relating to marriage merely recognize and regulate an institution that already exists.

But Isn't Marriage Just a Way of Recognizing People Who Love Each Other and Want to Spend Their Lives Together?
If love and companionship were sufficient to define marriage, then there would be no reason to deny "marriage" to unions of a child and an adult, or an adult child and his or her aging parent, or to roommates who have no sexual relationship, or to groups rather than couples. Love and companionship are usually considered integral to marriage in our culture, but they are not sufficient to define it as an institution. . . .

Why Should Homosexuals Be Denied the Right to Marry Like Anyone Else?
The fundamental "right to marry" is a right that rests with *individuals*, not with *couples*. Homosexual *individuals* already have exactly the same "right" to

marry as anyone else. Marriage license applications do not inquire as to a person's "sexual orientation.". . .

However, while every individual person is free to get married, *no* person, whether heterosexual or homosexual, has ever had a legal right to marry simply any willing partner. Every person, whether heterosexual or homosexual, is subject to legal restrictions as to whom they may marry. To be specific, every person, regardless of sexual preference, is legally barred from marrying a child, a close blood relative, a person who is already married, or a person of the same sex. There is no discrimination here, nor does such a policy deny anyone the "equal protection of the laws" (as guaranteed by the Constitution), since these restrictions apply equally to every individual.

Some people may wish to do away with one or more of these longstanding restrictions upon one's choice of marital partner. However, the fact that a tiny but vocal minority of Americans desire to have someone of the same sex as a partner does not mean that they have a "right" to do so, any more than the desires of other tiny (but less vocal) minorities of Americans give them a "right" to choose a child, their own brother or sister, or a group of two or more as their marital partners.

Isn't Prohibiting Homosexual "Marriage" Just as Discriminatory as Prohibiting Interracial Marriage, Like Some States Used to Do?

This analogy is not valid at all. Bridging the divide of the sexes by uniting men and women is both a worthy goal and a part of the fundamental purpose of marriage, common to all human civilizations.

Laws against interracial marriage, on the other hand, served only the purpose of preserving a social system of racial segregation. This was both an unworthy goal and one utterly irrelevant to the fundamental nature of marriage.

Allowing a black woman to marry a white man does not change the definition of marriage, which requires one man and one woman. Allowing two men or two women to marry would change that fundamental definition. Banning the "marriage" of same-sex couples is therefore essential to preserve the nature and purpose of marriage itself. . . .

How Would Allowing Same-Sex Couples to Marry Change Society's Concept of Marriage?

As an example, marriage will open wide the door to homosexual adoption, which will simply lead to more children suffering the negative consequences of growing up without both a mother and a father.

Among homosexual men in particular, casual sex, rather than committed relationships, is the rule and not the exception. And even when they do enter into a more committed relationship, it is usually of relatively short duration. For example, a study of homosexual men in the Netherlands (the first country in the world to legalize "marriage" for same-sex couples), published in the journal *AIDS* in 2003, found that the average length of "steady partnerships" was not more than 2 years (Maria Xiridou et al., in *AIDS* 2003, 17:1029–1038).

In addition, studies have shown that even homosexual men who are in "committed" relationships are not sexually faithful to each other. While infidelity among heterosexuals is much too common, it does not begin to compare to the rates among homosexual men. The 1994 National Health and Social Life Survey, which remains the most comprehensive study of Americans' sexual practices ever undertaken, found that 75 percent of married men and 90 percent of married women had been sexually faithful to their spouse. On the other hand, a major study of homosexual men in "committed" relationships found that only seven out of 156 had been sexually faithful, or 4.5 percent. The Dutch study cited above found that even homosexual men in "steady partnerships" had an average of eight "casual" sex partners per year.

So if same-sex relationships are legally recognized as "marriage," the idea of marriage as a sexually exclusive and faithful relationship will be dealt a serious blow. Adding monogamy and faithfulness to the other pillars of marriage that have already fallen will have overwhelmingly negative consequences for Americans' physical and mental health. . . .

Don't Homosexuals Need Marriage Rights So That They Will Be Able to Visit Their Partners in the Hospital?

The idea that homosexuals are routinely denied the right to visit their partners in the hospital is nonsense. When this issue was raised during debate over the Defense of Marriage Act in 1996, the Family Research Council did an informal survey of nine hospitals in four states and the District of Columbia. None of the administrators surveyed could recall a single case in which a visitor was barred because of their homosexuality, and they were incredulous that this would even be considered an issue.

Except when a doctor limits visitation for medical reasons, final authority over who may visit an adult patient rests with that patient. This is and should be the case regardless of the sexual orientation or marital status of the patient or the visitor.

The only situation in which there would be a possibility that the blood relatives of a patient might attempt to exclude the patient's homosexual partner is if the patient is unable to express his or her wishes due to unconsciousness or mental incapacity. Homosexual partners concerned about this (remote) possibility can effectively preclude it by granting to one another a health care proxy (the legal right to make medical decisions for the patient) and a power of attorney (the right to make all legal decisions for another person). Marriage is not necessary for this. It is inconceivable that a hospital would exclude someone who holds the health care proxy and power of attorney for a patient from visiting that patient, except for medical reasons.

The hypothetical "hospital visitation hardship" is nothing but an emotional smokescreen to distract people from the more serious implications of radically redefining marriage.

Don't Homosexuals Need the Right to Marry Each Other in Order to Ensure That They Will Be Able to Leave Their Estates to Their Partner When They Die?

As with the hospital visitation issue, the concern over inheritance rights is something that simply does not require marriage to resolve it. Nothing in current law prevents homosexual partners from being joint owners of property such as a home or a car, in which case the survivor would automatically become the owner if the partner dies.

An individual may leave the remainder of his estate to whomever he wishes—again, without regard to sexual orientation or marital status—simply by writing a will. As with the hospital visitation issue, blood relatives would only be able to overrule the surviving homosexual partner in the event that the deceased had failed to record his wishes in a common, inexpensive legal document. Changing the definition of a fundamental social institution like marriage is a rather extreme way of addressing this issue. Preparing a will is a much simpler solution.

Don't Homosexuals Need Marriage Rights So That They Can Get Social Security Survivor Benefits When a Partner Dies?

. . . Social Security survivor benefits were designed to recognize the non-monetary contribution made to a family by the homemaking and child-rearing activities of a wife and mother, and to ensure that a woman and her children would not become destitute if the husband and father were to die.

The Supreme Court ruled in the 1970s that such benefits must be gender-neutral. However, they still are largely based on the premise of a division of roles within a couple between a breadwinner who works to raise money and a homemaker who stays home to raise children.

Very few homosexual couples organize their lives along the lines of such a "traditional" division of labor and roles. They are far more likely to consist of two earners, each of whom can be supported in old age by their own personal Social Security pension.

Furthermore, far fewer homosexual couples than heterosexual ones are raising children at all, for the obvious reason that they are incapable of natural reproduction with each other. This, too, reduces the likelihood of a traditional division of labor among them.

Survivor benefits for the legal (biological or adopted) *children* of homosexual parents (as opposed to their partners) are already available under current law, so "marriage" rights for homosexual couples are unnecessary to protect the interests of these children themselves. . . .

Even If "Marriage" Itself Is Uniquely Heterosexual, Doesn't Fairness Require That the Legal and Financial Benefits of Marriage Be Granted to Same-Sex Couples—Perhaps Through "Civil Unions" or "Domestic Partnerships?"

No. The legal and financial benefits of marriage are not an entitlement to be distributed equally to all (if they were, single people would have as much reason to consider them "discriminatory" as same-sex couples). Society grants benefits to marriage because marriage has benefits for society—including, but not limited to, the reproduction of the species in households with the optimal household structure (i.e., the presence of both a mother and a father).

Homosexual relationships, on the other hand, have no comparable benefit for society, and in fact impose substantial costs on society. The fact that

AIDS is at least ten times more common among men who have sex with men than among the general population is but one example. . . .

Isn't It Possible That Allowing Homosexuals to "Marry" Each Other Would Allow Them to Participate in Those Benefits as Well?

Opening the gates of "marriage" to homosexuals is far more likely to change the attitudes and behavior of heterosexuals for the worse than it is to change the lifestyles of homosexuals for the better. . . .

What About the Argument That Homosexual Relations Are Harmful? What Do You Mean by That?

Homosexual men experience higher rates of many diseases, including:

- Human Papillomavirus (HPV), which causes most cases of cervical cancer in women and anal cancer in men
- Hepatitis A, B, and C
- Gonorrhea
- Syphilis
- "Gay Bowel Syndrome," a set of sexually transmitted gastrointestinal problems such as proctitis, proctocolitis, and enteritis
- HIV/AIDS (One Canadian study found that as a result of HIV alone, "life expectancy for gay and bisexual men is eight to twenty years less than for all men.")

Lesbian women, meanwhile, have a higher prevalence of:

- Bacterial vaginosis
- Hepatitis C
- HIV risk behaviors
- Cancer risk factors such as smoking, alcohol use, poor diet, and being overweight . . .

Do Homosexuals Have More Mental Health Problems as Well?

Yes. Various research studies have found that homosexuals have higher rates of:

- Alcohol abuse
- Drug abuse
- Nicotine dependence
- Depression
- Suicide

Isn't It Possible That These Problems Result From Society's "Discrimination" Against Homosexuals?

This is the argument usually put forward by pro-homosexual activists. However, there is a simple way to test this hypothesis. If "discrimination" were the cause of homosexuals' mental health problems, then one would expect those problems to be much less common in cities or countries, like San Francisco or the Netherlands, where homosexuality has achieved the highest levels of acceptance.

In fact, the opposite is the case. In places where homosexuality is widely accepted, the physical and mental health problems of homosexuals are greater, not less. This suggests that the real problem lies in the homosexual lifestyle itself, not in society's response to it. In fact, it suggests that increasing the level of social support *for* homosexual behavior (by, for instance, allowing same-sex couples to "marry") would only increase these problems, not reduce them. . . .

Haven't Studies Shown That Children Raised by Homosexual Parents Are No Different From Other Children?

No. This claim is often put forward, even by professional organizations. The truth is that most research on "homosexual parents" thus far has been marred by serious methodological problems. However, even pro-homosexual sociologists Judith Stacey and Timothy Biblarz report that the actual data from key studies show the "no differences" claim to be false.

Surveying the research (primarily regarding lesbians) in an *American Sociological Review* article in 2001, they found that:

- Children of lesbians are less likely to conform to traditional gender norms.
- Children of lesbians are more likely to engage in homosexual behavior.
- Daughters of lesbians are "more sexually adventurous and less chaste."
- Lesbian "co-parent relationships" are more likely to end than heterosexual ones.

A 1996 study by an Australian sociologist compared children raised by heterosexual married couples, heterosexual cohabiting couples, and homosexual cohabiting couples. It found that the children of heterosexual married couples did the best, and children of homosexual couples the worst, in nine of the thirteen academic and social categories measured. . . .

Do the American People Want to See "Marriages" Between Same-Sex Couples Recognized by Law?

No—and in the wake of the June 2003 court decisions to legalize such "marriages" in the Canadian province of Ontario and to legalize homosexual sodomy in the United States, the nation's opposition to such a radical social experiment has actually grown.

Five separate national opinion polls taken between June 24 and July 27, 2003 showed opponents of civil "marriage" for same-sex couples outnumbering supporters by not less than fifteen percentage points in every poll. The wording of poll questions can make a significant difference, and in this case, the poll with the most straightforward language (a Harris/CNN/Time poll asking "Do you think marriages between homosexual men or homosexual women should be recognized as legal by the law?") resulted in the strongest opposition, with 60 percent saying "No" and only 33 percent saying "Yes."

Even where pollsters drop the word "marriage" itself and use one of the euphemisms to describe a counterfeit institution parallel to marriage, we see a decline in public support for the homosexual agenda. The Gallup Poll, for instance, has asked, "Would you favor or oppose a law that would allow homosexual couples to legally form civil unions, giving them some of the legal rights of married couples?"

This question itself is misleading, in that it downplays the legal impact of "civil unions." Vermont, the only U.S. state to adopt "civil unions" (under coercion of a state court), actually gives *all* "of the legal rights of married couples" available under state law to people in a same-sex "civil union"—not just "some." But despite this distortion, a 49-percent-to-49-percent split on this question in May 2003 had changed to opposition by a margin of 58 percent to 37 percent when the *Washington Post* asked the identical question in August 2003.

Even the percentage of Americans willing to declare that "homosexual relations between consenting adults" (never mind homosexual civil "marriage") "should be legal" dropped from 60 percent to only 48 percent between May and July of 2003. The biggest drop in support, a stunning 23 percentage points (from 58 percent to 35 percent), came among African Americans—despite the rhetoric of pro-homosexual activists who seek to frame the issues of "gay rights" and same-sex unions as a matter of "civil rights." . . .

POSTSCRIPT

Should Same-Sex Couples Be Able to Marry?

Part of this discussion is that marriage is a civil right, not an inherent or moral one. Those supporting marriage rights for lesbian and gay couples cite the struggles of the civil rights movement of the 1960s in their current quest for equality for all couples. Among the points they make is that up until 1967, it was still illegal in some states for people of different races to marry. Many opponents find the idea of comparing same-sex marriage to the civil rights struggles of the 1960s and earlier is offensive, that it is like comparing apples and oranges. Many of these individuals believe that sexual orientation is chosen, rather than an inherent part of who one is—unlike race, which is predetermined. Most sexuality experts, however, agree that while we do not know for sure what "causes" a person to be heterosexual, bisexual, or homosexual, it is clear that it is determined very early in life, perhaps even before we are born. Regardless, is marriage a civil right? A legal right? An inherent right?

A final concern deals with mental health issues. What if Kurdek's research had found a different pattern of results indicative of more mental health and relationship issues among same-sex couples than heterosexual couples? Would such findings be a reasonable basis for arguing against same-sex marriage? Currently no heterosexual has to pass a "mental health test" in order to marry. Additionally, heterosexual couples do not have to demonstrate a "healthy" relationship in order to either marry or remain married. Finally, given that on at least some dimensions Kurdek found that same-sex couples actually functioned better than heterosexual couples. Is it possible that heterosexual couples could learn something from same-sex couples?

Suggested Readings

George Chauncey, *Why Marriage? The History Shaping Today's Debate over Gay Equality* (Basic Books, 2004).

Linda Hollingdale, *Creating Civil Union: Opening Hearts and Minds* (Common Humanity Press, 2002).

Jonathan Rauch, *Gay Marriage: Why It Is Good for Gays, Good for Straights, and Good for America* (Owl Books, 2004).

A. Sullivan and J. Landau, *Same-Sex Marriage: Pro and Con* (Vintage Books, 1997).

ISSUE 11

Can Lesbian and Gay Couples Be Appropriate Parents for Children?

YES: American Psychological Association, from *APA Policy Statement on Sexual Orientation, Parents, and Children*. Adopted July 2004.

NO: Timothy J. Dailey, from "State of the States: Update on Homosexual Adoption in the U.S." *Family Research Council* (2004)

ISSUE SUMMARY

YES: The American Psychological Association's Council of Representatives adopted this resolution that was drafted by a task force of expert psychologists. The resolution, based on a thorough review of the literature, opposes any discrimination based on sexual orientation and concludes that children reared by same-sex parents benefit from legal ties to each parent.

NO: Timothy J. Dailey, senior research fellow at the Center for Marriage and Family Studies, provides an overview of state laws pertaining to adoption by lesbian or gay parents. He points to studies showing that children do much better in family settings that include both a mother and a father, and that the sexual behaviors same-sex parents engage in make them, by definition, inappropriate role models for children.

Currently, there are thousands of children awaiting adoption. In many cases, there are strict requirements as to who can and cannot adopt. In one country, for example, a heterosexual couple must be married for at least four years—and if they already have one child, they can only adopt a child of a different sex. Most countries do not allow same-sex couples or openly lesbian or gay individuals to adopt children.

In the United States, same-sex couples can adopt in a number of ways. Some will adopt as single parents, even though they are in a long-term, committed relationship with another person, because the state or agency does not permit same-sex couples to adopt together. Others will do what is called "second parent" adoption—where one partner is the biological parent of the child, and the other can become the other legal parent by going through the court system. In other cases, the biological parent must terminate her or his own rights so that there can be a "joint adoption." Both parents jointly adopt the child and become equal, legal parents. This applies to unmarried different-sex couples, too.

There are a range of feelings about who should or should not parent children. Some individuals feel that children should be raised by a man and a woman who are married, not by a gay or lesbian individual or couple. Starting with the premise that homosexuality is wrong, they feel that such a relationship is an inappropriate context in which to raise children. For some of these opponents of lesbian and gay parenting, homosexuality is defined by behaviors. Opponents believe that children would be harmed if they grew up in gay or lesbian families, in part because they would grow up without a mother figure if raised by gay men or without a father figure if raised by lesbians. Additionally, because they fear that sexual orientation and behaviors can be learned, they also fear that a child raised by a lesbian or gay couple will be more likely to come out as lesbian or gay her or himself.

Other people do not believe that a person's sexual orientation determines her or his ability to parent. Whether a person is raised by one parent, two men, two women, or a man and a woman is less important than any individual's or couple's ability to love, support, and care for a child. They oppose the concept that a heterosexual couple in which there is abuse or where there are inappropriate sexual boundaries would be considered preferable to a lesbian or gay couple in a long-term, committed relationship who care for each other and their children. They point to the fact that most lesbian, gay, and bisexual adults were raised by heterosexual parents. Therefore, they believe, being raised by a lesbian or gay couple will not create lesbian, gay, or bisexual children, any more than being raised by a heterosexual, married couple would guarantee heterosexuality.

Some state laws support same-sex couples' right to adopt children, and some do not. In New Jersey, California, Connecticut, and Massachusetts, for example, joint or second parent adoption is currently available. In Utah, married heterosexual couples are given priority for foster or adoptive children, and in Mississippi, there is a law that outright bans a same-sex couple from being able to adopt children.

As you read this issue, think about what you think the characteristics of a good parent are. Can these characteristics be found only in heterosexual relationships, or can they be fulfilled by a same-sex relationship? Does the gender of a same-sex relationship affect your feelings on the subject? For example, do you find two women raising a child more or less threatening than two men?

In the following selections, the American Psychological Association's resolution concludes that there is no empirical evidence to support the claim that children raised by same-sex parents are harmed psychologically and that all children benefit from legal ties to both parents. Timothy J. Dailey asserts that gay men are sexually promiscuous, and are therefore poor role models and parents for children. Lesbians, he believes, are ineffective parents because they are raising a child without the presence and influence of a father figure, which theorists, he maintains, argue is vital to the psychosocial development of children, male and female.

YES

American Psychological
Association

APA Policy Statement on Sexual Orientation, Parents, & Children

Research Summary

Lesbian and Gay Parents

Many lesbians and gay men are parents. In the 2000 U.S. Census, 33% of female same-sex couple households and 22% of male same-sex couple households reported at least one child under the age of 18 living in the home. Despite the significant presence of at least 163,879 households headed by lesbian or gay parents in U.S. society, three major concerns about lesbian and gay parents are commonly voiced (Falk, 1994; Patterson, Fulcher & Wainright, 2002). These include concerns that lesbians and gay men are mentally ill, that lesbians are less maternal than heterosexual women, and that lesbians' and gay men's relationships with their sexual partners leave little time for their relationships with their children. In general, research has failed to provide a basis for any of these concerns (Patterson, 2002, 2004a; Perrin, 2002; Tasker, 1999; Tasker & Golombok, 1997). First, homosexuality is not a psychological disorder (Conger, 1975). Although exposure to prejudice and discrimination based on sexual orientation may cause acute distress (Mays & Cochran, 2001; Meyer, 2003), there is no reliable evidence that homosexual orientation per se impairs psychological functioning. Second, beliefs that lesbian and gay adults are not fit parents have no empirical foundation (Patterson, 2000, 2004a; Perrin, 2002). Lesbian and heterosexual women have not been found to differ markedly in their approaches to child rearing (Patterson, 2002; Tasker, 1999). Members of gay and lesbian couples with children have been found to divide the work involved in childcare evenly, and to be satisfied with their relationships with their partners (Patterson, 2000, 2004a). The results of some studies suggest that lesbian mothers' and gay fathers' parenting skills may be superior to those of matched heterosexual parents. There is no scientific basis for concluding that lesbian mothers or gay fathers are unfit parents on the basis of their sexual orientation (Armesto, 2002; Patterson, 2000; Tasker & Golombok, 1997). On the contrary, results of research suggest that lesbian and gay parents are as likely as heterosexual parents to provide supportive and healthy environments for their children.

Paige, R. U. (2005). Proceedings of the American Psychological Association, Incorporated, for the legislative year 2004. Minutes of the meeting of the Council of Representatives July 28 & 30, 2004, Honolulu, HI. Retrieved November 18, 2004, from the World Wide Web http://www.apa.org/governance/

Children of Lesbian and Gay Parents

As the social visibility and legal status of lesbian and gay parents has increased, three major concerns about the influence of lesbian and gay parents on children have been often voiced (Falk; 1994; Patterson, Fulcher & Wainright, 2002). One is that the children of lesbian and gay parents will experience more difficulties in the area of sexual identity than children of heterosexual parents. For instance, one such concern is that children brought up by lesbian mothers or gay fathers will show disturbances in gender identity and/or in gender role behavior. A second category of concerns involves aspects of children's personal development other than sexual identity. For example, some observers have expressed fears that children in the custody of gay or lesbian parents would be more vulnerable to mental breakdown, would exhibit more adjustment difficulties and behavior problems, or would be less psychologically healthy than other children. A third category of concerns is that children of lesbian and gay parents will experience difficulty in social relationships. For example, some observers have expressed concern that children living with lesbian mothers or gay fathers will be stigmatized, teased, or otherwise victimized by peers. Another common fear is that children living with gay or lesbian parents will be more likely to be sexually abused by the parent or by the parent's friends or acquaintances.

Results of social science research have failed to confirm any of these concerns about children of lesbian and gay parents (Patterson, 2000, 2004a; Perrin, 2002; Tasker, 1999). Research suggests that sexual identities (including gender identity, gender-role behavior, and sexual orientation) develop in much the same ways among children of lesbian mothers as they do among children of heterosexual parents (Patterson, 2004a). Studies of other aspects of personal development (including personality, self-concept, and conduct) similarly reveal few differences between children of lesbian mothers and children of heterosexual parents (Perrin, 2002; Stacey & Biblarz, 2001; Tasker, 1999). However, few data regarding these concerns are available for children of gay fathers (Patterson, 2004b). Evidence also suggests that children of lesbian and gay parents have normal social relationships with peers and adults (Patterson, 2000, 2004a; Perrin, 2002; Stacey & Biblarz, 2001; Tasker, 1999; Tasker & Golombok, 1997). The picture that emerges from research is one of general engagement in social life with peers, parents, family members, and friends. Fears about children of lesbian or gay parents being sexually abused by adults, ostracized by peers, or isolated in single-sex lesbian or gay communities have received no scientific support. Overall, results of research suggest that the development, adjustment, and well-being of children with lesbian and gay parents do not differ markedly from that of children with heterosexual parents.

Resolution

WHEREAS APA supports policy and legislation that promote safe, secure, and nurturing environments for all children (DeLeon, 1993, 1995; Fox, 1991; Levant, 2000);

WHEREAS APA has a long-established policy to deplore "all public and private discrimination against gay men and lesbians" and urges "the repeal of all discriminatory legislation against lesbians and gay men" (Conger, 1975);

WHEREAS the APA adopted the Resolution on Child Custody and Placement in 1976 (Conger, 1977, p. 432);

WHEREAS Discrimination against lesbian and gay parents deprives their children of benefits, rights, and privileges enjoyed by children of heterosexual married couples;

WHEREAS some jurisdictions prohibit gay and lesbian individuals and same-sex couples from adopting children, notwithstanding the great need for adoptive parents (Lofton v. Secretary, 2004);

WHEREAS There is no scientific evidence that parenting effectiveness is related to parental sexual orientation: lesbian and gay parents are as likely as heterosexual parents to provide supportive and healthy environments for their children (Patterson, 2000, 2004; Perrin, 2002; Tasker, 1999);

WHEREAS Research has shown that the adjustment, development, and psychological well-being of children is unrelated to parental sexual orientation and that the children of lesbian and gay parents are as likely as those of heterosexual parents to flourish (Patterson, 2004; Perrin, 2002; Stacey & Biblarz, 2001);

THEREFORE BE IT RESOLVED That the APA opposes any discrimination based on sexual orientation in matters of adoption, child custody and visitation, foster care, and reproductive health services;

THEREFORE BE IT FURTHER RESOLVED That the APA believes that children reared by a same-sex couple benefit from legal ties to each parent;

THEREFORE BE IT FURTHER RESOLVED That the APA supports the protection of parent-child relationships through the legalization of joint adoptions and second parent adoptions of children being reared by same-sex couples;

THEREFORE BE IT FURTHER RESOLVED That APA shall take a leadership role in opposing all discrimination based on sexual orientation in matters of adoption, child custody and visitation, foster care, and reproductive health services;

THEREFORE BE IT FURTHER RESOLVED That APA encourages psychologists to act to eliminate all discrimination based on sexual orientation in matters of adoption, child custody and visitation, foster care, and reproductive health services in their practice, research, education and training ("Ethical Principles," 2002, p. 1063);

THEREFORE BE IT FURTHER RESOLVED That the APA shall provide scientific and educational resources that inform public discussion and public policy development regarding discrimination based on sexual orientation in matters of adoption, child custody and visitation, foster care, and reproductive health services and that assist its members, divisions, and affiliated state, provincial, and territorial psychological associations.

References

Armesto, J. C. (2002). Developmental and contextual factors that influence gay fathers' parental competence: A review of the literature. *Psychology of Men and Masculinity, 3,* 67–78.

Conger, J. J. (1975). Proceedings of the American Psychological Association, Incorporated, for the year 1974: Minutes of the Annual meeting of the Council of Representatives. *American Psychologists, 30,* 620–651.

Conger, J. J. (1977). Proceedings of the American Psychological Association, Incorporated, for the legislative year 1976: Minutes of the Annual Meeting of the Council of Representatives. *American Psychologist, 32,* 408–438.

DeLeon, P. H. (1993). Proceedings of the American Psychological Association, Incorporated, for the year 1992: Minutes of the annual meeting of the Council of Representatives August 13 and 16, 1992, and February 26–28, 1993, Washington, DC. *American Psychologist, 48,* 782.

DeLeon, P. H. (1995). Proceedings of the American Psychological Association, Incorporated, for the year 1994: Minutes of the annual meeting of the Council of Representatives August 11 and 14, 1994, Los Angeles, CA, and February 17–19, 1995, Washington, DC. *American Psychologist, 49,* 627–628.

Ethical Principles of Psychologists and Code of Conduct. (2002). *American Psychologists, 57,* 1060–1073.

Fox, R. E. (1991). Proceedings of the American Psychological Association, Incorporated, for the year 1990: Minutes of the annual meeting of the Council of Representatives August 9 and 12, 1990, Boston, MA, and February 8–9, 1991, Washington, DC. *American Psychologist, 45,* 845.

Levant, R. F. (2000). Proceedings of the American Psychological Association, Incorporated, for the Legislative Year 1999: Minutes of the Annual Meeting of the Council of Representatives February 19–21, 1999, Washington, DC, and August 19 and 22, 1999, Boston, MA, and Minutes of the February, June, August, and December 1999 Meetings of the Board of Directors. *American Psychologist, 55,* 832–890.

Lofton v. Secretary of Department of Children & Family Services, 358 F.3d 804 (11th Cir. 2004).

Mays, V. M. & Cochran, S. D. (2001). Mental health correlates of perceived discrimination among lesbian, gay, and bisexual adults in the United States. *American Journal of Public Health, 91,* 1869–1876.

Meyer, I. H. (2003). Prejudice, social stress, and mental health in lesbian, gay, and bisexual populations: Conceptual issues and research evidence. *Psychological Bulletin, 129,* 674–697.

Patterson, C. J. (2000). Family relationships of lesbians and gay men. *Journal of Marriage and Family, 62,* 1052–1069.

Patterson, C. J. (2004a). Lesbian and gay parents and their children: Summary of research findings. In *Lesbian and gay parenting: A resource for psychologists.* Washington, DC: American Psychological Association.

Patterson, C. J. (2004b). Gay fathers. In M. E. Lamb (Ed.), *The role of the father in child development* (4th Ed.). New York: John Wiley.

Patterson, C. J., Fulcher, M., & Wainright, J. (2002). Children of lesbian and gay parents: Research, law, and policy. In B. L. Bottoms, M. B. Kovera, and B. D. McAuliff (Eds.), *Children, social science and the law* (pp. 176–199). New York: Cambridge University Press.

Perrin, E. C., and the Committee on Psychosocial Aspects of Child and Family Health (2002). Technical Report: Coparent or second-parent adoption by same-sex parents. *Pediatrics, 109,* 341–344.

Stacey, J. & Biblarz, T. J. (2001). (How) Does sexual orientation of parents matter? *American Sociological Review, 65,* 159–183.

Tasker, F. (1999). Children in lesbian-led families—A review. *Clinical Child Psychology and Psychiatry, 4,* 153–166.

Tasker, F., & Golombok, S. (1997). *Growing up in a lesbian family.* New York: Guilford Press.

Timothy J. Dailey    **NO**

State of the States: Update on Homosexual Adoption in the U.S.

The legal status of homosexual adoption varies from state to state, and is constantly changing due to court decisions and new state laws addressing the issue. Further complicating the issue are gay activist organizations that present misleading accounts of court rulings and laws reflecting unfavorably on homosexual parenting.

States that Specifically Prohibit Gay Adoption

Three states, Florida, Mississippi, and Utah, have passed statutes specifically prohibiting homosexual adoption. The advocates of gay adoption downplay the Utah statute, asserting that it was not intended to prevent adoption by homosexuals. Liz Winfeld, writing in the *Denver Post,* discusses claims that the Utah law was aimed squarely at homosexuals: "Not true. Utah disallows any unmarried person from adopting regardless of gender or orientation."[1]. . .

In fact, the Utah law was enacted specifically to close loopholes in Utah adoption laws that were being taken advantage of by homosexual couples seeking to adopt children. . . .

The ensuing fight led to the legislature passing a statute barring homosexual adoptions. . . .

States that Specifically Permit Gay Adoption

USA Today reports that seven states, including California, Connecticut, Illinois, Massachusetts, New Jersey, New York, Vermont, and the District of Columbia permit homosexuals to adopt.[2] However, at present the inclusion of California on this list is inaccurate.

States that Permit Second-Parent Adoption

Homosexual couples have adopted children through "second-parent" adoption policies in at least twenty states. There is no evidence that homosexuals in the remaining states are permitted to adopt children, a fact admitted by the gay activist Human Rights Campaign (HRC): "In the remaining 24 states, our research has not revealed any second-parent adoptions."[3]

At least one state has reversed its policy of permitting second-parent adoptions. In November 2000, the Superior Court of Pennsylvania ruled that same-sex couples cannot adopt children.[4] In addition, a court decision in California has reversed that state's policy of permitting homosexuals to adopt children. On October 25, 2001, the 4th District Court of Appeal (San Diego) ruled that there was no legal authority under California law permitting second-parent adoptions.[5] . . .

Homosexual Households in the United States

There are widely varying and unsubstantiated claims about the numbers of children being raised in gay and lesbian households. . . .

- The U.S. Census Bureau reports that there are 601,209 (304,148 male homosexual and 297,061 lesbian) same-sex unmarried partner households, for a total of 1,202,418 individuals, in the United States.[6] If one million children were living in households headed by homosexual couples, this would mean that, on average, *every* homosexual household has at least one child.
- However, a survey in *Demography* indicates that 95 percent of partnered male homosexual and 78 percent of partnered lesbian households do *not* have children.[7] This would mean that the one million children presumed to be living in homosexual households would be divided among the 15,000 (five percent of 304,148) male homosexual and 65,000 (22 percent of 297,061) lesbian households that actually have children. This would result in an astounding 12.5 children per gay and lesbian family.

The cases highlighted by the media to generate sympathy for homosexual adoption typically feature "two-parent" homosexual households. Of course, some children are also being raised by a natural parent who identifies himself or herself as homosexual and lives alone. Nevertheless, the hypothetical calculations above give some indication of how absurdly inflated most of the estimates are concerning the number of children being raised by homosexuals. Far from being the proven success that some claim, homosexual parenting remains a relatively rare phenomenon.

Implications for Homosexual Parenting

Demands that homosexuals be accorded the right to . . . adopt children fit into the gay agenda by minimizing the differences between homosexual and heterosexual behavior in order to make homosexuality look as normal as possible. However, as already shown, only a small minority of gay and lesbian households have children. Beyond that, the evidence also indicates that comparatively few homosexuals choose to establish households together—the type of setting that is a prerequisite for the rearing of children. Consider the following:

- HRC claims that the U.S. population of gays and lesbians is 10,456,405, or 5 percent of the total U.S. population over 18 years of age.[8] The best available data supports a much lower estimate for those who engage in same-sex sexual relations.[9] However, assuming the higher estimate for the purposes of argument, this would indicate that *only 8.6 percent* of homosexuals (1,202,418 out of 10,456,405) choose to live in a household with a person of the same sex.

- HRC asserts that "30 percent of gay and lesbian people are living in a committed relationship in the same residence."[10] Assuming HRC's own figures, that would mean over three million gays and lesbians are living in such households, which, as shown above, is a wildly inflated estimate over the census figures. It is worth noting that the HRC claim amounts to a tacit admission that 70 percent of gays and lesbians choose not to live in committed relationships and establish households together.
- HRC claims that the numbers of gay and lesbian households were "undercounted" by the census. However, if true, it would represent an unprecedented, massive undercount of 260 percent on the part of the U.S. Census Bureau.

The census figures indicate that only a small minority of gays and lesbians have made the lifestyle choice that is considered a fundamental requisite in any consideration regarding adoption, and only a small percentage of those households actually have children. The evidence thus does not support the claim that significant numbers of homosexuals desire to provide a stable family setting for children.

The Nature of Homosexual "Committed Relationships"

Gay activists admit that the ultimate goal of the drive to legitimize homosexual marriage and adoption is to change the essential character of marriage, removing precisely the aspects of fidelity and chastity that promote stability in the home. They pursue their goal heedless of the fact that such households are unsuitable for the raising of children:

- Paula Ettelbrick, former legal director of the Lambda Legal Defense and Education Fund, has stated, "Being queer is more than setting up house, sleeping with a person of the same gender, and seeking state approval for doing so. . . . Being queer means pushing the parameters of sex, sexuality, and family, and in the process transforming the very fabric of society."[11]
- According to homosexual writer and activist Michelangelo Signorile, the goal of homosexuals is to redefine the term *monogamy*.

For these men the term 'monogamy' simply doesn't necessarily mean sexual exclusivity. . . . The term 'open relationship' has for a great many gay men come to have one specific definition: A relationship in which the partners have sex on the outside often, put away their resentment and jealousy, and discuss their outside sex with each other, or share sex partners.[12]

- The views of Signorile and Ettelbrick regarding marriage are widespread in the homosexual community. According to the *Mendola Report,* a mere 26 percent of homosexuals believe that commitment is most important in a marriage relationship.[13] . . .

Even those who support the concept of homosexual "families" admit to their unsuitability for children:

- In their study in *Family Relations,* L. Koepke et al. observed, "Even individuals who believe that same-sex relationships are a legitimate choice for adults may feel that children will suffer from being reared in such families."[14]
- Pro-homosexual researchers, J. J. Bigner and R. B. Jacobson describe the homosexual father as "socioculturally unique," trying to take on "two apparently opposing roles: that of a father (with all its usual connotations) and that of a homosexual man." They describe the homosexual father as "both structurally and psychologically at social odds with his interest in keeping one foot in both worlds: parenting and homosexuality."[15]

In truth, the two roles are fundamentally incompatible. The instability, susceptibility to disease, and domestic violence that is disproportionate in homosexual relationships would normally render such households unfit to be granted custody of children. However, in the current social imperative to grant legitimacy to the practice of homosexuality in every conceivable area of life, such considerations are often ignored.

But children are not guinea pigs to be used in social experiments in redefining the institutions of marriage and family. They are vulnerable individuals with vital emotional and developmental needs. The great harm done by denying them both a mother and a father in a committed marriage will not easily be reversed, and society will pay a grievous price for its ill-advised adventurism.

Notes

1. Liz Winfeld, "In a Family Way," *Denver Post,* November 28, 2001.
2. Marilyn Elias, "Doctor's Back Gay "Co-Parents," *USA Today,* February 3, 2002.
3. "Chapter 4: Second-Parent Adoption," in *The Family* (Human Rights Campaign, 2002). . . .
4. Ibid.
5. Bob Egelko, "Court Clarifies Decision on Adoptions," *San Francisco Chronicle,* November 22, 2001. The decision is under review by the California Supreme Court.
6. "PCT 14: Unmarried-Partner Households by Sex of Partners" (U.S. Census Bureau: Census 2000 Summary File 1).
7. Dan Black et al., "Demographics of the Gay and Lesbian Population in the United States: Evidence from Available Systematic Data Sources," *Demography* 37 (May 2000): 150.

8. David M. Smith and Gary J. Gates, "Gay and Lesbian Families in the United States: Same-Sex Unmarried Partner Households," *Human Rights Campaign* (August 22, 2001): 2.

9. Dan Black et al., "Demographics of the Gay and Lesbian Population," "4.7 percent of men in the combined samples have had at least one same-sex experience since age 18, but only 2.5 percent of men have engaged in exclusively same-sex sex over the year preceding the survey. Similarly, 3.5 percent of women have had at least one same-sex sexual experience, but only 1.4 percent have had exclusively same-sex sex over the year preceding the survey." (p. 141.)

10. Ibid.

11. Paula Ettelbrick, quoted in William B. Rubenstein, "Since When Is Marriage a Path to Liberation?" *Lesbians, Gay Men, and the Law* (New York: The New Press, 1993), pp. 398, 400.

12. Michelangelo Signorile, *Life Outside* (New York: HarperCollins, 1997), p. 213.

13. Mary Mendola, *The Mendola Report* (New York: Crown, 1980), p. 53.

14. L. Koepke et al., "Relationship Quality in a Sample of Lesbian Couples with Children and Child-free Lesbian Couples," *Family Relations* 41 (1992): 228.

15. Bigner and Jacobson, "Adult Responses to Child Behavior and Attitudes Toward Fathering," Frederick W. Bozett, ed., *Homosexuality and the Family* (New York: Harrington Park Press, 1989), pp. 174, 175.

POSTSCRIPT

Can Lesbian and Gay Couples Be Appropriate Parents for Children?

Parenting is an area that has so many unknown factors, influences, and outcomes. Two-parent, high-income families sometimes have children who grow up with emotional and/or behavioral problems. Single parents can raise healthy, well-adjusted children. Some heterosexual couples raise children effectively and some do not; some lesbian or gay couples raise children effectively, and some do not. Some parents abuse their children; most do not.

While there is much research exploring correlations between economic health, number of parents, and other factors, literature reviewing the connections between a parent's sexual orientation and her or his ability to parent remains inconclusive. There are studies maintaining that children need to be raised by a married, heterosexual couple, and there are studies asserting that a same-sex couple can do just as effective a job.

There is also insufficient information about sexual orientation itself, and the effects that having a lesbian, gay, or bisexual parent may or may not have on a child. The lack of information and plethora of misinformation breed fear. When people are afraid, they want to protect—in this case, people who do not understand the bases of sexual orientation feel they need to protect children. In doing so, they sometimes make decisions that are not always in the best interest of the child. For example, in 1996, a divorced heterosexual couple living in Florida was battling over custody of their 11-year-old daughter. The male partner had recently completed an eight-year prison sentence for the murder of his first wife, and had married his third. His ex-wife, however, had since met and partnered with a woman. A judge determined that the man and his new wife would provide a more appropriate home for the child than the child's mother because she was in a relationship with another woman. In the end, the judge believed that the child would do best in a home with a mother and a father, even though the father was convicted of second-degree murder and accused of sexually molesting his daughter from his first marriage.

How do you feel about this? If you feel that heterosexual couples are more appropriate parents than same-sex couples, how would the fact that one of the heterosexual partners had committed a capital crime affect your opinion?

Sometimes, we argue for what we think "should be" in a given situation. A challenge arises when comparing the "should be" to the "is"—what we think is best as opposed to the reality. If you feel that heterosexual married couples make the best parents, what should be done with those same-sex couples who are providing a loving, stable home for their children? Would it be best to leave the child where she or he is, or do you think the child would be better

203

off removed from her or his existing family structure and placed with a heterosexual couple? Clearly, this is a discussion and debate that will continue as more and more same-sex couples not only adopt, but also have biological children of their own.

Suggested Readings

Jane Drucker (2001). *Lesbian and Gay Families Speak Out: Understanding the Joys and Challenges of Diverse Family Life*. HarperCollins: New York.

Noelle Howey, Ellen Samuels, Margarethe Cammermeyer, & Dan Savage (2000). *Out of the Ordinary: Essays on Growing Up with Gay, Lesbian, and Transgender Parents*. St. Martin's Press: New York.

Patricia Morgan (2002). *Children as trophies? Examining the evidence on same-sex parenting*. The Christian Institute: Newcastle upon Tyne, NE, UK.

ISSUE 12

Are Fathers Essential for Children's Well-Being?

YES: Sarah S. McLanahan and Marcia J. Carlson, from "Welfare Reform, Fertility, and Father Involvement," *The Future of Children Journal* (2002)

NO: Peggy Drexler, from *Raising Boys Without Men* (Rodale Books, 2005)

ISSUE SUMMARY

YES: Sarah S. McLanahan and Marcia J. Carlson examine the negative effects of father-absence in children's lives and offer suggestions for how to increase father involvement.

NO: In contrast, Peggy Drexler studied what she terms "maverick" moms to show how boys can succeed in homes without fathers.

$\mathbf{F}$or decades there has been active debate about parenting roles and responsibilities. What does it mean to be a responsible parent? Is one sex naturally better at parenting than the other? Are there essential characteristics of fathering versus mothering? Is having parents of two sexes necessary for the well-being of children? Should mothers work or engage in other activities outside the family? Should fathers move beyond the provider or breadwinner role and become more involved in the physical and emotional care of their children? Should fathers emulate mothers' traditional nurturing activities? Or, should fathers uphold their role as masculine role models for their children? Are fathers essential?

The twentieth century saw significant changes in the American family. Well over half of mothers are currently in the paid workforce. More than half of all new marriages end in divorce. One-third of all births are to single women. The traditional family ideal in which fathers work and mothers care for children and the household characterizes less than 10 percent of American families with children under the age of 18.

Mothers' increased labor force participation has been a central catalyst of change in the culture of fatherhood. Mothers began to spend less time with children, and fathers began to spend more time. Thus, the cultural interest in fatherhood increased, and it was assumed that fathers were becoming more nurturant and more essential. The history of the ideals of fatherhood reveals that fathers have progressed from distant breadwinner to masculine sex-role model to equal coparent.

Despite changes in the *ideals* of fatherhood, some family scholars observe that fathers' behavior has not changed. Rather, it appears that mothers' behavioral change may be responsible for the change in the culture of fatherhood. A recent review of comparisons of fathers' and mothers' involvement with their children (in "intact" two-parent families) reveals a gap: fathers' engagement with their children is about 40 percent that of mothers'; fathers' accessibility is about two-thirds that of mothers. Fathers' lesser involvement is even more characteristic of divorced and never-married families. Nearly 90 percent of all children of divorce live with their mothers. Most single-parent fathers are "occasional" fathers. More than one-third of children in divorced families will not see their fathers at all after the first year of separation. Only 10 percent of children will have contact with fathers 10 years after divorce. Yet at the same time, research has documented the important ways in which fathers influence their children. But does this mean that fathers are essential?

Some contend that fathers are not mothers; fathers are essential and unique. Many reject a gender-neutral model of parenting, arguing that mothers and fathers have specific roles that are complementary; both parents are essential to meet children's needs. Proponents of this model assert that fatherhood is an essential role for men and pivotal to society. They maintain that fathers offer unique contributions to their children as male role models, thereby privileging their children. Moreover, fathers' unique abilities are necessary for children's successful development.

The following selections advance two models. McLanahan and Carlson's paper suggests that father-absence plays an essential role in the economic welfare of children and their mothers. They contend that fathers serve as not only a financial resource but an emotional resource as well for children. They conclude that welfare policy reform is necessary and make several policy recommendations to increase the presence of fathers in children's lives. Their arguments are premised on the assumption that men bring something special to the parent-child relationship. In contrast, Peggy Drexel's study of boys raised without fathers challenges traditional views of fathering. Her results suggest that boys can thrive without fathers. Responsible parenting can occur in a variety of family structures, including single parents and same-sex parents. Drexel challenges four myths about traditional families and shows that single mothers can be successful, and does so without bashing fathers.

YES ↩

YES

Sara S. McLanahan and
Marcia J. Carlson

Welfare Reform, Fertility, and Father Involvement

The Personal Responsibility and Work Opportunity Reconciliation Act of 1996 represented a historic shift in U.S. policy toward poor families and children. In addition to requiring that low-income parents assume greater responsibility for their own economic well-being through increased work, the reform legislation included provisions to discourage births outside of marriage, to promote and strengthen two-parent families, and to encourage father involvement (at least with respect to financial support). These provisions reflect—and contribute to—a growing awareness of the importance of fathers for children.

Until recently, discussions about welfare policy have largely excluded fathers, except with respect to their frequent failure to pay child support. Despite rising concerns since the 1980s about the negative consequences of out-of-wed-lock childbearing and single-parenthood (particularly for children, but also for society), most policy and research about families on welfare have focused only on single mothers. However, recent research on fatherhood has pointed to the range of contributions that fathers can make in their children's lives, as well as to the barriers that some fathers face in providing economic and emotional support for their children.

Recent Trends and Effects on Children

Several major demographic trends in the latter half of the twentieth century have affected the composition of families in the United States, especially low-income families. In particular, declining marriage rates, increasing divorce rates, and increasing rates of births to unmarried women have combined to increase the likelihood that children will spend time living away from their fathers. Although many unmarried parents work together to raise their children by cohabiting or maintaining frequent contact, father involvement for most low-income families in this situation is not necessarily stable. . . .

. . . [T]rends suggest the emergence of a new family type—the "fragile family," comprised of unmarried parents who are working together to raise their children either by cohabiting or maintaining frequent contact. Such families are deemed fragile because of the multiple risks associated with nonmarital child-bearing, including poverty, and to signify the vulnerability of the parents'

From *The Future of Children Journal*, vol. 12, no. 1, 2002, pp. 148, 150, 152–156, 159–160. A publication of the David and Lucile Packard Foundation. Reprinted by permission.

relationship. Union dissolution rates are much higher among cohabiting couples than among married couples; this is true particularly in the United States, but also in Western European countries, where cohabitation is even more prevalent.

Fathers as Resources for Children

The consequences of not having a father have been a source of long-standing concern to society, but the focus of research on fathers has evolved as the larger cultural meaning of fatherhood has changed over time. Only in the last several decades have scholars begun to examine father involvement more broadly. Early studies focused on the effects of *father absence,* defined as the father not living with the child. In this "deficit model," children in mother-only (or "father-absent") families were compared to children in two-parent ("father-present") families without directly measuring what fathers—whether living with their children or not—were actually contributing to their children's lives. . . .

In the 1980s, with the emergence of a "new" fatherhood model (particularly among the middle class) in which there were greater expectations for fathers' emotional investment and active participation in parenting, studies began to investigate the potential *positive* effects of father involvement. The first studies in this area focused on fathers' financial support and found that the payment of child support is positively associated with children's well-being. . . .

A growing literature in sociology and child development has investigated the effects of fathers' nonmonetary involvement as well, such as participating in shared activities with the child and developing a close, high-quality relationship with the child. Positive father involvement, particularly by fathers who live with their children, has been linked to less-frequent child and adolescent behavioral problems, including delinquency, substance use, anxiety, and depression. . . .

Not surprisingly, fathers who do not live with their children see them less often, which decreases the likelihood that the father and child will develop a close relationship. Also, fathers who do not share the child's household are less likely to contribute financial resources to support their child, as they have less ability than a father living with the child has to monitor the allocation of resources by the mother. Particularly following divorce, absent fathers may become less altruistic toward their children over time. Divorced parents also may be less able to reinforce one another in child rearing, further diminishing the father's role. Although these findings refer to formerly married couples, the consequences are likely similar for unmarried couples following a separation. . . .

Policies Designed to Promote Father Involvement

As family demographics and the social environment have changed, public policy also has evolved in an attempt to mitigate the consequences of family instability and, in some cases, to reshape the demographic trends themselves. Most recently, the 1996 federal welfare reform law gave new emphasis to two primary categories of programmatic interventions intended to promote father involvement: 1) programs designed to discourage nonmarital fertility and thus decrease the formation of "father-absent" families; and 2) programs intended to increase nonresident fathers' support for and involvement with their children.

Programs to Discourage the Formation of Father-Absent Families

Efforts to reduce the rising number of father-absent families have focused primarily on preventing unwanted pregnancy among unmarried women, especially teenage girls. This approach is guided by the awareness that when a pregnancy is unintended, the father is less likely to live with the child and provide "positive parenting." In contrast, when a pregnancy is intended and births are spaced appropriately, better maternal and child health outcomes are likely, and assurance is greater that the child will be loved and nurtured by both the mother and the father. Most births to unmarried couples, however, are unintended. . . . Therefore, reducing the incidence of unintended pregnancy among unmarried couples represents a promising strategy to reduce the likelihood that a child will grow up without a father's involvement in his or her life. Pregnancy prevention efforts fall into three main categories: family planning, teen programs, and family caps. . . .

Overall, though pregnancy prevention programs have met with some success, they have not fundamentally abated the high levels of nonmarital fertility and the formation of father-absent families. This is because nonmarital fertility has risen for reasons that reflect larger cultural shifts in attitudes, values, and practices—simply because couples lack information about sex or access to contraceptive technology. As described in the section on demographic trends, consensual unions other than marriage have become more accepted and prevalent, increasing the likelihood that children will be born outside of marriage.

Programs to Encourage Greater Father Involvement

Because "father absence" is the defining characteristic of most single-parent families, public policy has attempted to compensate for the resources that children lose when the father is not in the household. The most obvious resource deficit is economic—without fathers' income, female-headed families are much more likely to be poor. Initially, policies were designed to compensate for the loss of the father's income directly with cash assistance and in-kind benefits such as food stamps and Medicaid. Then, as single mothers increasingly were women who were separated and divorced from their partners, as opposed to being widowed, policymakers began to consider seeking resources from fathers. Programs were initiated to collect child support from unmarried fathers and, more recently, to increase their earnings so that they can pay child support. Only recently has policy attention to fathers broadened beyond financial support to incorporate nonmonetary investments in children as well. . . .

Until very recently, poor noncustodial fathers of children on welfare were largely ignored by social policymakers and disconnected from resources that might help them become more involved in their children's lives. The child support system has operated solely as an enforcement agency collecting money from fathers (and punishing those who fail to pay) rather than as a social service organization attempting to balance responsibility with appropriate services and supports (and providing incentives to pay). This is changing as the confluence of three factors—demographic changes that have increased the number of fragile families; growing awareness of the difficulties faced by low-income fathers and families; and greater understanding of the benefits to children of father involvement—has led to the development of programs that more effectively promote fathers' financial and emotional involvement with their children.

Representing an important first step toward developing such programs, in March 2000 the U.S. Department of Health and Human Services approved 10 state demonstration projects to "improve the opportunities of young, unmarried fathers to support their children both financially and emotionally." These new programs serve both divorced fathers and new fathers in fragile families. They have varied emphases, but they generally are designed to improve fathers' parenting skills and employment capabilities, and to ensure that fathers have access to their children. Initial assessments of these new programs have found that enrolling fathers and sustaining their participation over time present particular challenges. More rigorous evaluations have yet to determine the nature and magnitude of the impacts across various program types. . . .

Conclusion

This article has highlighted the changing composition of families in the United States, particularly the fact that many children will spend some time living away from their father during childhood. Because fathers offer important financial and emotional resources to children, it is important to encourage greater father involvement, especially among fathers who do not live with their children. Recent trends and concern for such children have stimulated a variety of new public policies and programs to promote fathers' involvement with their children, both financially and emotionally.

Public policy, supported by sound research, can improve the likelihood that fathers will be involved with their children, both by discouraging the formation of father-absent families in the first place, and by increasing incentives and supports for positive father involvement. For example, programs designed to reduce the rising number of father-absent families by focusing on preventing unwanted pregnancies, especially among teens, appear to be most successful when they seek to alter adolescents' life opportunities in addition to providing family planning education or services. Also, although early efforts to encourage father involvement yielded disappointing results, newer programs that are better targeted and timed to the birth of a child appear to hold greater promise for improving the circumstances of low-income fathers and families.

Raising Boys Without Men

For as long as any of us can remember, parenting theory and popular culture have promoted the notion that Mommy and Daddy—the traditional family unit—produce the best sons. That message has become louder in recent years. In 1992, President George H. Bush announced that children "should have the benefit of being born into families with a mother and father," citing the number and the gender of parents and their biological bond as central to optimal family life. And his son has supported a constitutional amendment to ban gay marriage and thus produce the hallowed nuclear family. Whether conservative politicians and religious leaders like it or not, the family structure has changed—dramatically—and the Bush definition of family seems, well, less than definitive.

Across the country, a lightning bolt has split the trunk of the family tree, and it is growing in new and challenging directions.

Some have labeled this a family crisis, though as Laura Benkov, Ph.D., points out in her book *Reinventing the Family*, "A careful look at other places and other times reveals [the nuclear family] to be but one of many possible human arrangements." Further, according to historian Stephanie Coontz, "Families have always been in flux and often in crisis; they have never lived up to the nostalgic notions about 'the way things used to be.' " We cannot roll back history, nor—once we tear away prevailing misconceptions about the American family—would we want to. So get ready for a little myth-bashing reality check.

> **Myth #1: Families of the past didn't have problems like families do today.** The reality is that desertion, child abuse, spousal battering, and alcohol or drug addiction have always troubled a significant number of families. Many of those perky housewives from 50 years ago depended on mother's little helper (tranquilizers, mood enhancers, and alcohol) to see them through their mind-numbing days. In other words, the good old days weren't what they are cracked up to be.
>
> **Myth #2: The 1950s male-breadwinner family is and always has been the only traditional family structure in America.** Families have regularly been torn apart and reassembled throughout human history. Not until the 1920s did the majority of children in this country live in a home where the husband was the breadwinner,

the wife was a full-time homemaker, and the kids could go to school instead of working for their wages.

Myth #3: The sexual revolution of the 1960s caused the rise in unwed motherhood. The reality is that the sharpest increase in unwed motherhood occurred when it tripled between 1940 and 1958. During the Great Depression, abandonment rates rose, with husbands leaving their wives (and children if they had them). Out-of-wedlock sex shot up during World War II. And below the surface, the underpinnings of traditional marital stability continued to erode. After this shift, nontraditional families (including divorced families, stepfamilies, single parents, gay and lesbian families, lone householders, and unmarried cohabiting couples) would never again be such a minor part of the family terrain that we could count on marriage alone as our main institution for caring for dependents.

While women's out-of-wedlock sex and the breakdown of the nuclear family are issues for politicians who see it as the root to society's ills, women—whether in lesbian relationships, widowed, divorced, or as single mothers by choice—are transforming the way we think about unwed mothers. In my neighborhood and neighborhoods all across this country, single mothers and mothers in pairs are at the forefront of what it means to re-create the new American family. They are a galvanizing force in American society as our nation struggles to accommodate a broader and more useful— yet no less loving—definition of family.

Myth #4: Children of divorced or unwed mothers are sure to fail. The reality is that it's how a family acts, not the way it's made up, that determines whether the children succeed or fail. The number of times you eat dinner with your kids is a better guide to how well they'll turn out than the number or gender of the parents at the dinner table. Marriage is no longer the gold standard when it comes to being a good parent. Though residual condemnation still hits here and there, Dr. Benkov points out that raising children without being married has "emerged as a potentially positive decision, not an unwanted circumstance." We all can understand the appeal of a perfect mom-and-dad family. But we have to wonder, how many children and parents in this country actually live there?

Diversity is taking over America. The U.S. Census Bureau reported that in 2000 only 23.5 percent of households in the United States contained families with a married mom and dad and their children. The percentage of all households that were unmarried in 1950 was 22 percent; in 2000 that number had reached 48 percent. Figures released from the 2000 census show that mothers raising sons (and daughters) alone or in pairs in this new world are just as prevalent as the 1950s Donna Reed mom-and-dad version. The number of families headed by single mothers increased 25 percent between 1990 and 2000, to more than 7.5 million households.

This new breed of mothers without fathers is likely to be financially secure, straight or gay, and of any age and any race. The median age for unmarried mothers is late twenties, and the fastest-growing category is White women. Whether these women are divorced or never married, mothering singly and in pairs has not only entered the popular culture and become acceptable; it also is now considered chic. High-profile moms like Angelina Jolie, Isabella Rossellini, Wendy Wasserstein, Camryn Manheim, and Diane Keaton are parenting sons and daughters without husbands, and lesbian moms such as comedian Rosie O'Donnell and singer Melissa Etheridge are coming out with their partners and are mothering together. Few of these women have men as full-time parenting partners. Yet despite their deviation from what's been deemed a "normal" family pattern, the media routinely refer to their motherhood in a positive light. . . .

The Tarnished Gold Standard

Conservative critics tell us that family life is on the verge of being atomized, that our children are corrupted, that our moral codes are crushed. As we all know, there's a serious movement to define legal marriage as the union of one man and one woman, the conservative ideal for marriage—and for family making. Many in the so-called marriage movement (and, I would argue, in the clinical research field as well) take a pessimistic view of children raised by parents who are not a traditionally married couple. The mom-and-dad family may have its problems, conservative advocates of family values agree, but they pronounce the presence of a strong male family figure to be vital to a child's development.

Marriage proponents, however, ignore the dark side of matrimony. While overall both adults and children get a host of benefits from good marriages, the situation for kids in bad marriages is quite the opposite. Married couples in conflict don't always provide what's best for their children. Further, according to Philip Cowan, Ph.D., professor of psychology at the University of California at Berkeley, the way husbands and wives treat each other has as much impact on their children's academic confidence, social adjustment, and behavior problems in school as the way the parents treat the children. A high-conflict marriage or a marriage that isn't working can negatively affect children in a way that might never happen in a single-mom family.

In addition, social scientists have confused family structure with economic factors that can influence behavior and performance. Researchers who analyze the data of boys having problems, for example, see that a large percentage of these kids come from single-mother homes and assume that mothers' single status has caused their boys to fail. Think back to the days when mothers were blamed for their children's having illnesses they didn't cause. I believe the same thing is happening with single moms and two-mom households: They're blaming the mom instead of the economic situation of the family. A study by researchers at Cornell University found that single mothering did not automatically spell trouble in school for elementary-age sons. How much schooling the mother received and her abilities had the biggest influence on her children's school performance—not the fact that the boys were without fathers.

Similarly, it had been assumed that boys from divorced families had more problems than children of two-parent, mom-and-dad families, until a 2000 study reported by the New York University Child Study Center discovered that the same boys had been demonstrating behavioral problems even prior to the divorce. When the researchers controlled for earlier behavior problems, the differences between boys from intact families and from divorced families were significantly reduced. The researchers concluded that to blame the boys' difficulties after the divorce on the actual divorce or separation limited the scope of understanding. The likely turmoil that preceded the split had to be considered a contributing factor to any problems observed in the boys after the divorce.

So now we have seen a series of bad raps against mothers. I would say that ever since Eve, women have been blamed for the evils of the world (and she gave Adam the apple even before the children were born!). The mother is labeled overprotective when she worries about her children, negligent if she doesn't worry; smothering or bossy if she engages in her children's lives, selfish or icy if she doesn't; overly self-involved if she pursues a career or holds down a job, overly involved with her kids if she doesn't. She can't seem to get it right, and if anything goes wrong with the children, it's her fault.

Snap Judgments

If you think that's a problem, consider how much more severe the judgment is on single or lesbian mothers. Because the economics have not been factored into the difficulties single mothers face, many people assume that single mothers are bound to have trouble raising their sons. And the prejudice against lesbians carries over into the expectation that they can't raise healthy sons. These are the biggest myths of all.

In my research . . . I have found there is absolutely no reason to expect that single or gay moms cannot raise sons on their own. These maverick moms and their families are living their lives with an everyday consciousness of the problems they and their sons face. They are not ideologues working out a theory about different ways to parent in our culture. They are real mothers raising real boys, boys who should not be marginalized in the least. These boys may not live with biological fathers, but they are in no way illegitimate. The families their moms have created are as real and as legitimate as any other, and have much to teach everybody who cares about children. . . .

Throughout my research and the writing of this book, I have come to take a stand against the recent tide of opinion and the rash of books asserting that boys must have a father in the home in order to grow to full manhood. Instead, I have found that loving, growth-encouraging parenting is what boys (and girls, for that matter) need. A good parent, whether mother or father, will enable a boy to develop to his full potential as a young man, as long as his individuality, his manliness, his courage, and his developing conscience are respectfully and fully supported.

The families I studied were all in some way on the fringes of the societal mainstream, and the sons all suffered in one way or another from the ignorance or prejudice of others. Teachers didn't accept drawings of their families; other children teased them about their families; there was a presumption that boys raised by lesbians would be sissies and that sons raised by single mothers would be automatically vulnerable to the worst elements in our society. Then there was a terrible libel against these mothers, that they have no standards or morals.

I found that this very marginalization was a source of tears and concern. But it was also a source of strength for the mothers and their sons.

The boys and mothers I studied had all the ups and downs of every family. Just like the rest of the boys on the planet, they fought, they cried, they got into trouble, they had school problems, they got furious with their parents, they didn't do what they were told. But there was something different in the quality of their relationships, both at home and in the world.

They had a wider range of interests and friendships than the boys I studied from heterosexual parents, and they appeared more at ease in situations of conflict. They developed their "boyishness" at a normal rate, but their sense of justice and fairness and their ability to express their feelings were off the charts. They admired many kinds of men, from scientists to sports heroes, and they accepted their own quirks and interests (and those around them) more readily than did boys from traditional families.

My research showed that it's the quality of parenting, not the gender of the parents, that counts. And yes, two-parent families—including both the mom-and-dad variety and the two-mom variety—work well when they work well.

Does this mean that fathers are not important? Of course not. Do I mean to bash fathers? Under no circumstances. This book describes the strengths of these maverick mothers and how their sons used emotional skillfulness as an antidote to the stigma of being raised by lesbian or single moms. The truth as I see it is that the love, the respect, and the understanding their parents offered was what made for strong and resilient young men. . . .

[There is a] music of love and communication that surrounded the sons of maverick mothers. It is also the secret of sound children: You listen carefully, you respond the best way you can, you foster the children's interests, and you give them loving correction. You know what your own behavior says to them and what good Observers they are.

E. M. Forster said it best 80 years ago on *Two cheers for Democracy*: "Only connect!" This is the message of the maverick mothers. It's a lesson for us all. Mothers and fathers alike need to connect with their sons, not as clones of themselves, but as free-standing personalities. And they need to understand what their sons are going through, supporting their best instincts and teaching them how to be better men.

What kind of men will the boys I studied become? Only a fortune-teller can answer that question with certainty. But I see that the qualities they exhibited at a young age will serve them well.

From Howard Gardner's path-breaking work on the varieties of intelligence to Daniel Goleman's book on emotional intelligence, the world of social science is emphasizing the importance in interpersonal savvy in life and work. The boys I came to know already exhibited high emotional IQs. They might be a step ahead of many others when they enter the world of work.

And then there's the mountain of medical research about the importance to physical health of having intimate relationships throughout life. These boys already had an extraordinary capacity for closeness. Of course, they could shut down as teenagers (many boys do). But the chances are good that when they emerge as young men, they will once again be at home with intimacy.

These boys will bear close watching over the years to come. And like Judith Wallerstein and others, I will continue to listen to them and spend time with them as they mature. My bet is that living through all the vicissitudes of adolescence, dealing with the prejudices against their families, filling out forms that have no blanks for their family types, and surviving the torments of first love and disappointment will be very hard for these boys. But they already have a set of competencies to meet these difficulties.

We know that many successful women give credit for their courage and energy to the loving support of their fathers. I am beginning to suspect that the same dynamic between mother and son may have a similar effect.

"I've always loved and respected my mother. I thought she was a super-hero," Bruce Addison, then 34, said to me, remembering those economically and emotionally challenging years when his mother raised him and his siblings on her own and worked long hours running different mortgage bro-kering businesses. "I've never met or read about a woman who is as powerful as she is. She'll tell you that she muddled through it and what have you, but I certainly didn't get that sense. She really lived with purpose. She instilled in me a great deal of that sense of purpose."

What a different view this is from the traditional mother bashing we know so well. Perhaps mothers have been blamed for communicating the cultural norms of the day. Those "smothering mothers" of the past were mes-sengers of the family values of the time: Do what I tell you; go into your father's business; you have to be a doctor/lawyer/banker; no, theater isn't manly enough for you; don't cry—be a man!

By redefining manhood, mothers have the chance to redefine not only the American family but also the face of our society. "My hope is that my sons are going to be the kind of people who will understand that others haven't nec-essarily had the advantages they have, and not exploit or be blind to the fact that they have had a leg up, but instead use their privileges for good things," one such mother told me. "That is the kind of man who can change the world."

POSTSCRIPT

Are Fathers Essential for Children's Well-Being?

Researchers have explored under what conditions optimal father involvement is possible. Some state that the three necessary conditions are: (1) when a father is highly motivated to parent, (2) when a father has adequate parenting skills and receives social support for parenting, and (3) when a father is not undermined by work and other institutional settings. The reconstruction of fathering, whatever the redefinition, has proven to be very difficult, contested by many cultural forces.

At issue is the assumption that there is something natural and thus rooted in the basic nature of women and men that makes a two-parent family, with a mother and father, essential and ideal for children's well-being. The fundamental assumption of different parenting styles and roles of men and women have led to debates about whether "fathers can mother." That is, can men and should they begin to fill the role of nurturer? The result is that men's "job description" as fathers is less clear than expectations of women as mothers. Therefore, fathering is very sensitive to context (including the marital or coparental relationship, children, extended family, and cultural institutions). The role of mother is especially delimiting. Mothers often serve as gatekeepers in the father-child relationship. Father involvement is often contingent on mothers' attitudes toward, expectations of, and support for the father.

Many mothers are ambivalent about active father involvement with their children. The mothering role has been a central feature of adult women's identity, so it is no wonder that some women feel threatened by paternal involvement in their domain, which affects their identity and sense of control. In the absence of social consensus on fathering and counterarguments about the deficits of many fathers, many mothers are restrictive of father involvement. However, some maintain that responsible mothering will have to evolve to include support of the father-child bond.

In addition, with increasing latitude for commitment to and identification with their parental role, men are increasingly confused about how to exercise their roles as fathers. This also makes them sensitive to contextual factors such as others' attitudes and expectations. Worse yet, they frequently encounter disagreement among different individuals and institutions in their surrounding context, further complicating their role choices and enactment.

Four other contextual forces challenge a redefinition of fathering. (1) Legal notions of fatherhood disregard nurturing. Adequate fathering is primarily equated with financial responsibility. (2) Concepts of masculinity conflict with nurturant parenting. Nurturant fathers risk condemnation as being "unmanly."

How can nurturant fatherhood fit into notions of maleness and masculinity? (3) Homophobic attitudes further obstruct nurturant fatherhood. Ironically, active legal debate about sexual orientation and parenting might be influential in reconstructing fatherhood. Is there a model of shared parenting within the gay community? (4) Nurturing by fathers and mothers has typically functioned in a single-parent model, whether with a two-parent marriage or with parents living in separate households. One parent usually does most, if not all, of the nurturing. Interestingly, it is the case that nurturance is a better predictor of effective parenting than is sex. Gender neutrality and equality in parenting is undefined. How would you conceptualize a model of shared parenting (taking care not to discriminate against single-parent families)? What would parental equality look like in practice? Is it essential that children be exposed to both female and male role models? If so, why? If women and men were not expected to conform to a specific set of expectations associated with their sex would the sex of the people raising children matter? Which benefits the child more, a heterosexual set of parents who are bound by strict gender-related conventions which results in an over-bearing, abusive father, or a loving single father or loving, nurturing gay parents?

Suggested Readings

W. D. Allen and M. Connor, "An African American Perspective on Generative Fathering," in A. J. Hawkins and D. C. Dollahite, eds., *Generative-Fathering: Beyond Deficit Perspectives* (Sage Publications, 1997).

D. Blankenhorn, *Fatherless America: Confronting Our Most Urgent Social Problem* (Basic Books, 1995).

S. Coltrane, *Family Man: Fatherhood, Housework, and Gender Equity* (Oxford University Press, 1996).

Cynthia R. Daniels, *The Unexpected Legacy of Divorce: The 25 Year Landmark Study* (New York: Hyperion, 1998).

Lucia Albino Gilbert and Jill Rader, "Current Perspectives on Women's Adult Roles: Work, Family, and Life," in Rhoda K. Unger, ed., *Handbook of the Psychology of Women and Gender* (Hoboken, NJ: John Wiley & Sons, Inc., 2001), pp. 156–169.

F. Daniel McClure and Jerry B. Saffer, *Wednesday Evenings and Every Other Weekend: From Divorced Dad to Competent Co-Parent. A Guide for the Noncustodial Father* (Charlottesville, VA: The Van Doren Company, 2001).

Ross Parke and Armin Brott, *Throwaway Dads: The Myths and Barriers That Keep Men from Being the Fathers They Want to Be* (New York: Houghton Mifflin, 1999).

Janice M. Steil, "Family Forms and Member Well-Being: A Research Agenda for the Decade of Behavior," *Psychology of Women Quarterly,* 25 (2001): 344–363.

ISSUE 13

Is Fetal Sex Selection Harmful to Society?

YES: Dena S. Davis, from *Genetic Dilemmas: Reproductive Technology, Parental Choices, and Children's Futures* (Routledge, 2001)

NO: Rosamond Rhodes, from "Ethical Issues in Selecting Embryos," *Annals of the New York Academy of Sciences* (2001)

ISSUE SUMMARY

YES: Dena S. Davis argues that fetal sex selection is an ethical issue because it is really about gender selection that promotes traditional stereotypes and can interfere with a child's right to an open future.

NO: Rosamond Rhodes describes the acceptable scope of fetal sex selection, as well as professional responsibilities of practitioners of reproductive medicine.

Gender is influenced before conception, in making decisions to carry a fetus to term. The potency of sex and gender as explanations for differences between males and females escalates early in life. By early childhood, a host of differences are observed between boys and girls as children internalize a sense of themselves and others as gendered. Concern has been raised about inequities and deficits resulting from the effects of sex and gender.

Research has consistently documented the preference and desire for sons in twentieth-century America and in other cultures. In many cultures, such as India and China, maleness means social, political, and economic entitlement. Men are expected to support their parents in their old age. Moreover, men remain with their family throughout life; women, upon marriage, become part of the husband's family. Thus, women are traditionally seen as a continuing economic burden on the family—particularly in the custom of large dowry payments at weddings. In some cultures if a bride's family cannot pay the demanded dowry, the brides are often killed (usually by burning). Although dowries and dowry deaths are illegal, the laws are rarely enforced.

In such cultures, there is an expressed desire for male children and an urgency to select fetal sex. Recently, sex-determination technology is most commonly used to assay the sex of fetuses, although in many cultures the use of such technology has been banned. When the fetus is determined to be female, abortion often follows because of cultural pressures to have sons. Such sex-determination practices have led to many more male than female infants being born. The gap grows even wider because of a high childhood death rate of girls, often from neglect or killing by strangulation, suffocation, or poisoning. Furthermore, women are blamed for the birth of a female child and are often punished for it (even though, biologically, it is the male's sperm, carrying either X or Y chromosomes, that determines sex).

Research shows that in contemporary America, 78 percent of adults prefer their firstborn to be a boy. Moreover, parents are more likely to continue having children if they have all girls versus if they have all boys. Faced with having only one child, many Americans prefer a boy. But there is also a high preference for a "sex-balanced" family—the "perfect" family having a firstborn son and a second-born daughter. The availability of sex-selection technology in the last quarter of the twentieth century was met with growing interest and widespread willingness to make use of the technology.

Available technologies for sex selection include preconception, preimplantation, and postconception techniques. Preconception selection techniques include folkloric approaches like intercourse timing, administering an acid or alkaline douche, and enriching maternal diets with potassium or calcium/magnesium, all thought to create a uterine environment conducive to producing male or female fetuses. There are also sperm-separating technologies whereby X- and Y-bearing sperm are separated, and the desired sperm are artificially inseminated into the woman, increasing the chance of having a child of the chosen sex.

Preimplantation technologies identify the sex of embryos as early as three days after fertilization. For sex-selection purposes, the choice of an embryo for implantation is based on sex. Postconception approaches use prenatal diagnostic technologies to determine the sex of the fetus. The three most common technologies are amniocentesis (available after the 20th week of pregnancy), chorionic villi sampling (available earlier but riskier), and ultrasound (which can determine sex as early as 12 weeks but is not 100 percent accurate).

The American demand for social acceptance of sex-selection technologies has increased in the last decade. Preconception selection techniques are becoming quite popular in the United States, and preimplantation technologies (though more expensive) are also more frequently used. It has become more and more socially accepted to use prenatal diagnostic technologies to determine fetal sex. But incidence rates for sex-selective abortions are difficult to obtain. There is mixed opinion about the frequency of sex-selective abortions, tinged by political controversy.

In the following selections Dena Davis asserts that fetal sex selection is always unethical, that parents are really not interested in the genitalia that their infants are born with. What they are really choosing is an "ideal," defined by gender role expectations: a boy dad can play ball with or a girl who can wear mom's wedding gown when she marries. In contrast, Rosamond Rhodes argues that there are conditions under which fetal sex selection is ethical; gender imbalance in the population is one such condition. There are cases in which a genetic disease is sex-linked, in which case sex-selection to avoid the disease is acceptable.

YES

Dena S. Davis

Genetic Dilemmas: Reproductive Technology, Parental Choices, and Children's Futures

Sex Selection and Reproductive Choice

A common argument asserts that, whatever the causes and consequences of sex selection, choosing the sex of one's baby with available technology is part of a couple's basic right to reproductive choice. In a 1985 study two researchers presented 295 American geneticists with the case of a couple who have four daughters and requested prenatal diagnosis so that they could abort a fifth pregnancy if the fetus was a girl. Sixty-two percent of the geneticists surveyed responded that they would accede to the couple's request. When asked why, the geneticists stated that they perceived sex choice as a "logical extension of parents' rights to control the number, timing, spacing, and quality of their offspring."

In the case of arguments that rest on parental choice, the most common opposition focuses on the dangers of turning children into commodities. Parents become consumers whose goal is the perfect child, with the assumed corollary that children who are considered to be less than perfect will be devalued. Thus just as yuppie consumers purchase the perfect house, the perfect sport utility vehicle, and the perfect bottled water, they may also purchase the perfect baby. Maura Ryan, in a feminist critique of unlimited parental choice, points out that assisted reproduction is expensive and burdensome and wonders "how parents might look upon offspring when they enter the process with the belief that a certain kind of child is *owed* to them and after they have paid a high price for that child." Some ethicists worry that if sex selection is accepted, the next step will be selection to avoid short children, nearsighted children, or children whose intelligence is merely average. Like the inhabitants of Garrison Keillor's mythical Lake Wobegon, we want to believe that "all our children are above average." The result could be a return to the excesses of the eugenics movement. . . .

As I said earlier, the challenge I have set myself is to argue against sex selection in the absence of abortion, and even in the instance where girls are as desired as boys. In the United States, where genetic counseling embodies a culture of autonomy and where population control is not a pressing issue, a subtle but powerful argument can still be made that sex selection is wrong because it abrogates the child's right to an open future. Why, after all, do parents have strong preferences for girls or boys, even if those preferences are merely in the context of "family balance," the one rationale that some ethicists are willing to find blameless if not compelling?

In a 1990 study of 281 American undergraduates, only 18 percent indicated a willingness to use sex selection technology if it was "an inexpensive device or pill" that would allow them to select the sex of their first child. (However, of those who would use the technology, 73 percent preferred boys. It is also possible that if the question had been posed in terms of willingness to use the technology to select their *second* child, more people would have said yes.) In a 1989 study Nan Chico surveyed 2,505 letters to Ronald Ericsson, a Montana physician who patented an early version of the sperm-sorting technique. Chico found that most couples interested in the process already had at least one child and were seeking "mixed" families. There was almost a fifty-fifty split in requests for girls and boys. Ten years later Ericsson reports a larger number of requests for girls than for boys, despite the fact that his process has a higher success rate for producing boys. Microsort, the Virginia company that sorts sperm by a process that first dyes them and then "zaps" them with an ultraviolet laser, reports that many more couples are interested in having girls than boys. (Microsort accepts only couples who are trying to "balance" their familes, that is, they already have at least one child and are attempting to have a child of the sex underrepresented in their family.)

Parents whose preference for one sex or the other is compelling enough for them to take active steps to control the outcome must, I submit, be committed to certain strong gender-role expectations of the children they will raise. As Rothman points out, the genetic test selects for *sex*, that is, for a child with XX or XY chromosomes, but what the parents are really selecting for is *gender*, the social role of being a boy, girl, man, woman. When people go out of their way to choose, they don't want just the right chromosomes and the attendant anatomical characteristics, they want a set of characteristics that go with "girlness" or "boyness." Rothman says, "I've heard women say that they want the kind of relationship that they had with their mothers; they think they can't have that kind of relationship with a son. I've heard women talk about wanting to have the frills, the clothes, the manicures together, the pretty mother-daughter outfits, the fun of a prom gown and a wedding gown, that come with girls." Lisa Belkin, who surfed the Web sites devoted to discussions of gender choice, said that women who want girls "speak of Barbies and ballet and butterfly barrettes. They also describe the desire to rear strong young women." If parents want a girl badly enough to go to all the trouble of sperm sorting and artificial insemination, they are likely to make it more difficult for the actual child to resist their expectations and follow her own bent. Rothman says, "[W]hen you start from the premise that one can 'determine' fetal sex in the sense that it can be chosen, then the stereotypes predict the choice: people who want an active, vigorous, achieving child will have boys. And when they want a sweeter, quieter, more loving child, they will have girls." Of course, it is probably impossible to raise children without some gender stereotyping, but the more we can manage to do so, the more we can give our children the gift of the most open possible future, the one least trammeled by notions of how girls and boys (and women and men) are "supposed" to behave. As feminist activist Letty Cottin Pogrebin says, "Instead of dividing human experience in half, locking each child in the prison of either 'masculine' or 'feminine' correctness, and creating two separate definitions of human integrity, the nonsexist parent celebrates the *full* humanity of each girl or boy."

This point holds even for those who would argue that gender stereotypes have been breaking down dramatically in the years since Rothman and Pogrebin wrote. For example, the 1996 Olympics exhibited exhilarating performances by women athletes, the U.S. Supreme Court has required the Virginia Military Institute and the Citadel to admit women, and the current administration in Washington includes our first female attorney general and our first female secretary of state. But such optimism does not invalidate Rothman's point. If stereotypes are breaking down, why is it so important to have a child of the "desired" sex? If someone wants a daughter so that she can be groomed to be the first female navy admiral, that is still perceiving her primarily in terms of gender.

Because gender is only one among many characteristics, but one that carries very heavy baggage in our society, to view a child primarily through its gender narrows the child's ability to choose his or her own path through life. The same would be true if we could choose a child's height, musical ability, or aptitude for nuclear physics. At present, however, the one thing we can pinpoint and control is gender. Maura Ryan, arguing more generally against unfettered procreative liberty, challenges a framework where a desire

> for a particular type of child . . . is seldom weighed appropriately against the reality of the child-to-be as a potential autonomous human being. At what point does a being, who has been conceived, gestated, and born according to someone's specifications, become himself or herself? And if a child comes into the world primarily to fulfill parental need, are there limits to what a parent may do to ensure that the child will continue to meet the specific expectations?

Knowledge of Fetal Sex and the Child's Right to an Open Future

In the process of doing a chromosomal analysis to rule out Down syndrome and other problems, or in the course of a routine ultrasound, it is impossible for a lab technician *not* to determine the fetus's sex. The custom in the United States at this time is for this piece of information to be transmitted from the lab to the physician, who typically asks the couple if they wish to know the sex of their baby-to-be. Although women have reported mixed feelings on this subject, the vast majority of women who have had amniocentesis, CVS, or ultrasound do end up learning the sex of their fetus. Because all women over thirty-five are counseled to consider amniocentesis, as well as younger women with medical indications or family histories of genetic disease, this means that a great many women in America today know their baby's sex before it is born.

In fact, it is quite common for people to ask a pregnant woman if she is carrying a boy or girl, or for parents to announce their baby's name when he or she is still months away from making an appearance.

Few commentators see this practice as an ethical issue (at least when parents have no plans to act upon this knowledge to abort a fetus of the undesired sex). It is certainly a strange development, in that it calls into question many common customs. Of course, friends and relatives will still be delighted to get that dramatic phone call from the happy parents telling them that mother and baby are healthy, but without the news that it is a girl or a boy, the announcement lacks a certain something. And the obstetrician does not say, as she holds the baby up for the mother to see, "It's a baby!" However odd these issues seem, we will leave them for anthropologists (and marketers of infant goods) to worry about.

In my view, there *is* an ethical issue here, albeit a very subtle one. There is some evidence to show that for parents who know the sex of their fetus, sexual stereotyping begins even before birth. Joan Callahan describes a conversation with a woman whose daughter had recently learned that the baby she was carrying was a boy:

> The woman had no discernible preference for a boy grandchild over a girl grandchild, but she was delighted to know that her grandchild would be a boy because, she said, she could now "begin getting ready for him." When asked what that meant, she saw immediately that it meant certain colors for blankets and sweaters, certain sorts of toys and room decorations. Long before he was even born, this child would be started on a "boy track," surrounded by blues and trains, never pinks and dolls.

Pregnancy, perhaps especially when amniocentesis has freed one from at least some of the attendant anxieties, is a time rich with dreaming. If the fetus is quiet while one is listening to Bach, that shows great musical talent, while every fetal kick means that an Olympic soccer player is in the making. Just as the early developing embryo is totipotent, which is to say that each of its cells has an unlimited capacity to differentiate into different tissues and organs, so too the very early developing parent entertains a vast range of possibilities. In our heavily gendered culture, many of those dreams are lost and others become locked in the minute the baby is born and the sex is known.

Most social scientists agree that gender socialization begins at birth. Studies show that adults treat babies they think are male or female very differently from the first day of life. Experiments with babies from birth to a year show adults (men and women) interacting quite differently with the exact same baby, depending on whether or not they have been told that the (diapered) baby is a girl or a boy. Based on the baby's supposed sex, they offered it different toys, spoke in a different tone of voice, and interpreted the baby's behaviors quite differently. (When "boy" babies cried, for example, they were thought to be angry, while "girl" babies who cried were thought to be scared.)

These new techniques make it possible for gender socialization to begin *before* birth. Barbara Katz Rothman, in an ingenious study, asked women to decribe the movements of their fetus during the final trimester. Women who did not know their baby's sex before birth used a variety of adjectives, without any pattern connected to the sex of their baby. However, when women knew their fetus's sex, a distinct pattern emerged. The movements of female fetuses were much less likely to be described as "strong" and "vigorous." The word *lively* was used often to describe females, but never males, although parents who did not know the sex of their fetus were equally likely to describe male or female fetuses as strong or lively. Some masculine-sounding descriptions were used for female fetuses, but feminine-sounding descriptions were never used for males. This is in keeping with our culture, where tomboys are more acceptable than sissies and a girl in boy's pajamas looks cute, while a boy in a girl's nightgown sets off alarm signals.

Thus it seems that knowing the baby's sex before it is born encourages the kind of gender stereotyping that threatens to limit the child's right to an open future. This is such a subtle argument that it hardly justifies frustrating parents' right to know should they demand access to the information. However, Rothman points out that the urge to know the fetus's sex often arises from the parents' awareness that the doctor or lab technician already knows. Rothman comments:

> It is not simply that the information is now knowable. It is also that it is known. It is known to the medical personnel, and once the sex of the fetus becomes part of the medical record, it makes sense to treat it just as one would other information on that record. Nancy said she asked the sex because: "I want all the information available to the physician to be available to me."

One way to discourage the practice of reporting fetal sex while still respecting the rights of parents who insist on knowing is to adopt a policy suggested by Wertz and Fletcher in the context of discouraging actual sex selection. They propose that information about fetal sex remain in the lab and not be routinely reported to the doctor. Therefore the doctor also would not know, and few patients would be prompted to ask for the information. The information would be available for parents who ask, but reporting it to parents would no longer be routine. This would also avoid the now rather common occurrence of parents who have asked not to know accidentally being told by overenthusiastic nurses and physicians.

Conclusion

Sex selection, even in the absence of abortion, raises serious concerns of justice in the context of developing countries and societies in which there is a dramatic preference for boys. But even in countries such as ours, where preference for boys may soon be a nonissue, I believe that sex selection presents an ethical problem because it promotes gender role stereotyping and encourages parents to invest heavily in having certain types of children. This combination of investment and stereotyping makes it more difficult for the child to grow and develop in ways that are different than, perhaps even in conflict with, parental expectations. Just *knowing* the fetus's sex, even outside of any attempt to predetermine it, may exacerbate gender stereotyping by allowing parents to begin the tracking process before the baby is born. Thus policies that encourage sex selection or predetermination should be discouraged.

Rosamond Rhodes

 **NO**

Ethical Issues in Selecting Embryos

Introduction

People involved in assisted reproduction frequently make decisions about which of several embryos to implant or which of several embryos to reduce from a multiple pregnancy. Physicians involved in embryo transfers or pregnancy reductions have to choose which embryos will have a chance of developing into a baby and which will not. Currently, the embryos that look healthiest are most often the ones to be implanted and the ones that appear unhealthy or are conveniently positioned are the ones that are most commonly discarded or reduced.

Developing technology will enable doctors to know more about the embryos among which they are selecting. Embryos can already be selected because of their gender or because they do not have some specific genetic anomaly. But, being able to do something does not mean that it should be done. In the case of selecting embryos, people have already raised questions about the ethical acceptability of using sex as a selection criterion. Disabilities activists have challenged the morality of using criteria related to illness, disease, or disability. And fiction writers and others with vivid imaginations have raised questions about possible future uses of diagnostic technology in fashioning future human beings. They spark reflection about whether it is acceptable to select an embryo because its genes promise great intelligence, aggressiveness, physical prowess, and blue eyes. These issues also change significantly when we consider them from the perspective of different decision makers. Is the selection of embryos a choice for physicians to make or should it be left to government, to insurance providers, or to parents? If the choice is to be made by persons other than the physician, when should a physician cooperate with their choice and when should a physician refuse to act on their grounds for embryo selection?

With the possibility of selecting against kinds of humans, people worry about the morality of using the new technology. They are anxious about the ethical borders that might be crossed, they are apprehensive about eugenics, concerned about reinforcing negative social attitudes about gender and disability, and uneasy about producing humans without intending to allow them to live and to develop. The religiously inclined are concerned about meddling with the "sanctity of life." As Paul Ramsey explained, "the value of human life is ultimately grounded in the value God is placing on it. . . . [The] essence

From *Annals of the New York Academy of Science*, 2001, pp. 360–367. Copyright © 2001 by New York Academy of Sciences, U.S.A. Reprinted by permission.

[of human life] is [its] existence before God and to God, and it is from Him." For believers, selecting embryos sounds dangerously close to playing God, trespassing in His domain, or treading on the sanctity of life.

In response to such concerns from so many disparate perspectives, specialists in assisted reproduction have been hesitant in making their techniques available on request, because of uncertainty about making decisions on the ethical frontier and concerns about their moral reputation. Nevertheless, this paper will argue that, for the most part, we must resist the movement to proscribe or prohibit embryo selection. Our society's commitment to liberty requires that we allow individuals to make choices according to their own lights, and in the absence of actual substantial evidence that such practices cause serious harm or at least a demonstration of a significant likelihood of untoward repercussions, we are not justified in denying individuals the option.

In this presentation, I review some of the important considerations for allowing embryo selection and arguments that have been put forward for rejecting embryo selection criteria based on sex or genetic characteristics. I discuss the subject of choosing our offspring in terms of the centrality to ethics of liberty and autonomous choice and in terms of well accepted ideas about limiting liberty because of harm to others. In light of these remarks, I shall present a position on the acceptable scope of embryo selection, on who should be making the choices, and on the professional responsibilities of those who practice reproductive medicine.

Liberty

From its inception, our society has embraced the value of liberty. Freedom has been our creed and the foundation for building our government both because of its inherent value and because it is such a crucial component of happiness. In particular, reproductive freedom is a very important human value. Through reproductive choice people are allowed to act on their own values and to try to create their own image of happiness. For the most part, people want the liberty to choose their own reproductive partners, the timing of their reproduction, and their rate of reproduction.

While there has been a great deal of discussion about the concept of liberty, John Stuart Mill's account has been given significant weight in moral and political philosophy, and in this discussion, because of the strength of his arguments and their analytic power, I will follow his account. As Mill has explained, for people who extol liberty, "the sole end for which mankind are warranted, individually or collectively, in interfering with the liberty of action of any of their number is self-protection." This principle for limiting legislative and policy intervention with liberty has become known as the "harm principle." It demands that no action be forbidden unless it can be shown to cause harm to others in the enjoyment of their rights. . . .

Although anything one person does may give another affront, upset, or sadness and thereby cause some harm, only those actions that "violate a distinct and assignable obligation to any person or persons" may be proscribed by legislation. . . .

Embryo Selection, Rights, and Harms

Rights.   With respect to embryo selection, the question relevant to Mill's criterion is whether someone's use of the technology would violate anyone else's rights? To answer, we must consider all of those who we could anticipate might have rights violated. As far as I can foresee, those who might be harmed by the production of selected offspring would include the perspective children, their peers, and those in the community who would be upset by people overstepping the line into God's domain. Under any circumstances of implanting only a few of several embryos or reducing a pregnancy of one or more of several embryos, only some of the possible embryos will actually become children. Without invoking a theological argument about fertilized eggs having a right to life, it is hard to imagine that the destruction of a non-selected embryo would involve a violation of rights. None of the others who might claim some harm would suffer any violation of rights.

Devaluation and discrimination.   Some disabilities activists worry that by selecting against embryos with genetic abnormalities we would diminish our appreciation of people with disabilities. Similarly, some feminists worry that by allowing people to select against females we would encourage sexist attitudes and support gender discrimination. These concerns do not meet Mill's standard for prohibiting individual choice. First, it is not at all clear that the imagined untoward effects will actually occur, and if the attitudes did arise in a few instances, it is not clear that their limited social impact could justify limiting reproductive liberty. These are empirical matters, and a significant amount of evidence would have to be amassed before the concern reached the level of meriting a restrictive social policy. Second, it seems that no one has a right to prevent the existence of the selected others who might, in some way, be preferred or superior to themselves and, just by living, make the less desired or inferior feel unappreciated. That embryo selection technology might be the means to enable fewer females or fewer individuals with disabilities to be born does not, therefore, violate the rights of women, or people with disabilities, or anyone else.

Religious concerns.   The religious concern over interfering with the sanctity of life also fails to meet Mill's criterion for legislating against a practice. While liberty allows individuals the freedom to choose a religious perspective and the freedom to live according to the religious views they embrace, it limits individuals' infringement on the similar rights of others. In other words, no one may impose his own religious views on others. So while no one has the right to interfere with anyone else's religious practice, the others whom he respects have no right to intervene in his living by his own religious or nonreligious standards. The religious liberty guaranteed by the harm principle does not extend rights to control the lives of others, and so those whose religious sensitivities are upset by the prospect of other people meddling with the creation of human life cannot claim that harm as grounds for limiting others' procreative practice.

Justification.   Some people base their objections to embryo selection on the particular moral justification that people may offer for their choice. Yet, while we may consider some reasons better than others, efforts to constrain peoples' moral judgments are rejected by Mill as illegitimate "moral legalism." Many people consider the medical reason of wanting to avoid having a child with a serious genetic disease and the nonmedical reason of family balance as good reasons for embryo selection. Putting these "good" reasons aside, it is important to point out that we do not question the reasoning that motivates nontechnology-assisted reproduction. The ordinary desire to have biologically related offspring is not challenged even in the face of overpopulation and the large numbers of orphaned children around the world. Without aid and without society's interference people have children in order to pass along their genes, or to pressure a partner into marriage, or to get an apartment, or to keep a marriage together, or to get an inheritance, or to have a real live doll to play with, or to have somebody to love. It is not even clear which reasons are "good" reasons and which are not. But it is clear that privacy and respect for autonomy require that people be allowed to follow their own reasons. So reasons for procreation should be irrelevant to policy makers. And, at least since Hobbes's writings in the seventeenth century, it has been understood that law could only govern action and not thought or belief.

Further Considerations

In sum, I find no persuasive argument for restricting embryo selection (or, similarly, preconception sex selection) as long as there is no empirical evidence of significant social harm from allowing the technology to be freely available. Yet, I would like to press this conclusion in several directions to show what more might be said in defense of sex selection or selecting embryos for other reasons, such as to avoid having a child with a serious genetic disease.

Impact.   Significant social harms from resulting gender imbalance in the population would count against allowing access to embryo selection technology. Yet, in an environment resembling contemporary U.S. society, it is hard to imagine that the number of births that employed the technology could be large enough to have a demographic effect. Since the cost, inconvenience, discomfort, risks, and loss of privacy entailed by the procedure would be likely to make embryo selection a rarely employed technology, and since there would be a variety of motivations and procreators, the numbers of individuals produced by the technology in our society (or an other that was sufficiently similar to ours) would not be great enough or similar enough to have any significant impact on demographics or on social attitudes towards females or people with disabilities. While studies show that people have preferences about gender and birth order, in actual decisions about using embryo selection those considerations will have to be balanced against the others that mitigate against it. Only those for whom gender or avoiding a genetic disease is extremely important are likely to avail themselves of the technology.

Consequences. Any conclusion about the social impact of a practice has to take all of its effects into account. While my guess is that embryo selection is likely to have only a negligible societal impact, nevertheless, if we were to evaluate that effect we would have to assess all of its consequences, those that count as harms as well as those that count as benefits. Although gender imbalance in the population may turn out to be a harm at some point, other effects of embryo selection are likely to be beneficial. (1) Embryo selection for gender is likely to be used by parents who want an additional child to be of a different gender than other children in the family. Without assisted reproductive technology, "try again" has been the method to achieve that goal. Embryo selection (and preconception sex selection [PSS], if it should be effective) has the social advantage of not adding to society's overpopulation problems. (2) By helping couples achieve the gender balance they want with fewer children, embryo selection (or PSS) can benefit families by easing the economic and human burdens of providing for a large family. Today, when few enjoy the support of an extended family to help with the chores of everyday life and when both parents are typically employed outside the home, additional children tax a family's limited resources. (3) Potential parents, that is, autonomous adults, are in the best position to assess the kind of rearing and companionship experience that would be valuable to them. For those to whom gender or the avoidance of a child with disabilities makes a significant enough difference to justify embryo selection (or PSS), the gender- or genetic-selected child is likely to provide a more rewarding experience. (4) Children produced by embryo selection (or PSS) are also more likely to be attentively reared and to have a good childhood because their parents have chosen the kind of child who they are more likely to nurture well.

Context. Some objectors to embryo selection find the idea of choosing one's offspring, rather than accepting whichever ones happen to arrive, to be immoral *per se* or to support discrimination and therein be immoral. Sympathetic moral imagination can, however, help us to appreciate that embryo selection (or PSS) can be moral or, in some cases, may be obligatory. Consider the hypothetical case of George and Katherine. Many years ago, George had engaged in pederastic behavior. He was apprehended for his assaults on young boys, tried, convicted, and punished for his crimes. After years of psychotherapy he now understands and deeply regrets his previous behavior. He no longer experiences any sexual attraction for young boys. In fact, he has fallen in love with Katherine and they want very much to have a family. After fully discussing George's past and considering their options, they decide that they don't want to chance having a boy. The risk of triggering some old feelings would be far too costly for both George and a son, and George and Katherine would both be very happy as parents to a girl. Because of age-related factors, Katherine needs to use assisted reproductive technology and her obstetrician discusses the option of embryo selection with the couple. They opt for selecting only female embryos for implantation.

As I see it, the behavior of George and Katherine is morally responsible. They consider the value of a child in their lives, the conceivable danger to themselves and their future offspring, and how to minimize the possibility of related harms. Their choice exemplifies far-sighted prudence, appropriate care and concern, and ethical responsibility. It would be immoral for people in their situation to ignore the risks or to eschew embryo selection out of concern for appearing to display sexism. This case makes the point that sex selection is not necessarily immoral and it is not necessarily an act of unacceptable sex discrimination. The circumstances and the reasons for choosing selection can make a significant difference, and there is likely to be a broad array of situations in which embryo selection is ethically acceptable.

Prohibition. Moral imagination can also be used to make a further point. There is a significant difference between judging that a particular act is unethical and deciding that the practice should be legally prohibited. If we could know enough about the situations and reasons involved in other people's procreative decisions, we might decide that some were ethically unacceptable. While that information could be sufficient for our judgment about a particular case, it would not be sufficient to justify legislation that would limit the liberty of everyone. Allowing people to live their lives by their own lights and to make some bad or even unethical decisions is inherent in our valuing liberty. A demonstration of actual overriding harms is the only legitimate justification for constraining liberty.

Selfishness. Finally, we should consider the place of personal satisfaction in moral decisions, particularly in reproductive decisions. The most obvious social problem of serious gender imbalance is that those in the gender majority will be less likely than otherwise of having a heterosexual mating with all its attendant promise of personal satisfaction. And the reason most people want to have children involves the promise of personal satisfaction associated with being a parent. Such pleasure motivate us. They are importantly constitutive of well-being, and the pleasure associated with securing such basic goods is typically taken into account in moral and political philosophy. In the context of recognizing the importance of personal satisfaction as a moral consideration, we should notice that demeaning the pleasure that some people associate with having a child of a particular gender or devaluing the pain that some people associate with having a child with a genetic disease as unethically selfish requires justification. Those who want to decry embryo selection have to explain why the desire to have a child of a particular gender or a child without a genetic disease is unethical while the selfish desire to have any child is ethically acceptable.

Who Makes the Choice

My argument, so far, has focused on the unacceptability of government or policy restrictions on embryo selection. The questions that remain involve the proper scope for patient and physician choice. The answers require an understanding of physician professional responsibility and the doctor-patient relationship, subjects that may be even more controversial than the ones addressed so far.

The uncontroversial features of physician professional responsibility involve the doctor's commitment to: (1) using the scientific method and guiding practice by the knowledge provided by science, (2) relying on the cooperative model of practice involving a team of health care providers, and (3) pursuing the moral goal of acting for the patient's good. But, as soon as we recognize that a physician and a patient could have very different views of the good, we confront the controversial problem of whose view of the good should rule? When the doctor cares most about avoiding risks of physical harm and the patient cares more about some other component of her well-being, the doctor's and the patient's values are likely to clash. The issue raised by such conflict involves decisions about the appropriate goals and scope of medicine. These are lofty abstract philosophical questions. But the answers have very practical implications when it comes to embryo selection.

A physician may feel comfortable in going along with some patient requests for embryo selection and also be inclined to refuse the service in other cases. Taking personal comfort as the standard suggests that different obstetricians can each have their own personal standard for providing embryo selection and that there are no professional criteria to be used as a guide in these decisions. While physicians may be comfortable with this Lone Ranger approach to bioethics, recognizing that there are standards for professional behavior points us in another direction.

When we consider a patient's abortion decision or a patient's decision to undergo assisted reproduction with its attendant risks and harms, we can appreciate that a patient's values and goals play an important role and often rightly determine the course of treatment. Some people take a narrow and rigid view of the appropriate goals of medicine as promoting health, curing disease, or preserving life. However, thinking about abortion, assisted reproduction, or even plastic surgery provides a different view of the appropriate goals of medicine, something akin to the use of medicine's special knowledge, skills, and privileges to help promote a set of socially defined goods. This view allows a significant place for the patient's conception of the good in medical decision making. In other words, as long as the treatment requested provides an accepted good, and so long as it is likely to achieve the patient's goals without causing significant harm, the requested treatment should be provided and the patient's view of the good should rule.

Obstetrics has been called upon to promote reproductive choice as a socially accepted good and as an appropriate use of medicine's special knowledge, skills, and privileges. Embryo selection certainly fits within that widely appreciated class of goods. As such, patients should expect access to the technology and cooperation from their physicians in offering and providing the option. Regardless of whether the physician shares the patient's conception of the good and regardless of whether the physician feels comfortable with the decision, the patient's choice should rule, at least in most cases, and the physician would not be justified in withholding the technology.

While the reasons I have offered leave me "comfortable" with this conclusion for cooperating with gender selection and selection against genetic disease, I am inclined to give the opposite answer when it comes to genetic selection for dwarfism or deafness. In those cases, because such disabilities are so widely seen as harms, disabilities, and disadvantages, I think physicians would have good reason for not cooperating with a parental request for embryo selection.

Conclusion

In these remarks I have put forward a framework for thinking about the ethics of embryo selection. I have argued that the reasons for restricting the use of the technology are not sufficiently compelling to overcome our commitment to protecting liberty and reproductive liberty in particular. Furthermore, I have urged a view of the doctor-patient relationship that takes the values of patients very seriously and, therefore, accepts patient choice as ruling almost always in reproductive decisions. I suggest that the limitation on this freedom is the traditional stand against doing harm. In the case of embryo selection even though a resulting deaf child or dwarf would not be harmed in the sense that the particular resulting child would not be made worse off, I have broadly interpreted the concept of doing harm to include deliberately selecting a child who is likely to be impaired as creating a harmful outcome.

While a number of my conclusions may invite disagreement, my further agenda in this paper was to suggest that disputes in bioethics are to be settled by giving reasons that other reasonable people could accept. I see this view of morality as preferable to an attitude that accepts moral matters as settled on the grounds of claims about personal comfort or uneasiness. Recalling that the practice of medicine involves the cooperation of a team of physicians and other health care providers, forging a moral consensus among those who will be called upon to act becomes a significant concern. Understanding ethics in terms of reasons invites us to share our concerns and to reason together in defining moral positions in reproductive medicine.

POSTSCRIPT

Is Fetal Sex Selection
Harmful to Society?

A primary focus of critics' concern about sex-selection technologies (and cultural biases toward males) is their impact on population sex ratios. A skewed sex ratio, they fear, will cause dire consequences for a society, particularly for heterosexual mating (although it is ironic that the same class of reproductive technological advances not only facilitate sex selection but also make reproduction less reliant on conventional heterosexual mating). But what about social concerns about sex selection? How will the increasing frequency of the use of sex-selection technologies impact families? How will it affect gender assumptions and sex discrimination?

Is the acceptability of sex-selection conditional? If Americans were not as biased toward having just boys or just girls, and therefore the population sex ratio would not be threatened, would sex selection be acceptable to control the birth order of the sexes, to ensure a mixture of boys and girls, or to have an only child of a certain desired sex? Sex-selection technology might reduce overpopulation by helping families who already have a child of one sex "balance" their family with a second child of the other sex, rather than continue to have children "naturally" until they get the sex they want. Is using sex selection as a "small family planning tool" an acceptable use of sex-selection technologies? Many feel that using sex selection to balance a family is not sexist. But others argue that it is sexist because it promotes gender stereotyping, which undermines equality between the sexes.

Some feminists argue that sex selection for any reason, even family-balancing perpetuates gender roles and thus the devaluation of women. Some people in the disabilities right movement have joined with this perspective suggesting that if it is permissible to select against female embryos (is sex per se a genetic "abnormality?"), then so it is permissible to select against embryos with genetic abnormalities of all types; and who is to define what is "abnormal"—height, IQ? Then the door is open to increasing discrimination against people with disabilities.

Should abortions solely for the purpose of sex selection be allowed? This is a profound dilemma for many pro-choice feminists for whom a woman's right to choose an abortion for any reason is opposed to gross sex discrimination in the form of sex-selective abortions (usually of female fetuses). It is interesting to note that when parents choose to abort based on fetal sex in an effort to "balance" their family, sex selection is regarded as more acceptable than when only female fetuses are aborted because of a preference for males. What assumptions about sex and gender underlie this judgment?"In these selections the effects of sex and gender on fetuses, children, and adolescents are examined. Is fetal sex selection ethical? Are sex differences located in biology and/or culture? Can children's gender roles be redefined?

Suggested Readings

K. M. Boyd, "Medical Ethics: Principles, Persons, and Perspectives: From Controversy to Conversation," *Journal of Medical Ethics, 31* (2005): 481–486.

John Harris, "Sex Selection and Regulated Hatred," *Journal of Medical Ethics, 31* (2005): 291–294.

S. Matthew Liao, "The Ethics of Using Genetic Engineering for Sex Selection," *Journal of Medical Ethics, 31* (2005): 116–118.

Rosamond Rhodes, "Acceptable Sex Selection," *American Journal of Bioethics, 1* (2001): 31–32.

Susan M. Wolf, *Feminism and Bioethics: Beyond Reproductions* (New York: Oxford University Press, 1996).

See also the following organizations' statements on sex selection:

1. The American College of Obstetricians and Gynecologists Committee on Ethics, *"Committee Opinion: Sex Selection,"* Number 177 (November 1996).

2. FIGO [International Federation of Gynecology and Obstetrics], "Recommendations on Ethical Issues in Obstetrics and Gynecology by the FIGO Committee for the Study of Ethical Aspects of Human Reproduction, July 1997.

3. The Ethics Committee of the ASRM [American Society for Reproductive Medicine], "Sex Selection and Preimplantation Genetic Diagnosis," *Fertility and Sterility,* Volume 72, Number 4 (October 1999).

4. The Ethics Committee of the ASRM, "Preconception Gender Selection for Nonmedical Reasons," *Fertility and Sterility,* Volume 75, Number 5 (May 2001).

Internet References . . .

About Women's Issues

This website addresses a number of issues related to gender and the world of work.

http://womensissues.about.com/od/
genderdiscrimination/i/isgendergap.htm

International Labour Organization (ILO)

The ILO is dedicated to reducing poverty and promoting opportunities for women and men to obtain decent and productive work. This website provides a comprehensive bibliography of materials related to gender issues and women at work.

http://www.ilo.org

World Alliance for Citizen Participation

CIVICUS: World Alliance for Citizen Participation is an international alliance of over 1000 members from 105 countries that has worked for over a decade to strengthen citizen action and civil society throughout the world, especially in areas where participatory democracy and citizens' freedom of association are threatened.

http://www.civicus.org/new/default.asp

Gender at Work

The website for Gender at Work was created in June 2001 by AWID (Association for Women's Rights in Development), WLP (Women's Learning Partnership), CIVICUS (World Alliance for Citizen Participation), and UNIFEM (United Nations Fund for Women). They state "We aim to develop new theory and practice on how organizations can change gender-biased institutional rules (the distribution of power, privileges and rights), values (norms and attitudes), and practices. We also aim to change the political, accountability, cultural and knowledge systems of organizations to challenge social norms and gender inequity."

http://www.genderatwork.org

From 9 to 5: Gender in the World of Work

*T*here are few places other than the workplace where gendered patterns are more apparent. There are sex-segregated jobs: "pink" collar jobs for women and "blue" collar jobs for men. Within occupational categories there is sex-stratification, with men more often holding the higher, more prestigious and better-paying positions, such as anesthesiologist versus pediatrician, or corporate lawyer versus family lawyer. Women on average make $ .75 for each man's dollar; this holds across race, ethnicity, social class, educational level, and work status (full-time or part-time). Such disparities provoke heated discussion. Are they the result of discrimination against women in the workplace or are they justifiable differences based on natural talents? In what ways does gender influence women's and men's efforts to balance work and family interests and responsibilities? Why do we ask the question about the impact on children of mothers working outside the home but never the question of the impact of fathers working? What are the ramifications of this question for poor people, especially women? Are these women to be blamed for their status as single mothers on welfare? As you explore the issues raised in this section consider the competing, or perhaps complementary, explanations for gender differences in the workplace: biologically based differences that lead to differences in interests, motivations, and achievement level and/or culturally based differences, such as discrimination in hiring and promotion practices, the devaluing of women's work, the social rejection of competent women, and the lack of role models and mentors.*

Are biologically based explanations justified in the face of differential experiences in the workplace based on race, ethnicity, class, culture, and other status-defining attributes, such as disability status or sexual orientation? How do media images of the workplace affect our understanding of the workplace?

- Does the "Mommy Track" (Part-Time Work) Improve Women's Lives?
- Can Social Policies Improve Gender Inequalities in the Workplace?
- Is the Gender Wage Gap Justified?
- Are Barriers to Women's Success as Leaders Due to Societal Obstacles?

ISSUE 14

Does the "Mommy Track" (Part-Time Work) Improve Women's Lives?

YES: E. Jeffrey Hill, Vjollca K. Märtinson, Maria Ferris, and Robin Zenger Baker, from "Beyond the Mommy Track: The Influence of New-Concept Part-Time Work for Professional Women on Work and Family," *Journal of Family and Economic Issues* (2004)

NO: Mary C. Noonan and Mary E. Corcoran, from "The Mommy Track and Partnership: Temporary Delay or Dead End?" *The Annals of the American Academy of Political and Social Science* (2004).

ISSUE SUMMARY

YES: Brigham Young University colleagues E. Jeffrey Hill and Vjollca K. Märtinson, along with Maria Ferris of IBM and Robin Zenger Baker at Boston University, suggest that women in professional careers can successfully integrate family and career by following a new-concept part-time work model.

NO: In contrast, Mary C. Noonan, an assistant professor in the department of sociology at the University of Iowa, and Mary E. Corcoran, a professor of political science at the University of Michigan, document the various costs of the mommy track for female attorneys, including lower salaries and decreased likelihood of promotion to partner.

Women account for about 47 percent of the workforce in the United States and work approximately the same number of hours as men (35–50 hours/week); 60 percent of all women over age 16 are in the workforce. However, women earn less than men on average; this is true across full-time and part-time work, as well as across race, class, and educational levels. One explanation for the earning discrepancy is that women experience more job discontinuity due to family obligations, such as taking time off for childbirth, as well as dual-career conflicts, such as following a spouse who relocates to improve his job status. That is, women are expected to choose family over career in any work-family conflicts. Job interruptions and lower wages can result in women experiencing lower self-esteem and a reduced sense of accomplishment.

Often these patterns are attributed to women's own choices and that they "deserve" less. However, others have suggested that society would benefit from recognizing that the childbearing years are also the years during which one is most likely to make the greatest career advancements. Thus, if women get off the career track to have children, they begin to lag and struggle to ever get back on the track. As a solution to this problem, the "mommy track" was proposed in 1989, a phrase coined in the *New York Times* to describe a "career and family" path that would serve as a viable alternative to the traditional "career primary" path typically followed by men. The "career and family" path was intended to offer women—only temporarily, flexible schedules, with reduced salaries and less responsibilities, while they tended to family matters, with the opportunity to return later to the fast track. The debate is whether the mommy track adequately allows for a temporary delay in women's career trajectory or if it really is a dead end. Skeptics question whether it is ever possible to truly get back on the fast track following a timeout for family. Although the concept of the mommy track was to prevent women from being unfairly treated, many argue that all it has done is perpetuate the stereotype that women, who chose, even temporarily, family over career, are not really committed to the workplace. As recently as July 2007, a *U.S. News & World Report* article was focused on how the mommy track can derail a career. In the selections that follow Hill and colleagues use data from a study of IBM workers to argue that women in professional careers can successfully integrate family and career by following a new-concept part-time work model. The selection by Noonan and Corcoran counters with data from University of Michigan law school graduates to show the costs of the mommy track for female attorneys, including lower salaries and decreased likelihood of promotion to partner.

YES ↵

E. Jeffrey Hill, Vjollca K. Märtinson,
Maria Ferris, and Robin Zenger Baker

Beyond the Mommy Track: The Influence of New-Concept Part-Time Work for Professional Women on Work and Family

The demographic composition of the United States workforce now includes more dual-earner couples who have responsibility to care for children, as well as more dual-professional couples who both have careers, not just jobs. In addition, the trend is toward longer work hours for many segments of American workers, especially for highly educated managers and professionals. The United States is one of the countries with the highest percentage of employees working 50 hours per week or more. This creates what has been termed a time famine for today's families. The time deficit is especially severe for women who choose to have children while pursuing a full-time career in a professional occupation.

Becoming a mother can make having a balanced life very difficult for a professional woman. Some new mothers try to do it all, continuing to work long hours in their professional careers while at the same time investing heavily in their family career. This option often takes a toll in stress and health. Others opt for, or are channeled into the so-called mommy track, moderating their ultimate career aspirations in order to raise their children. Some of these women choose to drop out of the workforce completely or for some period of time. Others take less demanding jobs in order to have more time and energy for their children. Still others choose part-time work.

Voluntary part-time employment after childbirth or adoption is consistently cited as a desirable option to facilitate work and family balance, especially for women. Studies show that part-time work options, especially for women, are increasing, and that this work is associated with lower work-to-family interference, better time-management ability, and improved life satisfaction. However, most professional women do not opt for reduced-hours options because, like other work-life programs, the economic costs in the form of forgone wages and career advancement are perceived to be too great. Generally these part-time jobs are of lower status with less pay and fewer career opportunities.

Because job prestige, income, and career opportunity are important to many professional women, some companies have begun to offer new-concept

From *Journal of Family and Economic Issues*, vol. 25, no. 1, March, 2004, pp. 121–126, 129–133. Copyright © 2004 by Springer Journals (Kluwer Academic). Reprinted by permission.

part-time employment options, call[ing] it customized work; it [is] a growing trend. In contrast to most part-time jobs, these are high-status, career-oriented reduced-hours options that conserve pro-rated professional salaries and benefits. The hope is that this option might ameliorate the tendency toward mommy track career outcomes and convince women to continue to make professional career contributions as they embark on their family career. [O]ffering reduced work schedules that fit well with employee needs is an important weapon in "winning the war for talent" by retaining "professional employees and managers with critical skills."

Work and Family Balance

Research offers support for the notion that flexible work arrangements allowing individuals to integrate and overlap work and family responsibilities in time and space are instrumental in achieving a healthy work and family balance. Examples of outcomes associated with negative work-to-family spillover include withdrawal from family interaction, increased conflict in marriage less knowledge of children's experiences, less involvement in housework, shorter period of breast-feeding for mothers with full-time employment, depression, greater likelihood to misuse alcohol, and overall decrease in the quality of life.

Less research has focused on family-to-work spillover, the "neglected side of the work-family interface." Examples of outcomes associated with negative family-to-work spillover include more pronounced psychological distress at work due to poor marital and parental role quality, decreased job satisfaction, greater likelihood of leaving the company, and increased absenteeism. $6.8 billion worth of annual work loss in the United States as a result of the absenteeism that is associated with marital distress [has been documented].

Part-Time Employment

The most persistent work characteristic that predicts work-family imbalance is long work hours, especially for women. For those financially able to do so, part-time work seems an obvious option for dealing with the problems associated with long work hours. In fact, many professionals desire to work fewer hours. More than half of the companies in America have a part-time option for parents to transition back to the workforce after childbirth or adoption. A recent study shows that 8% of men and 21% of women employees in the United States work part time. However, due to work responsibilities, perceived diminished career opportunities, and reduction in salary and benefits, relatively few professionals choose to work less than full time. The emergence of new-concept, part-time work, attempts to address these concerns. "These jobs are viewed as permanent, have career potential, include fringe benefits, and their rate of pay is prorated relative to that of comparable full-time jobs." Though many studies examine part-time work in general, relatively few have specifically examined professional women who work reduced hours while their children are young in these new-concept, part-time professional positions. This study attempts to fill that gap.

Research Questions

This study will expand the extensive literature on part-time employment by exploring the influence of new-concept part-time options, used by professional women who are mothers of preschoolers, on work-family balance and perceived career opportunity. In essence, we speculate that these new-concept part-time jobs will enable female professionals to go beyond the mommy track and successfully start their family careers while they simultaneously move forward in their occupational careers. We will attempt to answer the following specific research questions for a sample of new mothers in professional positions:

1. What is the relationship between new-concept part-time work and work-family balance?
2. What is the relationship between new-concept part-time work and perceived career opportunity?
3. How do part-time professional women and full-time professional women differ in how they allocate time to work, child care, and household chores?
4. How do part-time professional women and full-time professional women differ in total income and pay rates?
5. What do those participating in new-concept part-time positions perceive they would have done, had that option not been available?

Method

The data for this paper came from a work and life issues survey administered on-line by IBM in the United States in 1996. The focus of this study was female professionals with preschool children (birth to age 4) who utilized the new-concept part-time option. Originally the study was to look at part-time work for men as well, but there were insufficient male responses for reliable statistical analyses.

Internal surveys revealed that IBM employees perceived the flexibility to choose when, where, and how many hours are worked to be the most beneficial IBM offering to enhance work-family balance. In 1991, as part of an overall flexibility initiative, IBM implemented the Flexible Work Leave of Absence Program, which enabled employees to reduce their scheduled work hours from 40 to 20–32 hours per week. This qualified as a new-concept, part-time program because those participating continued in their same professional position, received pro-rated pay and benefits equivalent to what they had received when working full time, and were eligible for promotion and recognition. This research was conducted when the maximum length of part-time employment allowed by IBM was five years.

Data Collection and Sample

A 9% representative sample of all IBM employees in the United States was invited to take this online survey; 58% (N = 6,451) responded. Sample respondents were similar to the broader U.S. population of workers, except that this IBM sample was more highly educated and more highly paid than national norms. The option of part-time employment was probably more feasible in this population than in the overall population.

The survey was administered electronically. IBM has conducted on-line surveys since 1986, and survey data indicate a high degree of confidence in confidentiality and anonymity. For confidentiality reasons, the electronic mail addresses were deleted from the data before data were sent to the survey administrator. . . .

Results

Results related to the research questions are summarized below.

Relationship Between New-Concept Part-Time Work and Work-Family Balance

Being in a new-concept part-time position vis-à-vis a full-time position was strongly and positively correlated to work-family balance. This relationship was maintained in multivariate analyses after controlling for occupational level, family income, age, and job flexibility.

Relationship Between New-Concept Part-Time Work and Perceived Career Opportunity

Being in a new-concept part-time professional position vis-à-vis a full-time position was not significantly correlated to perceived career opportunity. No significant relationship was found in multivariate analyses after controlling for occupational level, family income, age, and job flexibility.

Allocation of Time to Work, Child Care and Household Chores

Those in new-concept part-time professional positions reported that they worked an average of 23 fewer hours per week than those in full-time professional positions (26.3 hours per week vs. 49.3 hours per week). They reported slightly more hours per week in child care (27.3 vs. 25.5) and in household chores (16.1 vs. 13.5).

Differences in Total Income and Pay Rates

Those in the new-concept part-time professional positions reported $20,022 less annual family income than those in full-time professional positions ($100,568 per year vs. $120,590 per year). They also reported $26,624 less annual individual income ($37,954 per year vs. $64,578 per year). When converted to an hourly pay equivalent, those in new-concept part-time professional positions earned slightly more per hour than those in full-time professional positions ($27.94 per hour worked vs. $25.36 per hour worked).

What Professional Women Report They Would Have Done Had the Program Not Been Offered

Most of those participating in new-concept part-time professional positions (74%) reported they would have left IBM if this program had not been available. Almost three-fifths (59%) reported they would have left IBM to find a job with more flexibility. Almost one-fourth (23%) reported they would have left the workforce altogether. Only about one-fifth (19%) reported they would have stayed with IBM and continued to work full time.

Discussion

In this study we consider the possibility that new-concept part-time professional positions might be an alternative to the mommy track. We consider whether this option may better enable professional women to embark on their family career with less stress and fewer negative consequences to long-term career prospects.

Personal / Family Implications

It was not surprising that mothers in new-concept part-time professional positions reported much better work-family balance than those working full time. Considering they work 23 fewer hours per week, it would have been surprising if the part-time group did not report better balance. However, it was surprising that they did not report less perceived career opportunity. This is counter to what would be expected had they been working in traditional part-time jobs based on previous research. Why is this so? It may be the higher status, greater responsibility, and pro-rated pay of new-concept part-time professional positions creates an environment where the employee feels in the loop of future career opportunities.

The personal decision for a professional woman to work a part-time schedule is a matter of trade-offs. This study quantifies some of the advantages and disadvantages for this population. The most obvious advantage of new-concept part-time work for professional women is that more than four and one-half hours per work day are freed up for personal and family needs. This extra time was certainly a major factor in why work-family balance was less problematic for the professional women working part time.

An interesting finding is that women in the full-time group reported an average of almost as many hours in child care as the part-time group (26 vs. 27 hours per week) and almost as much time doing household chores (14 vs. 16 hours per week). Apparently both full- and part-time professional women take the time needed to care for home and family responsibilities. The real benefit for the part-time women, therefore, appears to be the extra 19 more hours per week available to use in individual activities that might reduce stress, such as additional sleep, recreation, and other renewal activities. The literature cited earlier indicates that possible benefits for these new mothers include less marital conflict, increased period of breast-feeding after the birth of an infant, less depression, and better monitoring of children.

The most obvious disadvantage for a new mother considering a new-concept part-time professional position is reduced income. This study documents that the salaries of the part-time professionals averaged about 41% less (about $27,000 less per year) than the full-time professionals. However, because they reported working 47% fewer hours (26 vs. 49 hours per week), their pay equivalent was actually higher than the full-time group ($27.94 vs. $25.50 per hour). The family income of the part-time group was only about 17% less than the full-time group (about $20,000 less per year).

Organizational Implications

Companies today are engaged in what is known as a talent war to "recruit and retain professional employees and managers with critical skills." Data from this study support the notion that offering new-concept part-time professional positions may be a useful weapon in that war. Difficulty managing the demands of work and personal/family life is very problematic, especially for professional women who have chosen to have children. It is considered to be the most important reason why professional women with preschool children would choose to leave their job. Of the reduced-hours group in this study, 23% reported they would have left their job to stay home full time had the part-time work option not been available. Another 58% said they would have left their job to work for another company that offered greater flexibility. Only 19% indicated they would have continued working full time for the company. It appears that new-concept part-time employment is a strategy that may have enabled 81% of these women to stay employed with IBM, rather than going to work for someone else or leaving the workforce altogether.

In summary, the results of this study indicate that new-concept part-time employment offers the promise of enabling professional women opportunities to better balance work and family life while maintaining career opportunity. This option appears to be a true win-win solution to help mitigate the personal toll of increased work demands, with relatively few costs. If visionary business leaders and empowered individuals adopt greater flexibility, we may see the end to the zero-sum game and set up a virtuous cycle in which work-family balance programs leverage on each other to promote individual well-being, family solidarity, and organizational success.

Limitations

One limitation of this study is that respondents all worked for IBM in the United States. IBM employees, in general, are highly educated, have higher salaries, and have more experience with computer technology than the general population. For these reasons, the degree to which these results may be generalized to other companies and in other parts of the world is uncertain. Even if the IBM sample is representative of employees working for large corporations, it may not be representative of the majority of professional women who work for smaller firms or are self-employed. In addition, most IBMers work in or near urban centers, so the applicability of this research to those who work in rural settings is uncertain.

Conclusion

Just as flexibility in family processes diminishes potential family stress, so flexibility in work processes may be key in helping employees effectively manage contemporary stress associated with work and family demands. In fact, this study documents that new-concept, part-time positions may provide the time professional women need at the beginning of their family career when children require the greatest parental investment. Given that these women represent key talent required for meeting business objectives, data like these can reinforce management's efforts to provide greater flexibility in the workforce, especially when the results are so clear and the costs of such efforts are relatively small. Just as important, these data may help encourage professional women to take advantage of the flexibility offered so they can more effectively care for their young children. As more companies offer viable new-concept part-time options and more employees use these options, perhaps we can move beyond the mommy track to enable women to contribute their best to both work and home, at the same time.

Mary C. Noonan and
Mary E. Corcoran

 **NO**

The Mommy Track and Partnership: Temporary Delay or Dead End?

More than 40 percent of recent law school graduates are women, and almost 40 percent of associates in large firms are women. In 2003, women made up 63 percent of Berkeley Law School's graduating class, 51 percent of Columbia Law School's graduating class, and 47 percent of Harvard Law School's graduating class. Despite the rapid feminization of law since the 1970s, women associates are far less likely than male associates to become partners. According to a recent American Bar Association Commission report, the most pervasive underrepresentation of women lawyers is among partners in law firms. Only 16 percent of partners in law firms are women. . . .

Women now graduate from top law schools and enter prestigious law firms at roughly the same rates as do men. [W]omen "start strong out of the gate." But after leaving law school and entering firms, women increasingly fall behind men. Why is this? [It has been] asserted that women associates make partner at lower rates than do male associates because women face "multiple glass ceilings" that men do not at many stages of the career hierarchy. One such stage is the decision to remain in a firm long enough to be considered for partnership. Partnership typically occurs after six to eight years at a firm, but many women associates drop out of large law practices by their fourth year. Donovan claimed that "the single most important element of women's inability to make partner is the high attrition rate of women from firms . . . women cannot make partner if they have left the firm." Foster (1995, 1658) stated that "attrition perpetuates the glass ceiling as fewer women are available for promotion and more men remain in decision-making positions as a result."

High attrition in the first years after joining firms is not the only reason offered for women's underrepresentation in partnership ranks. [G]lass ceilings operate at other career stages as well—resulting in lower promotion chances for women associates who remain in firms and in lower earnings and equity shares for women who become partners.

[T]he following institutional factors may marginalize women associates: "rainmaking" demands (i.e., generating new clients for the firm), lack of mentors, sexual harassment and discrimination, high work hours, and part-time work tracks that permanently derail lawyers from partnership tracks. [F]emale associates have fewer opportunities than male associates to develop "social capital" within law firms. Researchers who interview women lawyers find that

From *The Annals of the American Academy of Political and Social Science*, vol. 596, no. 1, 2004, pp. 130–135, 137, 139–142, 146–149. Copyright © 2004 by Sage Publications. Reprinted by permission.

many report experiencing sex discrimination within the firm. [B]oth men and women lawyers identify sex discrimination as one of the main reasons for women's early attrition from private firms and lower rates of promotion to partnership. [W]omen lawyers report lower levels of discrimination at the "front door" (hiring) than on the job (salary, promotion, and assignments).

The primary personal factor identified as constraining women's partnership chances is that some cut back labor supply (e.g., work part-time for a period, take a family leave, work fewer hours per year) to balance the demands of motherhood with the demands of practicing law. As Donovan put it, "The most notorious reason for women to leave [a firm] is motherhood." [C]hild care responsibilities and family leave policies play a significant role in career decisions—jobs, specialties, cases, and work hours—for women but not for men. Common reasons women report for leaving the field of law are the lack of flexibility offered by law firms, long hours, child care commitments, and the stressful nature of the work. Men are less likely to cite "work-family conflict" as a reason for leaving law and are more likely to state the desire to use different skills.

As these authors noted, the distinction between institutional and personal constraints is fuzzy. For instance, a woman associate may "choose" to work part-time for several years, and this choice may reduce her chances of making partner. But this choice may be a response to discrimination within a firm, or this choice may be all that is available in a firm. Furthermore, the "choice" itself may be strongly conditioned by the expectations of others—family, colleagues, the larger culture—expectations that do not constrain men's labor supply choices. . . .

[Many] authors hypothesized that work-family conflicts lead women to reduce their labor supply in ways that increase their chances of exiting law firms and reduce their chances of becoming partners. Two studies of attrition from law firms and several studies of partnership have used relatively recent data on lawyers' outcomes to test this hypothesis.

What do these researchers find? First, sex strongly predicted exits from law firms and promotion to partnership even when controlling for law school quality, academic distinction in law school, *potential* work experience (i.e., years since called to the bar, years since law school graduation), legal specialization, having taken a leave for child care, marital status, children, current work hours, and measures of social capital. Second, labor supply matters. Having taken a family leave was more common among women and reduced chances of partnership in [a] sample of Toronto lawyers. A work-family constraint lowered women's but not men's chances of partnership in [a] sample of Chicago lawyers. Current work hours positively predicted partnership.

The usefulness of this research in assessing for the extent to which women's labor supply choices reduce their chances of becoming partners is limited given the relatively weak measures of labor supply used. No study had a measure of years worked part-time to care for children. Yet [it has been] argued that choosing to work-part time on a "mommy track" can stigmatize women as "not serious" and permanently damage chances of becoming partners. . . . No study had a measure of years practicing law. Instead, all of these prior studies included a measure of potential experience (years since called to the bar or years since law school graduation), but actual years practiced is likely lower for women than for men. . . . Those who do not make partner might well cut back work hours.

Given the limitations of the labor supply measures used in past research, it may be surprising to learn that even with these weak controls for labor supply, mothers are no less likely than childless women to become partners. This does not mean that *sex* does not matter for partnership; mothers and childless women are equally *less* likely than men to become partners.

We use detailed information on the fifteen-year careers of graduates of the University of Michigan Law School to investigate sex differences in promotion to partnership. Because women may be disadvantaged relative to men at multiple career stages, we examine three steps in the partnership process: (1) the decision to attrite early from private practice, (2) the attainment of partnership among those who do not attrite, and (3) determinants of partners' earnings. Because we have direct measures of the labor supply choices made to handle child care responsibilities (e.g., months time out for kids, months worked part-time for kids, and years worked in law), we can more precisely estimate the extent to which cutbacks in labor supply are associated with reduced chances of becoming partner for women who start out in private practice than have past researchers. If, after controlling for sex differences in these precise measures of labor supply, women still have higher early attrition rates from private practice than men, women who stay in private practice are still less likely to be promoted than men, and women who become partners still have lower earnings than men, then this is strong indirect evidence that glass ceilings constrain women's opportunities at multiple points in their legal careers. In addition, if after controlling for labor supply, motherhood has no further effects on early attrition, partnership among stayers, and wages of partners, then it seems unlikely that parenting concerns account for the remaining sex differences in early attrition, partnership, and earnings.

Examining women's experiences at multiple stages of their careers after they first enter firms is important because the experiences of women long-termers in a firm likely inform the career decisions made by new women entrants. If cutting back on labor supply has derailed the partnership of older women, then new entrants who are concerned about balancing work and family may quit private practice for another legal setting. If older women who have not cut back labor supply are less likely than men with similar work histories to become partners, and if women partners earn less than men partners with similar work histories, then even new women entrants who are not concerned about balancing family demands may decide their opportunities are restricted and leave. . . .

We use a sample of University of Michigan Law School graduates to examine these questions. The law school surveys all graduates fifteen years after graduation about their earnings, work hours, work histories (including interruptions and years worked part-time), work settings, and families. These survey data are matched with law school records, giving additional information on graduates' performance while in law school.

The sample includes the graduating classes of 1972 to 1985. Outcomes are observed from 1987 to 2000. The average response rate across all years was

60 percent for women and 64 percent for men. We exclude women and men with missing data on the variables used in the analyses (about 18 percent of the total sample). We use three samples in our analyses: those who spent at least one year in private practice (433 women and 1,876 men), those who spent at least four years in private practice (354 women and 1,694 men), and those who were partners in their fifteenth year (144 women and 1,116 men). . . .

Women were less likely than men to have tried out private practice for at least one year (82 vs. 87 percent), to have stayed in practice for four or more years (67 vs. 79 percent), and to have made partner (27 vs. 52 percent). Among graduates who did not attrite early (those with four or more years' of private practice), 40 percent of women and 65 percent of men were partners.

. . . At three years of experience, the gap between the percentage of men and women still in private practice is minor—94 versus 89 percent, respectively. The gap widens to approximately 10 percentage points after four and five years of work experience. We suspect that this is the period when women become discouraged about their chances of making partner. Between five and eightyears, the years in which partnership decisions are typically made, the gap widens another 10 percentage points, reaching nearly 20 percent at year eight. It seems likely that women leave private practice at higher rates after five to eight years of practice either because they expect not to make partner or they do not make partner. The gender gap in attrition is constant over the period from eight to fifteen years.

. . . Sex differences in family characteristics were large: women were more likely to be childless, less likely to be married, and more likely to be married to a lawyer. Women, on average, also worked significantly fewer hours than men—1,966 hours versus 2,493 hours. Women and men were equally likely to have had a mentor and were equally satisfied with the balance of family and work in their lives.

Sex differences in the labor supply of parents are striking. Only 19 of the 1,574 fathers in our sample had worked part-time, and only 17 had taken a leave from work to care for children. In contrast, 47 percent of mothers had worked part-time and 42 percent had taken a leave from work. Mothers who had worked part-time averaged forty-two months of part-time work over the fifteen years since law school graduation, and those who took a leave from work averaged twenty-four months not working. Fathers worked more hours in year fifteen than did mothers—2,519 versus 2,005 hours. . . .

Although women lawyers were more likely than men lawyers to cut back labor supply, 56 percent of women lawyers *never* worked part-time or took a leave. This 56 percent consists of childless women (29 percent of the sample) and mothers who never worked part-time or took time out to care for children (27 percent of the sample). Women who had not worked part-time or dropped out worked high hours—roughly twenty-four hundred at year fifteen. . . .

Women are more likely than men to exit, even after controlling for GPA, marriage, children, labor supply, mentoring, and satisfaction. GPA and years practiced law are significantly associated with lower rates of leaving for both men and women. Marriage, children, time out, and part-time work are not significantly associated with rates of leaving for women or men. . . . Men who left are more likely than men who stayed to be satisfied with their work-family balance at the fifteenth year; this is not true for women. Further analyses show that, for women, having children, taking time out of work, and working part-time are all positively associated with work-family satisfaction. Women who leave private practice are more likely to take time out of work, women who stay in private practice are more likely to work part-time, and both groups are equally likely to have children. Therefore, it appears that both women "leavers" and "stayers" have balanced their work and family lives in different ways, but both approaches are equally satisfying. Since very few men who remain in private practice actually work part-time, it may be that—for men—work-family satisfaction only comes through leaving the stressful world of private practice for other less demanding lines of work.

Sex also affects promotion rates for lawyers who remain in firms for at least four years. Women are less likely than men to be promoted to partner, even when GPA, race, years practiced law, months part-time, months nonwork, marital status, number of kids, mentorship, and satisfaction are controlled. . . . [M]arriage and children are *positively* associated with the probability of becoming partner when experience measures are included. . . . GPA, years practiced law, and having a mentor are positively associated with partnership, and months not worked is negatively associated with partnership. The effects of time out on partnership are significantly larger for men, and the effects of GPA on partnership are significantly larger for women. Part-time work significantly decreases the likelihood of becoming a partner for women but not for men; however, the difference in the effect is not large enough to be statistically different by sex. Having a lawyer as a spouse increases women's but not men's chances of becoming a partner. . . .

The "base" lawyer is a white man who is married with children, has an average GPA, 13.5 years of private practice experience, no leave, no part-time experience, a mentor, is satisfied with his work-family balance, and has a spouse who is not a lawyer. This "base" lawyer has a 9 percent chance of leaving private practice before his fourth year and a 57 percent chance of making partner if he remains in private practice for at least four years. A woman with these same characteristics has a 15 percent chance of leaving practice within four years and a 40 percent chance of making partner if she remains in private practice for at least four years. Thus, "being female" increased the predicted chances of attrition by 6 percentage points and reduced the chances of becoming partner by 17 percentage points.

Conclusion and Discussion

In this article, we use data on graduates of the University of Michigan Law School, a highly ranked law school that provides specialized training and access to well-paid jobs, to examine sex differences in the path to partnership. These men and women started off on an equal footing in the legal marketplace. Despite this, men were almost twice as likely as women to become partners.

How did this happen? The pattern is one of cumulating disadvantages. Women fell behind men in each stage in the progression to partnership. . . .

Some argue that women are more likely than men to select themselves out at each stage of the partnership process because men and women handle family responsibilities differently. Certainly, a large minority of women in our sample cut back labor supply to deal with family responsibilities, and virtually no men did so. These cutbacks in labor supply were negatively associated with partnership chances and with partners' earnings. But we found large gaps between the early attrition rates, chances of partnership, and annual earnings of men and women partners with the *same* work histories. . . . At most, one-quarter to one-third of the male/female differences in early attrition and promotion and one-half of the earnings gap between men and women partners are due to labor supply differences. These estimates of reductions may be on the high side since women's labor supply choices are likely influenced by the options firms offer and by women's perceptions of sex differences in promotion opportunities.

A family leave of one year reduced women's chances of making partner by one-third and reduced women partners' earnings by 28 percent. But law school performance and connections had equally strong effects on women lawyers' careers. A woman with a B+ average GPA in law school was 1.5 times as likely to attrite early as was one with an A average (14 vs. 9 percent) and was less likely to make partner (35 vs. 49 percent). Women with mentors were almost 1.5 times as likely to become partners as were those without mentors (35 vs. 24 percent), and women married to lawyers were 1.8 times as likely to make partner as women who were not married to lawyers (54 vs. 35 percent).

The few male lawyers who reduced their labor supply to care for children fared badly economically. A year of leave reduced men's predicted chances of making partner from 58 to 0 percent, and a year of part-time work reduced male partners' predicted earnings by 41 percent. The meaning of these drops is unclear. These could be very unusual men, or it could be that male lawyers who behave in nontraditional ways face high penalties. If the latter were true, it is not surprising that so few male lawyers reduce labor supply. . . .

One could argue that parenting responsibilities reduce women's productivity at work in ways not captured by these analyses. But controlling for labor supply, mothers had the same early attrition rates, promotion rates, and earnings as did childless women; and ever-married women were more likely to be promoted than never-married women. It seems implausible that women's commitment to home and hearth accounts for the remaining sex-based gaps in early attrition, partnership, and partners' earnings.

This brings us to sex-based differences in the ways women are treated in law firms. Posited that direct discrimination and sexual harassment, as well as a wide array of embedded institutional practices, marginalize women within law firms. We could not directly test this proposition, . . . [b]ut our finding of large sex differences at each stage of the progression to partnership, controlling for labor supply differences, suggests that women are disproportionately selected out and discouraged at each of these stages. This is strong indirect evidence that women face multiple glass ceilings.

Researchers who have conducted in-depth, in-person interviews with associates and partners in law firms describe two sets of mechanisms that could systematically disadvantage women. One set constrains associates' labor supply choices and determines the effects these choices have on partnership. For instance, although firms offer part-time tracks, official policies differ on whether part-time work counts for partnership and on whether part-timers can return to partnership tracks. Even when the official policy is that family leaves and part-time work do not disqualify women from partnership, several studies find that some women reported being assigned less important cases and being labeled as less motivated after having worked part-time (Epstein et al. 1995; Gannon 2003). This social stigma and fear of not being taken seriously likely keeps many lawyers from pursuing part-time options. . . . A second set of mechanisms can systematically disadvantage women in ways that are unrelated to their actual labor supply choices. [H]igh rainmaking demands, a lack of mentoring, sex discrimination, disproportionate shares of pro bono work, and mixed messages about personal style all may reduce women's chances of making partner.

It is easy to describe institutional arrangements that might make law firms more family-friendly. A report in the *Harvard Law Review* (1996) suggested reducing "billable hours" requirements, billing approaches that move away from reliance on billable hours to other indicators of performance, officially counting part-time work toward partnership, developing a work climate in which individuals who work part-time and take family leaves are not stigmatized, part-time partnership, employer-assisted emergency day care, and mixed compensation (compensation consisting partly of time and partly of money).

It is equally easy to list approaches that can change institutional barriers to women's mobility. To the extent that sex discrimination and sexual harassment limit women's chances, there may be legal avenues to pursue. Of course, the individual costs of pursuing such strategies may be high. Other strategies include programs that improve the mentoring women associates receive, broaden the criteria for partnership, and reduce the extent to which women's personal styles are viewed as less effective in a legal setting. We find mentoring has a big impact on women's partnership chances.

Implementing family-friendly policies and changing embedded institutional policies that disadvantage women may require shifts in law firm culture. This is the rub. The *Harvard Law Review* study (1996, 1381) warned that such changes can "conflict with (firms') institutional norms" and that "law firms and their clients are understandably reluctant to challenge deeply ingrained business practices." [T]hree social processes—traditionalism, stereotyping, and ambivalence—contribute to this institutional inertia.

The *Harvard Law Review* study (1996, 1376) succinctly summed up the dilemma facing women associates: "Women cannot reach true equality within firms as large numbers of women are considered atypical because they fail to conform to the male-based definition of the ideal worker." Despite this gloomy assessment, the *Harvard Law Review* study contended that the benefits to changing firm culture may be powerful enough to overcome inertia. The *Harvard Law Review* report argues that high hour demands have led to a "time famine" among lawyers and that this "lack of time" can adversely affect health by increasing stress and can inhibit professional development by reducing available time for community service, pro bono work, scholarship, and education.

POSTSCRIPT

Does the "Mommy Track" (Part-Time Work) Improve Women's Lives?

The irony of the mommy track–fast track debate is that it is based on the assumption that women have a choice regarding work. In fact, most women have no choice. Either they are single parents or part of a family that needs two pay-checks to meet the family's financial needs. Thus, for large numbers of working women this is a meaningless debate. Choice is reserved for the educational elite according to Mary Blair-Loy in *Competing Devotions*. Rather, the debate serves to perpetuate stereotypes regarding women's commitment to family over work. The reality is that most working women have little control over the hours they work. Indeed, for the lowest income jobs working hours are not family-friendly hours. Consider the schedules of waitresses and housekeeping staff, for example.

It is worth noting that the family–career conflict that is receiving so much attention currently is in fact a rather current phenomenon. Claudia Goldin (2004) has suggested that this "conflict" has changed over time. For women graduating from college in the early 1900s the choice was clear: family or career. From 1920 to 1945 many women opted for a "job then family" model. From about 1946 to the 1960s, the pattern was reversed to "family then job." In the late 1960s the language shifted from "job" to "career," with a pattern of "career then family" dominating through the 1980s. Since then the trend has been toward "career and family." Goldin contends that these shifts have been possible due largely to increased career opportunities for women, especially white collar jobs, with improved contraceptive methods also making it easier for women to control their fertility.

Some scholars have suggested that it is the issue of care-giving that needs to be rethought in our society. If society as a whole were committed to the well-being of children, then conceptualizations of child care might well rest on a foundation of shared community support, freeing up all parents to provide quality care to their children. No longer would the parent who wants/needs to stay home with a sick child or attend preschool graduation be looked upon as less than the ideal worker. Only when there is a shift in perceptions of who is responsible for child care will even the subtle, but nevertheless powerful, effects of the assumption of women holding the primary responsibility for children subside.

Suggested Readings

Claudia Goldin, "The Power of the Pill: Oral Contraceptives and Women's Career and Marriage Decisions," *Journal of Political Economy* (August, 2002).

Janet C. Gornick and M. K. Meyers, *Families that Work: Policies for Reconciling Parenthood and Employment* (Russell Sage Foundation, 2003).

Kjell Erik Lommerud and S. Vagstad, *Mommy Tracks and Public Policy: on Self-fulfilling Prophecies and Gender Gaps in Promotion* (Center for Economic Policy Research, 2000).

Mary Blair-Loy, *Competing Devotions: Career and Family among Women Executives* (Harvard University Press, 2003).

Jeanne Marecek, "Mad Housewives, Double Shifts, Mommy Tracks and Other Invented Realities," *Feminism and Psychology* (vol. 13, 2003).

Phyllis Moen (ed.), *It's about Time: Couples and Careers* (Cornell University Press, 2003).

ISSUE 15

Can Social Policies Improve Gender Inequalities in the Workplace?

YES: **Hilda Kahne,** from "Low-Wage Single-Mother Families in This Jobless Recover: Can Improved Social Policies Help?" *Journal of Social Issues and Public Policy* (2004)

NO: **Hadas Mandel and Moshe Semyonov,** from "A Welfare State Paradox: State Interventions and Women's Employment Opportunities in 22 Countries," *American Journal of Sociology* (2006)

ISSUE SUMMARY

YES: Hilda Kahne, professor emerita at Wheaton College in Massachusetts and a member of the Scholars Program and a Resident Scholar at Brandeis University, makes the argument that incomplete education and few training programs, rather than gender discrimination, makes it more difficult for low-wage single mothers to raise their earnings.

NO: In contrast, Hadas Mandel of the department of sociology and anthropology and Moshe Semyonov of the department of sociology and labor studies anthropology at Tel Aviv University review extensive data from 22 countries and conclude that social policies have the counterintuitive impact of decreasing women's opportunities for access to more desirable and powerful positions.

According to the U.S. Census Bureau there are an estimated 9.8 million single mothers in the United States, a number that had tripled in the past 25 years and, as of 1998, there were an estimated 948,000 teen mothers age 15 to 19. About five-sixths of all single parents are women. Approximately 42 percent of single mothers have never married. From 1960 to 1980 the rate of divorce doubled, and although the rate has leveled off since, an increasing number of women find themselves in the role of single mother. Children, because they usually live with their mothers, are affected. Approximately two-thirds of divorces involve children and over one-half of children in the United States will experience parents' divorce. For these children their standard of living declines 30 to 40 percent and 25 percent of divorced mothers will fall into poverty within five years. Contributing to this poverty is the likelihood of not receiving child support even when entitled to it. Factors contributing to divorce, as well as single parenthood, for women include younger age of marriage, social attitudes more accepting of divorce, cohabitation and single-parenthood, as well as women's greater independence because of more opportunities in the workforce. At the same time, and perhaps ironically, the employment rates for single mothers has decreased from 73 percent in 2000 to 69.8 percent in 2003, and the steepest loss has been for black mothers.

Numerous debates surround these numbers. Issues being discussed include teen sexuality and unintended pregnancy as well as marriage initiatives. There is a strong belief among religious conservatives as well as economists that there is a relationship between marital stability, job stability, and earnings. One dimension of these debates relates to gender and whether welfare and work policies should be gender sensitive. There are stereotypes of welfare recipients, typically women, as lazy and irresponsible. However, stories of individual welfare recipients call welfare recipient stereotypes into question. In fact, it is common for poor women to combine welfare with work or to get welfare benefits between jobs. Many women use welfare to help them get more education—a critical factor in moving out of poverty. Many factors conspire against poor women: they can't find employment; they can't secure high enough pay, particularly if they have children in their care; they are financially penalized if married; and they have to endure public condemnation and discrimination.

Nevertheless, stereotypes of welfare mothers remain rigid and condemning. These stereotypes reflect three dominant perspectives or beliefs about the causes of poverty and wealth: (1) individualism contends that individuals are responsible for their own lot in life. Those who are motivated and work hard will make it. Those who do not make it (i.e., welfare recipients) have only themselves to blame; (2) social-structuralism asserts that due to economic or social imbalances (e.g., in education, marriage and family life, and even welfare programs themselves), opportunities are restricted for some people, overriding individual agency and affecting the likelihood of success; and (3) "culture of poverty," most often associated with African Americans who are thought to have developed a culture—some would say counterculture—of poverty with values, traits, and expectations that have developed from the structural constraints of living in poverty and that may be intergenerationally transmitted. Such logic demonstrates what social psychologists call the "fundamental attribution error;" that is, the tendency to blame individuals for their outcomes while ignoring the situational context. A focus on social structural factors leads to a discussion of the effectiveness of social policies. Can social policies help lift womens from poverty? This is apparent in the selections that follow.

Kahne suggests that wage-related social policies should be developed to improve educational and training opportunities for low-wage single mothers, thereby increasing their earning potential. In contrast, Mandel and Semyonov argues that although policies have indeed increased women's entry into the job market, they have failed to give women increased access to higher paying, more attractive jobs. This would suggest that current policies may actually contribute to gender-related inequalities in the world of work.

YES

Hilda Kahne

Low-Wage Single-Mother Families in this Jobless Recovery: Can Improved Social Policies Help?

This article focuses on the experience of low-wage single-mother families and how they are affected by the current soft economy and jobless recovery that continues to display many of the earmarks of a recession. It suggests that these effects, bringing uncertainty and stress and often temporary loss of income and asset value for many people, are worse for low-wage earners, including single-mother families. They face a difficult labor market and must compete with more-skilled unemployed workers for available jobs, while carrying considerable family responsibilities, often with limited education and no income reserves for coping with emergencies. In the short run they need financial support through an updating of existing social policies that take account of changing economic realities and life style requirements. But their more permanent need is to increase earning ability that can only be assured if training and education programs make possible an increase in their skills and job versatility. . . .

Changing Economic Context

Long Run

The long-run changing economic context provides a valuable backdrop for understanding the linkage between production and well-being of societal groups. In a recent study of productive and related institutions over time, Michael Piore describes the changing nature of four key institutions between the 1950s and today—the family, corporate enterprises, trade unions, and the government. During the earlier period the family was structurally stable and defined as including a male earner and female homemaker. Corporate enterprises were organized for mass production with a labor force having defined skills and tasks. A strong trade union movement negotiated terms of employment. And a federal government provided regulatory legislation and oversight as well as a safety net for persons needing social support. . . .

From *Analyses of Social Issues and Public Policy*, vol. 4, issue 1, 2004, pp. 47–48, 52–56, 58–65. Copyright © 2004 by Blackwell Publishing, Ltd. Reprinted by permission.

More Recent Trends

Given Piore's insightful observations about long-run changing societal trends, what can be said about the shorter-run influences on the well-being of poor single-mother families and the possibility of their achieving an adequate standard of living as a participant in the creation of society's goods and services? How will they be affected by current changing trends? At present, 50% of persons in poverty live in female-headed families and of all female-headed families, over 25% have incomes below the poverty level. Can their existence be made more economically secure through policies that move them further toward economic independence? . . .

Female family heads experienced unemployment rates higher than the overall average. By February 2003, their unemployment rate was 9% compared with a rate of 5.8% for all workers. The higher rate was partly due to the lesser stability of frequently held low-skill jobs that were often temporary or contingent or part time. It was also probably higher than for other groups because some skilled laid-off workers, at least until they found other work, took low-skill jobs, replacing traditional low-skill workers who were then shuffled to the back of the queue and lacked needed abilities to compete for other openings. It was especially high for single mothers who lacked a high school degree—18% in 2002. In addition to high rates, unemployment has shown a continuing increase in its length. Women's long-term unemployment rates now match those of men. . . .

The causes of the growth in income disparity are multiple and economists do not agree on the relative importance among them. Growing earnings inequality undoubtedly explains much of it with rewards given for high skills and educational levels. Bonuses and stock option benefits have also increased income, especially at the high managerial levels, as have relatively greater tax reductions for high-income groups. Some of the disparity has also been due to the effects of technological changes and of globalization. At the other end of the income stream, changes in family structures, erosion of the value of the minimum wage, and a decline in union bargaining strength have undoubtedly had negative effects on income distribution. Continued gender wage discrimination can intensify these effects. But, whatever the causes of growing inequality, the fact remains that in recent years the inequality in income distribution has increased despite the economic growth that has taken place in society as a whole. Although in the past all groups benefited from rising productivity in reduced unemployment and rising wages, this has not happened in recent years. The distribution of income has become more, rather than less, unequal.

Changing Family Structures and Economic Status

. . . The family, as we know, has been a true anchor of social life. But its form and the roles of its members have varied across cultures and nations and through historical time. . . . [I]n the United States, at least, it is "structure" that statistically defines a family unit. Government data on families reflect particular structural forms and have yet to take account of the features that highlight the cohesion that family units represent.

Family data for the United States is reported by the U.S. Census as part of household data. The Census defines a family as two or more people related by birth, marriage, or adoption who reside together. Female householders were 12% of all households and almost one-fifth of all families in 2001. About 60% of all single householders are single parents. The U.S. Bureau of Labor Statistics also reports on several categories of female singlehood such as single women (with or without children), single mothers with one or more children (own and/or step and/or adopted), and female householders (who may or may not have children). If a single mother with children is living in her mother's residence, she may be excluded from a single-family head accounting. Thus, discussions about categories of female family heads must be carefully defined and interpreted.

. . . No regular account is taken of blended families as a category, not infrequently composed of two or more clusters of stepchildren. Nonfamily households that have grown at twice the rate of family households, although not considered to be "families," often fulfill the role of a family unit. Sometimes single mothers and children live in a grandparent household; increasingly, the grandparents alone are the parent figures. But they are not included as a distinct family form in statistics. Widows are often subsumed under other categories such as "single mothers" or "elders." In fact, there are characteristics and issues that are unique to them.

Whereas in the 1950s, about 90% of all families were married couples, with a large majority of wives being homemakers, by 2001, only 76.3% of all families were married couples and over one-half of wives were in the paid labor force. By way of contrast, 10% of all families were female householders with no husband present in 1959; in 2001, they numbered 13.1 million or 17.7% of all families. . . .

For middle-class traditionally married parents, it is often difficult to understand the complexities required of a single parent who must meet not only work demands of inflexible work hours and required production schedules, but also the many immediate family demands that involve time and money and issues of child safety. . . .

But more than this, a high proportion of single-mother families experience low income and high rates of poverty because of limited education and/or job skills. Their treatment as low-paid workers is often further marked not only by wage disadvantage relative to men in comparable jobs, but also by more frequent lay-offs, involuntary part-time work, job severance, and lack of health and pension benefits and severance pay. Their situation can be further compromised by the absence of child support and accompanying stress and always the complexities involved in having to combine paid work with home responsibilities. Income reserves with which to meet emergencies are often absent. Single-mother parenting and poverty reflect a connection that is only somewhat mitigated in recent years by the rising labor force participation of single mothers. . . .

The rapid growth of single-mother families, and their association with high rates of poverty, has led to a number of research studies seeking to identify the causes for the strong growth trend in this family structure. . . .

One factor influencing the rapid growth of the group has been the weakening of the time linkage between marriage and having a child. This extension of time between the two events, found to be true for both white and black women who marry, is perhaps encouraged by the wish to participate in the labor market. But among less-educated black women who do not marry and who have fewer skills, marriage may be postponed but child bearing prior to marriage is not and is more likely than for white women, though both groups more commonly than in the past have children before or without marriage. Other factors may also play a role in the growth of single-mother families, though with varying intensity and direction at any one time. For example, a poor labor market experience of low-skill men (in wages or employment) as well as a low production of marriageable men relative to women can lead to marriage avoidance and an increase in the pool of single mothers. Divorce, greater sexual freedom, the availability of cohabitation as a prelude or alternative to marriage, and a lack of effective birth control availability and usage can also influence the result. Not all factors have the same intensity and direction at any one time—but the fact of their multiplicity and differing strength for specific population groups has made for complexity in explaining growth trends of low-wage single-mother families. What is clear is that single parenting, for low-skill women especially, has grown in size and results for them, as for other single-mother heads, in a complexity of life's functioning and often financial difficulty and poverty in achieving and retaining economic self-sufficiency for the family reliant on the earnings of one low-wage earner who must fulfill and reconcile both work and home demands.

Poverty: Consequences for Single-Mother Families

Changes in family structures, reinforced by the fact that economic growth in itself does not ensure a dispersal of its benefits to all members of society, have resulted in increasingly wide differences in family incomes. Poverty is often the consequence for single-mother families. . . .

[W]e can expect that with increasing income inequality, reduced job creation and prolonged unemployment for those who lose jobs, that family poverty will be a concern for some time to come, even if economic improvement begins for more skilled groups. The interaction of the growth of economically challenged family structures, combined with an uncertain economy with high unemployment, and the lack of adequate social supports including skill training, will continue to frustrate the efforts of poor families to regain an economic foothold in society.

Social Policy Directions

Existing Social Policies to Improve Incomes

A broad range of wage-related social policy measures need consideration and improvement in order to address effectively the downward sliding position and earnings inadequacy of many single-mother families. Each in some way compensates for inadequate wages and has merit. But none provides a means for permanently increasing the skill and productivity, and hence earnings, of the single-mother providers. This concluding section evaluates existing wage-related income-supportive measures and points the way to policies that can help to establish what is most important—an earned income economic independence for the family unit.

1. *Unemployment Insurance.* Unemployment insurance fulfills a distinctive need of helping to stabilize an economy in troubled times and to providing partial earnings replacement to maintain consumer spending for regular workers who experience involuntary temporary job loss. . . .

   Problems in coverage and eligibility for unemployment benefits arise not only because of changes in the law, but because of the changing nature of work and of labor force work patterns since the law's original enactment. Originally, unemployment was viewed as a temporary employment rupture due to cyclical and seasonal variation in employment patterns. But with changing technological and globalization effects causing major and long-term need for structural adjustments, unemployment can require permanent change in job location and work skills. At the same time, regular full-time uninterrupted work affiliation with an employer, by choice or necessity, is no loner the norm for many workers, especially women, who are more likely to work in service and retail industries where nonstandard work is more common.

   Indeed, women and increasing numbers of men, may need to choose such jobs (part-time, part-year, temporary, or other contingent work offering limited benefits, as best) in an effort to balance work and family responsibility. . . . [Thus, t]he unemployment insurance program is in need of review and revision to adapt to the realities of today's work structures and work patterns and to the needs of all groups in the labor force.

2. *Minimum Wage.* Low wage earners need more than the national economic growth and full employment to assure a satisfactory standard of living. Their well-being also requires that they receive adequate earnings to enable them to support their families. Historically, minimum wage legislation has provided an earnings floor. . . .

   Two criticisms, in addition to the low level of the national minimum wage, are directed at the effectiveness of minimum wage policy in fulfilling its purpose. One criticism points to the low-wage teen-age individuals in the group, not all of whom live in poor families. But teenagers constitute only about one-fourth of the minimum wage workers. Their earnings, like those of other family members, help to meet a variety of expenditures, including family needs and education. They are entitled to equal pay for the equal work they perform.

   The second criticism concerns the claim that, consistent with traditional economic theory, an increase in labor costs resulting from an increase in the minimum wage will negatively impact employment levels. Some studies have supported this result. But other recent scholarly research does not show this and, in fact, indicates that employment levels sometimes even increase as a consequence of worker increased motivation and satisfaction when the minimum wage is raised. . . .

3. *Earned Income Tax Credit (EITC).* Complementing the income support provided by the minimum wage is the Earned Income Tax Credit, a form of negative income tax credit applied to wages paid to low-income earners. Non-wage earners are not eligible for these benefits. . . . Single-mother families have especially benefited from the law's provisions. These benefits are viewed as being responsible for the large increase in their labor force participation in recent years.

Under the provisions of the federal law, a small credit is available to low-income single persons with no children and to childless couples. Substantially more, computed on a graduated scale, is payable to one-child families, and higher amounts to families with two or more children. . . .

The tax credit receives high praise from all political sectors. It is seen as providing a major stimulus for low-income single-mother heads of families and others to engage in paid work in order to qualify for an earned income benefit. And it provides a major boost to incomes of the 18.6 million low-wage family recipients. . . .

4. *Training and Education: A Missing Policy Link.* Each of these existing social supports has worthy goals and provides a measure of income support for the low earnings received by a worker or the absence of wages of a regular labor force participant temporarily and involuntarily unemployed. At present, the EITC is the strongest nation-wide measure in this category, giving tax credit and income rebate support specifically for low-earning family units. It provides a stimulus to potential earners in poor families to engage in paid work, with the result that poverty and the degree of family income inequality nationally can be somewhat lessened. It has been a major cause of the reduction of poverty for children and families.

Still, none of the national social policies, though supportive, has as a goal an increase in wages to a level adequate for family self-sufficiency. It is this that should be the long-run goal of social policy. This is what is needed to complement the income policies that buttress and supplement existing low wages.

Low wages and the increasing disparity in wages between low and high earners are thought by many economists to be linked in a major way to the relatively greater demand for more highly skilled and technically proficient workers. This demand is expected to continue to grow in the future as globalization and the use of technology intensify. Although wage supportive policies can buttress income for low earners, it is education and training that raise worker productivity and enable a move to more skilled jobs at higher wages. An added benefit of such a policy would be reducing the inequality in the distribution of income that now exists. . . .

Training and education programs are neither inexpensive nor easy to implement. Well-conceived programs must not only respond to employer and community skill needs but must take place for a period of time long enough to develop well-honed workplace talents. But all of society would benefit from the increased productivity that results from such programs. And the ameliorative social support that now buttresses low earnings would have as its complement a social policy that would both reduce national disparities in family incomes and, at the same time, make possible a permanent rise in the family standard of living for previously low-income families. That would be a welcome achievement for low-wage single mothers who have shown in earlier training programs an ability to respond well relative to other groups to training opportunities that have been offered them . It is time to develop constructive legislation to provide this meaningful steppingstone for single mother earners and other low-income groups to higher skills and more adequate family income.

Hadas Mandel and
Moshe Semyonov

 **NO**

A Welfare State Paradox: State Interventions and Women's Employment Opportunities in 22 Countries

In recent decades, an increasing number of researchers have begun studying the role played by the state in affecting women's economic activities and labor market positions. The growing research on this topic points to the role of the state as legislator and implementer of social and family services, as well as to the role of the welfare state as an employer. These two bodies of literature operate under the premise that the welfare state, whether as a legislator or as an employer, strongly affects women's participation rates and economic opportunities. More specifically, researchers have suggested that progressive social policies and a large public service sector are likely to provide women with better opportunities to join the economically active labor force, and, indeed, to increase women's economic activities.

Whereas the impact of the welfare state on women's labor force participation is widely studied, little research has further investigated the ways that state interventions affect women's occupational opportunities. To address this lacuna, we seek in this article to examine systematically the impact of the welfare state on women's integration into the labor market, their working time, and their opportunities to attain powerful and elite occupational positions. We argue that the state, in its roles as a legislator and implementer of family policies, and in its role as an employer, creates sheltered labor markets for women—labor markets in which women's rights are protected and secured. By so doing the welfare state contributes to increased women's labor force participation, enhances the economic independence of women and mothers, and strengthens their power within the household and in society at large. However, these state actions do not enhance women's occupational and economic achievements, since none of them seriously challenge the traditional distribution of market-family responsibilities between men and women. On the contrary, adjusting the demands of employment to women's home duties or allowing working mothers reduced working hours and long leaves from work are likely to preserve women's dominant roles as mothers and wives. As such, these interventions

From *American Journal of Sociology*, vol. 111, no. 6, May 2006, pp. 1910–1919, 1940–1942.
Copyright © 2006 by University of Chicago Press, Journals Division. Reprinted by permission.

impede women's abilities to compete successfully with men for powerful and lucrative occupational positions.

In what follows we first develop the theoretical rationale in which our arguments are embodied. Next, we test our theoretical expectations with data for 22 industrialized countries, and, finally, we discuss the findings in light of sociological theories on welfare-state policies and gender inequality. By doing so, we will be in a position to better understand the ways through which the welfare state affects the economic participation and occupational attainment of women.

Theoretical Considerations

The Welfare State and Women's Labor Force Participation

The massive entrance of women into the labor markets of Western societies in recent decades has been affected not only by market forces but also by state interventions. The impact of the state on women's employment opportunities is multidimensional and can be attributed to a series of factors, especially to the roles of the state as a legislator, as a provider of social services, and as an employer. The extensive literature on the topic is generally divided into two separate bodies of research, one that focuses on the role of the state as an implementer of family services, and one that focuses on the role of the welfare state as an employer.

In this study we combine the two bodies of research in order to better capture the effects of state interventions on women's employment opportunities. Specifically, we focus on the role of the state as a legislator and as an activator of programs aimed to decrease the conflict between family responsibilities and work, in addition to its role as an employer. For the sake of simplicity we will use the term "welfare state" to refer to all three roles.

In its role as a legislator and family service provider, the state implements and activates a variety of support systems and provides services and benefits targeted mostly at families with children. These programs and benefits, often referred to in the literature as "family policies," reflect both the state's responsibility for the care of young children and its effort to facilitate employment for mothers, by providing women with the necessary conditions to combine work with family responsibilities.

Comparative studies that focus on the relations between family policies and women's labor force participation find a positive correlation between the two. For example, in the Scandinavian countries, which represent the social democratic welfare regime, women's high levels of employment are supported by generous family policies in the form of universal benefits to working mothers. These characteristics stand in contrast to the other welfare regimes (i.e., liberal or market economies and the conservative welfare regime), in which family policies are less developed and women's labor force participation rates are usually lower. The reduced role of the state as a family service provider in the latter regimes leaves a greater role either to the family itself or to the private market.

Variation in the scope of family policies is evident across countries, as well as across welfare regimes. While ranking countries on continuous scales of family policies, Gornick and her associates found a positive and strong association between family policy indices and mothers' rates of labor force participation, reaffirming the argument that such state interventions are likely to facilitate women's, especially mothers', economic activity.

A different body of research links women's economic activities to the role of the welfare state as an employer. Specifically, the rise of the welfare state has led to a substantial expansion of public employment, especially in health, education, and social services. As a provider of public services— a sector overwhelmingly dominated by women—the state has become a major employer of women. By offering a large supply of care and service jobs (which are traditionally designed for women and which partly replace their care duties at home) along with convenient working conditions, the public service sector facilitates women's entry into the labor force by reducing their domestic responsibilities on the one hand, and by supplying them with new job opportunities on the other hand.

The Welfare State and Gender Occupational Inequality

Whereas researchers agree that both the development of family policies and the extension of public services enhance women's opportunities to become economically active, we know very little about the implications of the welfare state for women's occupational opportunities. In what follows we argue that state activities, while facilitating women's entrance into the labor market, do not facilitate their entry into high-authority and elite positions. Rather, the very same characteristics—generous family policies and a large public service sector—seem to reproduce the gendered division of labor and, in effect, decrease women's chances of joining desirable occupational positions. Put differently, state efforts to facilitate and protect women's work may result in lowering and hardening what is usually referred to in the sociological literature as "the glass ceiling."

State-provided benefits can affect women's occupational opportunities and influence their working patterns in a variety of ways. Paid maternity leaves, for example, although often viewed as paving the way for mothers back to the labor market, and thus strengthening women's ties to the labor market, actually remove mothers from paid employment for several months. In countries where family policies are particularly generous (e.g., Finland and Sweden) paid maternity leave can last for an entire year, and in many other places (e.g., Austria, Belgium, France, Germany, Hungary, Italy, Denmark, and Norway) paid maternity leave can be extended with reduced compensation for up to two years and even longer. Although paid maternity leave serves as a device through which women's employment rights are protected and secured, a long absence from paid employment may discourage employers from hiring women to positions of authority and power and thus handicap their ability to compete successfully with men for elite positions.

Likewise, institutional work arrangements, such as regulations mandating reduced working hours, can further depreciate women's economic outcomes.

Part-time employment, for example, is a common arrangement that enables women to combine paid employment with unpaid work. Consequently, part-time work has become one of the major forms of employment for women in most industrial societies, where about one-third of all employed women work on a part-time basis.

Although part-time employment is not a direct product of states' policies, it is reinforced by regulation and protected by the welfare state. This is, indeed, the case in many Scandinavian states. In these countries (with Finland as a notable exception), part-time employment has become a common practice for many mothers. Yet, unlike other countries where part-time employment serves as an institutional mechanism through which mothers are incorporated into paid work (e.g., the Netherlands, the United Kingdom, Germany, Belgium, and Australia), in Scandinavia part-time employees are entitled to full social benefits, paid vacation, and job security. The allocation of full benefits to part-time workers reflects the state's efforts to encourage and support women's economic activities, whether on a full-time or a part-time basis.

Part-time employment is not the only mechanism through which women's working hours are curtailed. In several European countries (e.g., Sweden, Denmark, France) working hours have been reduced through regulations that set the standard below the conventional 40 weekly hours. Although reduced working hours can contribute to decreasing the conflict between work and family responsibilities for both parents, women are more likely than men to utilize this option.

Occupational discrimination.—The tendency of women to adopt reduced working hour arrangements and their tendency to take parental leave are likely to restrict their opportunities for occupational mobility, as they foster employers' reluctance to hire women and to promote them to positions that require costly investment in firm-specific knowledge, as required in most powerful and elite positions. [Research] highlight[s] the importance of "on-the-job training" for occupational mobility, and its consequences for gender occupational and wage inequality. [This work] suggests that the limited access of women to firm-specific training is one of the most significant causes of their low occupational achievements compared to men.

One major explanation for the limited access of women to positions that require costly qualification and training periods can be cast within the framework of the "statistical discrimination model." According to this theoretical model employers have limited access to information on their candidates' characteristics and future productivity. Therefore when searching for workers to fill jobs that require high training costs, employers are likely to discriminate against employees belonging to groups with statistically lower average levels of expected productivity.

In this article we contend that in well-developed welfare states where women's eligibility for social rights supports their absence from work, the exclusion of women from jobs which require costly firm-specific investment will be more acute. In labor markets where women as a group are more protected by regulations and legislation, and where they enjoy social rights that interfere with their work continuity, employers are expected to prefer male workers for positions that require investment in firm-specific human capital. "If women have social rights that do not apply to men, or are seldom used by men, and the practice of these rights is unprofitable for employers, employers may choose to discriminate against female job applicants," as indeed has been demonstrated in many studies of gender inequalities in the Scandinavian labor markets.

The restricted ability of qualified women to enter high-paying jobs, and their limited promotion opportunities in positions of power and authority, can be viewed as part of the glass ceiling phenomenon—"the unseen, yet unbeatable barrier that keeps minorities and women from rising to the upper rungs of the corporate ladder, regardless of their qualifications or achievements." Following other studies that have dealt with the glass ceiling in this study we empirically define "powerful" or "high-level" positions as management positions. We argue that the invisible barriers of the "glass ceiling"—the barriers that prevent women from moving into positions of high authority and high earnings in organizations—are expected to be greater in well-developed welfare states where women are more protected by legislation that supports their absenteeism from the labor force and allows them reduced working hours.

The state as an employer.—The role of the welfare state as an employer completes our argument. With the expansion of public social services, many services have been transferred from the private sphere to the state domain. This process has a twofold effect on employment opportunities for women; first, it enables mothers to allocate more time to paid work, and second, it provides women with new job opportunities. Moreover, the public-welfare sector offers white-collar and service jobs, many of which are "female-typed" service and semiprofessional occupations. It also offers flexible employment hours and programs that tolerate paid absenteeism. As such, the public service sector has become one of the most preferred segments of employment for women. The nature of jobs in the public service sector, coupled with favorable and convenient work conditions, appears to channel women in disproportionate numbers into feminine occupational niches and away from lucrative and powerful positions. Hence, the expansion of the public service sector is likely to increase gender occupational segregation.

Several studies have demonstrated that the overrepresentation of women in the exceptionally large Swedish and Danish public sectors contributes to the lessening of their economic gains. Feminist scholars have also pointed out that the rise of the welfare state, accompanied by a massive entrance of women into the labor force, did not alter the traditional division of labor between men and women. Rather, it actually transferred the gendered division of labor from the private sphere into the public domain. In this process traditional gender roles are perpetuated; women are disproportionately channeled to public services and care roles, while men get hold of more desirable jobs. Hernes referred to this process in terms of "the family 'going public'" where "women have become clients and employees of a highly developed welfare state with a large public service sector."

In fact, a high concentration of women in the protected public sector and the practice of statistical discrimination by employers are not mutually exclusive but rather interdependent. Women's job preferences are influenced by both employers' behavior and labor market opportunities. In labor markets where employers are reluctant to hire women to powerful and high positions, it is less likely that women would be motivated to compete with men for such positions. On the other hand, a large public service sector, which offers job protection and convenient working conditions, is likely to attract women. Although we cannot distinguish between employees' and employers' preferences, these two mechanisms are interrelated; their negative impact on women's occupational attainments are expected to be more pronounced in countries with a highly developed welfare state.

To sum up our arguments: we contend that the massive entrance of women into the labor force of well-developed welfare states has not been accompanied by their equivalent entrance into powerful and desirable positions. On the contrary, in highly developed welfare states the "glass ceiling" has become lower and wider. Social rights attached to women's employment in advanced welfare states are likely to increase employers' tendency to discriminate against women in recruitment to powerful and elite positions in the private sector. Likewise, in a large "protected" public sector women are likely to be relegated mostly to female-typed service jobs. Although under these conditions the concentration of women in feminine niches can be seen as a rational choice, we tend not to view it as a purely free choice, mainly because job preferences are shaped by labor market opportunities, which cannot be separated from employers' discrimination.

Although some of these arguments have been advanced in the feminist literature for quite some time, they have not been systematically tested with cross-national comparative data. Thus, in the analysis that follows we provide a cross-national empirical examination of the hypotheses that developed welfare states—measured quantitatively by their family policies and size of the public service sector—are characterized by high rates of labor force participation among women, while at the same time they also exhibit a high concentration of women in female-typed occupations and low access for women to positions of power, authority, and high economic rewards.

Data Sources, Variables, and Measures

Our data set has information on both individual-level and country-level characteristics. The individual-level variables were obtained from the Luxembourg Income Study (LIS), which serves as an archive for comparable microdata sets for a large number of industrialized countries. The analysis reported here was restricted to the 22 countries that provided detailed information on demographic and labor market attributes of men and women, ages 25–60, during the middle to end of the 1990s. Information on welfare state characteristics was obtained from a variety of secondary sources. . . .

The individual-level variables included in the analysis are those traditionally employed in models predicting economic activity: gender, marital status, education, age, number of children, and the presence of preschool children. . . .

The dependent variables used in the analysis include two indicators of women's rate of labor force participation, an indicator for the amount of participation (i.e., part-time work vs. full-time employment), and three indicators of gender occupational inequality. The two indicators of participation are rate of labor force participation among women ages 25–60 and rate of participation among mothers of preschool children, respectively. [A] distinction between four categories of employment: full-time employment (more than 39 weekly hours), reduced-hours employment (30–39 weekly hours), half-time employment (15–29 weekly hours), and marginal employment (under 15 weekly hours). Gender occupational inequality was measured by the net odds (women relative to men) to be employed in an occupational category, according to three variables. The first variable captures women's access to powerful and elite positions by the net odds of women (relative to men) to attaining "managerial occupations." Since definitions of managers can vary across countries, and in order to capture confidently elite and top positions, an alternative is to estimate women's access to "lucrative-managerial occupations." While managerial occupations were defined according to the standard classification of occupations for each country, lucrative-managerial occupations were restricted to those that ranked in the top three deciles of the occupational earnings distribution. The third variable captures women's occupational segregation. We measured the net odds of women (relative to men) of being employed in "female-typed occupations." Female-typed occupations were defined according to two combined criteria: the relative proportion of women in an occupational category at the two-digit occupational classification level and a statistical significance test.

The key independent variable utilized in the analysis is an index that reflects the overall protection that the welfare state provides to working mothers. It is designed to capture state interventions that affect the employment of women via both family policies and state employment. . . .

The three indicators were combined to construct the index: the number of fully paid weeks of maternity leave (number of paid weeks multiplied by the percentage of wage replacement during the leave), the percentage of preschool children in publicly funded day-care facilities, and the percentage of the workforce employed in the public welfare sector (public health, education, and welfare). Each of the three components captures somewhat different aspects of the state's activities. Maternity leave policy indicates the benefits that the state offers to working mothers, while publicly funded child-care facilities and the size of the public service sector capture the prevalence of social services provided by the state and the demand for female labor. We believe that when combined into an index the three components represent a broad phenomenon that transcends the unique effect of each component. . . .

Integrative Analysis

An important limitation of previous comparative research in this area is that the multiple dimensions of women's labor market integration are usually studied in isolation from one another. Our comprehensive approach reveals that no country or group of countries approximates unambiguous gender equality. As anticipated, the social-democratic model of women's integration into the labor market is accompanied by their crowding in female-dominated occupations and their relative exclusion from managerial occupations. On the other hand, the liberal model is less effective in mobilizing women into employment but is more open to their entry into elite positions. Finally, the conservative model typically disadvantages women in both respects.

To underline the cross-national diversity of the opportunity structures that women face, we conducted a factor analysis procedure using all dependent variables utilized in the analysis (labor force participation, working hours, managerial occupations, lucrative-managerial occupations, and female-typed occupations). Two significant factors, representing two unrelated configurations of gendered employment patterns, emerged from the analysis. The first factor, which we dub "participation/segregation," loads strongly on female participation rates, concentration of women in female-typed occupations, and on reduced working hours rather than full-time employment. In our data set Sweden and Finland have the highest scores on this factor while the former socialist countries, Switzerland, and Luxembourg generate the lowest scores. The second factor captures "equality of opportunity"; it singles out gender equality in access to managerial jobs and also a tendency toward full-time employment among working women. In this respect, the North American countries stand at the top of the scale while the Netherlands and Norway are placed at the bottom.

The thesis advanced in this paper suggests that the two labor market profiles (captured by the two factors) should be closely related to the scope and character of the welfare state. In line with our expectations, the correlation between the [Welfare State Intervention Index] (WSII) and the "participation/segregation" factor is positive ($r = .555$) while the correlation between the WSII and the "equality of opportunity" factor is negative ($r = -.524$). Furthermore, when clustering the countries using the two sets of factor scores, we find that most of them fall into one of three distinctive configurations whose membership [reflects] welfare regimes. Of the 16 countries available for the factor analysis, three with the lowest WSII scores (United States, Canada, and Switzerland) form a liberal cluster characterized by exceptionally high rates of entrance into managerial positions ("equality of opportunity" factor). The Scandinavian countries, representing the social-democratic regime, with the highest scores on the WSII, also have exceptionally high scores on the "participation/segregation" factor and below-average scores for "equality of opportunity." Finally, most of the Continental states and Ireland (representing the conservative welfare state regime) cluster with intermediate levels of WSII and below-average scores on both factors.

Conclusions

The objective of the present research has been to provide a systematic examination of the impact of welfare state activities on the labor force participation of women and on gender occupational inequality. Utilizing data from 22 industrialized countries we found the impact of welfare states on women's employment opportunities to be complex and to vary from one aspect of economic activity to another (i.e., labor force participation and occupational inequality). This impact, therefore, can be properly understood and delineated only when the interrelations among the multiple aspects of women's economic activity are simultaneously considered.

Consistent with theoretical expectations and with previous studies, the data show that women's rate of labor force participation tends to be higher in countries with progressive welfare states. Apparently, expansion of family-oriented services, availability of public child-care facilities, and a large public service sector provide women with better opportunities to become economically active. By increasing the incorporation of women into the paid economy, the welfare state has significantly contributed to increasing women's economic independence, and, by implication, to strengthening their power within the household and the society at large.

However, once women have become economically active, benefits to working mothers and high demand for female labor in the public services serve to restrict their occupational achievements. Our data show that in countries characterized by a progressive welfare system women are disproportionately underrepresented in managerial positions and overrepresented in female-typed jobs. We contend that family-friendly policies and employment practices assume the primacy of women's familial responsibilities. As such they are designed to allow women time off for the care of young children through extended maternity leaves and support of part-time employment. These policies, in turn, discourage employers from hiring women for managerial and powerful positions and foster women's attachment to female-typed occupations and jobs with convenient work conditions. Although we cannot empirically separate employer discrimination from women's employment preferences, we have suggested that the two are interrelated and jointly have detrimental consequences for women's occupational achievements.

Paradoxically, therefore, the same welfare state activities that promote one dimension of gender equality appear to inhibit another dimension. This trade-off can best be understood in relation to specific welfare regimes. The social-democratic regime promotes women's integration into the labor market by providing them with convenient and flexible working conditions. However, this goal is achieved at the cost of greater occupational segregation and restricted opportunities for women to enter the most desirable positions. By contrast, the market-oriented liberal regime neither restricts nor supports women's economic activities, and no special work arrangements are mandated for mothers. In the liberal market economies women, like men, are expected to work continuously and on a full-time basis. These conditions may not meet the justified desire of many women for family-supportive working arrangements, and may discourage mothers from joining the labor force. At the same time, women who become economically active are in a better position to compete for high-status managerial jobs than are their counterparts in social-democratic countries.

POSTSCRIPT

Can Social Policies Improve Gender Inequalities in the Workplace?

A related controversy surrounds the incidence of conception and childbirth while the mother is a welfare recipient (i.e., "subsequent births"). Traditionally, welfare policies grant monetary benefits to families based on the number of children. Thus, the birth of another child would earn the family increased financial support. Critics charge these women with intentionally having additional children so as to increase their financial benefit and view them as irresponsible and promiscuous (though, on average, welfare recipients have fewer children than individuals not on welfare). Critics fear that subsequent births will promote long-term dependency on federal aid. The 1996 federal welfare reform law allows states discretion to adopt strategies for inhibiting subsequent births.

States have adopted a variety of programs that operationalize supposed solutions to the subsequent birth problem. Efforts include family caps on welfare benefits, enhanced family-planning services, directive counseling (telling mothers they should not have another baby and instructing them in how to prevent pregnancy), and financial incentives for young mothers who do not become pregnant. Additional incentives and programs aimed at keeping women from having additional children and keeping young women from having sex include the "Illegitimacy Bonus," which rewards states that reduce their out-of-wedlock birthrate while also reducing abortion rates for all women, not just those on welfare; the "Abstinence-Only Standard," which offers financial incentives to states that teach abstinence as the expected or only standard; requiring unmarried mothers under the age of 18 to live with their parents; and enforcing child support by performing paternity tests to identify biological fathers and forcing women to turn in fathers of their children or lose benefits, regardless of the risk of physical or emotional harm to the woman or her children.

Most controversial are family cap provisions, which preclude a welfare recipient from receiving additional case benefits for a child conceived while the recipient parent was on welfare (albeit the child would be eligible for Medicaid coverage and other benefits). The desired outcome of family cap provisions would be fewer out-of-wedlock births.

Supporters of family caps believe that the traditional rule that welfare benefits are determined on the basis of the number of children in a family actually provides a financial incentive to have children while on welfare. Therefore, family caps are implemented to send a message to these women that they should not have more children until they can support them.

Opponents of family caps consider them to be in violation of a mother's right to determine whether or when to have children. Others fear that family caps will increase welfare families' hardship and increase abortion rates. Interestingly, some evaluation studies of such programs also look for higher abortion rates as an outcome signifying program success. In fact, program evaluation research to date has been underwhelming, resulting frequently in inconclusive or disappointing results.

Another criticism is that efforts at the "rational econometric control" of reproduction are ignorant of the complexities involved in becoming pregnant. Typically, two individuals are involved in a social interaction that is not always volitional and often includes an array of pressures. To what degree can reproduction be controlled by incentive pressures? It is also noteworthy that males' role in fertility is largely ignored in programs aimed at reducing subsequent births.

Welfare legislation and statistics raise serious questions about gender dynamics and differentials. Why are most welfare recipients women? How is the societal construction of "mother" and "father" related to welfare statistics and policies? How is socioeconomic class associated with women's reproductive rights and freedoms? How do existing gender inequalities contribute to single mothers low-income status? How does racism amplify the problems for women of color?

Selected Readings

Children's Defense Fund, "Families Struggling to Make It in the Workforce: A Post Welfare Report" (December 2000).

Diane F. Halpern and S. E. Murphy, eds., (2005). *From Work-Family Balance to Work-Family Interaction: Changing the Metaphor* (Mahwah, NJ: Lawrence Erlbaum Associates, Inc. Publishers, 2005).

Diane F. Halpern, "How Time-Flexible Work Policies Can Reduce Stress, Improve Health, and Save Money," *Stress and Health*, 21, (2005).

K. Edin, L. Lein, T. Nelson, and S. Clampet-Lundquist, "Talking With Low-Income Fathers," *Poverty Research News*, 4, (2000).

M. C. Lennon, J. Blome, and K. English, "Depression and Low-Income Women: Challenges for TANF and Welfare-to-Work Policies and Programs," *Research Forum on Children, Families and the New Federalism, National Center for Children in Poverty* (Columbia University, 2001).

Martha Fetherolf Loutfi, ed., *Women, Gender and Work: What Is Equality and How Do We Get There?* (New Delhi: Rawat Publications, 2002).

Gary N. Powell, ed., *Handbook of Gender and Work* (Thousand Oaks, CA: Sage, 1999).

ISSUE 16

Is the Gender Wage Gap Justified?

YES: June O'Neill, from "The Gender Gap in Wages, circa 2000," *American Economic Review* (2003)

NO: Hilary M. Lips, from "The Gender Pay Gap: Concrete Indicator of Women's Progress Toward Equality," *Analyses of Social Issues and Public Policy* (2003)

ISSUE SUMMARY

YES: June O'Neill suggests that the gender gap is largely due to nondiscriminatory factors, most notably those associated with women's choices due to the division of labor in the home.

NO: Hilary M. Lips documents the continuing gender gap in wages and argues that a continuing undervaluing of women's work due to stereotypes and prejudice maintains the wage gap.

"**E**qual pay for equal work," "Equal pay for comparable work": These two phrases have been hallmarks of the women's movement's list of rights to which women are entitled. And there are several federal laws, enforced by the U.S. Equal Employment Opportunity Commission (EEOC), that are supposed to protect women from discrimination in their compensation. The Equal Pay Act states, "Employers may not pay unequal wages to men and women who perform jobs that require substantially equal skill, effort and responsibility, and that are performed under similar working conditions within the same establishment" but the act does allow for differences in pay under certain conditions: "Pay differentials are permitted when they are based on seniority, merit, quantity or quality of production, or a factor other than sex." These are known as "affirmative defenses" and it is the employer's burden to prove that they apply. Questions arise from these declarations. What constitutes "substantially equal"? By what criteria are judgments of "merit, quantity and quality of production or a factor other than sex" made? Classic studies in social psychology have shown repeatedly that the same work, whether it is an essay, a painting, or a resume, when attributed to a man receives a more favorable evaluation than when attributed to a woman. Decisions are made on a daily basis regarding who gets hired, who gets a pay raise, and who gets a promotion. To what extent do women's personality, interests, and choices affect these decisions and what extent do sexism and discrimination affect these decisions? Is the world of work so constructed that its practices and policies result in discrimination against women? These practices might include policies that require out-of-town travel to get a promotion and for the single mother in particular to have adequate childcare. Or these practices might include tolerance for sexual harassment that forces a woman to quit her job or suffer in silence because she cannot afford to lose her job. Or perhaps there are policies that are intolerant of a single mother missing work because she has a sick child. So, under such institutional barriers to success women may be forced to forego certain careers and occupations "choosing" those more compatible with the gender roles society expects them to fulfill. Or, alternatively, perhaps it is the way women are constituted that makes the difference. Are women by nature less ambitious, less competitive, less assertive, and as a consequence less effective leaders? If so, they may freely choose careers and occupations that are more suited to their nature, careers and occupations that just happen to pay less.

In the following selections June O'Neill argues that women make employment choices that ultimately determine their wages. She suggests that the division of labor in the home plays a large role in the choices women make. She suggests that discriminatory factors are negligible. Hilary Lips could not disagree more. Lips argues that the continued undervaluing of women's work and prejudice against women in the workplace result in a continuing unjustifiable gender wage gap.

June O'Neill

The Gender Gap in Wages

The transition of women into the U.S. labor market was surely one of the most profound economic and social changes of the 20th century. In 1900 about 20 percent of women were in the labor force. This percentage rose to about 34 in 1950 and reached 61 percent in 2000; not far below the 75-percent participation rate of men. A key element in this change was the dramatic rise in market work among married women with children under the age of 18, whose labor-force participation increased from a rate of 18 percent in 1950 to 71 percent in 2000.

However, for much of the last 50 years the rise in women's labor-force activity and its growing convergence with that of men, did not appear to be matched by a narrowing of the gender gap in pay. Between 1955 and 1980, the most commonly cited measure of that gap, the female-to-male ratio of median annual earnings of full-time year-round workers, hovered around 60 percent. But using the same measure, the ratio began to rise after 1980, reaching 69 percent in 1989 and 74 percent in the mid 1990's, after which it leveled off. Based on a more appropriate measure, average hourly wage rates (available since 1979), the gender gap is smaller, but the pattern of change is similar, and the ratio rises from 66 percent in 1979 to 80 percent in 1993 and then stabilizes.

Through the years the gender gap in wages frequently has been a source of public concern and a puzzle to researchers. In this paper I examine evidence from the Current Population Survey (CPS) and the National Longitudinal Survey of Youth (NLSY79) on recent trends and current sources of the gender gap.

I. Unique Factors Underlying Gender Differences in Skills

In comparing the earnings of different demographic groups it is usually important to examine the effect of productivity differences between the groups that might account for any earnings differential. In the case of differences in earnings between racial and ethnic groups of the same sex, productivity differences most often stem from differences in the quantity and quality of education and other human capital acquired at home as well as in school. Differences in productivity between men and women, however, are not likely to be due to

From *American Economic Review*, vol. 93, no. 2, May 2003, pp. 309–314. Copyright © 2003 by American Economic Association. Reprinted by permission.

differences in educational background. Sisters and brothers are exposed to the same parental background and attend schools of the same quality. Their current educational attainment and their cognitive skills, as measured by achievement test scores, are similar.

Instead, the main source of productivity differences between women and men stems from the lesser amount of time and energy that many women can commit to labor-market careers as a result of the division of labor within the family. Even though women's home responsibilities have fallen dramatically over the past 50 years, they are nonetheless, still significant. Consequently, women are less likely than men to work continuously after leaving school and therefore are less likely to gain experience that can only be acquired on the job. In addition, anticipation of child-related work interruptions and the need to coordinate home responsibilities with market work are likely to influence choice of occupation and type of firm.

One can argue whether the source of these gender role differences is a form of discrimination rather than an outcome of biological and other deeply rooted psychological and cultural factors. However, by the time they are old enough to make choices, many women make different choices than men regarding the extent of career attachment.

Current data continue to show the strong effect of the presence of children, particularly young children, on work participation and on hours of work among those who do work. In March 2001, at ages 25–44, the prime period for career development, 34 percent of women with children under the age of six were out of the labor force, compared to 16 percent of women without children. Thirty percent of employed mothers worked part-time, compared to 11 percent of women with no children. Among men, however, the presence of children is associated with an increase in work involvement. Only 4 percent of men with children under the age of six are out of the labor force, and among employed fathers only 2 percent work part-time.

The expectation of withdrawals from the labor force and the need to work fewer hours during the week are likely to influence the type of occupations that women train for and ultimately pursue. More subtle factors such as the level of stress at work and the ability to take unplanned time off for family emergencies are also likely to influence the choice of occupation and work place. Thus, certain characteristics of jobs may affect women's occupational choices because they are particularly compatible or incompatible with women's dual home/market roles. These adaptive occupational choices will tend to lower the market earnings of women relative to men.

For example, some occupations require lengthy investment in skills with applicability only to highly specific market activities (e.g., aerospace engineer, surgeon, top management in large complex organizations). The payoff to such investments is obviously reduced when years in the labor force are reduced. Moreover, skills depreciate during periods of withdrawal from work and the rate of depreciation is likely to vary depending on the rate of technological change and obsolescence of the skills acquired. Fields such as physics, where knowledge depreciates rapidly have disproportionately fewer women. Other types of schooling and training are more general in their applicability to different situations and impart skills that are less prone to depreciate. For example, nursing and teaching skills are valuable to mothers and can be practiced widely in different settings with relatively little additional firm-specific training.

Certain characteristics of the workplace are more compatible with women's home responsibilities than others. The depreciation in skills and earnings related to complete withdrawal from the labor force may be ameliorated by work situations that accommodate the need for less demanding work while raising a family. Part-time work is the most obvious manifestation of this adjustment. Even if a woman does not always work part-time she may be more likely to choose an occupation or job setting that provides a shorter or more flexible work week in the event it may be needed, or a more informal work setting where time off for unpredictable events is acceptable.

Both work attachment and the choice of occupation are expected to be important determinants of women's earnings and important factors underlying the gender wage gap. . . .

II. Findings from the Current Population Survey: 1979–2001

The CPS analysis is based on data from the CPS outgoing-rotation-group files (CPS ORG) merged with data on occupational characteristics from the Department of Labor's Fourth Dictionary of Occupational Titles (DOT), 1991 revision. The analysis includes part-time and full-time wage and salary workers, ages 20–60.

The major changes that have occurred during the 1979–2001 period in the gender differential in earnings-related characteristics are as follows. Women continue to be much more likely than men to work part-time (19 percent versus 5 percent in 2001), although that difference narrowed. With respect to education, women gained relative to men at the college level. By 2001 they were somewhat more likely than men to be college graduates and were almost as likely to receive a higher degree. Women also have been entering occupations requiring more job-specific skills, as measured by SVP (specific vocational preparation), the time required to attain the average level of proficiency in an occupation—a DOT variable. The gender gap in SVP declined by almost half between 1984 and 1994 and has since declined further, but at a slower rate.

However, despite these changes, women and men remain in occupations that are disproportionately female or male. In 2001 women, on average, worked in occupations in which the percentage of female employees was close to 68 percent; men worked in occupations that were only 30-percent female. The percentage female in an occupation is one simple way of measuring the characteristics of an occupation that are conducive to women's particular needs. However, in the CPS analysis I have taken the more direct path of including specific characteristics of occupations as individual variables.

Returns to "potential experience." —As a number of studies have shown, there is evidence that the years of work experience of employed women increased during the 1980's. In fact, the narrowing of the work-experience gap was a key factor causing the gender wage gap to narrow during the 1980's. Nonetheless, longitudinal data show that a significant experience gap remains. . . . Actual experience is reasonably close to potential experience for men. For women that is not the case. The return to potential experience is typically lower for women than for men, and the fact that the difference between actual and potential experience is larger for women than for men likely accounts for at least part of the difference in returns. Therefore, if women's actual experience has been catching up to their potential experience, one would expect that the effect of potential experience on the female wage rate would increase over time for women, and more so than for men, if the return to experience generally was rising for other reasons. [T]hat is in fact what has happened. . . .

Occupational characteristics explain a substantial portion of the wage gap. . . . The female/male wage ratio, increased from 84 percent in 1983 to 90 percent in 2001; the unadjusted ratio rose from 70 percent to 80 percent over the same period.

III. Findings from the NLSY

Analysis of data from the NLSY permits a more complete assessment of the extent to which important differences in human capital and job and occupational characteristics can explain the gender gap in wages. The analysis uses the 2000 NLSY when the cohort has reached ages 35–43.

. . . Here are the highlights:

(i) . . . Years of schooling and scores on the AFQT (Armed Forces Qualification Test) explain hardly any of the differential because women and men differ little in these characteristics.
(ii) Actual work experience accounts for much of the gap. . . .
(iii) The addition of occupational and workplace characteristics reduces the unexplained portion of the gap.

I have conducted additional analyses of the NLSY cohort separately by schooling level. Gender differences in work experience are much greater at the high-school level than they are for college graduates. Consequently, work experience accounts for a particularly large share of the gap. . . .

The unadjusted wage gap is larger for college graduates than it is at the high-school level. The field of college major, a harbinger of occupational choice, accounts for a significant amount of the gap.

IV. Concluding Comments

Understanding the gender gap in pay is important because even in the absence of any labor-market discrimination it is unlikely that the wage rates of women and men would be equal. As I have shown in this paper, the unadjusted gender gap can be explained to a large extent by nondiscriminatory factors. Those factors are unlikely to change radically in the near future unless the roles of women and men in the home become more nearly identical. Thus an unadjusted gender gap may be with us for quite a while.

Hilary M. Lips  **NO**

The Gender Pay Gap: Concrete Indicator of Women's Progress Toward Equality

Media reports sometimes suggest that the gender pay gap is disappearing. Contrary to this optimistic conclusion, data released by such sources as the U.S. Census Bureau, the U.S. General Accounting Office, and the Internal Revenue Service (IRS) suggest that a significant gap between women's and men's earnings persists. According to the latest figures from the U.S. Census Bureau, women earned 73.25% of men's earnings in 2000. The IRS reported that the ratio of men to women in particular salary brackets is highest at highest income levels: For salaries of $1 million or more, the ratio of men to women is about 13:1, and it is necessary to drop down to the $25,000 to $30,000 range before the numbers of women and men in an income category are roughly equal. The U.S. General Accounting Office (2001) study, which focused on managers within a set of 10 industries between 1995 and 2000, found that, controlling for education, age, marital status, and race, women earned less than men in both 1995 and 2000 and that, in 7 of the 10 industries studied, the earnings gap between women and men had actually widened between 1995 and 2000. . . .

Research tells us that the pay assigned to work reflects, in certain important respects, the value that is attached to that work and to the person doing it. Thus, the gender pay gap may be thought of as an indicator of the regard in which women and their work is held by society, or even as an outcome variable in a grand social quasi experiment. The size of the gender pay gap is one of the most concrete ways of assessing women's progress toward equality. It is an indicator that should be of interest to psychologists.

Issues in Estimating and Reporting the Gender Pay Gap

One of the most basic issues in measuring and reporting the gender pay gap is the choice of measure used to indicate "average" income. Median income, less skewed by a few people making very high or very low earnings, is the indicator usually reported by U.S. government agencies such as the Census Bureau. . . .

From *Analyses of Social Issues and Public Policy*, vol. 3, no. 1, 2003, pp. 87–96, 100–106. Copyright © 2003 by Blackwell Publishing, Ltd. Reprinted by permission.

The types of wages or salaries used in comparisons are also controversial. Agencies may present comparisons using ordinary hourly or weekly wages. Ordinary wages exclude overtime pay, bonuses, and other perks and awards. This measure makes the wage gap look smaller because men are more likely than women to have access to these "extras." The use of weekly or hourly, rather than annual, earnings makes the gap look smaller because men may work more weeks or more hours than women. . . .

A second problem with the reliance on an hourly measure of income is that it assumes equivalency between women and men in their choice to limit or expand the number of hours they work. However, men may be given more opportunities than women to work extra hours for extra pay; women, if they have family responsibilities, may be less free to accept such opportunities if they are presented. . . .

A third problem with the reliance on hourly income is one of practicality and social significance. When a woman applies for a mortgage or a car loan, she is not asked about her hourly income. The income statistic that affects whether or not she gets the loan, and indeed what kind of life she is able to afford, is her annual income.

It is obvious that it is difficult to find a comparison that is both inclusive and fair to women. The best solution to the problems noted above seems to be using median annual earnings of full-time, year-round workers. However, this strategy ignores part-time workers—and most of those workers are women. . . .

Much of the data used by governments around the world to measure the earnings gap between women and men is based on a model that makes men's pattern of working the standard—the norm against which women's outcomes are judged. If women cannot fit that model, they are omitted from the comparisons or their lower pay is said to be justified. However, the model of full-time, year-round, continuous participation in the workforce is not neutral, but gendered. Use of this model as the norm ignores the issues of family and domestic responsibilities that make it impractical for many women to fit this full-time, year-round, continuous model. It also ignores factors such as stereotyping, streaming, and discrimination that tend to channel women into low-paying work that is often part-time or seasonal.

There is, however, a strong tendency to brush such issues aside when talking about pay equity. . . .

[G]ender [is treated] as a factor that can be separated from such issues as hours worked, type of job, and family responsibilities. Yet, gender is strongly and seemingly inextricably associated with these very issues. The assertion that such issues can be somehow factored out of the pay-equity equation trivializes the importance of the earnings gap and promotes the assumption that women's route to pay equity lies in simply adopting a more male-like lifestyle. . . .

Documenting the Earnings Gap

A careful examination of the earnings of women and men in the United States reveals a significant and persistent gap that is evident in a variety of different comparisons. [W]hen the U.S. Census Bureau's reported median annual income of all workers, full- and part-time combined, is considered, the pattern revealed is more than half a century of earnings gaps favoring men. When the data are limited to full-time, year-round workers only a strong and persistent gap is still evident. . . .

Because the U.S. Census Bureau (2000c) has broken data down by race and ethnicity, at least for recent decades, it is possible to examine the gender pay gap within major racial and ethnic groups. . . . Only Asian American men approached the earnings levels of European American men, and within each racial group, women's earnings were less than men's.

The gender gap in earnings can also be examined within education levels—a comparison that is very important, in view of the widely held belief that education is one key to a higher income. Higher levels of education are indeed associated with higher levels of income for women however, the earnings gap does not become smaller with higher levels of education. . . .

The Earnings Gap and Occupational Segregation

Some have argued that the gender wage gap is simply an artifact of occupational choice. They assert that the difference in women's and men's median earnings does not reflect any devaluing of women's work or discrimination against women. Rather, it is an accidental result of the fact that women and men choose different occupational paths with different reward structures.

To evaluate this argument, it is instructive to examine U.S. Bureau of Labor Statistics data on earnings of women and men in various occupational subcategories. [I]n the 10 occupations in which women formed the largest majorities of full-time workers in 2001 and for which comparative data were available, in all but 2 of the occupations in which women formed the majority of workers, men's earnings were always higher than women's.

Women fare no better in occupations in which they form a minority of workers. Men's earnings were higher within all but one [male-dominated] occupation, electrical and electronic engineering, in which women's earnings were slightly higher than men's. . . . Clearly the gender wage gap does not exist simply because women and men choose different occupations. Within occupations, even within occupations in which women form the great majority of workers, there is an overwhelming tendency for women to earn less than men.

It may be tempting to think that at the high levels of education and awareness that characterize professional occupations and their institutional contexts, the gender pay gap is negligible. . . . An interesting case is the pattern of compensation for women in the teaching profession. Teaching at the elementary and secondary school level is dominated numerically by women. Women teachers earned 95% or less of what men teachers earned—a smaller earnings gap than exists in other professions, but one that translates into a significant economic advantage for men over years of continuing employment. The gap cannot be attributed to lower qualifications among women. . . .

The issue of occupational segregation is one that has been raised with enthusiasm by many people interested in closing the gender earnings gap. A variety of initiatives have been mounted to convince girls to choose such male-dominated career paths as engineering, business, and computing. Yet, these data suggest that the tendency for women to be paid less persists regardless of occupation. The explanation may well lie partly in the tendency to undervalue work that is done by women—a tendency that has been documented in the laboratory by psychologists. . . . [E]ven if the earnings gap can be partly attributed to gendered patterns of occupational choices (leaving aside the issue of how free or constrained such choices may be), it may not be easy to eliminate it by simply trying to change those choices. It is likely that as women enter occupations in large numbers, the prestige and earnings associated with those occupations tend to drop, leaving the earnings gap intact. . . .

The Earnings Gap Reflects a Long-Standing Pattern of Undervaluing Women

Why, in the face of years of focus on pay equity, does the gender earnings gap persist? As noted above, the gap appears within groupings of race/ethnicity and nationality; it is not diminished at higher levels of education; it cannot be explained easily or completely by women's and men's choices with respect to occupations; and, *if* it is closing, it is doing so at a glacial pace. It seems an inescapable conclusion that the gap reflects, in large part, a continuing tendency to undervalue women and the work they do: Even when women predominate in an occupational domain and perform at least as well as men, their work is valued and rewarded less than men's. In further support of this conclusion, I offer an examination of the gendered patterns in one final type of compensation and recognition for work produced: literary awards.

Literary awards have some monetary value, but that is only the tip of the iceberg in terms of the very tangible benefits they bring. Because literary prizes sell books, the recipient of such an award receives notice and status that may allow her or him to command a more prestigious position, with higher pay, and to be more sure that his or her next book will be published and that it will be likely to command a larger advance. The person may also be in a position to attract and mentor high-quality students and to place them by recommending them to others. Thus, the pattern of such awards is not a trivial matter. These and other awards are part of the pattern of the gender earnings gap.

When women appear scarce in the highest-paid echelons of various positions, such as engineers, computer scientists, and CEOs of Fortune 500 companies, the following explanation is often offered: Perhaps not as many women as men have the ability, qualifications, and/or interest to pursue such positions or to perform at top levels. In the field of literary endeavor, however, no such argument can be supported by the evidence. The literature on cognitive performance indicates that in the realm of verbal skills, there is no suggestion that males generally outperform females. . . . Clearly, the realm of writing and literature is one in which women should be primed to sweep the awards. However, that is definitely not what has happened.

Gender Differences in the Receipt of Pulitzer Literary Awards

The high-prestige Pulitzer awards are an interesting case. The overall ratio of men to women receiving these literary prizes is 4.25:1 over the life of the prize. Over the 86-year life of these awards, there have been 30 years in which men have won all of them—and only 1 year in which no men have won. . . .

Men defy the odds in winning these prizes. Here is a domain where women *should* have the advantage, but still the deck seems to be stacked against them. How are we to explain men's continuing dominance of these prestigious awards? It appears to reflect two forces that are intertwined and that underlie female–male differences in all types of compensation: greater male access to structural and decision-making power, and greater valuing of male than female contributions. The unacknowledged bias in the system is apparently so wide, so deep, and so long-standing that it remains virtually invisible and unassailable, even after decades of consciousness-raising efforts by activist women.

If women cannot obtain their share of the rewards in a domain in which, by objective measures, they appear to perform at least as well as, if not better than, men, what are we to anticipate for the more general, and perhaps even more intractable, problem of the gender earnings gap? What *cannot* be anticipated is that the gap will simply disappear without intervention. . . .

What Can Be Done?

Whereas there are many interventions that might reduce the gender pay gap in particular contexts, four broad recommendations appear plainly appropriate:

[1] Supporting Comparable Worth

Legislation that mandates comparable worth—the notion that people performing work of equal value should be paid the same—is resisted because businesses fear it will mire them in bureaucratic red tape. Yet there are strong reasons to support it. Because women and men tend to be segregated into different jobs, many gender disparities in pay are not covered by the requirement of equal pay for equal work. And research shows that it is difficult to evaluate the worth of an occupation independent of the gender labeling of that occupation. . . .

Comparable worth, once mandated, can be implemented through formal job analysis and evaluation—something in which industrial-organizational psychologists have strong expertise. Job analysis, already used in many settings (including the federal government) to determine appropriate salary levels, is not without problems. However, it provides a concrete strategy for comparing gender-segregated jobs and compensating them more fairly.

[2] Encouraging Family-Friendly Workplace Policies

If women's work tends to be undervalued, there may be nowhere it is more undervalued than in the context of home and family. Since women still do most unpaid domestic, child-rearing, or dependent-care work, and the average U.S. woman is also employed, most women are juggling two or three jobs. They suffer real economic costs when they must decrease their commitment to employment in order to meet other obligations. . . .

To the extent that family work prevents women from advancing in their occupations, the refusal of employers to accommodate these dual responsibilities contributes to the earnings gap. And whereas some may question whether employers are morally bound to support women (or men) in meeting their non-employment-related obligations, such support and acknowledgment is, at least, not without precedent. Employers sometimes give credit for military service—why not for child rearing? Employers sometimes grant paid or unpaid leave for employees to work for charity or to run for and hold political office—why not for dependent care?. . .

[3] Improving the Position of Part-Time Workers

As noted above, a large percentage of women work part-time, and the gender pay gap is much larger when part-time workers are included. One way to begin lifting the status, pay, and benefits associated with part-time work is to place information about those issues in the foreground of discussions about pay equity. This suggestion does not mean, however, that pay-equity analyses should rely on average hourly earnings. As noted above, such an approach may conceal more subtle forms of pay inequity. Reports on women's earnings should not focus only on full-time workers, as this marginalizes and excludes from consideration a large group of women workers. . . .

[4] Education About Gender Bias

Social psychological research abounds with examples demonstrating that both women and men are biased against women in terms of selecting them for positions, promoting them to higher positions, and evaluating their contributions. Over the years, social psychologists have demonstrated, for example, that under certain conditions, people tend to evaluate men's work more favorably than women's; prefer to hire and promote males than females; are more critical of females than males in positions of authority; dislike women, but not men, who promote their own competence; respond negatively to assertive or agentic women; and sabotage women who try to assert leadership in groups. In many of these cases, respondents were not aware of their biases in the evaluation of women. . . . Because biases are often subtle and organizations complex, changes produced by such education may be slow. However, there is a wealth of evidence that education can lead to attitude change.

POSTSCRIPT

Is the Gender Wage Gap Justified?

Historically, poor women have always worked, perhaps as a housekeeper or a nanny or a seamstress in a sweatshop. In recent U.S. history, women were most likely to enter the workforce in masses during times of war. Their presence was needed to compensate for the lack of male laborers. Rosie the Riveter became the patriotic role model. However, after each of the two major world wars women were encouraged to return to their rightful place in the home with as much enthusiasm as they had been encouraged to leave the home; Suzi homemaker became the new cultural icon for women. Issues of women's equal treatment in the workplace did not really come to the forefront for debate until large numbers of women entered higher education, participated in the civil rights movement and the antiwar movement of the 1960s. The second wave of the women's movement was the result. Many believed that as more women obtained more education and began to climb the career ladder gender inequities would begin to dissipate. However, although in forty years there has been progress at the entry level for women, women at the top find themselves in a minority. The glass ceiling has not been broken. Some have suggested that women no longer "want it all"—career and family; rather, women are willingly choosing to opt out of the fast-paced, competitive rat race to be stay-at-home moms. There is evidence that some women with advanced degrees from some of the most prestigious institutions in the United States have done this. However, these women are married to highly successful men who generate enough income to maintain an upper-middle-class lifestyle. Other women have opted out of the corporate race to the top because they realized they were not going to break through the glass ceiling. Women are a fast-growing group to start their own businesses. However, such examples ignore the fact that the vast majority of people (women and men) do not have the resources to begin their own businesses nor can they maintain a comfortable lifestyle without two incomes, and for single mothers it is not a question of lifestyle but a matter of survival. Economists Lommerud and Vagstad evaluated the notions of the mommy track and the fast track. The mommy track had originally been proposed as a career path that recognized women's role as child-bearers; the idea was that a woman's career trajectory would be adjusted to allow for this reality without jeopardizing her chances of advancement. It did not work. Such a choice by women has resulted in subtle discrimination. Lommerud and Vagstad argued that a self-fulfilling prophecy occurred. An employer is more likely to put a male employee on the fast track, believing that he will not be distracted by child-care responsibilities like a female employee. As a result, they conclude that effort rather than talent is being rewarded. The man is expected to be on the fast track and to put forth more effort than his partner who is on the mommy track. They suggest that only permanent changes in public policy will remove the discrimination.

Suggested Readings

Francis Achampong, *Workplace Sexual Harassment Law: Principles, Landmark Developments, and Framework for Effective Risk Management* (Westport, CO: Quorum Books, 1999).

Jeanette N. Cleveland, Kevin R. Murphy, and Margaret Stockdale, eds., *Women and Men in Organizations: Sex and Gender Issues at Work* (Mahwah, NJ: Lawrence Erlbaum Associates, 2001).

Barbara A. Gutek and M. S. Stockdale, "Sex Discrimination in Employment," in F. Landy (ed.), *Employment Discrimination Litigation: Behavioral, Quantitative, and Legal Perspectives* (New York: Jossey Bass, 2005).

Catherine Hein, *Reconciling Work and Family Responsibilities: Practical Ideas from Global Experience* (Washington, DC: Brookings Institution Press, 2005).

International Labor Office, *Gender Equality and Decent Work. Good Practices at the Workplace* (Washington, DC: Brookings Institution Press, 2005).

Kjell Erik Lommerud and Steinar Vagstad (2000). *Mommy Tracks and Public Policy: On Self-Fulfilling Prophecies and Gender Gaps in Promotion* (London: The Centre for Economic Policy Research, 2000).

Linda Wirth, *Breaking through the Glass Ceiling: Women in Management* (International Labor Organization, 2001).

ISSUE 17

Are Barriers to Women's Success as Leaders Due to Societal Obstacles?

YES: **Alice H. Eagly and Linda L. Carli**, from "Women and the Labyrinth of Leadership," *Harvard Business Review* (September 2007)

NO: **Kingsley R. Browne**, from *Biology at Work: Rethinking Sexual Equality* (Rutgers University Press, 2002)

ISSUE SUMMARY

YES: Alice H. Eagly and Linda L. Carli contend that barriers exist for women at every stage of their career trajectories, resulting in, not a glass ceiling, but a labyrinth.

NO: Kingsley R. Browne asserts that the division of labor by sex is rooted in biologically based differences between women and men. Evolutionarily based natural selection has led to inclinations that make women and men better suited for different types of jobs.

Women continue to face career barriers. Although women hold 40 percent of managerial positions in the United States today, only 2 percent of Fortune 500 CEOs are women. The question remains as to why. Explanations tend to fall into one of two camps: human capital theory and discrimination theory. Human capital theories focus on obstacles from within the person. These theories focus on explanations such as differences in women's and men's abilities, interests, education, qualifications, personal investment in their careers, and leadership style, as well as choices related to family-work conflicts that are more likely to result in job discontinuity and turnover for women than for men. On the other hand, discrimination theorists focus on sociocultural factors that result in differential treatment of women and men. Three forms of employment discrimination have been identified: within-job wage discrimination (i.e., disparities within the same job, or unequal pay for equal work), valuative discrimination (i.e., lower wages in female- than male-dominated fields), and allocative discrimination (i.e., biases in hiring, promotion, and dismissal). This latter form of discrimination has invoked various descriptors of discrimination, including the "glass ceiling," "concrete wall," and "glass escalator." The image of the glass ceiling suggests that women ascend the career ladder with the top in sight, but at some rung on that ladder they hit the "glass ceiling." This image was transformed to that of a "concrete wall" to describe the even greater challenges faced by ethnic minority women. The "glass elevator" was a term coined to express the rapid career advancement of men who enter nontraditional, historically female-dominated fields, such as nursing. In the selections that follow the excerpt from Browne is an example of an explanation from the human capital perspective in which he argues that by nature women and men have different interests and talents that better suits them for different jobs. In contrast, Eagly and Carli's selection represents a discrimination theory perspective. In addition to describing all the various ways in which women can be targets of discrimination in the workplace, they coin a new term for allocative discrimination, the "labyrinth."

YES

**Alice H. Eagly and
Linda L. Carli**

Women and the Labyrinth
of Leadership

If one has misdiagnosed a problem, then one is unlikely to prescribe an effective cure. This is the situation regarding the scarcity of women in top leadership. Because people with the best of intentions have misread the symptoms, the solutions that managers are investing in are not making enough of a difference.

That there is a problem is not in doubt. Despite years of progress by women in the workforce (they now occupy more than 40% of all managerial positions in the United States), within the C-suite they remain as rare as hens' teeth. Consider the most highly paid executives of *Fortune 500* companies—those with titles such as chairman, president, chief executive officer, and chief operating officer. Of this group, only 6% are women. Most notably, only 2% of the CEOs are women, and only 15% of the seats on the boards of directors are held by women. The situation is not much different in other industrialized countries. In the 50 largest publicly traded corporations in each nation of the European Union, women make up, on average, 11% of the top executives and 4% of the CEOs and heads of boards. Just seven companies, or 1%, of *Fortune* magazine's Global 500 have female CEOs. What is to blame for the pronounced lack of women in positions of power and authority?

In 1986 the *Wall Street Journal's* Carol Hymowitz and Timothy Schellhardt gave the world an answer: "Even those few women who rose steadily through the ranks eventually crashed into an invisible barrier. The executive suite seemed within their grasp, but they just couldn't break through the glass ceiling." The metaphor, driven home by the article's accompanying illustration, resonated; it captured the frustration of a goal within sight but somehow unattainable. To be sure, there was a time when the barriers were absolute. Even within the career spans of 1980s-era executives, access to top posts had been explicitly denied. . . .

Times have changed, however, and the glass ceiling metaphor is now more wrong than right. For one thing, it describes an absolute barrier at a specific high level in organizations. The fact that there have been female chief executives, university presidents, state governors, and presidents of nations gives the lie to that charge. At the same time, the metaphor implies that women and men have equal access to entry- and mid-level positions. They do not. The image of a transparent obstruction also suggests that women are being misled about their opportunities, because the impediment is not easy for them to see from a distance. But some impediments are not subtle. Worst of all, by depicting a single, unvarying obstacle, the glass ceiling fails to incorporate the complexity and variety of challenges that women can face in their leadership journeys. In truth, women are not turned away only as they reach the penultimate stage of a distinguished career. They disappear in various numbers at many points leading up to that stage.

Metaphors matter because they are part of the storytelling that can compel change. Believing in the existence of a glass ceiling, people emphasize certain kinds of interventions: top-to-top networking, mentoring to increase board memberships, requirements for diverse candidates in high-profile succession horse races, litigation aimed at punishing discrimination in the C-suite. None of these is counterproductive; all have a role to play. The danger arises when they draw attention and resources away from other kinds of interventions that might attack the problem more potently. If we want to make better progress, it's time to rename the challenge.

Walls All Around

A better metaphor for what confronts women in their professional endeavors is the labyrinth. It's an image with a long and varied history in ancient Greece, India, Nepal, native North and South America, medieval Europe, and elsewhere. As a contemporary symbol, it conveys the idea of a complex journey toward a goal worth striving for. Passage through a labyrinth is not simple or direct, but requires persistence, awareness of one's progress, and a careful analysis of the puzzles that lie ahead. It is this meaning that we intend to convey. For women who aspire to top leadership, routes exist but are full of twists and turns, both unexpected and expected. Because all labyrinths have a viable route to the center, it is understood that goals are attainable. The metaphor acknowledges obstacles but is not ultimately discouraging.

If we can understand the various barriers that make up this labyrinth, and how some women find their way around them, we can work more effectively to improve the situation. What are the obstructions that women run up against? Let's explore them in turn.

Vestiges of prejudice.   It is a well-established fact that men as a group still have the benefit of higher wages and faster promotions. In the United States in 2005, for example, women employed full-time earned 81 cents for every dollar that men earned. . . .

One of the most comprehensive of these studies was conducted by the U.S. Government Accountability Office. The study was based on survey data from 1983 through 2000 from a representative sample of Americans. Because the same people responded to the survey repeatedly over the years, the study provided accurate estimates of past work experience, which is important for explaining later wages.

The GAO researchers tested whether individuals' total wages could be predicted by sex and other characteristics. They included part-time and full-time employees in the surveys and took into account all the factors that they could estimate and that might affect earnings, such as education and work experience. Without controls for these variables, the data showed that women earned about 44% less than men, averaged over the entire period from 1983 to 2000. With these controls in place, the gap was only about half as large, but still substantial. The control factors that reduced the wage gap most were the different employment patterns of men and women: Men undertook more hours of paid labor per year than women and had more years of job experience.

Although most variables affected the wages of men and women similarly, there were exceptions. Marriage and parenthood, for instance, were associated with higher wages for men but not for women. In contrast, other characteristics, especially years of education, had a more positive effect on women's wages than on men's. Even after adjusting wages for all of the ways men and women differ, the GAO study, like similar studies, showed that women's wages remained lower than men's. The unexplained gender gap is consistent with the presence of wage discrimination.

Similar methods have been applied to the question of whether discrimination affects promotions. Evidently it does. Promotions come more slowly for women than for men with equivalent qualifications. . . . Even in culturally feminine settings such as nursing, librarianship, elementary education, and social work, men ascend to supervisory and administrative positions more quickly than women.

The findings of correlational studies are supported by experimental research, in which subjects are asked to evaluate hypothetical individuals as managers or job candidates, and all characteristics of these individuals are held constant except for their sex. Such efforts continue the tradition of the Goldberg paradigm, named for a 1968 experiment by Philip Goldberg. His simple, elegant study had student participants evaluate written essays that were identical except for the attached male or female name. The students were unaware that other students had received identical material ascribed to a writer of the other sex. This initial experiment demonstrated an overall gender bias: Women received lower evaluations unless the essay was on a feminine topic. Some 40 years later, unfortunately, experiments continue to reveal the same kind of bias in work settings. Men are advantaged over equivalent women as candidates for jobs traditionally held by men as well as for more gender-integrated jobs. Similarly, male leaders receive somewhat more favorable evaluations than equivalent female leaders, especially in roles usually occupied by men.

. . . [A] general bias against women appears to operate with approximately equal strength at all levels. The scarcity of female corporate officers is the sum of discrimination that has operated at all ranks, not evidence of a particular obstacle to advancement as women approach the top. The problem, in other words, is not a glass ceiling.

Resistance to women's leadership.   What's behind the discrimination we've been describing? Essentially, a set of widely shared conscious and unconscious mental associations about women, men, and leaders. Study after study has affirmed that people associate women and men with different traits and link men with more of the traits that connote leadership. . . .

In the language of psychologists, the clash is between two sets of associations: communal and agentic. Women are associated with communal qualities, which convey a concern for the compassionate treatment of others. They include being especially affectionate, helpful, friendly, kind, and sympathetic, as well as interpersonally sensitive, gentle, and soft-spoken. In contrast, men are associated with agentic qualities, which convey assertion and control. They include being especially aggressive, ambitious, dominant, self-confident, and forceful, as well as self-reliant and individualistic. The agentic traits are also associated in most people's minds with effective leadership—perhaps because a long history of male domination of leadership roles has made it difficult to separate the leader associations from the male associations.

As a result, women leaders find themselves in a double bind. If they are highly communal, they may be criticized for not being agentic enough. But if they are highly agentic, they may be criticized for lacking communion. Either way, they may leave the impression that they don't have "the right stuff" for powerful jobs.

Given this double bind, it is hardly surprising that people are more resistant to women's influence than to men's. . . .

Studies have gauged reactions to men and women engaging in various types of dominant behavior. The findings are quite consistent. Nonverbal dominance, such as staring at others while speaking to them or pointing at people, is a more damaging behavior for women than for men. Verbally intimidating others can undermine a woman's influence, and assertive behavior can reduce her chances of getting a job or advancing in her career. Simply disagreeing can sometimes get women into trouble. Men who disagree or otherwise act dominant get away with it more often than women do.

Self-promotion is similarly risky for women. Although it can convey status and competence, it is not at all communal. So while men can use bluster to get themselves noticed, modesty is expected even of highly accomplished women. . . .

Another way the double bind penalizes women is by denying them the full benefits of being warm and considerate. Because people expect it of women, nice behavior that seems noteworthy in men seems unimpressive in women. For example, in one study, helpful men reaped a lot of approval, but helpful women did not. Likewise, men got away with being unhelpful, but women did not. . . .

While one might suppose that men would have a double bind of their own, they in fact have more freedom. Several experiments and organizational studies have assessed reactions to behavior that is warm and friendly versus dominant and assertive. The findings show that men can communicate in a warm or a dominant manner, with no penalty either way. People like men equally well and are equally influenced by them regardless of their warmth.

It all amounts to a clash of assumptions when the average person confronts a woman in management. . . . In the absence of any evidence to the contrary, people suspect that such highly effective women must not be very likable or nice.

Issues of leadership style.   In response to the challenges presented by the double bind, female leaders often struggle to cultivate an appropriate and effective leadership style—one that reconciles the communal qualities people prefer in women with the agentic qualities people think leaders need to succeed. . . .

It's difficult to pull off such a transformation while maintaining a sense of authenticity as a leader. Sometimes the whole effort can backfire. In the words of another female leader, "I think that there is a real penalty for a woman who behaves like a man. The men don't like her and the women don't either." Women leaders worry a lot about these things, complicating the labyrinth that they negotiate. For example, Catalyst's study of *Fortune* 1000 female executives found that 96% of them rated as critical or fairly important that they develop "a style with which male managers are comfortable."

Does a distinct "female" leadership style exist? There seems to be a popular consensus that it does. . . .

More scientifically, a recent meta-analysis integrated the results of 45 studies addressing the question [comparing three leadership styles]. . . . Transformational leaders establish themselves as role models by gaining followers' trust and confidence. They state future goals, develop plans to achieve those goals, and innovate, even when their organizations are generally successful. Such leaders mentor and empower followers, encouraging them to develop their full potential and thus to contribute more effectively to their organizations. By contrast, transactional leaders establish give-and-take relationships that appeal to subordinates' self-interest. Such leaders manage in the conventional manner of clarifying subordinates' responsibilities, rewarding them for meeting objectives, and correcting them for failing to meet objectives. Although transformational and transactional leadership styles are different, most leaders adopt at least some behaviors of both types. The researchers also allowed for a third category, called the laissez-faire style—a sort of non-leadership that concerns itself with none of the above, despite rank authority.

The meta-analysis found that, in general, female leaders were somewhat more transformational than male leaders, especially when it came to giving support and encouragement to subordinates. They also engaged in more of the rewarding behaviors that are one aspect of transactional leadership. Meanwhile, men exceeded women on the aspects of transactional leadership involving corrective and disciplinary actions that are either active (timely) or passive (belated). Men were also more likely than women to be laissez-faire leaders, who take little responsibility for managing. These findings add up to a startling conclusion, given that most leadership research has found the transformational style (along with the rewards and positive incentives associated with the transactional style) to be more suited to leading the modern organization. The research tells us not only that men and women do have somewhat different leadership styles, but also that women's approaches are the more generally effective—while men's often are only somewhat effective or actually hinder effectiveness.

Another part of this picture, based on a separate meta-analysis, is that women adopt a more participative and collaborative style than men typically favor. The reason for this difference is unlikely to be genetic. Rather, it may be that collaboration can get results without seeming particularly masculine.

As women navigate their way through the double bind, they seek ways to project authority without relying on the autocratic behaviors that people find so jarring in women. A viable path is to bring others into decision making and to lead as an encouraging teacher and positive role model. . . .

Demands of family life.   For many women, the most fateful turns in the labyrinth are the ones taken under pressure of family responsibilities. Women continue to be the ones who interrupt their careers, take more days off, and work part-time. As a result, they have fewer years of job experience and fewer hours of employment per year, which slows their career progress and reduces their earnings. . . .

There is no question that, while men increasingly share housework and child rearing, the bulk of domestic work still falls on women's shoulders. We know this from time-diary studies, in which people record what they are doing during each hour of a 24-hour day. So, for example, in the United States married women devoted 19 hours per week on average to housework in 2005, while married men contributed 11 hours. That's a huge improvement over 1965 numbers, when women spent a whopping 34 hours per week to men's five, but it is still a major inequity. And the situation looks worse when child care hours are added.

Although it is common knowledge that mothers provide more child care than fathers, few people realize that mothers provide more than they did in earlier generations—despite the fact that fathers are putting in a lot more time than in the past. . . . Thus, though husbands have taken on more domestic work, the work/family conflict has not eased for women; the gain has been offset by escalating pressures for intensive parenting and the increasing time demands of most high-level careers.

Even women who have found a way to relieve pressures from the home front by sharing child care with husbands, other family members, or paid workers may not enjoy the full workplace benefit of having done so. Decision makers often assume that mothers have domestic responsibilities that make it inappropriate to promote them to demanding positions. . . .

Underinvestment in social capital.   Perhaps the most destructive result of the work/family balancing act so many women must perform is that it leaves very little time for socializing with colleagues and building professional networks. The social capital that accrues from such "nonessential" parts of work turns out to be quite essential indeed. One study yielded the following description of managers who advanced rapidly in hierarchies: Fast-track managers "spent relatively more time and effort socializing, politicking, and interacting with outsiders than did their less successful counterparts . . . [and] did not give much time or attention to the traditional management activities of planning, decision making, and controlling or to the human resource management activities of motivating/reinforcing, staffing, training/developing, and managing conflict." . . .

Even given sufficient time, women can find it difficult to engage in and benefit from informal networking if they are a small minority. In such settings, the influential networks are composed entirely or almost entirely of men. Breaking into those male networks can be hard, especially when men center their networks on masculine activities. The recent gender discrimination lawsuit against Wal-Mart provides examples of this. For instance, an executive retreat took the form of a quail-hunting expedition at Sam Walton's ranch in Texas. Middle managers' meetings included visits to strip clubs and Hooters restaurants, and a sales conference attended by thousands of store managers featured a football theme. One executive received feedback that she probably would not advance in the company because she didn't hunt or fish.

Management Interventions That Work

Taking the measure of the labyrinth that confronts women leaders, we see that it begins with prejudices that benefit men and penalize women, continues with particular resistance to women's leadership, includes questions of leadership style and authenticity, and—most dramatically for many women—features the challenge of balancing work and family responsibilities. It becomes clear that a woman's situation as she reaches her peak career years is the result of many turns at many challenging junctures. Only a few individual women have made the right combination of moves to land at the center of power—but as for the rest, there is usually no single turning point where their progress was diverted and the prize was lost.

What's to be done in the face of such a multifaceted problem? A solution that is often proposed is for governments to implement and enforce antidiscrimination legislation and thereby require organizations to eliminate inequitable practices. However, analysis of discrimination cases that have gone to court has shown that legal remedies can be elusive when gender inequality results from norms embedded in organizational structure and culture. The more effective approach is for organizations to appreciate the subtlety and complexity of the problem and to attack its many roots simultaneously. More specifically, if a company wants to see more women arrive in its executive suite, it should do the following:

> **Increase people's awareness of the psychological drivers of prejudice toward female leaders, and work to dispel those perceptions.** . . .
>
> **Change the long-hours norm.** . . . To the extent an organization can shift the focus to objective measures of productivity, women with family demands on their time but highly productive work habits will receive the rewards and encouragement they deserve.
>
> **Reduce the subjectivity of performance evaluation.** . . . To ensure fairness, criteria should be explicit and evaluation processes designed to limit the influence of decision makers' conscious and unconscious biases.
>
> **Use open-recruitment tools, such as advertising and employment agencies, rather than relying on informal social networks and referrals to fill positions.** . . . Research has shown that such personnel practices increase the numbers of women in managerial roles.

Ensure a critical mass of women in executive positions—not just one or two women—to head off the problems that come with tokenism. Token women tend to be pegged into narrow stereotypical roles such as "seductress," "mother," "pet," or "iron maiden." . . . When women are not a small minority, their identities as women become less salient, and colleagues are more likely to react to them in terms of their individual competencies.

Avoid having a sole female member of any team. Top management tends to divide its small population of women managers among many projects in the interests of introducing diversity to them all. But several studies have found that, so outnumbered, the women tend to be ignored by the men. . . . This is part of the reason that the glass ceiling metaphor resonates with so many. But in fact, the problem can be present at any level.

Help shore up social capital. As we've discussed, the call of family responsibilities is mainly to blame for women's underinvestment in networking. When time is scarce, this social activity is the first thing to go by the wayside. . . . When a well-placed individual who possesses greater legitimacy (often a man) takes an interest in a woman's career, her efforts to build social capital can proceed far more efficiently.

Prepare women for line management with appropriately demanding assignments. Women, like men, must have the benefit of developmental job experiences if they are to qualify for promotions. . . .

Establish family-friendly human resources practices. These may include flextime, job sharing, telecommuting, elder care provisions, adoption benefits, dependent child care options, and employee-sponsored on-site child care. Such support can allow women to stay in their jobs during the most demanding years of child rearing, build social capital, keep up to date in their fields, and eventually compete for higher positions. . . .

Allow employees who have significant parental responsibility more time to prove themselves worthy of promotion. This recommendation is particularly directed to organizations, many of them professional services firms, that have established "up or out" career progressions. People not ready for promotion at the same time as the top performers in their cohort aren't simply left in place—they're asked to leave. But many parents (most often mothers), while fully capable of reaching that level of achievement, need extra time—perhaps a year or two—to get there. . . .

Welcome women back. It makes sense to give high-performing women who step away from the workforce an opportunity to return to responsible positions when their circumstances change. . . .

Encourage male participation in family-friendly benefits. Dangers lurk in family-friendly benefits that are used only by women. Exercising options such as generous parental leave and part-time work slows down women's careers. More profoundly, having many more women than men take such benefits can harm the careers of women in general because of the expectation that they may well exercise those options. Any effort toward greater family friendliness should actively recruit male participation to avoid inadvertently making it harder for women to gain access to essential managerial roles.

Managers can be forgiven if they find the foregoing list a tall order. It's a wide-ranging set of interventions and still far from exhaustive. The point, however, is just that: Organizations will succeed in filling half their top management slots with women—and women who are the true performance equals of their male counterparts—only by attacking all the reasons they are absent today. Glass ceiling-inspired programs and projects can do just so much if the leakage of talented women is happening on every lower floor of the building. Individually, each of these interventions has been shown to make a difference. Collectively, we believe, they can make all the difference.

The View from Above

Imagine visiting a formal garden and finding within it a high hedgerow. At a point along its vertical face, you spot a rectangle—a neatly pruned and inviting doorway. Are you aware as you step through that you are entering a labyrinth? And, three doorways later, as the reality of the puzzle settles in, do you have any idea how to proceed? This is the situation in which many women find themselves in their career endeavors. Ground-level perplexity and frustration make every move uncertain.

Labyrinths become infinitely more tractable when seen from above. When the eye can take in the whole of the puzzle—the starting position, the goal, and the maze of walls—solutions begin to suggest themselves. This has been the goal of our research. Our hope is that women, equipped with a map of the barriers they will confront on their path to professional achievement, will make more informed choices. We hope that managers, too, will understand where their efforts can facilitate the progress of women. If women are to achieve equality, women and men will have to share leadership equally. With a greater understanding of what stands in the way of gender-balanced leadership, we draw nearer to attaining it in our time.

Biology at Work: Rethinking Sexual Equality

Modern evolutionary biology and psychology pose an even more direct challenge to the [Standard Social Sciences Model] (SSSM) with their insight that human behavioral predispositions are ultimately attributable to the same cause as the behavioral predispositions of other animals—evolution through natural selection. The centrality of mating and reproduction to evolutionary success, coupled with the differential investment of mammalian males and females in offspring, makes behavioral and temperamental identity of the sexes highly improbable. Just as no farmer expects to see identical patterns of behavior from the mare as from the stallion, from the cow as from the bull, or from the hen as from the rooster, no social scientist should expect to see identical patterns of behavior from men and women.

Claims for the existence of a recognizable "human nature" or for predictable behavioral differences between the sexes should be inherently suspect only to those who believe that the forces that created humans were importantly different from those that created the rest of the animal kingdom. If males and females are at their core psychologically identical, they are unique among mammals. This is not to deny the importance of social influences or the fact that societies have certain emergent characteristics that no amount of atomistic study of individuals could ever predict. But it is critical to understand that some social practices are more likely to arise than others precisely because human *minds* are more likely to settle on some social practices than others and that males and females tend to have different psychologies independent of the influence of cultures that expect them to be different.

The Division of Labor by Sex

A proper understanding of psychological sex differences would go far toward an understanding of the modern workplace, the study of which has heretofore been heavily biased toward the SSSM orientation. One human universal that is apparently a product of human nature is the division of labor by sex. All societies label some work "men's work" and other work "women's work." Although the content of the categories is by no means fixed—what some cultures label "men's work" is "women's work" in others—there are, nonetheless, some consistent patterns. Big-game hunting and metalworking are almost always "men's work" and cooking and grinding grain are almost always "women's work." While some divisions are obviously related to physical capacity, this is not always the case. For example, carrying water is almost always "women's work," and manufacture of musical instruments is almost always "men's work."

Modern Western societies are breaking down these age-old divisions, so that workers increasingly find themselves in what anthropologists call an "evolutionarily novel environment"—an environment that differs from that in which our hominid ancestors evolved—in this case a workplace environment in which men and women work side by side and compete for position in the same status hierarchies. Today, almost all positions in the labor market are formally open to women, the primary exception being certain combat positions in the military. Nonetheless, a high degree of de facto occupational segregation continues to exist, so that in practice there are many occupations that remain "men's work" and "women's work." Thus, most men work mostly with other men, and most women work mostly with other women. Moreover, even in largely integrated occupations, men are more likely than women to achieve the highest organizational positions.

The architects of sexual equality appear to have assumed that lifting formal barriers to women in the workplace would result in parity with men because men and women inherently have identical desires and capacities. When prohibitions on formal discrimination have not resulted in sexual parity, hidden discrimination is often assumed responsible. If hidden discrimination can be disproved, then informal barriers, such as sexist attitudes of parents or teachers are identified as the culprit. If direct external forces must finally (and reluctantly) be abandoned because the paths that women's lives have taken must be attributed to their own choices, then their choice becomes a "choice" that is attributed to their internalization of "patriarchal" notions about the proper role of the sexes and to their life constraints. While the causal attribution may shift over time, what does not change is the persistent invocation of causes other than women's inherent predispositions. Given the human propensity for self-deception, it may not be possible to answer the question whether these shifting arguments reflect actual beliefs or are merely opportunistic arguments to advance a political agenda.

The social-role view of sex differences is that "men and women have inherited essentially the same evolved psychological dispositions" and that behavioral sex differences are simply results of "two organizing principles of human societies: the division of labor according to sex and gender hierarchy." How is it that a sexually monomorphic mind came up with the division of labor by sex and gender hierarchy? Certainly the social explanation is not the most parsimonious explanation for sex differences in behavior. Humans evolved from other creatures surely having sexually dimorphic minds. The notion that humans evolved away from the primate pattern of behavioral sex differences—presumably because it was advantageous to do so—but simultaneously replaced the preexisting biological pattern with cultural patterns having the same effect is difficult to credit. Moreover, the direction of causation in this explanation is implausibly unidirectional. Even if behavioral sex differences originated from a sexually monomorphic mind, one would expect that they would be reinforced through selection over the hundreds of thousands or millions of years that these social phenomena existed.

Stasis and Change

Trends in women's work-force participation are not easily explained in terms of broad themes such as "patriarchy," "subjugation of women," or even the waning power of a monolithic male hierarchy. The progress of women has not been uniformly slow or uniformly fast, as might be expected if it were solely a consequence of such wide-ranging forces; instead, the pattern has been much more complex, and it is that pattern that any theory of workplace sex differences must attempt to explain.

In some respects, the role of women in the work force has been massively transformed in just a few decades. In 1960, women constituted just one-third of the American work force compared to over 46 percent today. During that same period, the percentage of married women who work doubled to 61 percent. Only 4 percent of lawyers in 1970 were women, while today the figure for law school graduates exceeds 42 percent. The percentage of female physicians increased from 10 to 24 percent between 1970 and 1995, and the percentage of female medical students now exceeds 40 percent. In business, the change has been no less impressive. In 1972, women held only 18 percent of managerial and administrative positions, compared to 43 percent of such positions in 1995. These changes represent a genuine revolution in the American workplace.

Despite these striking advances, however, women are far from achieving parity in a number of areas. They constitute only 5 to 7 percent of senior executives in the largest corporations, and the average full-time female employee makes less than 75 cents for every dollar earned by the average full-time male, if factors that influence wages such as hours worked and nature of the occupation are not considered. Many occupations remain highly sex segregated. Among the occupations in the United States that remain 90 percent or more female are bank teller, receptionist, registered nurse, and preschool and kindergarten teacher. Among the occupations that are less than 10 percent female are engineer, firefighter, mechanic, and pest exterminator. Large numbers of women pursue education in some scientific fields—such as biology and medicine—yet far fewer are found in other scientific fields—such as mathematics, physics, and engineering. Despite frequent assertions that women are victims of widespread discrimination, for the past two decades unemployment rates of the two sexes have not diverged by as much as a percentage point.[14] Thus, women's progress has not been uniformly stifled nor has it uniformly advanced; instead it has been quite patchy.

The question is why. Part of the answer lies in the sexually dimorphic human mind. . . . The means by which any animal "makes a living" is intimately related to the animal's physical and psychological makeup. If the physical and psychological makeup of a species varies substantially by sex, we would expect that males and females may make their livings in a somewhat different manner. The culturally universal division of labor by sex appears to be a manifestation of that principle.

Even in today's relatively egalitarian Western societies, men and women tend to seek different jobs, favor different occupational attributes, and sometimes even perform the same jobs in a somewhat different manner.

Because workplace choices often influence both tangible and intangible rewards, systematically different preferences tend to result in systematically different rewards. A social environment in which individuals of both sexes are free to pursue their own priorities cannot therefore be expected, a priori, to produce identical rewards to members of the two sexes.

Sex differences in temperament and cognitive abilities, as well as occupational preferences, are at least partially responsible for a number of workplace phenomena that are sometimes labeled "problems"—the "glass ceiling," the "gender gap" in compensation, and occupational segregation. Although sex discrimination can also play a role, complete understanding of workplace patterns requires us to look honestly at other factors. Some individuals, for example, are more likely to seek, and make the requisite sacrifices and investments to achieve, the highest positions in business, government, and academia. Those who achieve positions of high status tend to be those for whom status is a high priority. Those who have high earnings tend to be those for whom high earnings are a sufficiently high priority that the sacrifices and tradeoffs necessary to achieve them are worthwhile. Because men and women vary systematically along these and other dimensions, occupational outcomes for men and women are not identical. Whether this is a problem or merely a fact is to some extent a value judgment. However, one's beliefs about the causes of the outcomes— for example, discrimination by employers or personal choice of the affected individuals—may influence the extent to which the outcomes are deemed acceptable. . . .

Conclusion

The evidence and arguments put forward in this book will be troubling to many. Some may believe that invocation of biology is implicitly (or perhaps even explicitly) a defense of the status quo—a paean to the virtue of existing arrangements or at least a testament to their inevitability. The defense, however, is more limited. It is that many of the workplace patterns that are laid at the foot of nefarious causes such as discrimination by employers or sexist socialization have causes that are less invidious and less attributable to an anti-female ideology than is commonly recognized.

A consensus about the causes of workplace patterns does not foreordain consensus about policy responses. One's values are important, and values are not directly derivable from scientific fact. Proponents of laissez-faire policies will likely draw free-market implications, while those more inclined toward governmental intervention may settle on more activist approaches. Everyone interested in workplace policy, however, whatever his political or social outlook, should desire an accurate understanding of the underlying causes of current patterns.

It would be a mistake to interpret average temperamental or cognitive sex differences as limitations on the potential of individual girls and women. Nothing contained in this book implies that women cannot or should not be corporate presidents or theoretical physicists, only that equal representation of women in these positions is unlikely to occur unless selection processes are modified with the specific purpose of guaranteeing proportional representation.

Sufficient overlap exists on most traits that there are few occupations that should be expected to remain the exclusive domain of one sex, but many occupations will remain overwhelmingly male or overwhelmingly female if people continue to select occupations on the basis of their preferences and abilities. Expansion of the choices available to women (and to men) increases the influence of individual preferences on workplace outcomes. To the extent that individuals' preferences differ, we should expect them to seek different workplace rewards. Because the average endowment of men and women differs— in temperament, cognitive ability, values, and interests—it would be astonishing if their occupational preferences and behaviors were identical.

Modern attitudes about preferences are somewhat conflicted. The value that Western liberals place upon individual liberty rests heavily on the assumption that the preferences of individuals differ. Each individual should be free, within broad limits, to pursue his own ends. There is, therefore, something vaguely illiberal about both the assumption that all individuals *should* have the same preferences and attempts to ensure the outcomes that would result if they did.

Some people believe that even if sex differences exist, there is harm in publicizing them because they can become self-fulfilling prophecies. Even if the "correct" ratio of professional mathematicians is, say, 5 males to 1 female, it is harmful to make that fact widely known, because then mathematics will be labeled a "male field," and girls will assume that it is *only* for males. Although that is a rational concern, it is not well supported empirically. Clark McCauley found, for example, that when asked to estimate the proportion of males or females in a number of sex-stereotyped occupations, subjects showed no evidence of stereotypic exaggeration. The correlation between estimates and actual percentages was high, indicating that people rank-ordered them accurately, but where the subjects erred, it was almost always in the direction of underestimating the difference between men and women in the occupation. Similarly, Mary Ann Cejka and Alice Eagly found that participants systematically underestimated the extent to which male-dominated and female-dominated occupations were segregated.

It may seem odd that this book implies the near-inevitability of disproportionate male representation at the highest levels in corporate and other hierarchies, at least under current incentives, at the same time that other writers are predicting seemingly contrary trends. In 1999, two books appeared on the market, coincidentally both by Rutgers University anthropologists: *The First Sex* by Helen Fisher and *The Decline of Males* by Lionel Tiger. Both chronicled changes in the workplace, in education, and in broader social forces such as increasing female control over reproduction. Fisher's book emphasized the positive—the ascendancy of females—but gave little attention to the social effects of the "displaced males" that ascendancy of females implies. Tiger analyzed many of the same trends, but his view was more pessimistic, as the specter of large numbers of marginalized males does not bode well for any society. Neither Fisher's nor Tiger's analysis is inconsistent with that provided here, however. [T]he gender gap in compensation shrinks with changes in work that favor women. Nonetheless, men will continue to dominate the scarce positions at the top of hierarchies as long as it is necessary to devote decades of intense labor-market activity to obtain them, even if women come to predominate in middle-management positions and even if men also disproportionately occupy the bottom of hierarchies. Men will similarly continue to dominate math-intensive fields, as well as fields that expose workers to substantial physical risks.

The extent of one's willingness to live with the sex differences in outcomes described here depends to some extent on one's definitions of equality. If current workplace outcomes are a cumulative consequence of millions of individual choices made by men and women guided by their sexually dimorphic psyches, are the outcomes of those choices rendered suspect because those sexually dimorphic minds incline men and women to make their choices in systematically different ways? This question resembles, if not entails, the familiar question of whether the equality that ought to be of importance to policy makers is "equality of opportunity" or "equality of result." Those who place primary importance on equality of opportunity may say that as long as both men and women are given the opportunity to pursue the opportunities that the workplace provides, the outcomes are unimportant. Those who look to group outcomes, on the other hand, may say that the critical question is what the different groups end up with. However, we cannot say that the "outcome" for women is deficient without specifying with precision what that outcome is. We cannot, that is, simply look at women's income and occupational attainment without also considering what they get in return for the occupational tradeoffs that they make.

The question of agency is at the core. Are women, like men, active agents in their own lives, making rational decisions based upon their own preferences? Or are they pawns of both men and society—making suboptimal "choices" that are forced on them by others? All indications are that the former is closer to the mark. Women, though somewhat constrained by life circumstances, as are men, make rational and responsible choices that are most compatible with their temperaments, abilities, and desires.

POSTSCRIPT

Are Barriers to Women's Success as Leaders Due to Societal Obstacles?

Women's leadership style has been cited frequently as a barrier to success at the top of the corporate ladder. Leadership can be viewed from either the human capital perspective or the discrimination perspective. The human capital view would suggest that women, due to their natures, simply do not have the dominance-related and assertive dispositions that are presumed to be correlates of leadership. From a discrimination perspective one can argue that women have not been given opportunities to learn and practice leadership skills. Furthermore, research shows that many people prefer a male to a female boss. The irony is that much of the research suggests that women's leadership styles, when they differ from those of men, can be more effective, although the job description rather than the sex of the person usually better predicts what type of leadership style one will use.

How can the contradictions between women being effective leaders and still have difficulty exercising leadership be resolved? Alice Eagly has suggested that the view of female leadership is complex and is mixture of advantage and disadvantage. On the one hand, women's styles have been described as transformative, in that they promote innovation, trust and empowerment in followers. On the other hand, expectations regarding competitiveness and toughness, coupled with old-fashioned prejudice against women can interfere with effective leadership, especially in male-dominated domains.

Suggested Readings

Jean Lau Chin, B. Lott, J. Rice, and J. Sanchez-Hucles, *Women and Leadership: Transforming Visions and Diverse Voices* (Teachers College Press, 2007).

E. E. Duehr and J. E. Bono, "Men, Women and Managers: Are Stereotypes Finally Changing?" *Personnel Psychology* (Winter 2006).

Robin. J. Ely, D. E. Meyerson, and M. N. Davidson, "Rethinking Political Correctness," *Harvard Business Review* (September 2006).

Anna Fels, "Do Women Lack Ambition?" *Harvard Business Review* (March 2005).

B. R. Ragins, J. M. Cornwell, and J. S. Miller, "Heterosexism in the Workplace: Do Race and Gender Matter?" *Group & Organizational Management* (vol. 28, 2003).

Internet References . . .

World Health Organization

The World Health Organization website provides access to many documents related to female genital mutilation.

http://www.who.int/mediacentre/factsheets/
fs241/en/

Information for Health

The INFO Project (Information and Knowledge for Optimal Health Project), based at the Johns Hopkins University Bloomberg School of Public Health's Center for Communication Programs, is focused on understanding how knowledge and information can improve the quality of reproductive health programs, practice, and policies.

http://www.infoforhealth.org/

National Organization to Halt Abuse and Routine Mutilation of Males

The website for the National Organization to Halt the Abuse and Routine Mutilation of Males: A Health & Human Rights Organization (NOHARMM) is dedicated to what it calls a campaign for genital integrity and provides information and links related to male and female circumcision.

http://www.noharmm.org/

Go Ask Alice!

Go Ask Alice! is a health question-and-answer site and is sponsored by Columbia University's health education program. The mission of this site is to provide in-depth, factual, and nonjudgmental information to assist individuals' decision making about their physical, sexual, emotional, and spiritual health. Questions about sexuality, sexual health, and relationships are frequent. This site includes hundreds of relevant links.

http://www.goaskalice.columbia.edu/

Relationship Factors in Polyamorous Women

This website reports the results of a recent study on polyamorous women by Dr. Rachel Robbins.

http://www.polystudy.com/

Gender and Sexuality: Double Standards?

*M*any contemporary scholars view sexuality as a cultural construction. *Cultures provide individuals with knowledge and "lenses" that structure institutions, social interactions, beliefs, and behaviors. Through cultural lenses or meaning systems, individuals perceive the "facts" of sex and gender. Conceptualizations of sex and gender and the importance of sex and gender as social categories vary from culture to culture. However, within a particular culture, because individuals are usually limited to their own cultural lens, definitions of sex and gender seem fixed or even natural. In fact, cultural scholars argue, culture so completely defines us that we are usually oblivious to its presence in our own society. We think of culture as something that other societies have.*

How do adolescents first experience sexual attractions—developing a "crush," falling in love, making the decision to "go all the way?" How does a child grow into a sexual being? What does it mean to be sexual? How does a child learn to think about his or her own genitals? These are profoundly personal and important questions, the answers to which are shaped by our cultural understanding of sexuality.

In this section, we examine cultural constructions of sex and gender, especially messages sent to children and adolescents. Specifically, how are cultural institutions and mores structured by cultural definitions of the importance of sex and gender and by cultural gender proscriptions? What does culture dictate about the significance and characteristics of the social categories "male" and "female"? Does one's standpoint or location within the culture prescribe one's sexual experiences? Consider how assumptions about the biological basis of sexuality as a prime force in human behavior influence how some cultures attempt to control female sexuality through circumcision. Does the assumption that the expression of sexuality is based on biological drives affect messages that are delivered via the media? How can media images of sexual expression operate as both informational and normative sources of influence? Is it possible to resist media images?

- Is Female Circumcision Universally Wrong?

- Should "Abstinence-Until-Marriage" Be the Only Message for Teens?

- Can Women's Sexuality Be Free from Traditional Gender Constraints?

ISSUE 18

Is Female Circumcision Universally Wrong?

YES: Gerald Mackie, from "Female Genital Cutting: A Harmless Practice?" *Medical Anthropology Quarterly* (2003)

NO: Carla Makhlouf Obermeyer, from "The Health Consequences of Female Circumcision: Science, Advocacy, and Standards of Evidence," *Medical Anthropology Quarterly* (2003)

ISSUE SUMMARY

YES: Gerald Mackie takes a scientific approach to challenge the argument that female genital cutting is not always harmful, citing multiple examples of physical and psychological harm.

NO: Carla M. Obermeyer argues that a lack of research precludes us from fully understanding female circumcision and claiming that it is responsible for a variety of harmful health outcomes. She includes examples of no harm.

According to the World Health Organization, female circumcision (also called female genital mutilation—FGM) involves the partial or total removal of the external female genitalia or other injuries to the female genital organs. These practices may occur for cultural, religious, or other nontherapeutic reasons. Is female circumcision a practice of some cultures that other cultures should respect? To what extent is it a fundamental violation of females' human rights? For those who conclude that it is, the basis of their claim is based on health concerns or on concerns surrounding the imposition of gender role constraints on women, the most fundamental being reduction in capacity for female sexual pleasure.

FGM is practiced primarily in Middle Eastern, African, Indonesian, and other Muslim countries. In Africa it is estimated that every year two million girls are subjected to FGM. The practice reduces their chances of having a normal sexual and reproductive life and jeopardizes their own survival, as well as that of their unborn children. Other complications include severe pain, shock, hemorrhage, urinary retention, ulceration of the genital region, and injury to adjacent tissue. Hemorrhage and infection can cause death.

The type of FGM and the age at which the practice is done varies across countries and regions, ranging from birth to early adulthood. The targeted age varies by the cultural meaning of the ritual. For example, if FGM is thought of as a rite of passage into adult womanhood, FGM is done at the age of 14 or 15. If FGM is done to control female sexuality, the procedure is performed at age 7 or 8. FGM has a disproportionate impact on girls of color. Mothers, grand-mothers, and other female kin typically control FGM. Women who are not medically trained usually perform the procedures.

There has been heated debate about FGM as being in violation of universal human rights. Are there certain fundamental, inviolable human rights that transcend all cultural boundaries? Cultural universalists argue *yes*. But cultural relativists respond *no*, arguing that Western liberal individualism has biased the delineation of human rights, and thus current delineations of human rights cannot be seen as universal but as Western impositions on non-Westerners. Cultural relativists also maintain that scholars' prioritization of human rights differs in Western and non-Western societies, whereby Westerners value civil and political rights over social and cultural rights; non-Westerners tend to do the opposite. Universalists retort that relativists' toleration of FGM and other harmful cultural practices perpetuates the violation of human rights and rein-forces the subjugation of women to the interests of their larger sociocultural group.

Some immigrants to the United States and Canada from Aboriginal, Christian, and Muslim families from some Muslim countries desire to continue the practice as a social tradition. It is also done at birth to some "inter-sex" infants for what are seen by some as medical reasons. One issue in the United States is the pressure to allow immigrants to continue this practice, where it is outlawed with prison sentences up to five years.

On the question of justified reaction to FGM, the universalist position has largely prevailed. Many legal and nonlegal strides have been made in the international campaign against FGM, including the passage of the Female Genital Multilation Act into U.S. law in 1996. On February 5, 2004, the World Health Organization reconfirmed its call to member states in the African region to eliminate female circumcision. In recognition of the first Interna-tional Day on Zero Tolerance to FGM (observed on 6 February 2004), the WHO Regional Director for Africa (AFRO), Dr. Ebrahim M. Samba said, "I appeal to all (African) countries and their (development) partners to ensure that this practice is eliminated in our continent." But now the question has shifted from whether or not FGM is a human rights violation to how FGM can be eradicated, effecting lasting social change. Some argue that relativists' sensitivity to the cultural context may be more effective in bringing about change *from within*, since culture itself is the most formidable obstacle. Universalist critics argue that assertive condemnation is necessary to convey the moral imperative of the eradication of FGM, anything short of this stance may be counterproductive. In the following selections, Gerald Mackie represents the universalist stance, and Carla Obermeyer advocates a cultural relativist position on bringing about the eradication of FGM. As you read these selections, consider with which position you are most comfortable and why.

YES

Gerald Mackie

Female Genital Cutting:
A Harmless Practice?

The stated purpose of a recent article in this journal (Obermeyer 1999) is to obtain a relative reduction of funding for research intended to assist affected peoples to abandon the practice of female genital cutting (FGC), labeled advocacy, and thereby obtain a relative increase of funding for the mass survey research preferred by the author, labeled science (p. 85). The article has entered public debate as warrant for the claim that FGC is of minimal harm, and, thus, that it should be legalized for minors in the United States (it is presently legal for consenting adults) and other immigrant-receiving countries; that claims for asylum based on FGC are spurious; and that international agencies such as WHO and UNICEF should cease supporting programs for abandonment of FGC in practicing areas of Africa.

The article speaks in the voice of science as the authoritative survey of the epidemiological, demographic, and anthropological evidence on the question. It was awarded the Polgar Prize by the Society for Medical Anthropology, for the best article published in volume 13 (1999) of the society's journal, *Medical Anthropology Quarterly.* The article is correct that some people have undifferentiated and exaggerated views about the forms, meanings, and risks of FGC, and that it would be better to have more research on the topic. Otherwise, many of its remarkable claims are mistaken, or so I shall argue. Because of the article's vigorous claim to authority, and because of its actual and possible effects on public policy and private health decisions, I call attention to ambiguities, inconsistencies, and errors that one ordinarily might leave unmentioned. . . .

Scientific Conclusions

The article presents itself as the scientific approach toward FGC, in opposition to the "moral advocacy" (p. 78) approach of policy makers, activists, and professionals in various fields concerned to end the practice. The article claims to be within the purely empirical scientific framework (p. 97), based on the sciences of epidemiology and demography, "two disciplines where the evaluation of empirical evidence is a central preoccupation" (p. 81). The moral advocacy position is said to lack nuance (p. 79) and moderation (p. 98).

According to the article, the moral advocacy position has aroused an international consensus and mobilization to end FGC based on two premises: (1) that the practices are widespread, and (2) that the practices have "extremely harmful consequences for those who undergo them" (p. 80). An unstated implication of such an argument is that if one of the premises were wrong, then the international consensus on advocacy would be wrong; the author states that the second premise is wrong. I say, however, that the international consensus and mobilization on FGC is based on two alternative premises: (1) that in general there is an absence of meaningful consent to the irreversible act of FGC, and (2) that complications are nontrivial. Liberals are reluctant to intervene against activities freely consented to by adults, or of trivial consequence. Prevalence is not morally relevant: If only one person suffers nontrivial complications in the absence of consent, then that is a matter for concern. Complications are relevant only if nontrivial, but such complications need not be precisely measured, especially frequent, or especially severe. . . .

The genius of epidemiology is to detect a causal relationship between an exposure, often subtle, and outcomes that are obscure, rare, or latent. There is no causal question, however, about the connection of the traumatic injury of FGC to immediate complications such as bleeding and infection, nor to many of the delayed complications cited in the literature. Nor is prevention obscure: Refrain from doing the FGC and the complications do not ensue. Effective strategies of prevention are a sociological question, not a medical one. Secondarily, epidemiology might establish frequencies and dose–response relationships. Such information might be very useful in crafting strategies of prevention, but it need not be, and in any case we would also want insights from many fields of inquiry, most of all from people involved in the practice and attempts to end it.

The [Obermeyer] article demands evidence that is *incontrovertible;* further, it states that those who claim nontrivial complications must present *irrefutable* (p. 91) and *indisputable* (p. 97) evidence for their case. An epidemiology textbook explains that since Hume it has been understood that induction fails to provide a foundation for conclusive causal inference (Rothman and Greenland 1998:22). Perhaps the author means that the claim must be beyond any reasonable doubt. But there is no reasonable doubt that FGC is a traumatic injury, nor, from an anatomical standpoint, that there are associated complications of nontrivial quality. Frequencies of complications are more vaguely apprehended, but, for purposes of public policy, these assessments should be made by the public-policy standard rather than by the laboratory standard of evidence. By either standard, the author has no warrant to claim as "fact that the most severe complications are actually rare events" (p. 93).

Similarly, the article's anticlimactic claim that FGC is "probably" not a matter of "relative safety," but that further studies are needed to attain greater certainty (p. 97), wrongly assumes that harm is harder to establish than safety and it commits an error of misplaced precision. There is insufficient evidence that FGC is safe. There is no reasonable doubt that FGC is harmful.

Theory: Idiographic or Comparative?

According to the [Obermeyer] article, "female genital surgeries" are practices that are ambiguous, variable, changing (p. 84); sociodemographic factors equivocally relate to them (p. 88); indeed, "it may not be possible to fully understand the complex forces that account for the persistence or decline of these practices" (p. 97). . . . The author believes that the only commonality among the practices is that they involve the cutting of women's genital areas (p. 89). But just as it is possible for the ethnographer to generalize despite the range of circumstances, motivations, and meanings across individual respondents, so is it possible for the comparativist to generalize across groups.

A commonality of major importance overlooked in the article is that FGC is found more or less contiguously within a zone of distribution, but is not found outside that zone (with a few exceptions that can be traced to diffusions in the historical era). Such a distribution demands theoretical attention. Also, adherents give different but overlapping reasons for the practice. When we look for patterns across lists, we notice that marriageability and tradition are offered as reasons in almost all groups. This commonality suggests that these two reasons usually play the causal role and that the remainder of reasons are either explained by marriageability and tradition or express non-causal associationist responses to the practice. . . .

The only way to abandon such a convention is if a critical mass of the families in an intramarrying group agrees to stop together at the same time, which preserves the marriageability of their daughters. This method worked to end the convention of footbinding in China. In Senegal, people in rural villages with almost no formal education were exposed in a basic education program to nondirective health, human rights, and other information that, among many other items, included information about FGC. They were further given information about how one village (later many) stopped FGC by means of collective deliberation culminating in public declaration that all would stop FGC at the same time. As predicted by the convention hypothesis, people in exposed villages decide to abandon FGC by the same process, and these are by far the largest abandonments in the FGC zone. Further abandonments now proceed through hundreds of villages by way of organized contagion. . . .

Trends and Variations

The [Obermeyer] article reports that in some places there is a (modest) decline in prevalence and shift to less severe forms. Elsewhere, persistence is robust (p. 87). There is an association of FGC with region and with ethnic group, but an equivocal association with urbanization, it says, and an equivocal association with education (p. 88). The equivocal association with education, it argues, "undermines a key presumption" in the literature, "that the spread of formal education, mass media, and 'modern' health care entails a convergence in worldviews towards biomedicine and the particular ways in which 'universal' values are defined . . . in international human rights documents" (p. 89). This discrepancy poses a puzzle to the intellect and imagination, it says (p. 89); FGC is perhaps even "unknowable" (pp. 97, 98).

The absence of an education effect on attitudes toward FGC is the second most important claim in the article (the first is the minimization of complications); the finding is now repeated in policy debates. The claim contributes to

Table 1

Beh = Behavior = Prevalence, Percent Respondents Cut; Att = Attitude = Percent Respondents Support Continuation of FGC.

Country:	CAR		CDI		Egypt		Eritrea		Mali		Sudan	
Education:	Beh	Att	Beh	Att	Beh	Att	Beh	Att	Beh	Att	Beh	Att
Sec'ary+	23	11	23	na	91	61	92	18	90	48	98	55
Primary	45	29	25	na	100	87	93	34	94	76	98	84
None	48	36	55	na	100	93	95	71	94	78	83	82

Sec'ary+ = Secondary education or better
CAR = Central African Republic, CDI = Ivory Coast
Source: Carr 1997:69–74

further inferences: that the understanding of advocates and generalizers is shallow and ethnocentric (p. 90), that FGC continues because it is of minimal harm (pp. 91, 92, 94), and that the association of genital organs with sexual enjoyment is a social construction peculiar to the Western worldview (p. 96).

[However, it] helps to display further DHS [Demographic Health Surveys] results in tabular and more complete form, as in Table 1. Looking at the columns labeled *Beh* (Behavior), indicating percentage cut, it is plain that in five of the six countries there *is* an education effect (Sudan is the exception, and I surmise that ethnicity confounds education in this case).

. . . Looking at the columns labeled *Att* (Attitude) in Table 1, it is plain that large proportions of the more educated do *not* support continuation of FGC, and in larger proportions than the less educated. . . .

There are many who oppose the practice of FGC but nevertheless intend it for their daughters. If behavior matched attitude, then, among women who oppose continuation of cutting, 100 percent in each country would intend not to have their daughters cut. . . . The DHS findings suggest that the mothers are caught in a convention trap. . . .

Empirical Science versus Moral Advocacy

The [Obermeyer] article discourages generalizations about FGC (except to the extent permitted by the scientific demographic and health surveys) and encourages attention to the heterogeneity disclosed by ethnographic reports. It recommends that we investigate and understand the motivations of people who do FGC, "without dismissing others as ignorant, irrational and cruel" (p. 93). Yet, in its discourse about *advocates,* the article makes broad and extremely negative generalizations. Their discourse is not "supported by the evidence" (p. 79), which suggests that the advocates are ignorant. The advocates fail "to gain an insider's view of those societies that practice such surgeries" (p. 89), which suggests that they are irrational, as does their "false sense of knowledge" and "sensationalizing accounts" (p. 90). Their "reactions of rejection and contempt," their "neocolonial thinking," and their domineering role in "ongoing political struggles about legitimacy and authority, at both the local and the global levels" (p. 90), suggest that they are cruel.

The article demands the highest standards of evidence for the uncontroversial proposition that FGC entails nontrivial complications but offers no such evidence for its controversial propositions about the advocates. The negative characterization of them violates two further canons of science.

First, other than an assertion that "many" (pp. 89–90) sources, publications, and discussions of FGC deserve such characterization, the article presents no data of any kind concerning the distribution of views among those who prefer FGC to end. Shouldn't we appreciate the heterogeneity of views among advocates? The term includes everyone in the world who would like for FGC to end and contains everyone from African individuals who have worked a lifetime for reform to high school students writing term papers in Peoria.

Second, there is no controlled comparison of advocates' attitudes with respect to matched issues. To make the point that advocates are unusually in the grip of illegitimate motivations, the article would have to measure, say, American advocates' attitudes with respect to FGC in Africa, and American advocates' attitudes with respect to an American issue, perhaps abortion. Do all pro-choice advocates have a thorough and detailed grasp of the relevant evidence? Do they all sympathetically understand the motives of pro-lifers, and discuss them in tones of reserve and respect?

To conclude, is the article's claim merely that public opinion has a shallow understanding of a topic distant from respondents' experiences? Or does it intend to lodge the serious charge that the most informed and most practically involved advocates are factually and morally mistaken?

Frequency of Health Complications

The article excludes from evidence of health complications all anatomical inference, all history, all journalism, all ethnography, all policy forums, all public health reports, all clinical observations, and all personal experiences. . . .

The article concludes, then, that health complications "are the exception rather than the rule" (p. 92). Death from malaria is the exception rather than the rule, but no physician would put it that way to a patient about to travel to a malarial zone. A more responsible statement for the public would be that "complications are common, and can be serious." Summarizing the DHS research, Carr states that "women commonly report cutting-related health problems" (1997:6). The DHS surveys that the article considers authoritative measured self-reported complications in the Central African Republic, Egypt, and Eritrea. The DHS analysis extrapolated from the sample to estimate that one million women in those countries would self-report complications (Carr 1997:41), and in its summary reported that "medical problems related to genital cutting are a public health issue of some magnitude" (Carr 1997:6). For those one million women, complications would be the rule not the exception. . . .

Perils of Survey Research

The [Obermeyer] article warns that respondent women may not be able to accurately distinguish among complications and may be subject to recall bias with respect to both the operation and potential complications. I want to add that there are other major problems of causal attribution that would bias toward serious underreporting of FGC complications, and these must be considered in research design.

If FGC is nearly universal within an intramarrying group, then respondents themselves have no comparison group. In the worst case, they would mistakenly consider even immediate complications as normal background, and this would bias against both recognition and recall of complications. Respondents without close knowledge of untreated women may not suspect a causal relationship between FGC and complications. Writing about complications of infibulation in Islamic Northeast Africa, Hicks observes:

> Women do not even correlate subsequent physical discomfort, pain, and related gynecological and obstetric problems with having been circumcised. Such physical problems are perceived as being the common lot of women. That is because the problems are, to one degree or other, prevalent among the majority of infibulated women, they are not viewed as unusual. Logically then, neither the act of infibulation nor related sequelae (unless requiring emergency treatment) are high priority issues for women in these societies. [1996:73]

. . . A survey among such women would show very different results before and after the discovery of a causal relationship (the article, however, considers schooling or contact with women's organizations a biasing factor; p. 100). An excisors' future work depends on the repute of her skills in carrying out the cutting. I learned in Senegal that excisors, those who perform FGC, often for compensation, will, sincerely or opportunistically, minimize or misattribute immediate complications, which further contributes to causal misattribution in the population. . . .

There seems to be a universal human reticence about discussing matters relating to human sexuality. This is exacerbated in some localities by norms of female modesty and further in some localities by powerful norms of secrecy concerning FGC and its meanings. . . .

Prior to sensitization, a causal relationship was not suspected by those involved in the practice and would never have been discovered, because women did not disclose to one another, let alone to local men or to outsiders, information about the FGC and associated (though unrecognized) complications; complete silence was the powerful norm. After sensitization, and the suggestion of a causal relationship, women began to share experiences about complications, and discovered, to their horror, that what they thought were unassociated or idiosyncratic harms were associated and unacceptably prevalent. . . .

Survey results would drastically undermeasure complications in locations where there is a strong norm of secrecy—the norm of secrecy is itself a secret—and would mislead, compared to other approaches. It would not do to have flawed surveys paraded as science alongside the dismissal of anatomical inferences, clinical reports, personal experiences, and other data as worthless information. Poorly designed survey research would also suffer from extreme selection bias on the question of severe complications. The survey would undercount all complications sufficiently severe to remove the woman by death from the measured population. Such selection bias also probably obscures causal attribution within practicing populations. If the survey measures only ever-married women, then those who survive but are unmarriageable due to complications also go unmeasured. Interviewing sisters or mothers about family fatalities would fail if respondents were unaware of a causal relationship between FGC and complications, which is no imaginary problem. And even if respondents were aware of causal connection, perceived culpabilities for the loss may inhibit reporting.

Survey research is not equivalent to facts.

Harms and Benefits

Next, the [Obermeyer] article maintains that assessments of benefits and harms are culturally variable and socially constructed. It cites the benefits of beauty, marriageability, sexual alteration, and group conformity. What is the evidence for such benefits? Notice again an inconsistent standard: citations to five ethnographers. If, on the question of *benefits,* we demanded the same standard of evidence that the article demands on the question of *complications*—that ideally designed and executed demographic and health surveys carried out widely across space and time confirm that FGC *inevitably* provides *incontrovertible* benefits— then we would have to conclude that its critical discourse about benefits is insufficiently supported. Ethnographers' reports contain descriptions of perceived benefits, harms, and complications; thus, if ethnographers' reports are our standard of evidence, then nontrivial complications are well established.

The article deplores generalizing theories of FGC but, inconsistently proposes one of its own: "the ill health and the death that these practices are thought to cause are difficult to reconcile with the reality of their persistence in so many societies" (p. 91, reiterated on pp. 92, 94). That a practice would persist because it is only minimally harmful seems to be a plausible hypothesis, but on reflection it is not. Do smoking and drinking persist because they are harmless? Does war? Did footbinding persist for a millennium because it was harmless? The convention hypothesis explains how certain harmful practices like FGC and footbinding stubbornly persist, and how they suddenly end. No other evidence is offered in the article to support the minimal-harm hypothesis.

A few simple observations will indicate the implausibility of the minimal-harm explanation for the persistence of FGC. . . . The minimal-harm hypothesis, would predict less persistence in groups with more severe FGC and more persistence in groups with less severe FGC. With the recent exception of organized abandonments in Senegal, where FGC has ended in groups regardless of severity of cutting, FGC is unusually persistent, for example, the severe practice of infibulation for 2,200 years among some Beja.

Inspection of DHS data does not suggest any relationship between severity of practice and proportion opposed to continuation of the practice. [Furthermore,] if complications were trivial, then education would not change attitudes. We have seen already, though, that more education means more opposition in attitudes toward continuation. . . .

The article suggests that education makes no difference in approval for the continuation of FGC, and from this it infers that the educated do not share the biomedical view of harm and the universalist view of human rights. The inference is confused: If one cannot escape from the tragic circumstance of having to suffer a harm in order to obtain a greater benefit, that does not mean that one believes there is no harm. Mothers worry and sorrow when daughters go under the knife. . . . For a girl to avoid the harm of FGC brings about for her the worse harm of unmarriageability.

The article . . . claims that ethnographic studies link FGC to "rites of passage and to the marking of membership in a social group such as a tribe or secret society" (p. 88). . . . [However,] contrary to expectation, FGC is *not* a rite of passage; . . . but rather a practice that is entirely oriented to marriageability.

A physician at a public health clinic in Senegal emphasized to me that the negative psychological consequences of FGC (for some individuals, not all) were not sufficiently appreciated. . . . Toubia and Izett (1998:31–33) say that the "cumulative evidence suggests that the [cutting] event is remembered as extremely traumatic and leaves a life-long emotional scar." . . .

Sexual Limitations

. . . Toubia, a physician originally from the Sudan, explains that, "by altering the normal anatomy of the sexual organs, FGM reduces the case with which sexual fulfillment is achieved, or makes it extremely difficult."

The [Obermeyer] article (pp. 96, 101) proposes, however, that Western anatomy's finding that the genital organs are related to sexual enjoyment is merely a social construction, as is female orgasm. The case reports on sexuality, it says, are from "unusual" women who have had contact with schooling or women's organizations. Further, case reports tend to be from groups with more severe cutting, and negative effects are improperly generalized to all forms of cutting. . . .

[In contrast,] numerous sources indicate that FGC is widely *intended* to limit female sexual capacity, often to encourage chastity or fidelity. The [Obermeyer] article, however, suggests that FGC is "not designed to obliterate sexual enjoyment," that humans in FGC cultures have a "very different conception of the link between an intact clitoris and orgasm," and that such a linkage is not a "physiological reality" but rather is "socially constructed" (p. 96). . . .

Conclusion

In sum, the article shifts standards of evidence without justification, and its hypotheses are falsified by evidence from sources it otherwise accepts. Its central conclusions are stated boldly, but dissolve with simple linguistic analysis. The conclusive proof it seeks of complications is not possible in any empirical investigation, and is not appropriate for evaluation of a health and human-rights issue such as FGC.

The claim that the advocates exaggerated estimates of prevalence is contradicted by evidence from a source otherwise relied on and considered ideal, as is the claim that more educated respondents do not adopt new attitudes on harm, bodily integrity, health, and informed consent. The article's extremely negative generalizations about the advocates are unjustified. Its claim of low frequency of health complications is unsupported by the laboratory standard of evidence demanded in the article, and is contradicted by the DHS data that it otherwise accepts. Its belief that evidence on health complications of FGC is peculiarly wanting is not tested against controlled comparisons, and it fails to consider more plausible alternative hypotheses to its proposal that the allegedly poor state of the evidence should be blamed on the advocates and on unnamed forces.

It is wrong to equate survey research to the facts: Survey research on FGC may underestimate harms because of norms of secrecy and of modesty, because of causal misattributions among respondents due to the local universality of the practice, and because of selection bias. It wants to explain FGC as a benefit, not grasping that to avoid the harm of FGC brings about the worse harm of unmarriageability. It minimizes the "discomfort" (p. 94) of "female genital surgeries" without reference to any source, a claim directly contradicted by a demographic study and by an ethnographic study cited elsewhere in its text. It suggests that FGC does not limit sexual capacity, but the very sources it cites in support, on examination, demand the opposite conclusion. It may take a relativist view toward biomedicine and morality, which would not cohere with its scientism and evaluative stance.

The article argues that the "international consensus" (p. 80) to support the abandonment of female genital cuttings is based on "the conviction that they have extremely harmful consequences" (p. 80). The article concludes that the evidence that they have extremely harmful consequences is insufficient (p. 97). Thus, the author is "motivated" (p. 80) to shift "resources" (p. 85) away from "groups working against the continuation of these practices" (p. 80).

I propose an alternative account: That the international consensus and mobilization to which the article objects is based primarily on something like the understanding that FGC is an irreversible limitation of a human capacity carried out in the absence of meaningful consent, that opposition is motivated by human-rights concerns. I argue that by appropriate standards of evaluation, FGC entails nontrivial complications. The foregoing debate over complications must not distract us, however, from the more important human-rights issues pertaining to FGC and the need to orient research toward the goal of abandonment.

Carla Makhlouf Obermeyer

The Health Consequences of Female Circumcision: Science, Advocacy, and Standards of Evidence

The opportunity to revisit a controversial article more than five years after it was written is an offer one cannot refuse. I appreciate the chance to clarify my position, dispel misrepresentations, and continue to insist on nuanced statements. Returning to the issue at this time is also the occasion to review the state of our knowledge in light of recent research, and I have chosen to devote part of this rejoinder to an update on the evidence. . . .

My Article Was Not an Attack against "Advocates"

. . . Although I expressed concern at the imbalance between research and advocacy, I did not portray them as being in competition. I see the two as complementary, and I referred to the "potential disparity between the mobilization of resources toward activism and the research base that *ought to support such efforts*" (p. 80; emphasis added). Although I disagreed with some specific claims in the advocacy literature, nowhere did I condemn advocacy efforts in general. I welcomed initiatives to bring together activists and researchers (p. 85). . . .

Mackie's argument is based on deliberately misreading my work and imputing to me misguided opinions and motivations. . . .

Nowhere did I say the things that are attributed to me. The supposed paraphrase has in fact been assembled from text found on three different pages. . . .

Mackie also engages in a detailed polemic about whether particular advocates more often under- or over-estimated the prevalence of circumcisions globally. This is irrelevant, because the point is not whose guesses were accurate, or whether some guesses were better than none, but, rather, that many estimates were made by individuals who did not have the requisite competence, and that advocacy efforts were not based on reliable evidence. . . .

It may be true that research on circumcision is not unique and that many other widely held beliefs are not sufficiently supported by evidence. But when I reviewed the evidence in 1996, it was certainly shocking to find out how little attention had been directed to documenting harmful effects, given

From *Medical Anthropology Quarterly*, vol. 17, no. 3, 2003, pp. 394–403, 408. Copyright © 2003 as conveyed via the Copyright Clearance Center. Reprinted by permission.

the global mobilization of attention and efforts toward eradicating female genital mutilation, precisely on the grounds that the operations caused death and ill health. It may well be more appropriate that advocacy efforts have since shifted to a discourse highlighting human rights, informed consent, and bodily integrity, and that research will be directed toward ascertaining how the practice violates these principles. This still does not dispose of the need for solid information on prevalence and health consequences. That was the goal of my article: to take stock of what was known about health effects and to assess how good the evidence was.

Claims about the Integrity of the Review Are Unfounded

Mackie repeatedly questions my use of sources, claiming that some reports, available at the time of writing, were excluded or presented inaccurately. But despite his sustained efforts over a three-year period to find fault with the quality of the review, he offers no credible evidence that I excluded reports about health effects, or that I misrepresented the findings of any study. I presented all the sources that were available to me and provided explicit criteria for inclusion and exclusion. My article included an extensive bibliography, so readers can easily verify that sources have been appropriately cited. While Mackie may disagree with my explicit exclusion of nonscholarly sources such as journalism or individual accounts, he cannot and does not point to any omissions or misrepresentations. . . .

Mackie contends that some of the sources that I cited in my discussion of the association between schooling and circumcision were insufficiently covered, and he tries to suggest that this was a deliberate attempt to conceal findings that did not support my argument. The point I had made was that whereas some studies showed lower prevalence of circumcision among educated women in some countries, in others, differences by education were very small or nonexistent (pp. 88–89). The lengthy discussion that Mackie engages in to try and disprove my point shows exactly the same results for each of the countries I had cited and provides similar figures from more recent surveys in two other countries. It unequivocally substantiates what I had said: that the direction of the association between schooling and prevalence is not uniform, that it is relatively weak, and that in several countries, the near totality of women with secondary schooling are circumcised.

The additional data that Mackie presents have no direct bearing either on the question of prevalence or on the question of health effects. The finding that in several countries, schooling is associated with lower expressed support for circumcision only allows us to speculate that practices may change in the future. And responses in surveys about the frequency of unspecified complications do not represent reliable evidence on health effects. It is for this simple reason, rather than other questionable motives, that I had not discussed such sources in detail. This example demonstrates how, despite his efforts, Mackie is unable to question the integrity of the review.

Multidisciplinarity Still Requires
Specific Standards of Evidence

Mackie repeatedly claims that my analysis shifts standards of evidence. This allegation stems from a misunderstanding of what is involved when combining different disciplines to analyze a complicated topic. Each of the three disciplines that were brought to bear on the issue—demography, epidemiology, and anthropology—uses specific methods to gather and analyze data. Although it is important to consider the results of all research together, one cannot indiscriminately mix evidence across fields. Multidisciplinarity requires a degree of competence in each discipline and is a risky undertaking because it can, as I had stated, "make one vulnerable to critiques of specialists from each of them" (p. 80). It is thus somewhat ironic that my article is criticized by someone who is not familiar with any of the three disciplines I drew on.

Mackie misunderstands my approach. He appears at times to think that I advocate surveys unconditionally, while at other times he refers to "the laboratory standard of evidence demanded in the article," and yet elsewhere he states that as a relativist I do not endorse the biomedical view. Perhaps my review confused him because it did not privilege a single discipline. I had said as much in the introduction of my article: that my analysis was "motivated by the conviction that a single approach is not sufficient in itself to understand the issue" (p. 80). Each discipline brings a different contribution to the study of this complex problem. All involve trade-offs in attaining "gold standards" of evidence, but good research is about balancing these trade-offs in light of the reality of the field situation.

Concerning the prevalence of female circumcision, the best evidence would come from large-scale observations, but because clinical research of this kind is neither feasible nor desirable, the next best thing is to assume that women know whether they have been circumcised and to ask them to report on their own condition. This assumption is known to be fairly reasonable, and demography has well-established methods for making inferences from samples to large populations. That is why my presentation of the data on prevalence relied on demographic surveys.

Surveys, however, are not a good way to measure health effects, and this is obvious to those who obtain the most elementary training in any of the health sciences. The reasons for this include recall bias and differences in perceptions of general health and symptoms across individuals and across cultures. Another important reason is that health conditions may be caused by various agents—for example, reproductive health problems may result from any number of factors, such as malnutrition, sexually transmitted infections, poor obstetric care, exposure to radiation or chemicals, etc.—and individuals suffering from health problems are usually not qualified to draw conclusions about the connections. To ascertain the increased risks associated with a given factor, the frequency of the health outcome has to be measured by means other than respondents' reports and comparisons have to be made between groups where the factor is found and groups where it is not. . . .

How to Measure, and Not to Measure, Health Effects

The best way to determine whether a given factor represents a risk for a given health effect is to examine the statistical association between the two. Because experimental or prospective designs are rarely feasible, the most commonly used method in epidemiology is the case-control study. It ascertains the extent of exposure in a sample of "exposed" and "unexposed" individuals, compares the frequencies of the hypothesized health effect in the two groups, and applies statistics to measure the strength of the association. [W]e would have to measure the frequency of the reproductive health problem among women who have been subjected to cutting or hitting, compared to those who have not. To determine the health effects of female circumcision, there is no substitute for studies that include a comparison group and provide sufficient numbers for statistical analyses.

Mackie does not understand why certain sources were excluded from my analysis, and he denounces my exclusion of "all history, all journalism, all ethnography, all policy forums, all public health reports, all clinical observations, and all personal experiences." Although each of these sources is valuable for particular purposes, they are not equally relevant to the analysis of health effects. Mackie lumps them together indiscriminately, showing little awareness of differences in the quality of the information they provide on health effects. The individual stories and case reports that he would rely on are certainly useful as a preliminary step, to draw attention to possible connections with health conditions. But although anecdotal evidence and individual reports can be important bases for formulating hypotheses, they have limited value when trying to establish associations. They may over- or underestimate health effects, depending on the population from which they are drawn. For example, reports from a clinic specializing in reproductive problems or surgical repair of lesions often overestimate complications because they come from facilities where the more complicated cases are referred; conversely, where awareness of health consequences is low, individuals may not report symptoms that they view as normal, and such reports underestimate complications. Thus, one cannot simply rely on an ad hoc collection of reports to convincingly establish increased risks, especially when measuring effects beyond those immediately observed.

Mackie consistently fails to distinguish the health effects of circumcision, measured by the methods of public health, from public policy judgments about preventing the practice and sociological analyses about abandonment. He argues that "proof of complications is not possible and not appropriate for human rights," and that because female circumcision is a social practice and not a pathogen or toxin, assessing the "frequencies of complications [. . .] should be made by the public-policy standard." Such assertions mix science and advocacy and confuse the domains of analysis of different disciplines. My article dealt with prevalence and health effects. It did not cover harmful effects other than health complications, nor address questions related to consent, ethics, or rights. That these dimensions of the practice are important does not mean that public policy or human rights standards can be substituted for epidemiological methods when measuring health consequences.

Ethnographic Reports Are Not Normative Statements or Scientific Endorsements

Throughout his critique, Mackie appears unable to refrain from entering public policy debates, even when reading descriptions of the practices found in other cultures. My article had included ethnographic reports on circumcision and relied on anthropology to help contextualize the practices and gain some insight into what they mean in the societies where they are found. Information about local views would help answer the question "How can they do this?" and lessen the reactions of horror or outrage that Shweder calls the "mutual yuck" response. Ethnographic descriptions are meant to give us a glimpse of the different valuations that surround circumcision and the way in which it is rationalized in the local culture. They are not arguments in a public policy debate. No one familiar with the anthropological approach could take my statement (p. 94) regarding the perceived benefits of circumcision as an endorsement of local beliefs, and then proceed to demand that I provide evidence for such benefits. Mackie also disagrees when I report (pp. 95–96) on local notions of gender and sexuality, or when I try (p. 94) to explain how individuals can disregard the risks of circumcision, mistaking my attempt to suspend belief and understand others' views for wholehearted approval.

The effort to set aside our own assumptions and consider foreign practices from the perspective of others is particularly challenging when dealing with the effects of circumcision on sexuality, and here Mackie does not seem to see the point of the exercise. My review of the very limited information documenting sexual effects led me to raise some questions about the experience of sex in cultures where women are circumcised. These questions arose from reports indicating that circumcised women said that they enjoyed sex and that some experienced orgasm. None of these reports were from studies specifically designed to address the many difficulties encountered in research on sexuality, and I was careful to say so (p. 95). But the unexpected finding in several of the studies—that sexual response persists despite the operations—casts some doubt on the blanket assertion that circumcision obliterates sexuality, and I called for careful research that would focus on the link between the physical reality of the operations and the experience of sex under those conditions.

I said that contemplating the possibility of such different notions of sexuality is unsettling, because it implies "that what is presented as an undisputable physiological reality may itself be socially constructed" (p. 96). Mackie interprets this as a complete denial of anatomy, an extreme constructivist view that rejects the connection between genital organs and sexual enjoyment. There is no room here for subtlety, and we are back to gross comparisons with cutting and amputating, along the lines of the domestic violence analogy.

My discussion of the consequences of circumcision on sexuality was not designed to provide answers, mainly because the evidence is so scant. I said that the practice of circumcision, and its consequences, strains our ability to understand, and, far from making definitive pronouncements about how others experience it, I had suggested that perhaps there were limits to how much we can understand it. That is why I had referred to the "unknowable" in the title of my article.

Anthropology's nonconventional ways of thinking about the contingency of social arrangements and ideas appear to be disturbing to Mackie. He finds it "worrisome" when I say that not everyone shares the biomedical point of view on circumcision. If I mention variations in the extent to which people in different societies think about risks to health, expect discomfort, or endure pain, he thinks I am denying that the operations cause pain. If I warn that conflating lesser and more extensive operations is an oversimplification, he concludes that I am opposed to comparisons and generalizations. Relativism makes him apprehensive, and he detects what he refers to as "undercurrents" of it when I put quotation marks around words like *facts, normal bodies,* or *healthy sexuality,* or use the word *powerful* to refer to the biomedical point of view. From all this, he deduces that I must be skeptical of science, of medicine, of universals, maybe even an adept of Foucault, for whom there is no truth or falsehood, right or wrong.

Oversimplification versus Nuanced Statements

Mackie is so impatient with the subtle distinctions I tried to make that he takes it on himself to restate my findings. He asks: "How might they read if we removed the ten qualifiers and readjusted phrasing?" And, of course, after such vigorous editing, they read exactly the way he would like them to read.

Instead of relying on Mackie to do so, let *me* sum up the "bottom-line" of the argument: Did I try to argue that circumcision was harmless from a health point of view as Mackie's title suggests? No, it depends on the type of operation: more extensive operations are more likely to cause damage. It also depends on the type of harm: some effects are well documented, others not. I offered comments to elaborate on these points.

First, I commented on the state of the available evidence that did not support some of the claims of harmful effects; I attributed this to the paucity and poor quality of the research rather than to the fact that the operations are completely safe (p. 97)—remember that it depends on the type of operation.

Second, I commented on the frequency of complications and said that serious complications were relatively infrequent. This is a statistical assessment, and it is made in contrast with claims that circumcision causes death and serious ill health. It was not meant to diminish the importance of individual pain and illness or to question the veracity of the many poignant stories and personal experiences. I had also qualified my statement about serious complications by saying that from a public health point of view, even low frequencies are too high if they are preventable (p. 92).

Finally, I commented on the context in which the debates about circumcision were taking place, pointing out the historical and political forces that shaped them.

Perhaps the reason my article has been controversial has to do with the passions that circumcision continues to elicit, with the surprise caused by the weakness of the evidence on what was thought to be patently obvious, and with the difficulty of accepting that the answer to the question of harmful effects is in shades of gray. I believe that as more evidence becomes available, it will confirm both the assertions that I did make and the caution I exercised in presenting my findings.

Update on the Evidence

A few months ago, I conducted a review of sources published between 1997 and 2002. Comparing the 440 recent sources to those reviewed in 1996 shows a small increase in the proportion of studies that present some evidence compared to those that do not. There remain fundamental problems in studies measuring health and other effects, such as lack of comparison groups, inconsistent numbers, or incomplete analyses, but there are a few well-designed studies and, one hopes, the start of a trend toward better research on health effects.

To facilitate comparisons with my 1999 article, I have prepared a summary table, grouping effects under headings similar to those I used in my earlier review: general health, bleeding, infections, reproductive problems, labor and delivery problems, lesions-scars-cysts, urinary problems, pain, and sexual problems. Findings have been separated depending on the type and strength of the evidence on which they are based. Studies that include a comparison group and provide information about statistical significance represent the strongest evidence. . . . Studies that do not include comparison group of women not subjected to circumcision are less conclusive. Many of these studies use loose definitions of effects and give no details about measurements in the field. This results in much less precise estimates of the frequencies of complications. . . .

In general, the quality of the information is better for measures that lend themselves to laboratory or clinical confirmation. Many of these come from a thorough study in the Gambia. The results indicate that some infections (bacterial vaginosis and herpes) are significantly more frequent among circumcised women, while others (syphilis) are significantly less frequent, and yet others (candida, chlamydia, or trichomoniasis) show no significant difference. Studies not including a comparison group show much wider, and less informative, estimates, for example 2–50 percent for edema, or 8–37 percent for unspecified infections.

Analyses of studies on infertility that have appeared in the last few years do not document significant differences, while studies of labor and delivery problems show mixed results: those with a comparison group do not find significantly higher risks of complications of labor and delivery, except where these are very loosely defined to include hospital practices such as c-sections and episiotomies; less rigorous studies suggest that difficulties in delivery, prolonged labor, c-sections, excessive bleeding, and various tears may be relatively frequent but do not make it possible to ascertain that the risks are statistically higher, or to estimate the magnitude of the increased risks. Studies of gynecological problems find that some are significantly more frequent (unspecified complications), others (prolapse) significantly less so. Regarding urinary problems, [one] study did not find significant differences, whereas studies without comparison groups show a wider range in reported frequencies, reflecting the lack of standardized definitions, and inaccuracies in measurement.

Bleeding and scarring are, to a certain extent, self-evident consequences of any surgical operation, and it is important to document how serious they are and the magnitude of the health risks they represent. There is a disparate set of studies on bleeding, but given the lack of clear definitions and measurements (e.g., what is bleeding compared to excessive bleeding, or hemorrhage), it is difficult to interpret their results. On lesions, scars, and cysts, there are several series of case reports, and a number of frequency-only studies reporting a range of figures, but [a] controlled study did not find significant differences.

Studies of pain have concentrated principally on dysmenorrhea, and, whereas [one] study found significantly higher frequencies among circumcised women, [and another] found higher frequencies among uncircumcised women but the difference was not significant. Other studies without a comparison group report widely divergent estimates (9–87 percent), again showing the difficulty of ascertaining effects with suboptimal research designs.

Problems with quality are especially apparent in studies that have investigated sexual effects. Unlike other complications that can, in principle, be measured in purely medical fashion, assessing the effect of female genital cutting on sexuality requires inputs from the individual herself. To ensure accuracy and allow systematic comparisons, data collection methods have to be especially careful with terminology, the phrasing of questions, the circumstances of the interview, and the quality of the conversation with the researcher.

In addition, attention has to be directed to contextual factors that reflect the values of a given culture and influence the meanings attached by the respondent to her experience: admitting to sexual pleasure may, in some settings, be regarded as inappropriate with strangers, or there may be gendered values related to interest in sex, or modesty considerations that influence responses. Unfortunately, none of the available studies has taken the necessary care to ensure that concepts related to sexuality can be appropriately defined and translated, none has documented the conditions of interviews and women's understandings and reactions. This considerably weakens their findings. . . . [One] controlled study found no differences in dyspareunia. Other studies have reported on problems with intercourse and orgasm, but it is not clear how different these frequencies would be in an uncircumcised group of women.

In general, the studies summarized in this review show that circumcision is associated with significantly higher risks of selected complications, but that for many possible complications, the available evidence does not show significant differences. The summary also highlights two simple points: (1) where complications are not precisely defined, widely divergent frequencies of complications are found, and (2) studies without comparison groups do not provide conclusive results.

It is not clear to what extent the paucity of significant results can be attributed to the difficulty of designing appropriate studies. Certainly, the fact that most of the research summarized here has been conducted in countries where the lesser operations are prevalent—Burkina, Central African Republic, Côte d'lvoire, Egypt, the Gambia, Kenya, Mali, and Tanzania—needs to be noted. Some of the studies I had reviewed in my 1999 article had been conducted on populations where infibulation is practiced (Sudan and Somalia), and they suggested that the more extensive operations may be associated with a greater likelihood of complications. I cannot, on the basis of this recent review, comment on this possibility, because none of the studies on infibulated women included a control group, and all have been limited to immigrant populations (Somali immigrants to Canada, Horn of Africa immigrants to Australia, and Sudanese/Somali women in Saudi Arabia). It is all the more important that future research make special efforts to separate lesser operations from the more extensive ones (i.e., infibulation compared to others) in order to establish to what extent more extensive surgeries cause greater harm.

Conclusion

Despite the accumulation of information on health effects, large gaps remain in our understanding of the extent of harm that is caused by the various operations subsumed under the heading of circumcision. This is mainly because most of the available studies are not designed to document these effects. Some careful studies have shown higher risks for a few well-defined complications but no difference for most others, whereas less rigorous studies yield much wider ranges of estimates for a greater number of, often loosely defined, conditions. There is no doubt that better-designed studies can go a long way toward improving our estimates of the health risks of the operations, but the current state of the evidence does not allow hasty pronouncements about all the harmful effects attributed to circumcision.

My 1999 article drew attention to the complexity of measuring harms to health, pointed to the weakness of our understanding, and showed the inadequacy of simplistic judgments. While we may feel strongly that these practices are wrong, and for a variety of reasons apart from their health effects, the debates about female circumcision remind us of one of anthropology's central tenets—that "we see the lives of others through lenses of our own grinding and that they look back on ours through ones of their own." The multiculturalism of today's world makes it all the more pressing that we engage in discussions that are informed by evidence and that we develop better ways to bring together different perspectives to focus on this complicated issue.

POSTSCRIPT

Is Female Circumcision Universally Wrong?

Why has FGM been practiced for so long? What sociohistorical changes have made possible the recent campaigns against FGM? What are the major obstacles to the worldwide eradication of FGM?

When should a cultural practice that is a departure from established American culture be accepted or disallowed in the United States? Imagine you are a pediatrician and one of your new patients is a small female child whose family just immigrated to the United States from Northern Sudan, where FGM is very prevalent. Her mother asks you to perform FGM on the child. What would be your response? How far do U.S. principles of familial privacy and personal autonomy extend in such a situation? Should the parent's decision about her/his child be respected or rejected? How does this situation differ from the performance of surgical "correction" to intersexual infants and children? To what degree should the child's health and well-being and legal inability to consent be weighed in the decision?

Now imagine you are a gynecologist and an adult Sudanese woman of legal consenting age comes to you and asks to be reinfibulated. If the procedure to which she is consenting is prohibited under law, are we unconstitutionally limiting her personal autonomy? After all, Americans place high value on bodily autonomy and privacy.

Consider a new twist on nonmedically based genital surgery. "Sexual-enhancement" surgery is the hottest new trend in plastic surgery, including labiaplasty and vaginal tightening. A Canadian surgeon Dr. Stubbs, who performs these procedures, suggests that this is a natural extension of women's quest for beauty (see Issue 16): "After all the benchmarks of beauty have been obtained—Barbie Doll breasts, youthful face, sporty thighs—it appears that for a certain segment of female society, tidy genitals are worth the $1,500 to $2,500 price tag. If the labia are oversized, asymmetrical, too loose or triangular, they don't measure up to the ideal and are a candidate for cutting." According to Dr. Stubbs, women seeking the surgery are either the 25- to 35-year-old trophy wives of sports figures for whom the sexual and physiological ideal is the price of entry into that world, or women of all ages who have abnormally large labia that may be interfering with their sexual confidence and performance (see http://www.noharmm.org/mommy.htm).

What is the relationship between FGM and elective genital surgery for sexual enhancement? Is it truly elective or just a newer form of cultural pressures to look and feel the "right way"? What position do you think the universalists' and the cultural relativists would take on this new trend?

Finally, what is the relationship between FGM and male circumcision? Is there really a difference?

Suggested Readings

C. L. Annas, "Irreversible Error: The Power and Prejudice of Female Genital Mutilation," *Contemporary Health Law and Policy* (1996).

Fauziya Kassindja, *Do They Hear You When You Cry?* (New York: Delta Books, 1998).

Ellen Gruenbaum, *The Female Circumcision Controversy: An Anthropological Perspective* (Philadelphia: University of Pennsylvania Press, 2001).

Mireya Navarro, "The Most Private of Makeovers," *New York Times* (November 28, 2004).

Rosemarie Skaine, *Female Genital Mutilation: Legal, Cultural and Medical Issues* (Jefferson, NC: McFarland, 2005).

C. J. Walley, "Searching for 'Voices': Feminism, Anthropology, and the Global Debate Over Female Genital Operations," *Cultural Anthropology* (1977).

ISSUE 19

Should "Abstinence-Until-Marriage" Be the Only Message for Teens?

YES: Bridget E. Maher, from "Abstinence Until Marriage: The Best Message for Teens," Family Research Council (2004)

NO: Debra Hauser, from *Five Years of Abstinence-Only-Until-Marriage Education: Assessing the Impact* (2004)

ISSUE SUMMARY

YES: Bridget E. Maher argues that far too much funding has gone into programs that teach young people about sexuality and contraception—programs that she concludes are ineffective.

NO: Debra Hauser, in an evaluation of numerous abstinence-only-until-marriage programs that received funding under the Title V Social Security Act, concludes that they show few short-term benefits and no lasting, positive effects; rather such programs may actually worsen sexual health outcomes.

In 1996, President Clinton signed the welfare reform law. Attached to this law was a federal entitlement program allocating $50 million per year over a five-year period to abstinence-only-until-marriage educational programs. This Act specifies that a program is defined as "abstinence-only" education if it:

- has as its exclusive purpose teaching the social, psychological, and health gains to be realized by abstaining from sexual activity;
- teaches that abstinence from sexual activity outside of marriage is the expected standard for all school-age children;
- teaches that abstinence from sexual activity is the only certain way to avoid out-of-wedlock pregnancy, sexually transmitted diseases, and other associated health problems;
- teaches that a mutually faithful monogamous relationship in the context of marriage is the expected standard of sexual activity;
- teaches that sexual activity outside the context of marriage is likely to have harmful psychological and physical side effects;
- teaches that bearing children out-of-wedlock is likely to have harmful consequences for the child, the child's parents, and society;

- teaches young people how to reject sexual advances and how alcohol and drug use increases vulnerability to sexual advances; and,
- teaches the importance of attaining self-sufficiency before engaging in sexual activity. (*Section 510(b) of Title V of the Social Security Act, P.L. 104–193*).

In order to access these funds, an entity must agree to teach all of these points, not just a few. Failure to do so would result in loss of the funding.

Those who support the teaching of comprehensive sexuality education disagree with the tenets that abstinence-only-until-marriage (AOUM) supports. They present research that demonstrates how comprehensive sexuality education programs help young people to delay the onset of risky sexual behaviors, and to use contraceptives more effectively once they do start engaging in these behaviors. Some argue that AOUM is exclusionary, excluding non-heterosexual youth; is fear- and shame-based, and is wildly out of touch with the reality in which young people are living. They are quick to point out that AOUM supports have yet to provide empirical evidence that their programs "work."

AOUM supporters believe that comprehensive sexuality education programs teach "too much, too soon." They believe strongly that providing information about abstinence, along with safer sex information, confuses teens, and gives them permission to become sexually active when the potential consequences for sexual activity are much more serious.

Take a look at the language of the legislation. The language refers to "sexual activity." We know that for many people "having sex" means only sexual intercourse. It does not include oral sex, for example. We know that many teens are having sexual intercourse outside of marriage, and although this number is going down, the number of youth engaging in oral sex is increasing. What does "sexual activity" mean to you? Would you be able to support the legislation if it included some behaviors, but not others? Are there some messages you agree with and not others? If you were an educator, would you be able to teach all eight points, especially given what you know about adolescent sexual behavior?

As you read these selections, think about any sexuality education classes you may have had—do you think they should have taught you more? Less? Consider, too, young people who are already sexually active. Would abstinence messages work for them? Did a more comprehensive program "fail" them?

In the following selections, Bridget E. Maher outlines some of the negative consequences of teen sex, and why abstinence is the only 100 percent effective option for avoiding those negative consequences. She argues that more comprehensive sexuality education programs, while purporting to teach about abstinence, actually rarely, if ever, do. Debra Hauser describes what she perceives to be flaws in the assertions made by AOUM proponents, such as the idea that if educators teach only abstinence, teens won't have sex. In reviewing abstinence-only programs, she concludes that although most show changes in attitudes towards abstinence, many actually discourage safe practices in youth who are sexually active and thereby increase the risks of the very problems the programs were designed to prevent.

YES

Bridget E. Maher

Abstinence Until Marriage: The Best Message for Teens

The federal government has provided some abstinence-until-marriage funding in recent years, but comprehensive sex education and contraception programs are vastly over-funded in comparison. In 2002, abstinence-until-marriage programs received $102 million, while teen-sex education and contraception programs received at least $427.7 million. In his last budget, President Bush proposed an increase of $33 million for abstinence-until-marriage programs, following upon his campaign promise to try to equalize funding between comprehensive sex education and abstinence programs. This is a good first step, but it still doesn't bring true parity between these programs. It's time for our government to get serious about fulfilling the president's promise to at least level the playing field with regard to funding of the positive and healthy message of abstinence-until-marriage versus that of promoting premarital sex and contraception.

Teens are greatly influenced by the messages they receive about sex in school. Unfortunately, the majority of schools teach "safe sex"—"comprehensive" or so-called "abstinence plus" programs—believing that it's best for kids to have all the information they need about sexuality and to make their own decisions about sex. Abstinence is downplayed while sexual activity and condom use are encouraged in these curriculums, because it's assumed that children are eventually going to have sex. A 2002 report by the Physicians Consortium, which investigated comprehensive sex programs promoted by the Centers for Disease Control, reveals that abstinence is barely mentioned and condom use is clearly advocated in these curriculums.

Abstinence-until-marriage programs, on the other hand, teach young people to save sex for marriage, and their message has been very effective in changing teens' behavior. Today, there are over one-thousand abstinence-until-marriage programs around the United States and one-third of public middle and high schools say that abstinence is "the main message in their sex education." Abstinence organizations do more than just tell teens to say no to unwed sex: they teach young people the skills they need to practice abstinence. Classes cover many topics including self-esteem building, self-control, decision-making, goal-setting, character education, and communication skills. Choosing the Best, Teen-Aid, Inc., and Operation Keepsake are just a few of the many effective abstinence programs in the U.S. . . .

Those who do not abstain from sex are likely to experience many negative consequences, both physical and emotional. Aside from the risk of pregnancy, teens have a high risk of contracting a sexually transmitted disease (STD). Each year 3 million teens—25 percent of sexually active teens—are infected with an STD. About 25 percent of all new cases of STDs occur in teenagers; two-thirds of new cases occur in young people age 15–24. Teens who engage in premarital sex are likely to experience fear about pregnancy and STDs, regret, guilt, lowered self-respect, fear of commitment, and depression. . . .

Public opinion polls show that teens value abstinence highly. Nearly all (93 percent) of teenagers believe that teens should be given a strong message from society to abstain from sex until at least after high school.[1] A 2000 poll found that 64 percent of teen girls surveyed said sexual activity is not acceptable for high-school age adolescents, even if precautions are taken to prevent pregnancy and sexually transmitted diseases.[2] Moreover, teens who have not abstained often regret being sexually active. In 2000, 63 percent of sexually active teens said they wish they had waited longer to become sexually active.[3]

Negative Consequences of Unwed Teen Sex

Teens need to be taught to save sex for marriage, because premarital sex has many negative consequences, both physical and emotional. One of the most obvious outcomes of engaging in premarital sex is having a child outside marriage; today, one-third of all births are out-of-wedlock.[4] Teen birthrates have declined since the early 1990s, but the highest unwed birthrates are among those age 20–24, followed by those 25–29.[5] This shows that many young girls abstain from sex while they are in high school, but not afterward.

Teen unwed childbearing has negative consequences for mothers, children, and society. Unwed teen mothers are likely to live in poverty and be dependent on welfare, and only about 50 percent of them are likely to finish high school while they are adolescents or young adults.[6] Children born to teen mothers are more likely than other children to have lower grades, to leave high school without graduating, to be abused or neglected, to have a child as an unmarried teenager, and to be delinquent.[7] Teen childbearing costs U.S. taxpayers an estimated $7 billion per year in social services and lost tax revenue due to government dependency.[8] The gross annual cost to society of unwed childbearing and its consequences is $29 billion, which includes the administration of welfare and foster care programs, building and maintaining additional prisons, as well as lower education and resultant lost productivity among unwed parents.[9]

Aside from the risk of pregnancy, teens have a high risk of contracting a sexually transmitted disease (STD). Each year 3 million teens—25 percent of sexually active teens—are infected with an STD.[10] About 25 percent of all new cases of STDs occur in teenagers; two-thirds of new cases occur in young people age 15–24.[11]

Chlamydia and gonorrhea are two of the most common curable STDs among sexually active teens. According to the Centers for Disease Control, gonorrhea rates are highest among 15- to 19-year-old females and 20- to 24-year old males, and more than five to 10 percent of teen females are currently infected with chlamydia.[12] If these diseases are untreated, they can lead to pelvic inflammatory disease, infertility, and ectopic pregnancy.[13] Studies have found that up to 15 percent of sexually active teenage women are infected with the human papillomavirus (HPV), an incurable virus that is present in nearly all cervical cancers.[14]

In addition to being at risk for STDs, unwed sexually active teens are likely to experience negative emotional consequences and to become both more promiscuous and less interested in marriage. Teens who engage in premarital sex are likely to experience fear about pregnancy and STDs, regret, guilt, lowered self-respect, fear of commitment, and depression.[15] Also, adolescents who engage in unwed sex at a younger age are much more likely to have multiple sex partners. Among young people between the ages of 15–24 who have had sex before age 18, 75 percent had two or more partners and 45 percent had four or more partners. Among those who first had sex after age 19, just 20 percent had more than one partner and one percent had four or more partners.[16] Premarital sex can also cause teens to view marriage less favorably. A 1994 study of college freshmen found that non-virgins with multiple sex partners were more likely to view marriage as difficult and involving a loss of personal freedom and happiness. Virgins were more likely to view marriage as "enjoyable.". . .[17]

"Safe Sex" or "Comprehensive Sex Education" Programs

In addition to the influence of their parents, teens are also affected by the messages on sex and abstinence that they receive in school. Unfortunately, the majority of schools teach "safe sex," "comprehensive," or so-called "abstinence plus" programs, believing that it is best for children to have all the information they need about sexuality and to make their own decisions about sex.[18] Abstinence is downplayed and sexual activity and condom use are encouraged in these curriculums, because it is assumed that kids are eventually going to have sex. A 2002 report by the Physicians Consortium, which investigated comprehensive sex programs promoted by the Centers for Disease Control, reveals that abstinence is barely mentioned and condom use is clearly advocated in these curriculums. Not only do students learn how to obtain condoms, but they also practice putting them on cucumbers or penile models. Masturbation, body massages, bathing together, and fantasizing are listed as "ways to be close" in one curriculum. . . .[19]

The Effectiveness of Abstinence-Until-Marriage Programs

Abstinence-until-marriage programs, on the other hand, teach young people to save sex for marriage, and their message has been very effective in changing teen's behavior. According to the Physicians Resource Council, the drop in teen birthrates during the 1990s was due not to increased contraceptive use among teens, but to sexual abstinence.[20] This correlates with the decrease in sexual activity among unwed teens. In 1988, 51 percent of unwed girls between the ages of 15 and 19 had engaged in sexual intercourse compared to 49 percent in 1995. This decrease also occurred among unwed boys, declining from 60 percent to 55 percent between 1988 and 1995.[21]

Today, there are over one thousand abstinence-until-marriage programs around the United States, and one-third of public middle and high schools say both that abstinence is "the main message in their sex education" and that abstinence is taught as "the only option for young people."[22] Started by non-profit or faith-based groups, these programs teach young people to save sex for marriage. However, abstinence organizations do more than just tell teens to say no to unwed sex: They teach young people the skills they need to practice abstinence. Classes cover many topics including self-esteem building, self-control, decision making, goal setting, character education, and communication skills. Sexually transmitted disease, the realities of parenthood and anatomy are also discussed.[23] The effectiveness of birth control may be discussed, but it is neither provided nor promoted in these programs.

Choosing the Best, an abstinence program based in Marietta, Georgia, and started in 1993, has developed curriculum and materials that are used in over two thousand school districts in 48 states. Students in public or private schools are taught abstinence by their teachers, who have been trained by Choosing the Best's staff. Appropriate for 6th through 12th graders, the curriculum teaches students the consequences of premarital sex, the benefits of abstaining until marriage, how to make a virginity pledge, refusal skills, and character education. Choosing the Best involves parents in their children's lessons and teaches them how to teach abstinence to their children. . . .

This abstinence program has contributed to lower teen-pregnancy rates in Georgia. In Columbus, Georgia, Choosing the Best's materials were used in all 8th grades for a period of four years. A study requested by the Georgia State Board of Education to examine the effectiveness of this curriculum found a 38-percent reduction in pregnancies among middle-school students in Muscogee County between 1997 and 1999. Other large school districts that did not implement Choosing the Best's program experienced only a 6-percent reduction in teen pregnancies during those same years.

Teen-Aid, Inc., based in Spokane, Washington, has been promoting abstinence until marriage and character education for over twenty years. This program seeks to teach young people the knowledge and skills they need to make good decisions and to achieve goals. Parent-child communication is a key component of the Teen-Aid curriculum, as parents are involved in every lesson. In 1999–2000, over 41,000 families in public schools, churches, and community organizations used these materials.

A 1999 study conducted by Whitworth College in Spokane, Washington found many positive results among teens in Edinburg, Texas who were taught the Teen-Aid curriculum. On the pretest administered to students before the course, 62 percent said "having sex as a teenager would make it harder for them to get a good job or be successful in a career," compared to 71 percent on the post test. When asked if they were less likely to have sexual intercourse before they got married, 47 percent responded yes on the pretest, compared to 54 percent after taking the course. . . .[24]

Operation Keepsake, a Cleveland, Ohio-based abstinence program started in 1988, has its "For Keeps" curriculum in 90 public and private schools in the greater Cleveland area. It is presently taught to over 25,000 students, including those in middle and high school, as well as college freshmen. Along with a classroom component, this program also includes peer mentoring, guest speakers, opportunities to make an abstinence pledge, and parental involvement.

Case Western Reserve University evaluated Operation Keepsake's program in 2001, finding that it is having a positive impact on adolescents' beliefs and behavior regarding abstinence. Over nine hundred 7th and 8th graders completed the pretests and posttests. According to the study, the program had "a clear and sustainable impact on abstinence beliefs" because students in the program had "higher abstinence-until-marriage values" at the follow-up survey than did those in the control group, who did not attend the abstinence program. . . .[25]

Virginity pledges are also successful in encouraging sexual abstinence among unwed teens. A 2001 study based on the National Longitudinal Study of Adolescent Health . . . found that teens who take a virginity pledge are 34 percent less likely to have sex before marriage compared to those who do not pledge, even after controlling for factors such as family structure, race, self-esteem, and religiosity. . . .[26]

Conclusion

These are only some of the many abstinence-until-marriage programs in the United States. Their success in changing young people's views and behavior regarding abstinence is due to their telling the truth about sex to young people: that it is meant to be saved for marriage and that it is possible to live a chaste life. Along with this message, they give kids the encouragement and skills they need to save themselves for marriage. . . .

Notes

1. "The Cautious Generation? Teens Tell Us About Sex, Virginity, and 'The Talk,'" National Campaign to Prevent Teen Pregnancy, April 27, 2000.

2. Ibid.

3. "Not Just Another Thing to Do: Teens Talk About Sex, Regret and the Influence of Their Parents," National Campaign to Prevent Teen Pregnancy, June 30, 2000.

4. Joyce A. Martin et al., *Births: Final Data for 2001*, National Vital Statistics Reports 51, December 18, 2002, National Center for Health Statistics, Table C.

5. Bridget Maher, *The Family Portrait: A Compilation of Data, Research and Public Opinion on the Family*, Family Research Council, 2002, p. 73, 162.

6. Rebecca Maynard, *Kids Having Kids: Economic and Social Consequences of Teen Pregnancy*, The Urban Institute, 1997, p. 2–5.

7. Ibid, p. 205–229, 257–281, Judith Levine, Harold Pollack and Maureen E. Comfort, "Academic and Behavioral Outcomes Among the Children of Young Mothers,"

Journal of Marriage and Family 63 (May 2001): 355–369 and Amy Conseur et al., "Maternal and Perinatal Risk Factors for Later Delinquency," *Pediatrics* 99 (June 1997): 785–790.

8. Rebecca A. Maynard, ed., *Kids Having Kids: A Robin Hood Foundation Special Report on the Costs of Adolescent Childbearing,* The Robin Hood Foundation, 1996, p. 19.

9. Ibid, pp. 20, 88–91.

10. The Alan Guttmacher Institute, "Teen Sex and Pregnancy," *Facts in Brief,* 1999.

11. Linda L. Alexander, ed., et al., "Sexually Transmitted Diseases in America: How Many Cases and at What Cost?" The Kaiser Family Foundation, December 1998, 8.

12. Centers for Disease Control, *Tracking the Hidden Epidemics: Trends in the United States 2000,* 4.

13. The Alan Guttmacher Institute, "Teen Sex and Pregnancy."

14. Ibid. See also the Kaiser Family Foundation, "HPV (Human Papillomavirus) and Cervical Cancer," *Fact Sheet,* July 2001.

15. Tom and Judy Lickona, *Sex, Love and You* (Notre Dame: Ave Maria Press, 1994), 62–77.

16. Centers for Disease Control, "Current Trends: Premarital Sexual Experience Among Adolescent Women—United States, 1970–1988," *Morbidity and Mortality Weekly Report* 39 (January 4, 1991): 929–932. . . .

17. Connie J. Salts et al., "Attitudes Toward Marriage and Premarital Sexual Activity of College Freshmen," *Adolescence* 29 (Winter 1994): 775–779.

18. Tina Hoff and Liberty Greene et al., "Sex Education in America: A Series of National Surveys of Students, Parents, Teachers, and Principals," Kaiser Family Foundation, September 2000, 16.

19. The Physicians Consortium, "Sexual Messages in Government-Promoted Programs and Today's Youth Culture," April 2002.

20. Cheryl Wetzstein, "Drop in Teen Birthrates Attributed to Abstinence," *The Washington Times,* February 11, 1999, A6.

21. Joyce C. Abma and Freya L. Sonenstein, *Sexual Activity and Contraceptive Practices Among Teenagers in the United States, 1988 and 1995,* Series 23: Data from the National Survey of Family Growth, National Center for Health Statistics, Washington, DC., April 2001, Table 1.

22. Tina Hoff and Liberty Greene et al., "Sex Education in America: A Series of National Surveys of Students, Parents, Teachers, and Principals," 14.

23. Barbara Devaney et al., "The Evaluation of Abstinence Education Programs Funded Under Title V Section 510: Interim Report," Mathematica Policy Research, Inc., April 2002, 14.

24. Raja S. Tanas, "Report on the Teen-Aid Abstinence-Education Program Fifth-Year Evaluation 1998–1999, Whitworth College, Spokane, WA, July 1999.

25. Elaine Borawski et al., "Evaluation of the Teen Pregnancy Prevention Programs Funded Through the Wellness Block Grant (1999–2000), Case Western Reserve University, March 23, 2001.

26. Peter S. Bearman and Hannah Bruckner, "Promising the Future: Virginity Pledges and First Intercourse," *American Journal of Sociology* 106 (January 2001): 859–912.

Debra Hauser

 **NO**

Five Years of Abstinence-Only-Until-Marriage Education: Assessing the Impact

Introduction

Since 1991, rates of teenage pregnancy and birth have declined significantly in the United States. These are welcome trends. Yet, teens in the United States continue to suffer from the highest birthrate and one of the highest rates of sexually transmitted infections (STIs) in the industrialized world. Debate over the best way to help teens avoid, or reduce, their sexual risk-taking behavior has polarized many youth-serving professionals. On one side are those that support comprehensive sex education—education that promotes abstinence but includes information about contraception and condoms to build young people's knowledge, attitudes and skills for when they do become sexually active. On the other side are those that favor abstinence-only-until-marriage—programs that promote "abstinence from sexual activity outside marriage as the expected standard" of behavior. Proponents of abstinence-only programs believe that providing information about the health benefits of condoms or contraception contradicts their message of abstinence-only and undermines its impact. As such, abstinence-only programs provide no information about contraception beyond failure rates.

In 1996, Congress signed into law the Personal Responsibility & Work Opportunities Reconciliation Act, or "welfare reform." Attached was the provision, later set out in Section 510(b) of Title V of the Social Security Act, appropriating $250 million dollars over five years for state initiatives promoting sexual abstinence outside of marriage as the only acceptable standard of behavior for young people.

For the first five years of the initiative, every state but California participated in the program. (California had experimented with its own abstinence-only initiative in the early 1990's. The program was terminated in February 1996, when evaluation results found the program to be ineffective.) From 1998 to 2003, almost a half a billion dollars in state and federal funds were appropriated to support the Title V initiative. A report, detailing the results from the federally funded evaluation of select Title V programs, was due to be released more than a year ago. Last year, Congress extended "welfare reform" and, with it, the Title V abstinence-only-until-marriage funding without benefit of this, as yet unreleased, report.

As the first five-year funding cycle of Title V came to a close, a few state-funded evaluations became public. Others were completed with little or no fanfare. This document reviews the findings from the 10 evaluations that Advocates for Youth was able to identify. Advocates for Youth also includes evaluation results from California's earlier attempt at a statewide abstinence-only initiative.

Available Evaluations

Ten states made some form of evaluation results available for review. For Arizona, Florida, Iowa, Maryland, Minnesota, Oregon, Pennsylvania, and Washington, Advocates was able to locate evaluation results from state Title V programs. For Missouri and Nebraska, Advocates located evaluation findings from at least one program among those funded through the state's Title V initiative. Finally, the evaluation of California's abstinence-only program was published in a peer-reviewed journal and readily available.

Funding*

During the first five years of abstinence-only-until-marriage Title V programming, the 10 states received about $45.5 million in federal funds. To further support the initiatives and to cover their required funding match, these states appropriated about $34 million in additional funds over the five years. In addition, California spent $15 million in state funds between 1991 and 1994 to support its abstinence-only initiative. In sum, the program efforts discussed in this paper cost an estimated $94.5 million in federal and state dollars.

Program Components

For the most part, Title V funds were administered through states' departments of health and then sub-granted to abstinence-only contractors within each state. Program components varied from state to state and from contractor to contractor within each state. However, all programs discussed in this document included an abstinence-only curriculum, delivered to young people in schools or through community-based agencies. Popular curricula included: *Education Now Babies Later (ENABL), Why Am I Tempted? (WAIT), Family Accountability Communicating Teen Sexuality (FACTS), Choosing the Best Life, Managing Pressures before Marriage,* and AC Green's *Game Plan,* among others. Some programs included peer education, health fairs, parent outreach, and/or *Baby Think it Over* simulators. Some states supplemented their educational programs with media campaigns, also funded through Title V.

Evaluation Designs

The 11 evaluations summarized in this document represent those Advocates for Youth could uncover through extensive research. The quality of the evaluation designs varied greatly. Most evaluations employed a simple pretest/posttest survey design. Slightly fewer than half (five) assessed the significance of changes from pre- to posttest, using a comparison group. Additionally, seven evaluations included some form of follow-up to assess the program's impact over time, although results are not yet available for two. Three of these seven also included a comparison group. For those programs that included follow-up, surveys were administered at three to 17 months after students completed their abstinence-only-until-marriage program. . . .

Summary of Results

Evaluation of these 11 programs showed few short-term benefits and no lasting, positive impact. A few programs showed mild success at improving attitudes and intentions to abstain. No program was able to demonstrate a positive impact on sexual behavior over time. A description follows of short- and long-term impacts, by indicator.

Short-Term Impacts of State Abstinence-Only Programs

In 10 programs, evaluation measured the short-term impact of the program on at least one indicator, including attitudes favoring abstinence, intentions to abstain, and/or sexual behavior. Overall, programs were most successful at improving participants' attitudes towards abstinence and were least likely to positively affect participants' sexual behaviors.

Attitudes endorsing abstinence   10 evaluations tested for short-term changes in attitudes.

- Three of 10 programs had no significant impact on attitudes (Maryland, Missouri, and Nebraska);
- Four of 10 showed increases in attitudes favorable to abstinence (Arizona, Florida, Oregon, and Washington);
- Three of 10 showed mixed results (California, Iowa, and Pennsylvania).**

Intentions to abstain   Nine evaluations measured short-term changes in intentions.

- Four of nine programs showed no significant impact on participants' intentions to abstain (California, Maryland, Nebraska, and Oregon);
- Three of nine programs showed a favorable impact on intentions to abstain (Arizona, Florida, and Washington);
- Two of nine programs showed mixed results (Iowa and Pennsylvania).**

Sexual behaviors   Six evaluations measured short-term changes in sexual behavior.

- Three of six programs had no impact on sexual behavior (California, Maryland, and Missouri).

- Two of six programs reported increases in sexual behavior from pre- to posttest (Florida and Iowa). It was unclear whether the increases were due to youth's maturation or to a program's effect, as none of these evaluations included a comparison group.
- One of the six programs showed mixed results (Pennsylvania).**

Long-Term Impacts of State Abstinence-Only Programs

Seven evaluations included some form of follow-up survey to assess the impact of the abstinence-only programs over time. Results from two of these are not yet available (Nebraska and Oregon). Of the remaining five, three were of statewide initiatives (Arizona, California, and Minnesota). Two were evaluations of programs within statewide initiatives (Missouri's *Life Walk* Program and Pennsylvania's LaSalle Program). All five evaluations included questions to assess changes in participants' attitudes and behaviors between pretest/posttest and follow-up. Four also measured changes in intentions to abstain. Three evaluations included a comparison group.

Attitudes endorsing abstinence   Five evaluations included assessment of changes in attitudes.

Four of five evaluations showed no long-term positive impact on participants' attitudes. That is, participants' attitudes towards abstinence either declined at follow-up or there was no evidence that participating in the abstinence-only program improved teens' attitudes about abstinence relative to the comparison groups, at three to 17 months after taking the abstinence-only program (Arizona, California, Missouri, and Pennsylvania's LaSalle Program).

Follow-up surveys in Minnesota showed mixed results.

Intentions to abstain   Four evaluations measured long-term intentions to abstain.

Three of four evaluations showed no long-term positive impact on participants' intentions to abstain from sexual intercourse. That is, participants' intentions either declined significantly at follow-up or there was no statistically significant difference in participants' attitudes relative to controls at follow-up (Arizona, California, and Minnesota).

In one of the four (Pennsylvania's LaSalle Program), evaluation showed a positive impact at follow-up on program participants' intentions to abstain relative to comparison youth.

Sexual behavior   Five programs measured long-term impacts on sexual behavior.

No evaluation demonstrated any impact on reducing teens' sexual behavior at follow-up, three to 17 months after the program ended (Arizona, California, Minnesota, Missouri, or Pennsylvania's LaSalle Program).

Comparisons of Abstinence-Only-Until-Marriage versus Comprehensive Sex Education

Two evaluations—Iowa's and the Pennsylvania Fulton County program—compared the impact of comprehensive sex education with that of abstinence-only-until-marriage programs.

- In Iowa, abstinence-only students were slightly more likely than comprehensive sex education participants to feel strongly about wanting to postpone sex, but less likely to feel that their goals should not include teen pregnancy. There was little to no difference between the abstinence-only students and those in the comprehensive sex education program in understanding of why they should wait to have sex. Evaluation did not include comparison of data on the sexual behavior of participants in the two types of programs.
- In Fulton County, Pennsylvania, results found few to no differences between the abstinence-only and comprehensive approaches in attitudes towards sexual behavior. Evaluators found that, regardless of which program was implemented in the seventh and eighth grades, sexual attitudes, intentions, and behaviors were similar by the end of the 10th grade.

Discussion

These evaluation results—from the first five-year cycle of funding for abstinence-only-until-marriage under Section 510(b) of Title V of the Social Security Act—reflect the results of other studies. In a 1994 review of sex education programs, Kirby *et al* assessed all the studies available at the time of school-based, abstinence-only programs that had received peer review and that measured attitudes, intentions, *and* behavior. Kirby *et al* found that none of the three abstinence-only programs was effective in producing a statistically significant impact on sexual behaviors in program participants relative to comparisons. In a 1997 report for the National Campaign to Prevent Teen Pregnancy, Doug Kirby reviewed evaluations from six abstinence-only programs, again finding no program that produced a statistically significant change in sexual behavior. This was again confirmed in 2000 when another review by Kirby found no abstinence-only program that produced statistically significant changes in sexual behaviors among program youth relative to comparisons. This failure of abstinence-only programs to produce behavior change was among the central concerns expressed by some authors of the evaluations included in this document. . . . It is important to note that a great deal of research contradicts the belief that changes in knowledge and attitudes alone will necessarily result in behavior change.

A few evaluators also noted the failure of abstinence-only programs to address the needs of sexually active youth. Survey data from many of the programs indicated that sexually experienced teens were enrolled in most of the abstinence-only programs studied. For example:

- In Erie County, Pennsylvania, researchers found that 42 percent of the female participants were sexually active by the second year of the program.
- In Clinton County, Pennsylvania, data collected from program participants in the seventh, eighth, and ninth grades showed a dramatic increase in the proportion of program females who experienced first sexual intercourse over time (six, nine, and 30 percent, respectively, by grade).
- In Minnesota, 12 percent of the eighth grade program participants were sexually active at posttest.
- In Arizona, 19 percent of program participants were sexually active at follow-up. Concurrently, Arizona's evaluators found that youth's intent to pursue abstinence declined significantly at follow-up, regardless of whether the student took another abstinence-only class. Eighty percent of teens reported that they were likely to become sexually active by the time they were 20 years old.

Abstinence-only programs provide these youth with no information, other than abstinence, regarding how to protect themselves from pregnancy, HIV, and other STIs.

A third, related concern of evaluators was abstinence-only programs' failure to provide positive information about contraception and condoms. Evaluators noted more than once that programs' emphasis on the failure rates of contraception, including condoms, left youth ambivalent, at best, about using them.

- In Clinton County, Pennsylvania, researchers noted that, of those participants that reported experiencing first sexual intercourse during ninth grade, only about half used any form of contraception.
- Arizona's evaluation team found that program participants' attitudes about birth control became less favorable from pre- to posttest. They noted that this was probably a result of the "program's focus on the failure rates of contraceptives as opposed to their availability, use and access."

Conclusion

Abstinence-only programs show little evidence of sustained (long-term) impact on attitudes and intentions. Worse, they show some negative impacts on youth's willingness to use contraception, including condoms, to prevent negative sexual health outcomes related to sexual intercourse. Importantly, only in one state did any program demonstrate short-term success in delaying the initiation of sex; none of these programs demonstrates evidence of long-term success in delaying sexual initiation among youth exposed to the programs or any evidence of success in reducing other sexual risk-taking behaviors among participants.

Notes

*   In federal fiscal year 2003, the 10 states discussed here with evaluations of Title V programs received $8,810,281 in federal funds. Under the law, states are required to provide matching funds of three state-raised dollars for every four federal dollars received. Thus in 2003, the 10 states supplied $7,268,060 in state dollars, bringing the total of public monies to Title V funded abstinence-only-until-marriage programs to $16,078,341.

**   Mixed results indicated that attitudes changed in both desired and undesired directions, either by survey questions within one initiative, or by individual programs within an initiative.

POSTSCRIPT

Should "Abstinence-Until-Marriage" Be the Only Message for Teens?

The Healthy People 2010: Understanding and Improving Health report (U.S. Department of Health and Human Services, 2000) suggests that as many as 50 percent of all adolescents are sexually active. The *National Youth Risk Behavior Survey* (1998) reported similar findings, with rates higher for boys than girls, and with 7.2 percent of youth having sexual intercourse before age 13. The *National Survey of American Attitudes on Substance Abuse IX: Teen Dating Practices and Sexual Activity* found that 28 percent of 12-year-olds have sexually active friends, and this rises to 79 percent for 17-year-olds. The high rates of sexual activity among young people are especially troubling, given that a large and disproportionate percentage of sexually transmitted diseases and unintended pregnancies occur among adolescents. Approximately 25 percent of teenagers who are active sexually will acquire a STD in a given year, nearly as many sexually active adolescent females (20 percent) become pregnant, and the overwhelming majority (85 percent) of these pregnancies are unplanned.

In reality we know that during the teen years, young people go through many powerful hormonal, emotional, and social changes. They discover sexual feelings without fully understanding their meaning or what to do with them. They often end up engaging in sexual activity that is not pleasant (especially females) and often do not practice safe sex (using condoms or dental dams, for example). There are powerful gender-related dating and sexual scripts that make it more difficult for adolescents to negotiate their sexual experiences. These scripts guide expectations: notions of "real" sex, who is supposed to initiate, and what the experience is supposed to be like (e.g., an ideal), as well as the consequences for engaging (or not) in sexual activity. Males may feel like they have to be sexually active to be seen as a "real" man and run the risk of being called "gay" if they refrain. Females have to deal with the stereotypes of "prude" or "slut." Many adolescent girls report they engage in oral sex to be popular.

Each side of the sexuality debate is working with what it considers to be a logical presumption. For AOUM proponents, the surest way to avoid an unintended pregnancy or STI is to not do anything sexually until in a committed, monogamous relationship—which, to them, is only acceptable within the context of marriage. If people do not engage in the behaviors, they cannot be exposed to the negatives. Since AOUM supporters also believe that marriage is a commitment that is accompanied by a promise of monogamy, or sexual exclusivity, it is, for them, the only appropriate choice for teens.

For comprehensive sexuality education proponents, the logic is that sexual exploration is a normal part of adolescents' development. They believe that the "just say no" approach to sexual behaviors is as unrealistic as it is unhealthy. Rooted in education, social learning, and health belief theories, comprehensive sexuality education programs believe that youth can make wise decisions about their sexual health if given the proper information. Comprehensive programs can address the psychosocial issues, and the role of gender-role expectations in ways that AOUM cannot.

Suggested Readings

Charles Abraham, Mary Rogers Gillmore, Gerjo Kok, and Herman P. Schaalma, "Sex Education as Health Promotion: What Does It Take?" *Archives of Sexual Behavior, 33* (2004): 259–269.

Paul Florsheim, (2003). *Adolescent Romantic Relations and Sexual Behavior: Theory, Research, and Practical Implications* (Mahwah, NJ: Lawrence Erlbaum Associates, 2003).

Douglas Kirby, "The Impact of Schools and School Programs upon Adolescent Sexual Behavior," *The Journal of Sex Research, 9* (2002): 27–33.

J. Mark Halstead and Michael J. Reiss, *Values in Sex Education: From Principles to Practice* (London: Routledge Falmer, 2003).

Karen J. Maschke, ed., *Reproduction, Sexuality, and the Family: Gender and American Law: The Impact of the Law on the Lives of Women* (New York: Garland Publishing, 1997).

ISSUE 20

Can Women's Sexuality Be Free from Traditional Gender Constraints?

YES: Elizabeth Sheff, from "Polyamorous Women, Sexual Subjectivity and Power," *Journal of Contemporary Ethnography* (2005)

NO: Yuko Yamamiya, Thomas F. Cash, and J. Kevin Thompson, from "Sexual Experiences among College Women: The Differential Effects of General versus Contextual Body Images on Sexuality," *Sex Roles* (2006)

ISSUE SUMMARY

YES: Elizabeth Sheff conducted an ethnographic study that suggests that engaging in nontraditional relationships can help women reject sexual objectification and enlarge their sexual subjectivity.

NO: In contrast, Yuko Yamamiya, Thomas F. Cash, and J. Kevin Thompson, in the department of psychology at Old Dominion University, suggest that the objectification of women's bodies in Western culture results in lower sexual self-efficacy and sexual difficulties.

Sexuality has been identified by feminists as a culturally important domain for gender relations and politics. In Victorian times, self-control, discipline, delayed gratification, self-sacrifice, and repression characterized sexuality. Religious authorities defined the moral boundaries of right and wrong sexual activities. Contemporary conservative religious perspectives continue to restrict sexuality to procreation in the family context. Women's individual pleasure, exploration, and sexual identity are seen as antithetical or even threatening to procreative sexuality within the family. The patriarchal influence of Victorian times castigated women into a role of sexual subordination and ignorance, shame, and passivity. The pleasures of the body were considered "dirty."

The locus of definition and control then shifted to a medical model, proscribing sexual activity outside of a procreative model as abnormal and evidence of illness. In the medical model, sexuality is seen as located within the person as a set of natural physiological drives. The dominant medical model of sexuality, the Human Sexual Response Cycle (HSRC) was advanced in 1966 by William Masters and Virginia Johnson. The HSRC describes the sequence of physiological changes that occur during sexual activity and presumes that the sexes have the same sexual response cycles. Critics argue that this model of sexuality is biased toward men's sexual interests. They argue that although men's and women's sexuality may be more similar than different physiologically, gender inequality is a social reality that impacts that HSRC. Furthermore, sexuality is not just an internal or genital sensation of desire, arousal, and orgasm. There are also important *social* sexual realities.

Some contemporary sexologists (scholars who engage in the scientific study of sexuality) challenge a biological or "natural" approach to sex by arguing that the sociocultural context is central in defining everything about sexual experience. The sociocultural context creates and shapes sexuality by defining "sexual scripts," which are enacted in physical performance. Sexual scripts, of which expectations are a key element, guide sexual behavior by helping participants define the situation and plot out appropriate behavior.

Males are socialized to be more sexually aware, active, assertive, and entitled. They learn to value varied sexual experience and sexual gratification, for which they are often rewarded with the esteem of peers. Females generally are socialized to limit sexual activity and to tie sex to romance and beauty in which there is greater concern for affection than for sex. They learn to value intimacy and emotional communion. Females are often treated as and consequently see themselves as sexual *objects,* not subjects with sexual agency of their own. Many scholars argue that sex role socialization creates fundamental gender differences and inequalities, leading to heterosexually based scripts and experience.

Indeed, it seems that females are in a no-win situation regarding their sexuality. While heterosexual females are rewarded early on for abstinence, later they receive pressure from male partners to have sex. Such females are considered "prudes" if they do not have sex, "sluts" or "loose" if they do have sex. Females learn that sex is "dirty" but they feel like their worth as a female is determined by their ability to attract and please males. HIV prevention educator Carolyn Laub explains how such sexual gender ideology is related to the practice of safer sex strategies and sexual risk. According to Laub, a female who is prepared for sex (e.g., carrying condoms) signals that she is sexually aware and therefore "easy" or dirty. Likewise, a female who talks with a potential sex partner about safer-sex issues may imply that she has been sexually active and therefore "loose."

The following selections illustrate a stark contrast between patriarchally delimitted women's sexuality and the possibility of sexual freedom and power for women. Elizabeth Sheff describes her study of polyamorous women—women who she says, by engaging in long-term romantic, sexual, and/or affective relationships with multiple people (female or male) simultaneously, are able to reject sexual objectification and find a subjective sexuality that is free of societal constraints. Her analyses suggest that polyamorous women report feelingless constrained by gender roles, an increased sex drive, deeper connections with other women, and more powerful. The Yamaniya selection links the objectification of women's bodies to a preoccupation with body image during sex. The association can result in lower self-confidence to refuse sex, reduced sexual assertiveness, lower sexual self-efficacy, and more difficult sexual decision making.

YES

Elizabeth Sheff

Polyamorous Women, Sexual Subjectivity and Power

In the shifting gendered and sexual social landscape of the early twenty-first century, multiple-partner relationships remain eroticized and undertheorized. Pornographic films and magazines frequently present images of multiple-partner sex, most often of multiple women or a man with several women. Rather than challenging gendered and sexual roles or enlarging women's sexual sphere, these scenes actually reinforce heteronormativity. These highly sexualized images fail to capture the lived experiences of the people, especially the women, who actually engage in multiple partner relationships. Feminist theorists have criticized such androcentric images of women's sexuality and have argued instead for an agentic female sexual subjectivity.

Polyamory is a form of relationship in which people have multiple romantic, sexual, and/or affective partners. It differs from swinging in its emphasis on long-term, emotionally intimate relationships and from adultery with its focus on honesty and (ideally) full disclosure of the network of sexual relationships to all who participate in or are affected by them. Both men and women have access to additional partners in polyamorous relationships, distinguishing them from polygamy. . . .

The study of polyamory is essential to forming a more complete understanding of women's sexual subjectivity and power. My analysis provides empirical evidence that suggests new complexities associated with multiple-partner relationships and expands sociological understanding of women's sexuality by investigating a previously unexamined area of sexual subjectivity. To explore polyamorous women's potential to enlarge the concept of sexual subjectivity through engagement in nontraditional relationships and their attempts to reject sexual objectification, I analyzed data based on seven years of participant observation and in-depth interviews. . . .

While social theorists have examined multiple-partner relationships in the context of bisexuality, open marriage, adultery, and swinging, these discussions have focused on variations within a conventional sexual framework. Analysis indicates that swingers maintain conservative attitudes regarding gender roles, heterosexuality, and politics. . . . Addition of polyamory to the catalog of women's sexual identities augments contemporary sociological

From *Journal of Contemporary Ethnography*, vol. 34, no. 3, June 2005, pp. 251–267, 269, 271–273, 275–280. Copyright © 2005 by Sage Publications. Reprinted by permission.

research by acknowledging an alternate form of sexuality that offers women expanded horizons of choice.

[S]exual subjectivity [is] "a person's experience of herself as a sexual being, who feels entitled to sexual pleasure and sexual safety, who makes active sexual choices, and who has an identity as a sexual being. Sexual desire is at the heart of sexual subjectivity." . . . Sexual subjectivity for girls and women contrasts heterocentric, patriarchal objectification in which female sexuality is commodified or colonized in the service and convenience of men. Sexual subjectivity is integrally linked with power—the power to appropriate sexuality, relational power, and social power connected to defining versions of sexuality outside rigidly controlled norms as deviant. Women with no access to their own sexual subjectivity have bodies that Tolman terms "silent," disempowered by being spoken for and defined by masculine ideas and desires. . . . Some women refuse the mandates of androcentric versions of sexuality and redefine themselves as sexual agents. . . .

By simultaneously challenging and participating in aspects of sexual subjectivity and sexual objectification, polyamorous women inhabit the borderland between *emphasized femininity,* or a version of womanhood that is "defined around compliance with this subordination and is oriented to accommodating the interests and desires of men" and an alternative, noncompliant form of femininity. . . .

If, conventional sexual arrangements are designed to silence women's authentic spirits, then an alternative erotic system could offer women a more authentic expression of sexual subjectivity from which to "rise up empowered." Through their involvement in polyamory, the women in my sample explored new roles and avenues of sexuality while shifting the balance of power in their relationships. . . . In this article, I explore the impact the alternate sexual system of polyamory exerts on some women's lives. In so doing, I detail some of the ways in which polyamorous women expand "normal" social roles, discuss their sexual lives and identities, and explore the novel and traditional forms of power polyamorous practice engenders for these women's relationships.

Method

This article is part of a larger project based on participant observation and in-depth interviews I conducted during a seven-year period (1996 to 2003). . . .

My data for this article come from extensive participant observation, including attendance at support group meetings, workshops, and national polyamorists conferences, as well as informal conversations and forty in-depth interviews (twenty women and twenty men). Reflecting mainstream polyamorous communities in the Western United States, my respondents were in their mid-30s to late 50s and tended toward middle- and upper-middle-class socioeconomic status, usually college educated, overwhelmingly white, and frequently employed as professionals in computer or counseling/therapy fields. I used semistructured interviews that lasted from one and one half to two hours, a format that yields data suitable for answering questions about members' interpretations, actions, and interactions. . . .

I analyzed the interview data and my field notes by adjusting analytical categories to fit the emerging theoretical concepts. Once the theoretical concepts emerged, I constructed clusters of participant's experiences to further develop my theories. I used subsequent interviews and field observation to verify the validity of these theories, as well as checking for the boundaries and variations of common themes.

[Concepts and Themes]

[1] Expanded Roles

Some polyamorous women who felt constrained and disempowered by monogamy reported a sense of release upon embarking on polyamorous relationships. Departure from accepted forms of relationships required polyamorous women to form new roles or expand roles previously available to them as monogamists. The women in my sample expanded their familial, cultural, gendered, and sexual roles.

[a] Family and monogamous culture.   Peck, a thirty-six-year-old white magazine editor and mother of three, rejected the traditional wifely role she observed in her family of origin and had originally replicated in her monogamous marriage: "Women got married, had children, raised the children and stayed in the home, that's what I was taught and brought up with. And that was the role I was following. . . . That period in my life, I was thinking and wanting things different and was starting to get my own empowerment as a woman, changing roles, and wanting more." "Wanting more" involved not only pursuing higher levels of education but also rejecting a form of sexuality and family that was not working for her and forging a polyamorous alternative. Polyamory provided the impetus for Peck to shift long-standing roles she found ill fit. . . .

[b] Gender roles.   The majority of the polyamorous women in my sample reported shifting gender roles resulting from, or precipitating, participation in polyamory. Yansa, a twenty-nine-year-old African American health care provider and stepmother of one, related her reasons for agreeing to monogamous relationships even though she knew she desired multiple partners.

> I didn't want to hurt my partner's feelings. I felt that I wanted to be the righteous one and do the right thing for them and for the relationship. . . . When we became committed and like kind of in a monogamous relationship I think the relationship immediately went down hill from there. And it was more of a situation where he had sown his wild oats. He was tired of playing around. I was the one, but I had just begun and it was like, quelled this desire and I was just like, this is not enough for me. And he was like, this is enough for me, and I said, we have a problem.

Yansa initially conformed to a traditionally feminine role of ignoring her own desire for multiple partners in favor of being "righteous" and engaging in the monogamy her partner desired. Eventually, she came to define their disparate needs as "a problem" and transitioned to a polyamorous relationship style and identity. . . .

[c] Sexual roles.   Sexuality was one of the primary areas in which polyamorous women reported expanding their roles. Julia, a forty-one-year-old Lebanese American software consultant, found polyamory to be instrumental in redefining the cultural ideal of sex and sexuality that failed her personally:

> My motive of expressing my sexuality has really changed a lot since finding polyamory. . . . On the face of it, you could just say that it's been limited a lot and the things that other people usually call sex, things that involve genital contact and bringing one another to orgasm, mostly I don't do that anymore because it's too emotionally wrought for me. It's too, I just can't do it with integrity anymore. . . . So for me, when I talk about any sexual relationships or interactions I have had they've been relationships dominated overwhelmingly by what other people might just call smooching or a lot of breathing and gazing into each other's eyes and caressing and things where for me arousal is what's enjoyable and orgasm is not.

. . . [P]olyamorous women rejected a sexual and gender system that separated people with a false emphasis on small differences between men and women. Many of these polyamorous women embraced forms of sexual subjectivity that allowed them to redefine mores and social institutions such as sexuality and monogamy to better fit their own needs. Some consciously refused the subject/object dichotomy that cast women as passive objects of men's sexual satisfaction. Others simply forged novel roles without theorizing a social context. . . .

[2] Sexuality

Polyamorous women frequently discussed sexuality in support groups, social gatherings, and with their partners. These discussions emphasized sexuality in relation to polyamorous women's high sex drives, connections with other women, and bisexual identities.

[a] High sex drive.   In direct opposition to cultural mandates of female sexual submission and a double standard that requires women restrain their sexual desires, a number of polyamorous women reported viewing themselves as highly sexual people. Louise asserted that

> I have such a high sex drive and literally feel I need sex on a regular basis to feel grounded, to feel clear, to feel good, and it's just, it's very, it's like exercise for me. It feels good. I enjoy it. . . . If I haven't had sex in a while, after about three to four weeks I start climbing the walls and I get very bitchy and I'm just not in a good mood and I don't feel good and I feel on edge. Whereas if I get sex on a regular basis, I'm calm, I'm fine, I'm happy.

This description of sexual appetite would be unremarkable coming from a man, but from a woman, it contrasts dominant cultural scripts mandating women's disinterest in sex except to meet masculine needs. . . . Risking defamation by eschewing the constraints of coupledom, polyamorous women reject the power dynamic embedded in the persistent sexual double standard that continues to limit women's sexual choices and stigmatize those who refrain from living by its mandates. . . .

[b] Connections with other women.   The majority of the women in my sample viewed sexuality as a source of unity with other women, even some who had previously experienced sexuality as divisive. Louise discussed the new sense of connection she had developed with women since finding the polyamorous community:

> One of the things that has probably been the best thing about finding the poly community is meeting women that I can relate to because I haven't had women friends before now. This is the first time in my life, with a few exceptions, that I have really had close women friends. It's been wonderful to meet women who are highly sexual who don't feel threatened that I'm highly sexual. . . . And it's brought me a closeness with women that I thought I'd never have.

. . . Facile connection with other women was not universal, however, and feelings of jealousy or strife often plagued relationships among polyamorous women. . . .

[c] Bisexuality.   Bisexual women were quite numerous in polyamorous communities. In fact, bisexuality was so common among women in the polyamorous community that they had a standing joke that it allowed them to "have their Jake and Edith too!" Bisexual women were also among the highest status members of the subculture because they were most often sought as additions to existing female/male dyads to create the coveted and elusive F/M/F (female, male, female) triad. While the high status of the role might have encouraged some women to experiment with bisexuality, others had identified as bisexual long before their association with the polyamorous community. Some polyamorous women sought independent sexual relationships with other women, while others preferred group sexual encounters involving both women and men. Women in polyamorous communities interacted with varying degrees of sexuality that created social space for multiple definitions of bisexuality to coexist. . . .

Even those women who questioned the legitimacy of their bisexual identity because of their greater attraction for men made it clear that they had felt attractions to and engaged in sexual relationships with women as well as men. . . .

Clearly, the relationship between gender and bisexuality within the polyamorous community is complex. On one hand, women were sometimes sexualized as "hot bi babes" and sought to endow a new level of eroticism upon established male/female sexual relationships. On the other hand, men were sometimes objectified as sex toys but excluded from emotional relationships. In the relationally intricate world of polyamory, both scenarios operated simultaneously. Still, in patriarchal societies, men generally retain greater social and financial power on average, endowing their definitions of a given situation with greater weight. Power remains a complex issue within polyamorous relationships.

[3] Power

While both men and women involved in polyamorous subcultures tended to view women as retaining more power in polyamorous relationships, women who had initiated the entree into polyamory themselves seemed more secure in their perceived enhanced power than did women who engaged in polyamory at the behest of their male partners. Yet both types of women endured stigma and the attendant loss of power that accompanies deviation from cherished social norms such as monogamy.

[a] Women in power. Some polyamorists perceived women to have greater power in polyamorous subcultures. Emmanuella felt women's greater control of sexuality within polyamorous communities endowed them with increased social power in a potentially highly sexualized setting.

> The women seem to have more of a sexual parlance because the women decide whether sex is available and there are still some incredibly conventional notions about who approaches whom. The men seem to swing between being very sort of kid in a candy store, elated, can't believe this whole practice is happening to them, but yeah, buddy, let's get it on of thing. And the other extreme is feeling very dour about the fact that their woman is participating in this and really uncertain whether they want to have that, but are going along with it because there might be sex involved. . . .

[b] Power shifts. Other polyamorous women viewed power as more equally shared. . . .

[Some] polyamorous women maintained the ostensibly equitable balance of power via rigorous communication, an esteemed ideal of polyamorous relationships. Some discussed a division of labor with their partner(s) that included some task division but ultimately established parity, while others explained how they shared all tasks with their partners and split everything equally.

Some women asserted that polyamorous men supported and indeed sought relationships based on equality in relationship. Louise said that she found that the polyamorous men "just think differently." She explained:

> They are much more nontraditional. They aren't looking, most men that I've seen that are polyamorous aren't looking for a relationship with a woman they can control or be in charge of. They like independent women who are highly sexual, who are exciting. They like that. That's why they're

attracted to this kind of lifestyle is because they like strong women. And because of that, they're looking for an equal relationship in most cases.

This perception of equality stood in sharp contrast to some other polyamorous women's experiences with both polyamorous and monogamous men who became increasingly uncomfortable with multiple-partner sexuality as the relationship became more serious. . . .

[c] Women disempowered.   Some polyamorous relationships retained elements of a traditional power structure in which men relied on their female partners to perform a greater share of the emotional maintenance. These relationships seemed to regularly self-destruct. Louise reported encouraging Max, her husband of thirteen years and the father of two of her children, to deepen emotional intimacy with her and facilitate her attempts at friendly contact with his other lovers. Max reported feeling that these demands were excessive and refused to meet them because they "invade my privacy." . . .

Some women reported an increased sense of insecurity in their relationships with the advent of polyamory. Shelly was eloquent regarding the numerous personal costs of polyamory. She had chosen to engage in polyamory at the behest of Sven, her forty-two-year-old white bisexual husband employed as a computer consultant. Sven hoped to find another bisexual man with whom he and Shelly could establish a long-term triad. This ideal relationship proved difficult to establish, and Shelly felt some emotional pain in connection with Sven's desire for outside relationships. . . .

Regardless of potential power shifts in intimate relationships, polyamorous women retained their positions relative to the power base of monogamous society. This created some problems for them, primary among which was the anomic pain borne of failing to fit in to a monogamous society. Many discussed the social intolerance and fear of censure that sometimes accompanied their polyamorous lifestyle. Dylan described this as "being profoundly unacceptable on many levels." Peck detailed the legal difficulties that plagued her when she was married to one man but had a child with another and wanted the "real" father's name listed on the birth certificate. Ultimately she chose to divorce, partially to disentangle herself from legal issues surrounding multiple-partner relationships. . . .

Conclusions

The polyamorous women who participated in this ethnographic study related their experiences of attempting to expand their social roles, explore sexuality (especially bisexuality), and create and maintain the assorted power arrangements associated with polyamorous relationships, with varied results. Many of the women in my sample discussed feelings of power, with feelings of empowerment and disempowerment coexisting in the same relationships. While very few of the respondents explicitly linked access to shifting power dynamics and social arrangements with race, the impact of race and class privilege cannot be ignored. The fact that the majority of these polyamorous women have considerable financial and cultural capital to fall back on should their nontraditional relationships fail made this complex and somewhat risky relationship style more accessible to them than it might have been to women with fewer social or personal resources. It is no coincidence, then, that women with class and race privilege reported feeling greater freedom in relationship style. The ample resources they commanded conferred increased ability to transgress social boundaries since their cultural cachet created the safety net that allowed them to challenge monogamous social norms while simultaneously weathering the storms of the complex relationship style. My findings thus support [the] conclusion that those with power are at greater liberty to alter the social fabric around them.

The women in my sample recognized and rejected the propensity to define female sexual desire in male terms. Many were aware of their transgressions and sought the company of others who supported their efforts to reshape dominant forms of female sexuality in a way that better met their needs. They experienced some success at a gynocentric redefinition of sexuality, gaining greater social power within polyamorous communities and relationships. By rejecting conventional social mores, polyamorous women were forced to create their own roles and examine their sexual relationships. . . .

Shifts in the base of relational power may have endowed polyamorous women with greater power because their ostensible greater ease in finding additional partners translated to greater capital within the relationship. . . . Increased access to other lovers amplifies the resources of the more sought-after lover. In this market-based relationship model, successful polyamorous women (and especially bisexual women) would indeed have greater power in their relationships because of their superior market worth. At least for some polyamorous women, the expanded horizons of choice conferred greater power than that which they experienced in monogamous relationships.

This dynamic could shift as the polyamorous population ages and elderly polyamorous women potentially outnumber their male counterparts. Such numerical imbalance might empower the relatively fewer men choosing from a comparatively larger pool of female partners. . . .

Though numerous women in my sample reported feelings of empowerment, they simultaneously discussed experiences that left them feeling disempowered in their own relationships or larger, monogamous society through the impacts of stigma. Sexuality remains a contested region, and women who challenge it often do so at a cost. The promise of sexual freedom, which theoretically accompanied the sexual revolution beginning in the 1960s, translated into increased sexual freedom for men, but not for women. Feminist theorists hypothesize that it "released" women's sexual appetites in the service of male sexual desire and retained an androcentric focal point. Many polyamorous women experienced the lingering affects of this stalled sexual liberation when they felt periodically objectified as sex toys. Others grated at the assumption that they would perform the majority of emotional management in an extremely high-maintenance relational style. While polyamorous women offered new visions of expanded sexual subjectivity and alternative roles for women, many continued to struggle under the yoke of an androcentric society that demands that women's sexuality function in the service of men. Even though they reported varying degrees of success in their attempts to create new roles and power dynamics within their own relationships, they continued to live with the impacts of stigma attributed by a monogamous society that views their actions as deviant. In both cases, they were unable to completely reform power dynamics in either their own relationships or society at large.

. . . Ultimately, polyamorous women's attempts at self-redefinition were active resistance to suppression. Even though their defiance was imperfect and left their emancipation unfinished, they still attempted to forge lives outside of the narrow confines allowed by heterocentric patriarchal culture. Any attempts at liberation serve to undermine the suppression of women and sexual minorities and are worthy of recognition in their myriad forms.

Yuko Yamamiya, Thomas F. Cash,
and J. Kevin Thompson

Sexual Experiences among College Women: The Differential Effects of General versus Contextual Body Images on Sexuality

In Western and Westernized cultures, women's bodies are objectified and evaluated (Wiederman, 2000). Women are socialized to endorse that "to be an adequate sex partner, one must conform to social norms regarding physical attractiveness and what's considered 'sexy'." Cultural objectification and sexualization of female bodies are thus internalized in women, which results in constant concerns over how their bodies appear in the eyes of others, particularly to men. When such concerns become extreme, women end up viewing their bodies critically—that is, they develop a negative body image.

Body image has been found to be associated with sexual experiences. For instance, women with body shame are more likely to engage in risky sexual behaviors, such as inconsistent condom use and a larger number of recent sexual partners. However, it has also been found that body dissatisfaction, perhaps a less severe manifestation of body image disturbance than body shame, is related to fewer and less satisfying sexual experiences. In fact, body-dissatisfied persons tend to avoid sexual activities, perceive themselves as sexually unskilled, and report more sexual distress, all of which may explain why they have had limited sexual experiences.

An important distinction in the body image literature is between general, dispositional body image evaluations and contextually specific body image experiences. In terms of sexual functioning, [it has been] recently found that body-exposure anxiety/avoidance in a sexual context was inversely associated with sexual functioning, defined as less consistency and quality in sexual arousal and orgasm. In contrast, dispositional body dissatisfaction was only weakly related to sexual functioning. [There are] few reliable relationships between dispositional body image and sexual functioning after controlling for other variables (e.g., self-esteem, depression, anxiety, and body mass).

Thus, there is suggestive evidence that women's body image, the quality of sexual experiences, sexual assertiveness, and sexual functioning are interrelated. However, as [it has been] stated, "the potential mediating role of body image [in sexual functioning] has not been explored." In the current study, a

From *Sex Roles: A Journal of Research*, vol. 55, nos. 5–6, September, 2006, pp. 421–427. Copyright ©
2006 by Springer Journals (Kluwer Academic). Reprinted by permission.

variety of variables that addressed different dimensions of body image, sexual functioning, and sexual attitudes were assessed to determine whether negative sexual experiences can be explained by either general body evaluation or contextual body image concern (or any other sexual variables). Based on previous work in this area, we hypothesized that women's general body image evaluation and contextual body image during sex would both be correlated with their self-efficacy in refusal of sex, sexual-assertiveness, and overall sexual functioning. Women who had greater discrepancies between their physical ideals and perceived self were expected to be less certain whether they would be able to refuse sex when they did not want to have sex, less able to tell their partner what they wanted during sex, and less able to function optimally in their sexual relationships. We especially focused on women in the present study because negative body image (both general and contextual) is found to have more detrimental effects on sexuality among women than men.

Moreover, we systematically asked participants about their experiences the first time they had sexual relations with their most recent partner. We hypothesized that body image evaluation, and especially contextual body image, would predict the quality of women's experiences when they initially had sex with their partner. More precisely, we expected those with more overall body dissatisfaction and greater appearance concern in sexual contexts per se to be more ambivalent in their sexual decision-making and less emotionally engaged during sex. In addition, we conducted mediational analyses to test whether contextual body image would mediate the relation between general body dissatisfaction and sexual assertiveness and self-efficacy.

Method

Participants

Participants were 384 college women. . . . Participants had to meet the following criteria: (1) heterosexual, (2) sexually active currently or in the past year, (3) unmarried, and (4) between ages 18 and 25 years. The mean age for the sample was 20 (*SD* −1.96). The majority was European American (58.1%); 18.2% were African American, 10.9% Hispanic/Latina, and 5.5% Asian. The majority (88%) had had one to three sexual partners in the past year, and 70.9% had had one to five sexual partners in their lifetime. Approximately one-half of the participants (44.3%) were currently with someone exclusively, whereas 23.5% were either dating more than one person or had only a non-dating sexual relationship.

Measures

Demographic questionnaire. This form asked participants' age, ethnicity, height, weight, how long they had been sexually active, the number of sexual partner(s) they had had in the past year and in their lifetime, the length of their longest sexual relationship, and the type of relationship they were in currently or had been during the past year (e.g., dating, cohabiting, engaged).

Body-image ideals questionnaire (BIQ). This 22-item questionnaire measures the extent to which one's current self matches an ideal via-à-vis 11 physical attributes and how important it is to meet each ideal. This scale has been found to be correlated significantly with other validated measures of body image evaluation and dysphoria, as well as with eating pathology.

Body exposure during sexual activities questionnaire (BESAQ). This 28-item self-report inventory assesses a person's anxious self-focus on appearance and exposure avoidance during sex. Respondents rate each item, such as "During sexual activity I am unaware of how my body looks." . . . Convergent validity is supported by its positive correlations with other measures of body image dissatisfaction/anxiety, and construct validity is reflected in its association with indices of sexual functioning. . . .

Sexual risk behavior beliefs and self-efficacy scales (SRBBS). The three-item Self-Efficacy in Refusing Sex (SER) subscale was used in this study, including items like "Imagine that you met someone at a party. He wants to have sex with you. Even though you are very attracted to each other, you are not ready to have sex. How sure are you that you could *keep from having sex*?" On a 3-point response scale that ranged from 1—"Not sure at all" to 3—"Totally sure," participants indicate their confidence in declining to have unwanted sex. A higher score indicates greater confidence. . . .

Sexual self-efficacy for female functioning (SSES-F). This 37-item scale assesses confidence in performing certain sexual actions or having certain sexual experiences in four sexual phases—interest, desire, arousal, and orgasm. Items include "Feel comfortable being nude with the partner," and degree of confidence is rated from 0 to 100. The measure has eight subscales, but an overall composite score may be calculated. This scale is found to have a good validity in relation to well-established measures of sexual functioning and sexual satisfaction.

The sexual awareness questionnaire (SAQ). The eight-item Sexual Assertiveness subscale of the SAQ was used to assess how assertive a woman believes she could be in terms of sexual desires that she wants to fulfill when having sex. An example of items is "I don't hesitate to ask for what I want in a sexual relationship." . . . This measure has been found to be related to higher sexual esteem and sexual satisfaction and lower sexual anxiety. . . .

First-time sexual experience questionnaire (FTSEQ). In the absence of an available measure, this questionnaire was developed for the present study to assess three qualitative aspects of sexual experience during the first sexual encounter with the most recent partner with whom the person had sexual relations: (1) extent of internal conflict or ambivalence; (2) degree of emotional detachment or disengagement during the sexual encounter; and (3) extent of uncertainty or concerns about acceptance by the partner after the sexual encounter. The original questionnaire contained 32 items and used a 5-point disagree-agree response scale, ranging from 1—"Definitely disagree" to 5—"Definitely agree."

Procedure

Participants anonymously completed a set of questionnaires either in a private laboratory office or on-line (120 participants completed paper-and-pencil questionnaires, 264 on-line questionnaires, 264 on-line questionnaires).

Results

Preliminary analyses

. . . [Analysis of the FTSEQ] showed that there were only two distinctive factors—ambivalence before having sex and emotional disengagement during sex. . . .

Bivariate analyses

Pearson correlation coefficients were calculated to determine the relationships among body image scales and sexuality indices. General body image (BIQ) and contextual body image during sex (BESAQ) were significantly related, BIQ scores were significantly negatively correlated with self-efficacy to refuse sex (SRBBS-SER), self-efficacy for sexual functioning (SSES-F), and sexual assertiveness (SAQ). These findings indicate that higher physical self-ideal discrepancies (i.e., dispositional body dissatisfaction) are associated with greater self-consciousness and exposure avoidance in sexual contexts and lower self-efficacy to refuse sex, to assert sexual desires during sex, and to function sexually. In addition, there were significant, albeit only modest, positive correlations between the scores on the BIQ and those on the FTSEQ scales for ambivalence and emotional disengagement. That is, greater general body dissatisfaction was modestly related to more ambivalence in sexual decision-making and more emotional engagement during sex.

BESAQ scores were significantly negatively correlated with SSES-F, and SAQ, but not with SRBBS-SER. Thus, when women were more body conscious and exposure avoidant in sexual contexts, their sexual assertiveness and confidence in sexual functioning were poorer, but their self-efficacy to refuse sex was not. Furthermore, the BESAQ was moderately positively correlated with both of the subscales of the FTSEQ. When women's appearance self-consciousness during sex was greater, they were more ambivalent in their sexual decision-making and less emotionally engaged during sex.

Multivariate analyses

To determine the extent to which each of the variables would account for the nature of women's sexual experiences, a series of standard multiple regressions was conducted. First, general body image evaluation (BIQ), contextual body concern during sex (BESAQ), sexual assertiveness (SAQ), and self-efficacy to function effectively during sex (SSES-F) were entered as independent variables with the self-efficacy to refuse sex (SRBBS-SER) as the dependent variable. Results showed that the overall effect for the SRBBS-SER was significantly [related to]. Thus, only a favorable dispositional body image evaluation significantly accounted for a general self-efficacy to refuse sex.

Second, the same variables were entered as independent variables with ambivalence towards having sex (FTSEQ1) as the dependent variable. The overall model was significant, [due to contributions from BIQ, BESAQ, and SSES-F.] . . . Thus, self-efficacy to function during sex and contextual body concern during sex significantly and uniquely accounted for initial ambivalence about having sex with the partner.

Finally, the same variables were again entered as independent variables with emotional disengagement during sex (FTSEQ2) as the dependent variable; overall model was significant, with . . . SSES-F [accounting for the significant.] In sum, sexual assertiveness, self-efficacy to function during sex, and contextual body concern during sex each significantly accounted for the women's degree of emotional disengagement during sex.

As the BIQ and BESAQ were significantly correlated with each other, with sexual assertiveness, and with self-efficacy to function during sex, mediational analyses were evaluated with contextual body image (BESAQ) as the mediator and the BIQ as the independent variable. . . . [A]ssociations between the BIQ and SAQ as well as BIQ and SSES-F were fully mediated by the BESAQ.

Discussion

In the present study, we evaluated how young, single women's dispositional and contextual body image experiences were related to various dimensions of their sexuality. Trait body image evaluation refers to one's general or typical feelings of satisfaction or dissatisfaction with various aspects of one's body. Results indicated that such body dissatisfaction was modestly associated with a lack of general self-efficacy to refuse sex, sexual unassertiveness, and lower confidence in sexual functioning. In contrast, sexually contextual body image pertains to women's self-consciousness about and avoidance of exposure of their body during sexual relations. Results revealed that such concerns per se were moderately related to less sexual assertiveness and confidence in sexual functioning. [B]ody image is not only related to more confident and satisfying sexual behavior, but contextual body image experiences are better predictors of sexual experiences than are trait-level evaluations of one's appearance.

In our study we uniquely asked participants to recall their first-time sexual relations with their most recent sexual partner, thereby focusing on a particular sexual encounter rather than reporting about participants' sexual experiences in general, over time, with various partners. Our results show that, although trait body image dissatisfaction modestly predicts women's ambivalence about and emotional disengagement during first-time sexual encounters, contextual body image predicts these experiences more strongly. In other words, those who are typically more physically self-conscious during sex are more uncertain or ambivalent when making a decision about whether to have sex and feel less emotional engagement during sex. Although causality cannot be conclusive, perhaps the anticipation of self-consciousness about body exposure during sex produces decisional conflict and then emotional detachment or avoidance vis-à-vis the sexual experience per se.

Whereas a more favorable overall body image may entail more general self-efficacy for refusal of sex across a range of potential partners, sexually contextual body image trumps dispositional body image in predicting the quality of experiences in an actual, first-time sexual encounter. In such encounters, women's contextual body image concerns and their poorer self-efficacy about their ability to function are related to greater ambivalence about their decision to have sex with the partner. Furthermore, their sexually contextual body image during sex, self-efficacy to function well during sex, and sexual assertiveness account for the emotional disengagement during sex with a partner for the first time. This may be because body self-consciousness and performance anxiety in sexual contexts distract women from fully committing themselves to, and immersing themselves in, sexual experiences with a new partner. Moreover, to the extent that a woman cannot and does not assert what she wants during sex, she is simply not enjoying the sexual experiences, as reflected in the emotional disengagement scores.

The results of our mediational analyses confirm that, although general body dissatisfaction may predispose sexually contextual body image experiences, the latter mediates women's sexual assertiveness and self-efficacy to function effectively during sex. That is, when a woman's dispositional body dissatisfaction entails body concern/anxiety in sexual situations, she is likely to have lower self-assertiveness to ask for a partner what she wants during sex and poorer self-efficacy to have arousal and orgasm during sex.

A secondary purpose of this study was to develop a new measurement to evaluate the quality of women's first-time experiences with a sexual partner, the First-Time Sexual Experience Questionnaire (FTSEQ). The value of such an assessment is that it taps a novel sexual encounter with a novel partner, rather than an aggregate of experiences across partners and sexual history. The two subscales of this new assessment capture continua of decisional ambivalence and emotional disengagement, and were highly internally consistent in the present sample. Both subscales were also significantly correlated with all measures of sexual and body image functioning. Of course, further validation research on the FTSEQ is needed. The results also support the reliability and validity of the Body Exposure during Sexual Activities Questionnaire (BESAQ) to measure physical self-consciousness and exposure avoidance in sexual contexts.

Among the limitations of the present study is the fact that we examined only evaluative body image, albeit dispositionally and contextually. Most worthy of research for understanding the role of body image in sexuality is the construct of body image investment or schematicity, which pertains to the degree of psychological importance persons' place on their appearance in determining their sense of self or self-worth. [Other research has found] that body dissatisfaction and appearance investment independently contributed to more anxious body focus and exposure avoidance during sex on the BESAQ, which in turn predicted the quality of sexual functioning.

The results of the present study support and extend extant evidence that women's body image has important implications for their sexual experiences. Can interventions to improve women's body image enhance their sexual functioning? Unfortunately, there is meager research to answer this question. [One study] found that women's reported sexual functioning improved as their body image improved following weight loss. [Others] found that cognitive-behavioral therapy not only improved dispositional body image but also lowered participants' body image concerns in sexual contexts per se. [Yet another study] found that the same treatment led to improved evaluations of sexuality. The potential of body image interventions to improve sexual functioning is an area that certainly warrants further research.

POSTSCRIPT

Can Women's Sexuality Be Free from Traditional Gender Constraints?

Within feminism, women's sexual freedom was initially advanced as a central cause. Shortly thereafter, women's sexual victimization was added to the feminist agenda. Many say that although women's sexual victimization is a critical cause, attention to it supplanted the advancement of women's sexual freedom.

Over the last three decades, women's sexuality has changed—by some accounts dramatically—in ways more commensurate with men's sexuality. In general, women are gaining greater sexual experience. They engage in intercourse at a younger age, they have more sex partners, they engage in sexual intercourse more frequently, and they are increasingly likely to engage in casual sex. Yet, despite this trend toward sex equality in behaviors, traditional gender socialization and the sexual double standard continue to act as an interpretive filter for sexual experience. Women continue to experience guilt and shame in response to sexual experience and be seen by others as "dirty" or promiscuous.

Caution must be exercised in defining sexual equality for women. Many argue for commensurate sexual permissiveness for males and females. But does that necessarily mean women achieving a sexuality akin to men? Competitiveness, assertiveness, and coercion often characterize males' sexual experience. Males' self- and peer-esteem are linked to sexual experience and performance. Many future-oriented sexologists caution that in striving for sexual equality, we must not limit ourselves to a preset "male" definition of sexual freedom.

Psychologist and sex researcher Leonore Tiefer argues that we need to encourage women's sexual experimentation and explore sexual possibilities. Furthermore, new ideas need to be developed about desire and pleasure. To facilitate this, there needs to be freely available information, ideas, images, and open sexual talk. Tiefer asserts that if women develop sexual knowledge and self-knowledge, they can take more responsibility for their own pleasure.

Traditional sex education programming has overlooked the possibility of female desire and sexual pleasure. Some argue that sex education programs can be used to help females not allow themselves to be treated as objects but think of themselves as sexual subjects. Women as sexual subjects would feel free to seek out sexual pleasure and know that they have a right to this pleasure. This argument supports the assertion that we also need to raise boys to avoid treating females as sexual objects. The challenge for sex education programming is to inform women about the possible risks of sexual relationships without supporting the double standard that limits, inhibits, and controls their sexuality.

Ideally, sex education programming would include education specifically about gender ideology, as it influences sexual perceptions, decisions, and experiences. Conformity to gender-based norms and ideals for sexual activity is the most important source of peer sexual pressure and risky sex among youth; youth "perform" gendered roles in sexual relations to secure gender affirmation.

Other scholars also argue that catalyzing women's sexual freedom necessitates more far-reaching changes in gender role socialization. Tiefer comments, "A person would have to feel comfortable, safe, and entitled in order to focus wholly on his or her tactile experience. Can we assume that most women can be thoroughly relaxed in sexual situations given the inequality of so many relationships, given women's concern with their appearance, given women's worries about safety and contraception?"

Advocates of sex education reform also call for incorporating definitions of "good sex"—sex that is not coercive, exploitative, or harmful. They caution not to impose rigid definitions of "sexual normality"; rather, identify some dimensions of healthy sexuality as examples upon which individuals can explore and develop their own unique sexual identity and style. It has been observed that a central practice in the social construction of gender inequality is *compulsory heterosexuality* or societal pressure to be heterosexual. Many sexual revolutionaries argue that an important condition of sexual freedom is freedom from pressures to be a particular "type" of sexual being.

What cultural pressures exist to be a certain kind of sexual being? How can these cultural pressures be transcended? What would women's sexuality be like if it were not so socially restricted? How do media images of the "ideal" woman contribute to these restrictions? Do you think, as Sheff's research suggests, that it is possible to be free of societal constraints?

Suggested Readings

Michael Basso, *The Underground Guide to Teenage Sexuality*, 2nd ed. (Fairview Press, 2003).

Boston Women's Health Book Collective, *Our Bodies, Ourselves: Updated and Expanded for the 90's* (New York: Touchstone, 1996).

Patricia Hill Collins, *Black Sexual Politics: African Americans, Gender, and the New Racism* (New York: Routledge, 2004).

Jean Kilbourne and Mary Pipher, *Can't Buy My Love: How Advertising Changes the Way We Think and Feel* (New York: Simon & Schuster, 2000).

K. Thompson and L. Smolak, *Body Image, Eating Disorders, and Obesity in Youth: Assessment, Prevention, and Treatment* (Washington, DC: American Psychological Association, 2001).

Leonore Tiefer, "Arriving at a 'New View' of Women's Sexual Problems: Background, Theory, and Activism," *Women and Therapy, 24* (2001): 63–98.

Deborah Tolman, *Dilemmas of Desire: Teenage Girls Talk about Sexuality* (Cambridge, MA: Harvard University Press, 2005).

Naomi Wolf, *The Beauty Myth: How Images of Beauty Are Used Against Women* (New York: HarperCollins, 2002).

Contributors to This Volume

EDITOR

JACQUELYN W. WHITE is professor of psychology and former director of Women's and Gender Studies, at the University of North Carolina at Greensboro. She received her Ph.D. in social psychology from Kent State University.

Dr. White has conducted research in the area of aggression and violence for over 30 years, publishing numerous articles and chapters. She has conducted one of the only longitudinal studies of sexual assault and dating violence among adolescents and college students (funded by NIMH, NIJ, and CDC). Recent publications reflect an ecological developmental perspective to aggression and violence. She is a frequent speaker at national and international conferences. She is co-editor with Dr. Cheryl Travis of the University of Tennessee on *Sexuality, Society, and Feminism: Psychological Perspectives on Women,* published by the American Psychological Association. She recently completed the "Gendered Aggression" chapter for the *Encyclopedia of Gender* (Academic Press) and "A Developmental Examination of Violence Against Girls and Women" for the *Handbook of the Psychology of Women and Gender* (Wiley).

In addition to her research activities, Dr. White served as the editor of the *Psychology of Women Quarterly* (2000–2004) and is a consulting editor for *Aggressive Behavior.* She has been president of the Southeastern Psychological Association, is currently the treasurer of the International Society for Research in Aggression and is the 2007–2008 president of the Society for the Psychology of Women Division 35 of the American Psychological Association. She has been a consultant on a project with the U.S. Navy examining the impact of pre-military experiences with physical and sexual abuse on military experiences. She has been the recipient of a number of awards, including the Women's History Committee Service Award given by the Commission on the Status of Women and the Greensboro YWCA and Kent State University's Honors Alumna of 2000. She was UNCG's 1996 Senior Research Excellence Award recipient, the highest research honor the university can bestow on a faculty member. She is also a fellow of the American Psychological Association.

AUTHORS

BRENDA ALLEN is associate dean of the department of communication at the University of Colorado at Denver. She conducts research on social identity and communication. She is also co-editor of the *International and Intercultural Communication Annual.* In 2004 she received the Francine Merritt Award for Outstanding Contributions to the Lives of Women in Communication from the National Communication Association. In 2006 she became the first recipient of the Annual Award for Outstanding Achievement for Commitment to Diversity at the University of Colorado, Denver.

AMERICAN PSYCHOLOGICAL ASSOCIATION'S COUNCIL OF REPRESENTATIVES is the elected governing body of the American Psychological Association. Among various activities it creates task forces charged with drafting resolutions based on research reviews that the Council can then consider for adopting as official APA policy.

ROBIN ZENGER BAKER has been a lecturer at the Boston University School of Management and has a Ph.D. in organization studies from UCLA.

BARRIE BONDURANT, a former professor of psychology at Lyon College, where she received the 2002–2003 Excellence in Teaching award, is a counselor at New River Valley Community Services in Blacksburg, Virginia. She has published several chapters and research articles related to violence against women.

LOUANN BRIZENDINE, M.D., is a neuropsychiatrist at the University of California, San Francisco. She is the founder and director of The Women's and Teens' Mood and Hormone Clinic at UCSF. She is working on a book entitled *The Male Brain,* due out in 2009.

KINGSLEY R. BROWNE is a professor at Wayne State University Law School. He specialized in labor and employment law when he was previously a partner in the San Francisco-based law firm of Morrison & Foerster. He has written *Co-ed Combat: The New Evidence that Women Shouldn't Fight the Nation's Wars* (Sentinel, 2007). His work deals primarily with employment discrimination law and the legal implications of evolved differences between the sexes.

ANNE CAMPBELL, professor of psychology at Durham University, studies sex differences in aggression with special emphasis upon female aggression. She is the author of *Mind of her own: The evolutionary psychology of women.* Oxford: Oxford University Press, 2002.

LINDA L. CARLI, Ph.D., is an associate professor in the psychology department at Wellesley College, where she has been since 1991. Her current research focuses on women's leadership, particularly the obstacles that women leaders face and ways to overcome those obstacles. Dr. Carli teaches a variety of courses, including organizational psychology, the psychology of law, and research in applied psychology.

MARCIA J. CARLSON is an assistant professor of social work and sociology at Columbia University. Her current research focuses on linkages among family structure, mother-father relationships, father involvement, and child well-being for a cohort of children born outside of marriage. She calls these family structures "fragile families."

THOMAS F. CASH, Ph.D., is currently a professor in the department of psychology at Old Dominion University. Dr. Cash's research interests focuses on the psychology of physical appearance as well as how our looks and our view of our own looks affect our lives. He also focuses on body-image assessment and cognitive-behavioral body-image therapy.

FREDERICK L. COOLIDGE, Ph.D., is currently a professor of psychology at the University of Colorado at Colorado Springs, where he has taught since 1979. His research interests include behavioral genetics, personality disorders, and paleopsychology.

MARY E. CORCORAN is professor of political science, public policy, social work, and women's studies at the University of Michigan. Her research focuses on the effects of gender and race discrimination on economic status and earnings and on welfare and employment policies.

TIMOTHY J. DAILEY, senior research fellow at the Center for Marriage and Family Studies, has a Ph.D. in religion and specializes in issues threatening the institutions of marriage and the family. He has authored three books, including *Dark Obsession: The Tragedy and Threat of the Homosexual Lifestyle* (Broadman and Holman, 2003).

ANTHONY D'AMATO is the Leighton professor of law at Northwestern University School of Law, where he teaches courses in international law, international human rights, analytic jurisprudence, and justice. He was the first American lawyer to argue and win a case before the European Court of Human Rights in Strasbourg, and is the author of over 20 books and over 110 articles.

DENA S. DAVIS is a professor at the Cleveland-Marshall College of Law at Cleveland State University. She was a Fellow in Bioethics at the Cleveland Clinic and has published in the areas of church and state and bioethics and teaches and conducts research in biomedical ethics, church and state, torts.

PATRICIA L. N. DONAT, professor of psychology and associate vice president of Academic Affairs at Mississippi University for Women, has published several chapters and articles related to her research interests in women's issues and violence against women.

PEGGY DREXLER, an assistant professor of psychology in psychiatry at the Weill Medical College of Cornell University, has been a clinician and lecturer at the New York Hospital/Cornell Medical School, and a researcher at Stanford University as a Gender Scholar. Her research focuses on the new American family.

ALICE EAGLY, a social psychologist, is the James Padilla Chair of Arts and Sciences, professor of psychology, faculty fellow of Institute for Policy Research, department chair of psychology, all at Northwestern University.

She has received numerous awards including the 2007 Interamerican Psychologist Award from Interamerican Society of Psychology for contributions to psychology as a science and profession in the Americas, as well as the 2005 Carolyn Wood Sherif Award from Society for the Psychology of Women for contributions to the field of the psychology of women as a scholar, teacher, mentor, and leader.

RICHARD B. FELSON, is a professor in the department of crime, law & justice and sociology at Pennsylvania State University, has received numerous grants, and published extensively in the field of aggression. He received the PSU 2004 Distinction in the Social Sciences Award from the College of Liberal Arts.

MARIA FERRIS currently works for IBM managing their Global Workforce Diversity and Work/Life programs. During her 27-year career with IBM, she has held a variety of staff and management positions within the HR organization in staffing, employee relations, management development, benefits, and diversity. She is a current member and former co-chair of the Conference Board's Work-Life Leadership Council and a founding member of the Leadership Forum for Women's Advancement.

MARK V. FLINN, Ph.D., is currently an associate professor in the department of anthropology at the University of Missouri, Columbia. His research interests include childhood stress, family relationships, and health. For the past sixteen years he has conducted a longitudinal study to identify specific psychosocial causes and consequences of childhood stress.

DAVID C. GEARY, Ph.D., is currently a Curators' professor for the department of psychological sciences at the University of Missouri, Columbia. Geary is the lead investigator on a longitudinal study of children's mathematical development and learning disabilities. Dr. Geary is also a member of the President's National Mathematics Panel.

CARLA GOLDEN, professor of psychology at Ithaca College has published several articles on women's issues, including articles related to sexual orientation. She is co-editor, along with Joan Chrisler and Patricia Rozee of *Lectures on the Psychology of Women* (McGraw-Hill, 2003), which received a distinguished publication award from the Association of Women in Psychology.

TARA L. GRUENEWALD, Ph.D., is currently an assistant professor in residence for the department of Geriatric Medicine at the University of California, Los Angeles. Her research interests include psychological and social factors that impact functioning and health outcomes in older adults, including the biological pathways through which psychosocial variables influence health.

REGAN A. R. GURUNG, Ph.D., is currently a professor at the University of Wisconsin, Green Bay, where he teaches both psychology and human development classes. His research interests include culture and health, impression formation and clothing, and pedagogical psychology.

DEBRA HAUSER, MPH, is the vice president of Advocates for Youth. Advocates for Youth is a national, nonprofit organization that creates programs and supports policies that help young people make safe, responsible decisions about their sexual and reproductive health.

JEFFREY HILL, Ph.D., has been an associate professor in the School of Family Life at Brigham Young University since 1998. His research interests include home and family living, and he teaches a variety of classes in the School of Family Life and a Work and Family class in the Marriott School of Management.

JANET SHIBLEY HYDE, Ph.D., is currently a professor of psychology and women's studies at the University of Wisconsin at Madison. Dr. Hyde's research spans the fields of the psychology of women, human sexuality, and gender-role development. Her current research project is the Wisconsin Study of Families and Work, which focuses on working mothers and their children. She is also working on the Moms and Math (M&M) Project, funded by the National Science Foundation, which focuses on studying mothers as they interact with their fifth- and seventh-grade children to complete math homework.

HILDA KAHNE, professor emerita at Wheaton College in Massachusetts and a member of the Women's Studies Research Center Scholars Program and a Resident Scholar at Brandeis University. Her research at the Women's Studies Research Center (WSRC) focuses on low-wage single-mother families and how their earnings can be increased to a level of long-run financial adequacy. In her earlier years, Dr. Kahne also held positions at Wellesley College, Radcliffe College, Harvard University, Harvard School of Public Health, and the Social Security Administration in Washington, D.C.

LAURA C. KLEIN, Ph.D., is assistant professor of biobehavioral health at Penn State University. Her research interests include the biobehavioral effects of stress on drug abuse in humans and animals, sex differences in neuroendocrine and behavioral stress responses, and nicotine regulation of stress reactivity.

LAWRENCE A. KURDEK, clinical psychology professor at Wright State University, is interested in developmental psychology and the effects of family structure and family process on children's and adolescents' development. He is also interested in the issue of relationship quality in gay, lesbian, and heterosexual couples. He has published over 150 referred journal articles and edited book chapters.

BRIAN P. LEWIS has been associated with Syracuse University and the University of California, Los Angeles.

HILARY M. LIPS, a professor of psychology and the director of the Center for Gender Studies at Radford University, has published numerous books and articles related to the psychology of gender, including *Sex and Gender: An Introduction* (Mayfield, 2000).

GERALD MACKIE, assistant professor of political science at the University of California, San Diego. He has been research fellow, Social and Political Theory Program, Research School of Social Sciences, Australian National

University, and junior research fellow in politics, St John's College, University of Oxford. He is the author of *Democracy Defended.*

BRIDGET E. MAHER, policy analyst at the Center for Marriage and Family Studies at Family Research Council. She has authored several Family Research Council publications including two editions of *The Family Portrait,* a comprehensive book of data, research, and polling on the family.

HADAS MANDEL, Ph.D., is a lecturer in the department of sociology and anthropology at Tel Aviv University. Her current research focuses on cross-country variations in gender inequality and their relationship to class inequality and the role of the welfare state.

VJOLLCA K. MÄRTINSON received her Ph.D. from the Marriage, Family, and Human Development Department at Brigham Young University in 2005.

SARAH S. McLANAHAN is professor of sociology and public affairs and director of the Bendheim-Thoman Center for Research on Child Well-being at Princeton University. She is editor-in-chief of *The Future of Children.* She is the author of many articles and books including *Fathers Under Fire: The Revolution in Child Support Enforcement* (1998). The James S. Coleman Fellow of the American Academy of Political and Social Sciences and the Distinguished Scholar Award from the American Sociological Association Family Section are two of the many honors she has received.

MARY C. NOONAN is currently a professor in the department of sociology at the University of Iowa, where she has taught since 2001. Her research interests include gender, family, work, stratification, and quantitative research methods.

JUNE O'NEILL, Wollman Professor of Economics and Finance at the Zicklin School of Business, is also the director of the Center for the Study of Business and Government, School of Public Affairs, at Baruch College, City University of New York. Dr. O'Neill is the chairwoman of the Board of Scientific Counselors of the National Center for Health Statistics. Between 1995 and 1999, she served a term as director of the Congressional Budget Office (CBO) in Washington D.C. O'Neill is currently a member of a panel of economic advisors for the CBO. She has authored books pertaining to welfare, income and earnings differentials, women in the economy, health insurance, social security, and education finance.

CARLA MAKHLOUF OBERMEYER, scientist for the World Health Organization's Department of HIV and adjunct associate professor in the Department of Population and International Health at Harvard University, has been chair of the Committee on Reproductive Health of the International Union for the Scientific Study of Population and a member of the U.S. National Science Foundation Senior Review Panel for Anthropology. Her research has addressed the links between health and social factors and has included population policy and gender in Arab countries, the Safe Motherhood initiative in Morocco, the health effects of female circumcision, and a multi-site study of therapeutic decision making at menopause. She is the author of three books: *Changing Veils: Women and Modernization in*

Yemen (1979); *Family Gender and Population in the Middle East* (1995); *Cross-Cultural Perspectives on Reproductive Health* (2001).

STEVEN PINKER is now the Johnstone Family Professor of Psychology at Harvard University. Until 2003 he was in the department of brain and cognitive sciences at MIT. His empirical studies focus on linguistic behavior. He also conducts theoretical analyses of the nature of language and its relation to mind and brain. He has authored several books including *The Blank Slate: The Modern Denial of Human Nature* (Penguin Books, 2003).

IGNACIO LUIS RAMIREZ, Ph.D., is a professor in the department of sociology at Texas Tech University. His research interests include violence in intimate relations. His teaching includes social problems as well as law and policing.

JUDITH REISMAN is president of The Institute for Media Education, author of, among other publications, the U.S. Department of Justice, Juvenile Justice study, *Images of Children Crime and Violence in Playboy, Penthouse and Hustler* (1989), *Kinsey, Sex and Fraud* (Reisman, et al., 1990) and *Soft Porn Plays Hardball* (1991), and *Kinsey, Crimes & Consequences* (1998, 2000). She is also a news commentator for *WorldNetDaily.com* and has been a consultant to four U.S. Department of Justice administrations, The U.S. Department of Education, and the U.S. Department of Health and Human Services.

ROSAMOND RHODES is a professor of medical education and director of bioethic education at the Mount Sinai School of Medicine. She was guest editor, along with Daniel A. Moros, on the theme of "Issues in medical ethics understanding professionalism and its implications for medical education" in the *Mount Sinai Journal of Medicine* (2002).

MOSHE SEMYONOV, Ph.D., is the Bernard and Audre Rapoport Chair in the sociology of labor department at Tel Aviv University as well as a professor at the University of Illinois at Chicago. He teaches in the departments of sociology and of labor studies. He is also the director of the University Institute for Diplomacy and Regional Cooperation. His research interests include labor market inequalities, labor migration in the global economy, and comparative social stratification. His current research focuses on structural sources of ethnic, gender and socioeconomic inequality (mostly in the labor market) and on the status of labor migrants across societies.

ELIZABETH SHEFF, assistant professor of sociology at Georgia State University, is currently studying issues of sexuality, gender, family, deviance, and communities. She has taught courses in sexuality, gender, families, introductory sociology, social theory, and research methods. Her current research interests involve examining the norms and ethics of practitioners of various types of sexual activities, including bondage, domination, and sadism.

DAVID L. SNOW, Ph.D., is a professor of psychology in the departments of psychiatry, child study center, and epidemiology and public health at Yale University School of Medicine and is director of the Consultation Center and Division of Prevention and Community Research in the Department of Psychiatry. His work has focused extensively on the design and evaluation of preventive interventions and on research aimed at identifying key risk and protective factors predictive of psychological symptoms, substance use, and family violence. He also has special interests in the protective and stress-mediating effects of coping and social support and in methodological and ethical issues in prevention research.

ELIZABETH SPELKE, the Marshall L. Berkman Professor of Psychology at Harvard University. Her most recent honors include the William James Award, American Psychological Society 2000; Distinguished Scientific Contribution Award, American Psychological Association, 2000; Ipsen Prize in Neuronal Plasticity, 2001; America's Best in Science and Medicine, *Time Magazine*, 2001; Fellow, American Association for the Advancement of Science, 2002. She is currently publishing research on numerical cognition in infants and young children.

PETER SPRIGG is vice president for policy at the Family Research Council. He oversees research, publications, and policy formulation, and coordinates the work of Center for Human Life and Bioethics and Center for Marriage and Family Studies. His areas of policy expertise are human sexuality and the homosexual agenda; religion in public life; and the arts and entertainment. He has authored *Outrage: How Gay Activists and Liberal Judges Are Trashing Democracy to Redefine Marriage* (Regnery, 2004).

MURRAY A. STRAUS, Ph.D., is currently a professor of sociology at the University of New Hampshire where he has taught since 1968. Dr. Straus is also the co-director for the Family Research Laboratory at the University of New Hampshire. He has been collaborating with researchers in 23 nations on a cross-national study of violence between partners in the dating relationships of university students.

SUZANNE C. SWAN, is an assistant professor in the department of psychology and the Women's Studies Program at the University of South Carolina. Before coming to the University of South Carolina, she was the director of Family Violence Programs at the Yale School of Medicine's Department of Psychiatry. She received her Ph.D. from the University of Illinois in 1997. Her recent work has focused on research with women who use violence in intimate relationships, with a particular emphasis on the contextual factors underlying women's violence. She teaches courses on the psychology of women, social psychology, and relationship violence.

SHELLEY E. TAYLOR, social psychologist and professor at the University of California, Los Angeles, is co-director of the Health Psychology program at UCLA and director of the social neuroscience lab. Her research interests are in the areas of social cognition and health. She has written several books and among several awards, including the American Psychological Association's Distinguished Scientific Contribution to Psychology Award and the Outstanding Scientific Contribution Award in Health Psychology.

LINDA L. THEDE recently completed a master's of science degree in neuropsychology at the University of Medicine and Science in Chicago. She is currently pursuing her doctorate of psychology with an emphasis in neuropsychology at the Colorado School of Professional Psychology.

J. KEVIN THOMPSON, Ph.D., is currently a professor in the department of psychology at the University of South Florida. His research interests include body image, eating disorders, and obesity.

JOHN A. UPDEGRAFF, Ph.D., is currently an assistant professor of psychology at Kent State University. His current research interests are health communication, how self-concept and motivations influence people's interpretations and reactions to everyday experiences, and the role of positive psychological states in coping with stress.

RICHARD WILSON, a former research fellow at the University of Sheffield, is currently a Medical Research Council-funded student in Medical Sociology at the Royal Holloway College at the University of London. He is also an assistant editor of the journal *Sexualities, Evolution and Gender.*

YUKO YAMAMIYA is a doctoral student at the University of South Florida. Her research interests are body-image disturbances among young population across different cultures, and social factors that influence body-image development. Her current research project is about men's internalization of sociocultural ideal of female media image and how the internalization levels affect the men's evaluation of "real-life" women in their lives.

SUSAN E. YOUNG, Ph.D., is currently a researcher at the Institute for Behavioral Genetics at the University of Colorado at Boulder. Her research interests include genetic and environmental factors underlying the development of conduct disorder, ADHD and substance use problems, and the links between executive cognitive function and developmental psychopathology.